Smart Home Automation with Linux and Raspberry Pi

Steven Goodwin

Apress·

Smart Home Automation with Linux and Raspberry Pi

ISBN-13 (pbk): 978-1-4302-5887-2

ISBN-13 (electronic): 978-1-4302-5888-9

Trademarked names, logos, and images may appear in this book. Rather than use a trademark symbol with every occurrence of a trademarked name, logo, or image we use the names, logos, and images only in an editorial fashion and to the benefit of the trademark owner, with no intention of infringement of the trademark.

The use in this publication of trade names, trademarks, service marks, and similar terms, even if they are not identified as such, is not to be taken as an expression of opinion as to whether or not they are subject to proprietary rights.

While the advice and information in this book are believed to be true and accurate at the date of publication, neither the authors nor the editors nor the publisher can accept any legal responsibility for any errors or omissions that may be made. The publisher makes no warranty, express or implied, with respect to the material contained herein.

President and Publisher: Paul Manning
Lead Editor: Michelle Lowman
Developmental Editor: Douglas Pundick
Technical Reviewer: Steve Potts, Michael Still
Editorial Board: Steve Anglin, Mark Beckner, Ewan Buckingham, Gary Cornell, Louise Corrigan, Morgan Ertel, Jonathan Gennick, Jonathan Hassell, Robert Hutchinson, Michelle Lowman, James Markham, Matthew Moodie, Jeff Olson, Jeffrey Pepper, Douglas Pundick, Ben Renow-Clarke, Dominic Shakeshaft, Gwenan Spearing, Matt Wade, Tom Welsh
Coordinating Editor: Anamika Panchoo
Copy Editor: Laura Lawrie
Compositor: SPi Global
Indexer: SPi Global
Artist: SPi Global
Cover Designer: Anna Ishchenko

Distributed to the book trade worldwide by Springer Science+Business Media New York, 233 Spring Street, 6th Floor, New York, NY 10013. Phone 1-800-SPRINGER, fax (201) 348-4505, e-mail orders-ny@springer-sbm.com, or visit www.springeronline.com. Apress Media, LLC is a California LLC and the sole member (owner) is Springer Science + Business Media Finance Inc (SSBM Finance Inc). SSBM Finance Inc. is a Delaware corporation.

For information on translations, please e-mail rights@apress.com, or visit www.apress.com.

Apress and friends of ED books may be purchased in bulk for academic, corporate, or promotional use. eBook versions and licenses are also available for most titles. For more information, reference our Special Bulk Sales–eBook Licensing web page at www.apress.com/bulk-sales.

Any source code or other supplementary materials referenced by the author in this text is available to readers at www.apress.com. For detailed information about how to locate your book's source code, go to www.apress.com/source-code/.

To mum and dad—for the first automated home I had;
where clothes washed themselves, and food cooked itself!

And to Holly—for making her parents wish that they,
too, had an automated home!

Contents at a Glance

Contents

About the Author

Steven Goodwin (London, England) has been involved in science and technology from an early age, building his first synthesizer while still in his teens. Since then, his projects have been wide and varied. He has built robots, musical instruments, chess sets, and has a house that can be controlled from the Internet where he is able to e-mail his PVR and control his light switches from work.

The growth of his desire for home automation led to the creation of the "Minerva" project, an open source suite of tools and protocols that made it possible to combine many different technologies, allowing them to interact in new and interesting ways. It is a project for which he is still the lead architecture and developer.

He is also an active member of the Linux, Free Software, and Open Source communities, having spoken at many conferences, including UKUUG, FOSDEM, NotCon, and the BBC Backstage OpenTech event. His articles have appeared in over 50 magazines, covering topics from programming to management (even including magic and beer!). He is also the author of two industry-standard textbooks for the games industry.

Currently, Steven is funding his passion for technology through the development of the SGX 3D engine, and his work with startups in London.

About the Technical Reviewers

Steve Potts Steve Potts graduated from Manchester University, England with a Bachelor's degree in Applied Computing and continued to study a Master's degree in Computing for Commerce and Industry at the Open University, UK.

His career has a foundation in the defense industry, squeezing an immense amount of failure-resistant software into a remarkably small footprint, which migrated into developing for handheld devices, mobile Internet, and the e-commerce web.

He is an accomplished technical editor, having worked on Java, XHTML, PHP, Wireless, and social media publications, including Apress's own "Building Online Communities" as well as the first edition of "Smart Home Automation with Linux."

Steve is delighted to hold the rewarding position of Software Engineer at BBC Sport in Salford, where he is responsible for delivering over 2.5 million data fragments per year to over 16 million unique devices per week, pushing the boundaries of better data faster.

He is still continuing to refit his house with home automation technology.

 **Michael Still** works at Rackspace, where he works on the Open Source OpenStack project as part of the Private Cloud team. He spends most of his time hacking on the libvirt virtualization layer in nova.

Before joining Rackspace in 2012, Michael spent six years as a Site Reliability Engineer at Google and one year as an Operations Engineer at Canonical. In both roles, he was responsible for maintaining and improving web systems with millions of users. He was also the director for linux.conf.au 2013, the largest Open Source conference in Australia.

Michael holds a Bachelor of Engineering with first class honors from the University of Cranberra in Australia, where he lives with his wife, three kids, and a ludicrous number of pets. In his spare time, he enjoys reading bad science fiction and working on OpenStack development.

Acknowledgments

For every word I've written, six have been discarded. Such is the nature of writing. For every ten programs I've downloaded, tried, and tested, nine have been discarded. Such is the nature of software. Finding a perspicuous overlap has been a long and arduous task, and one that I'd wish for no one to suffer in solitude. Fortunately, I didn't . . .

To those enduring the role of first-line support to my restless questions and curiosity, I thank you. Phil Downer, Mal Lansell, and Frank Scott will be collecting their magniloquent medals in due course!

The greatest of thanks go to those developers, reviewers, evangelists, and forum posters over whose shoulders we've all peered to learn and discover, with those active on UKHA_D, GLLUG, Lonix, FAB, and TULS having all played their part.

Thanks also to those manufacturers that have supplied me with test hardware to verify my assumptions about their wares. They include Kevin Toms from Phillips for early access to Hue and its SDK, Dr. Chris Dodge, Technical Director at RedRat Ltd, Alan Quinby of Keene Electronics Ltd, Benjamin Gilbert at Anders electronics, and Melanie Jeuken at Marmitek for the crystal-clear images of all the X10 kit. Also to Chris Vine at IntelliSoftware Ltd and Darren Daws at Txtlocal Ltd for allowing me to send junk text messages through their systems until I got it right!

My thanks also to Michelle Lowman, Douglas Pundick, Anamika Panchoo, Laura Lawrie, and their respective editorial teams at Apress for fixing my mistakes before my readers realize I've made them!

To my network of friends, colleagues, and associates: Janey Barnett, Darren Bolland, Dean Butcher, Barbara Cassani, David Eade, Martin Frost, Ed and Margaret Grabowski, Raffaella Garavini, Lucas Grange, Justine Griffith, Phillip Hart, Mike Knight, Kathryn McAnulty, Andy Leigh, Phil Lunt, Nat Morris, Colin Murphy, Shane O'Neill, Duncan Parkes, Cveta Rahneva, Tracey Spencer, Steve Shipton, Michał Skorupka, John Southern, Fiona Stewart, Bruno Baillorge and Josiane Baillorge Valverde, Dave Wall, and Betsy Weber. All without whom . . .

And, as always, to my family. Grandma, Shirley and Ken, Juliette and Dean and George and Matilda, Melanie and Dan and Grace and Rose, Mum and Dad, Angela and Colin, and Holly (who's probably still not old enough to understand it!)

—Steven Goodwin

Introduction

Home Automation is anything that your home does for you that makes living there more enjoyable or productive. A Smart Home is one that appears to apply intelligence to make that happen.

To my friends, family, and visitors, my home is both smart and automated; I can e-mail my light switches, receive tweets from my CD player, and have a personalized TV guide e-mailed to me every day.

To me, my home is a collection of existing open source software, some consumer-level hardware, and small pieces of glue code that make them all interact. The magic happens in the way they are combined, and it's those secrets that I'll be exposing in this book.

The most cogent phrase in this field is probably "the devil is in the details." Home Automation (HA) requires small confirmed tools that do a single, specific, job in much the same way that Unix utility software does one job, and does it well. Consequently, our decision to adopt Linux as the underlying operating system is no accident. Unlike the monolithic approach of Windows, we have large repositories of open source software that perform these individual jobs—SMS handling, media playback, X10 control, e-mail, web servers, speech synthesis, and everything in between is freely available—and, most importantly, interoperable.

Throughout the book I shall reference many different technologies and languages that I consider to be the most suitable to the task in hand. In some cases, this will refer to old technology that is no longer cutting-edge, as those are the devices that have been made to work effectively with Linux through (primarily) developer support. The glue code makes use of Perl, PHP, C++, and Bash. Each has been chosen according to the merits of the language and which modules made the task easier, and not with any presupposed advocacy.

The book begins by covering appliance control, and the whys, wherefores, and how to's of controlling devices such as your kettle, CCTV, light switches, and TV from a computer. A multitude of technologies including X10, C-Bus, ZWave, ZigBee, and Hue are covered and explained. We continue by looking at other devices that you can build, adapt, or hack yourself from existing technology. The Arduino, for example, can be employed as part of an automated doormat that reminds you to take your umbrella when the weather forecast spells rain, or can remind you that today is the day that the rubbish is collected.

We then look at media systems, discovering how to automate and replace the aging combination of VCR and TV guide by using UPnP, NAS, and computer-oriented solutions. They can automatically suggest TV shows, sending their recommendations to your e-mail inbox or mobile phone, and provide a method of recording them by the same means.

Afterward, we look at the technical considerations necessary when running a computer 24-7, the methods of wiring a home network, and preparing your home for the patter of tiny silicon feet! This is followed by the use and installation of communication protocols, which allow anything in your home to talk to anything else, and is our first step toward true technology homogeneity.

The final proverbial straight consists of the data sources that provide the information to make our home appear intelligent, and the software and processes necessary to combine everything learned into a unified whole. The specifics. The glue code. The details that make the magic work!

The coda then details the Raspberry Pi. Although the machine itself can be used anywhere a Linux machine can (and therefore the whole book is about the Raspberry, even if not explicitly detailed as such), this chapter concentrates on those elements that are specific to the Pi. After all, it's only one year since its release; it has become a media darling and Linux computer that the lay public aren't afraid of, introducing new users and programmers to a technological future that they can be part of. Its small size and low price point mean that many devices that couldn't be sensibly automated before are now connected to the Internet and home servers. My final chapter covers installation, hardware interfacing, software methodologies, and more ideas than you can shake a proverbial stick at!

I should like to end on a note of carefree abandon—learn to steal! Once you've learned the pieces of the puzzle, and how to combine them, there is very little new to invent. Every new idea you discover is a mere permutation of the old ideas. And ideas are free! Every cool feature discussed on TV shows, or presented in the brochures or web sites of commercial HA companies, can be taken, adapted, and implemented with the information presented here using very little effort. And then you will graduate from automated home, to smart home, to personalized smart home!

■ ■ ■

## CHAPTER 1

Appliance Control: Making Things Do Stuff

For most people, home automation begins and ends with the principle of appliance control. When any household device such as a video or TV is controlled by something other than a button on its front panel or its original remote control, it is deemed somewhat magical and a topic of further inquiry, particularly if the control is done remotely. Lights and toasters don't need to be controlled by a wall switch, and your TV doesn't need to be fed signals from your PVR, DVD player, or satellite receiver. Each device has its own idiosyncrasies and control methods, and each has specific functionality that cannot easily be abstracted into any general-purpose form of control interface. However, it is possible to control the vast majority of them using one of two basic methods:

- Mains line-powered control (light bulbs, toasters, electric teakettles)
- Infrared (IR) remote control (TV, video)

Although modern set-top boxes might have a serial, USB, or network socket on the back, these are in addition to the previous two methods, not exclusive of them. Therefore, being able to control IR signals and the power lines covers the majority of devices in the modern home. Even relatively unsophisticated appliances such as teakettles, which were built without any intention of them being controlled by another means, can be controlled remotely if you know how to control their power source. After all, if you ensure the teakettle is full of water and plugged into a wall-switched socket and the teakettle itself is switched on, then the only necessary task to start the water boiling is to flick the switch on the wall socket—something that can be governed by mains control. And it is these methods of controlling the mains power that I'll cover first.

X10

X10 is one of the methods I'll cover that allows you to remotely control the power of any device plugged into the standard ring main in your home. The lights, electric teakettle, and toaster are all examples of existing devices in this category. Additionally, I'll cover devices that were originally invented to be controlled by X10 such as motorized curtain rails. X10 achieved its market penetration by being fairly cheap and very easy to install.

About X10

X10 is a control protocol that sends data packets along the mains power line with messages such as "turn device on" or "dim to 50 percent." The data packets are applied to the power lines by a transmitter such as a computer interface or a custom-built remote control, and they're processed by a much simpler receiver device, such as a light switch, which in turn controls the power to the local device.

X10 works by encoding the data in high-frequency bursts (of 120KHz) and adding it to the existing power line. Because the mains supply in all countries is either 50Hz or 60Hz (with Japan and Tahiti using both!), these high-frequency signals are customarily lost by most devices that are looking only to consume power. On the other hand, a special device can be plugged into the power line that *is* interested in high-frequency bursts. It is consequently possible to recognize one binary digit of data every time the voltage goes from positive to negative, or vice versa.

■ **Caution**   Several devices are available that are based on this principle, with most do-it-yourself (DIY) stores stocking their own variant. If they do not contain the X10 logo, however, they are not compatible with X10 because their protocols differ. They can also conflict with each other.

Every device that is to be controlled by X10 must have an address. This address comprises two parts: a house code and a unit code. The *house code* is simply a letter, from A to P, and should be unique to your house. Obviously, with only 16 letters to choose from, the house code won't be unique to every house in the world, but it should be unique to any property that shares your immediate mains supply. This usually comprises your neighbors, and occasionally the property two or three doors down, because all your power lines converge in larger conduits under the road. Consequently, any house that shares these lines will also share X10 messages, making it possible to control your neighbors' appliances as well as (or instead of) your own. Currently, few enough people are involved in home automation (and specifically X10) for this to be a practical issue. You can provide yourself with some peace of mind right now by placing a filter between the electricity meter and the rest of the house mains. This is usually called a *whole house filter*, and several makes and models exist, such as the PZZ01, which permits 200A of current. Naturally, with the levels of current involved (and the law in certain countries), many people hire a qualified electrician to install such a device.

The second part of the address is the *unit code*, of which there are 16, and is represented by a hexadecimal digit between 0 and F. Although this might not seem a lot, 16 devices allows you to have two appliances (one light and one other) in every room of a moderately sized four-bedroom house. Most rooms will have only one—the light—while appliances such as TVs and radios are more likely to be effectively controlled through infrared or even Ethernet.

In addition to an address, every X10 receiver module fits into one of two broad types, either *lamp* or *appliance*. This is a difference that exists in the X10 module itself and that governs how it will deliver power to the device plugged into it and which messages it will accept. An appliance module simply provides on/off control to whatever is plugged into it and usually has a high enough power rating to accept most household appliances (ovens excepted). In contrast, a lamp module will also respond to brightness control messages, varying the voltage applied to the light bulb plugged into it. Consequently, plugging a toaster into a lamp module can be problematic and a potential fire risk. Adding a light to an appliance module, on the other hand, works fine and only suffers the limitation of losing the dimming functionality.

■ **Note**   Some types of light (such as fluorescent and power-saving bulbs) cannot generally work on lamp modules and must be used with appliance modules.

Each X10 message consists of three parts:

- A start message block (a nibble of 1110)
- An address (a house code and/or unit code)
- A command code (for example, "switch on")

There are several different commands, fitting mainly into two groups—house code messages directed toward all devices and unit code messages targeting a single appliance. As mentioned earlier, each X10 module is built to accept or ignore specific messages, usually according to whether it's designated a lamp or appliance module; however, appliance modules will also ignore the "all lights on" message but honor the "all units off," which is suggested by the subtle wording of the commands differentiating between *lights* and *units*. It is interesting to note that their inverse variants ("all lights off" and "all units on") do not exist. This is intentional. One of the intentions of "all lights on" was to act as a security feature. An accidental invocation of an "all *units* on" command might start a teakettle dry boiling or something similarly dangerous. Conversely, "all units off" provides a quick closedown procedure for the house.

Once the message has been sent, nothing else happens. Ever! The receiver does not generate an acknowledgment of the message, and the sender doesn't query the state of the recently controlled device to confirm its arrival. This is because the transmitting circuits are more complex and expensive than the receiver and because adding a message facility would add cost and bulk to the simplest of light switches. Some two-way switches do exist, providing a way for you to query their state, but they are more expensive.

However, in an attempt to ensure data validity, the message is sent twice, and both messages are compared for equality since electrical noise on the power line could have corrupted part of the signal. Consequently, it takes around 0.64 seconds for an X10 message to be received. Although this is an accepted facet of the protocol, it is not particularly friendly when guests are staying at your house, because when they try to turn on the light, it appears to have not worked . . . so they press the switch again and in doing so turn it off! To overcome this, many devices have a local switch that affects the light directly without sending an X10 message to do so. This is mostly true for X10 light switches that act like a normal in-wall switch but not an in-place X10 socket that is controlled by an existing (that is, normal) light switch.

Another problem that can occur with X10 is that of *dead spots*, where all messages can (and sometimes do) get swallowed because of the electrical noise generated by certain appliances. The power supplies for some MacBooks are known to have this issue. It is therefore sometimes necessary to move X10 devices to different sockets for them to work. X10 signals are also lost when there is a transformer in the circuit or you have a split phase system. Again, you may need to move both the transmitter and the receiver to the same side of the problem device.

■ **Note**   Before committing to an X10 installation, experiment with a couple of devices to ensure there is a location in the house that is capable of issuing an X10 message that can get heard in the vital majority of other areas.

General Design

Before buying and installing any devices, you must first consider what devices you want to control and how you want to control them. The important part of that question is not how *many* devices you will use but *how* they will be controlled. This can be as simple or as complex as you like. And there need not be a computer involved at all.

Simple Case

In this situation, your appliances will be controlled either by their local switches or by one or more wired controllers plugged into the mains. A wired controller is necessary here because you always need some way of introducing the X10 signals to the power line. There are some wired controllers (SD7233), which include timing circuits so they can automatically turn the lights on or off at particular times of day—sometimes within a randomized time frame to confuse potential burglars. These work well and provide a cheaper alternative to running a computer all day, every day.

Other than the basic timer functions, this setup can only be controlled by a human making physical contact with the controllers. It is the cheapest way to begin an exploration into X10, but appliances cannot be controlled remotely via web sites or e-mail or wirelessly from handheld controllers.

If aesthetics are important, there are some controllers (for example, TMD4, shown in Figure 1-11) that will fit into a wall outlet, allowing you to use the existing light switches to control multiple lights without a *Star Trek*-like controller on the coffee table. However, this requires the purchase of both an X10 switch (to send the message) and an X10 light fitting (to respond to it) and is usually overkill for such simple setups.

Standard Case

The next step after the simple case shown earlier is to utilize wireless controllers. Most of the equipment on the market uses radio frequency (RF, at 433MHz), allowing devices to be controlled from the garden, through walls, through floors, and through ceilings. The precise range varies according the materials through which the signal is traveling, the other devices operating in the 433MHz range such as TV senders or RFID readers, and the strength of the transmitter, with some mid-price devices having a 25-meter range when unobstructed.

Because RF has no connection to the power lines, it also requires the use of an RF-to-X10 gateway, which plugs into a wall socket, picks up the RF signals sent by any suitable controller, and places the data message onto the X10 power line. Although such devices have a configurable house code, their unit code is invariably hard-coded to one, so be sure to avoid using such a code for any devices if you plan on migrating from a simpler environment.

Adopting an RF-to-X10 gateway in this way provides a lot more scope for automation, because controllers are wireless and no longer need to be situated next to a power socket, enabling them to appear in bathrooms where such sockets contravene domestic housing regulations in many countries by being within 1.5 meter of a water tap, as is the case in the United Kingdom, for example. There are RF controllers that stick to walls, sit on desks, and even fit on key rings!

The primary issue with RF remote control is that rogue transmissions are very difficult to filter out,[1] meaning someone outside could conceivably control your inside lights.

Fully Automated

The big difference between this and the standard automated example is the inclusion of a computer interface, generally the CM11, covered later in this chapter and shown in Figure 1-14. This doesn't have an X10 address, but it passively monitors the messages on the power lines and passes them back to the computer via the serial or USB port. Similarly, the computer can use the device to place new messages onto the power lines, which will be picked up by the devices you already have. Once a computer is involved, the possibilities open up. I'll be covering these possibilities later in this chapter when covering the range of available X10 devices.

It is perfectly possible to have a fully automated solution using the computer that doesn't use RF wireless or suffer its problems. Instead of RF, you can use a more secure transport and protocol such as HTTPS through a web browser that could be on an iPod touch, iPhone, or other suitably connected handheld device such as a mobile phone to send the message to the computer, which is turn places suitable data on the power line.

Assigning Addresses

Because every automated device in your house needs an address, it makes sense to assign them something sensible and memorable at the start of the process. The most important thing to remember here is that your X10 configuration can grow as your budget increases, and you're more likely to add a couple of new appliances in your house than you are to add a couple of new rooms!

Determining a house code is simple enough. If you have a neighbor, or neighbors, with an X10 setup, then pick any letter that isn't used by them. It might sound obvious, but you should *talk* to them about whether they have one and what codes they're using. Just because you're not seeing any irrational behavior at the moment doesn't mean there won't be a conflict in the future. I would also avoid using P, since some devices (the TM13UAH, for example) considers P as "accept message on any house code," which could be confusing and problematic. My only other advice here is to avoid A, which is the default for most equipment. This has two benefits. First, it ensures that anyone "playing" with X10 devices in the neighborhood won't accidentally stumble onto your network and cause

---

[1] A Faraday cage works but is not generally practical in a home environment!

mischief. The second is that by switching away from the defaults, you can be sure that the system was successfully reprogrammed and is not working temporarily by a happy coincidence.

Producing assignments for the unit codes is a matter for your own judgment, but you cannot go far wrong by creating a *pattern*. I began by numbering my devices at 2 and worked around the rooms in my house in a counterclockwise order, starting upstairs and ending in the kitchen. I assumed two devices per room. My reasoning and thought processes were as follows:

- Start at 2 because 1 is used by the RF-to-X10 gateway.

- Two devices per room means each room starts at 2, 4, 6, 8, and so on, which is easy to remember.

- The only time I need to know the numbers by heart is when fumbling with the remote in the dark. This is when I'm in bed looking for a light switch. Because the master bedroom is upstairs, I start counting upstairs. And when lying in bed, I'm facing the rest of the house, with the second bedroom directly in front of me, and the third to its left, which makes a counterclockwise motion more natural.

- If the split between upstairs and downstairs hadn't occurred on unit code 8, I would have left a gap so that it did.

- I split the lounge/dining room into two logical rooms, even though it's one space. This means I can have up to four devices in the one space, which is likely to happen with larger open-plan areas.

- The kitchen is more likely to gain devices over time, so I kept that last in the list.

If you browse the selection of controllers available, you will notice that most have a selector switch that reassigns the buttons from 1–4 to 5–8, for example, or from 1–8 to 9–16. An alternate approach is to have the first bank (1–4, say) controlling only the lamps in the house, with the second (5–8) being used to control the appliances in the equivalent room, making it switch between "lamps and appliance" rather than "upstairs and downstairs." This ensures that although the first bank is selected, it's impossible to accidentally turn off an appliance when you mean to control the lights, and vice versa.

The final consideration concerns the physical size of the controller modules you plan on using, as many support only eight devices. If your most convenient numbering system happens to use devices 9–16, then you will either have to rethink your pattern or buy only larger controllers.

Using Multiple House Codes

It is possible to have two or more house codes within a single property, bringing the total number of household devices up to a maximum 256. That's enough for the largest of mansions! The only consideration with such setups is that a control message such as "all lights off" can be applied only to a single house code. For computer-based control, you can easily adapt the software to send two (or more) messages of the "all units off" variety, which affect all devices on the specified house code. However, if you've elected to use only stand-alone remote controls, such as the desktop controllers you will learn about later in this chapter, this can require some fiddling as you switch off each house code in turn. In this case, you would probably want to split up the house codes into the first floor, second floor, and so on, and have a separate controller for each floor.

Device Modules

I'll now cover the multitude of devices available on the market that can be controlled *by* X10, in other words, those that contain a receiver. These break down into three categories:

> *Internal*: Where the X10 receiver and the thing it controls are within the same physical form factor. An example is motorized curtain rails.

> *Local control*: The X10 receiver processes the message but controls the power to something directly wired into it. An example is light switches.

> *Plug-in modules*: These fit into a standard power socket, and an external device is plugged into them. The X10 logic determines whether to allow the flow of current between them. An example is appliance units.

Controlling Lights

This is by far the most common type of device, and accordingly there are several different devices to choose from, all known in X10 parlance as *lamp modules*. However, it should be noted that some lights cannot be attached to lamp modules at all. These include the fluorescent lighting strips found in most kitchens and their compact fluorescent lamp equivalents (often known as *energy-saving bulbs*) now making their appearances in homes around the country. To make matters worse, these bulbs can also introduce spikes on the power line that can turn off nearby X10 lights.[2]

The primary functional difference between the various lamp modules is whether the device in question supports dimming. When a light is dimmed, the alternating voltage is not reduced in amplitude. Instead, small portions of the power sine wave are removed, which effectively turns off the lamp for short periods of time. Consequently, the bulbs filament is charged and discharged many more times a second than usual, which creates a changing electromagnetic field. This can result in the filament starting to vibrate and creating an audible hum. This is not usually a problem with light bulbs (and you can always buy *rough service* bulbs that hold the filament steadier to prevent this movement), but it is dangerous to other appliances that are not built for it.

Note that many countries are phasing out the old incandescent light bulbs due to their relative inefficiencies, compared with newer alternatives, such as LED, compact fluorescent lamps, and halogen.

Lamp Module (LM12U)

This is a simple affair that requires zero installation. You simply plug it into a free wall socket, set the address using the dials on the front, and plug your lamp into the socket on the front, as shown in Figure 1-1.

---

[2] You can witness the noise introduced by observing the oscilloscope traces shown at http://jvde.us/x10/x10_cfls.htm.

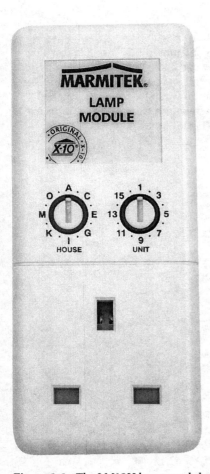

Figure 1-1. *The LM12U lamp module, 122 × 52 × 42mm*

This will support any incandescent lamp between 60 and 300 watts and can be switched on and off or dimmed by any X10 controller set to the same house code. The LM12U has a sister device, the AM12U, which works in the same work. The primary difference is that the AM12U is intended for appliances and therefore ignores any "dim" messages. The LM12U will also respond to two special messages, "all lights on" and "all units off," provided they are sent using a matching house code. This module, like many of the others featured here, is placed in series with the power line acting like a logical AND gate. That is, both the lamp's switch and the power switch at the wall must be on for the X10 "turn on" message to have any effect.

■ **Note** The code numbers given here are for the U.K. versions of these devices. Because of slightly—but significantly—different power systems used in various countries around the world, alternate modules are required according to your country. The LM12U in Italy, for example, is called the LM12I.

Bayonet Lamp Module (LM15EB)

This is also a simple zero-installation device but one that requires slightly more configuration. To install it, you plug it into an existing light socket and then reinsert the bulb (up to 150W) into its free end. Neither fluorescent lamps nor low-energy lamps should be used, though. The address is set by turning the lamp off and on again and then pressing the required house/unit code on the controller three times, once a second, within 30 seconds of it being switched back on. The light will come on once the code has been learned. There is also a screw-in version of the same device (LM15ES, with ES standing for *Edison screw*), although it is the bayonet version (LM15EB) that's shown in Figure 1-2.

Figure 1-2. *The LM15EB, 45 × 45 × 95mm*

LM15EBs lack the dimming facility of the larger LM12U, but because they extend only 62mm farther than a traditional fitting, they are small enough to hide inside most lampshades, allowing the room to maintain its existing aesthetic qualities.

Again, the module acts like an AND gate, allowing the light to shine only when both the X10 command for "on" has been sent and the light switch would normally be on.

Wall Switch (LW10U)

As you can see from Figure 1-3, these are complete replacements for a standard light switch, which means you are limited in styling to white plastic. However, they are easy to fit into existing recessed switch boxes with only 16mm protruding from the wall. The unit's address is set from a pair of dials placed behind the rocker switch and can be accessed by gently prying it off with a screwdriver. Care should be taken, however, because the plastic lugs that hold the switch onto the case are quite flimsy and would only suffer three or four removals before breaking.

Figure 1-3. *The LW10U, 85 × 85 × 30mm*

In addition to being controlled remotely by "on," "off," "dim," and "bright" commands, the same functionality is available locally through the switch. Touching it once switches the light to full on or off, whereas keeping it held down will dim the light (if it is bright) or brighten it (if it is dim). Alas, the last brightness is not kept when you switch it off and then on again, nor can you slightly increase the brightness of a dim light without first making it fully dark, but local control means the light comes on immediately after pressing the button so as to not confuse any guests.

This device also responds to the "all lights on" and "all units off" messages for matching house codes.

MicroModule with Dimmer (LWM1)

This module is a turbocharged version of the LM10U and is shown in Figure 1-4. It works in the same way as the LM10U but is small enough to fit *inside* the wall outlet, allowing you to use any switch fascia you prefer.

Figure 1-4. *The LWM1, 40 × 40 × 15mm*

It supports all the existing functionality of the LM10U but can also remember the last brightness setting, allowing the light to be smoothly changed when it's first switched on, which helps increases the bulb life.

■ **Note**   The cheaper modules switch on at full brightness, so if you enjoy mood lighting, then this is a variant worth considering.

Furthermore, this is one of the few devices in this section that supports two-way X10 communication. This means that you can send a message to the device asking for its current brightness state, and it is able to reply. This is unavailable with most other devices, meaning that you (or more specifically, your controller device) must remember the last message it sent, hoping it arrived, in order to emulate the querying of the lamp's state. And even this result might be flawed if the brightness was changed locally. In most cases, however, this functionality is unnecessary because you rarely want to know whether the light is on. If you're going to bed, then you're not interested is whether the light is on or not, only whether you can switch it off. Unless you have a very large house, you can usually see a single light on in an otherwise pitch-black house and therefore know whether you need to resend the "all units off" message.

The downside of this device is that it costs around three times that of the LM10U. However, there is a midrange product in the LW12 that features the same specification but without two-way communication.

DIN Rail Dimmer (LD11)

This is a (very) high-power module, capable of controlling devices up to 700W, and it is consequently suitable for mains halogen as well as traditional mains lighting. Instead of being used in place of a switch (like the LWM11) or in connection with the bulb (like the LM15EB), this device is remotely placed near the fuse box, with the LD11 output cables running into the light directly. This is a switch terminal on the LD11 that allows the appliance to be switched on and off, as if it were local. However, with four (potentially) long cable runs from the appliance to the LD11 (two for power and two for control, as visible in Figure 1-5), its purpose isn't so obvious.

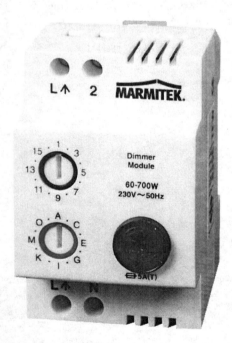

Figure 1-5. *The LD11, 50 × 80 × 70mm*

The primary purpose for the LD11 is mood lighting, thanks to its support for halogens, and scene lighting, thanks to its soft dimming and memory functions. Because they are generally placed away from the devices themselves, you get a much cleaner install. The cost in cabling is thankfully offset by the cheaper cost of the module.

If you use the LD11 to power lighting sockets, only lamps must use them, as the dim feature will destroy many other types of appliance. To aid in this, you can use nonconventional plugs and sockets for the lamps and LD11-fed outlets. If your country uses square pin plugs, source some rounded pins, and vice versa.

Appliance MicroModule (AWM2)

This module uses the A prefix because it is primarily intended to control appliances; however, its function is also suited to lights. The AWM2, shown in Figure 1-6, sits inside a standard wall outlet and supports two switches. One switch controls the locally connected lightbulb (and sends an equivalent X10 message onto the power line), while the other switch sends an X10 "on" or "off" messages to the *next* address in sequence. So, if your AWM2 is configured to E2, you can also control E3 from the same switch. By installing two identically configured units at the top and bottom of the stairs, you can control both the upstairs and downstairs lights from either location with no rewiring. And because this is an internal module, you can use any switch facing your choose. Note, however, that this device doesn't support dimming.

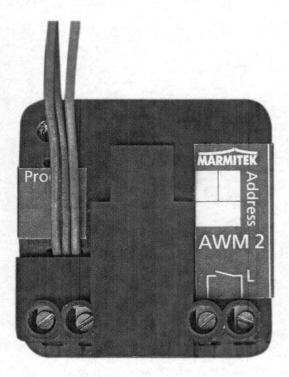

Figure 1-6. *The AWM2, 46 × 46 × 18mm*

Controlling Appliances

For appliances that are supplied without X10, such as teakettles, toasters, and HiFi units, a second type of device is needed. These function in much the same way as the LM12U or LM15EB/LM15ES, whereby the device is plugged into an existing power socket and the appliance in question is plugged into the X10 module. As mentioned previously, these require the switch on the wall socket to remain permanently on, along with any switch on the appliance itself. This further implies that any device plugged into such a module that could be controlled remotely must be safe at all times. In the case of the teakettles, for example, it must contain enough water so it won't boil dry.

Appliance Module (AM12U)

Like its sister module, the LM12U, this is a very simple "plug in and go" device that, although it looks the same (see Figure 1-7), has three very important differences:

- It has no dimmer support
- It can control fluorescent lights
- It can operate at much higher loads (up to 500W for incandescent lamps, 1A for inductive[3] appliances like fans, and 16A for resistive loads[4] such as heaters)

Figure 1-7. *The AM12U, 52 × 122 × 33mm*

Consequently, its intended purpose is to automate units such as fans and teakettles. However, high-power devices such as vacuum cleaners and fan heaters rarely work on these modules because of the back-EMF created by the collapsing magnetic field around the motor when it is switched on or off. This back-EMF generates a large voltage spike that can blow the fuse in the AM12U (if you're lucky) or the device (if you're unlucky).

---

[3]Inductive loads use magnetic fields and are usually characterized by motors or solenoids.
[4]Resistive loads convert electrical current into other forms of energy, such as heat.

There is an in-wall version of this, called the AW12U, with a similar specification.

■ **Note** You can often use these devices to automatically power-cycle routers and modems when the Internet connection is unavailable, often from the router being choked or when it simply crashes.

Appliance MicroModule (AWM2)

This is the same module featured previously (and in Figure 1-6) as a suitable candidate for light control, because it can also be used to control appliances. Apart from its smaller size (46 × 46 × 18mm), its main benefit over the AM12U is that it has a much higher power rating, making it possible to power fan heaters and their ilk. The given power specification on this unit is 2kW for incandescent lamps, 3A for inductive appliances, and 16A on resistive loads.

As mentioned previously, this device is mounted in wall outlets, making it more difficult to circumvent. Consequently, this module allows you to switch off a child's TV or stereo system at night without them simply unplugging it, as they might with an AM12U.

Table 1-1 gives a breakdown of the previously referenced devices.

Table 1-1. *Basic X10 Modules*

Appliance	Name
AM12U	Appliance Module (plug)
AWM2	Appliance MicroModule (in wall)
LD11	DIN Rail Dimmer
LM10U	Wall Switch
LM12U	Lamp Module
LM15EB	Bayonet Lamp Module
LM15ES	Screw-In Lamp Module
LWM1	MicroModule with Dimmer
LW12	In-Wall Module with Dimmer (like LWM1, but no two-way comms)
TMD4	MicroModule Transmitter Dimmer (four-switch, in-wall, no power handler)

Internal Devices

These devices are rare and usually fit in the novelty category. One good case is REX-10, a barking dog alarm system! On receipt of a suitable X10 message (for example, from a motion detector), this device plays the noise of a dog barking followed, a few moments later, by the sending of an X10 message to switch a light on. As an idea it's good, but it is very difficult to configure these hardwired devices as effectively as you could with a short computer program or simple script.

Combination Devices

I'll briefly cover some devices that, although they are not supplied with X10 control, are invariably used with it. It should also be noted that the mains control could equally well come from an alternative power control method (for example, C-Bus).

Electronic Curtain Rails: Retrofit

You can automate many curtains by simply wrapping the U-shaped pulling cords around an electric motor. Naturally, the devil is in the details, so there are a few prebuilt motor and pulley systems on the market that are able to open and close curtains, mounted into a head rail. They include the Regency PowerMotion, Universal Curtain Motor (UCM), and the Add-a-Motor 80 (CM80).

Using a retrofit solution requires you to have a good existing head rail, because this determines the maximum weight of the curtain the motor is able to handle—if it gets stuck, then the motor could burn out. The specific weight will vary between devices, but a good guide is that head rails with ball bearings will manage curtains up to 30 kilograms, while those without might stop at 10 kilograms.

All of these devices require manual installation to fix the cords to the motor, configure the open and closed positions of the curtains, and adapt the electronics to incorporate a separate X10 receiver. Depending on the device, this might involve a simple AWM2 or AM12U unit or possibly an in-line module.

Controlling the curtains once installed is a simple on/off affair, requiring some additional control logic to automatically position them as "50 percent open," for example; however, you can always issue an "off" command manually to stop them from opening any further. There are switches designed specifically for curtain control, such as the Marmitek X10 Motor Drive Switch (SW10), which repurposes the standard X10 messages of "on," "off," and "bright" to be "fully open," "fully closed," and "partially open," respectively.

■ **Tip**   You should not leave control curtains unattended in the first few days after installation, because the motor might try to move them too far and burn out.

Electronic Curtain Rails: Prebuilt

One such solution here is the Silent Gliss AutoGlide. This provides a made-to-measure curtain track with a premounted motor and a remote-control unit. Because the curtain track is custom-made, you must know in advance the size and shape of your window since DIY adaptations are not possible and bending it (to fit in a bay window) is possible only by the manufacturer. The motor can be controlled by an X10 appliance module using a similar amount of DIY to the retrofit versions.

Stand-Alone Controllers

Having lots of remotely controlled lamps and appliances isn't much use unless you have some way of controlling them. All the devices covered in this section contain an X10 transmitter in some form that places an X10 data message onto the power lines, which is in turn picked up by any of the X10 modules covered previously.

Tabletop Transmitter Modules

These modules all provide a way to send X10 messages from a basic keypad to a specific device. Because they are powered by mains, the signal can be placed directly on the power lines, avoiding the need for an RF-to-X10 gateway. This group supports the largest selection of devices, with each adding its own unique selling points. I'll cover only a small selection here.

Mini Controller (MC460)

This is a standard, but functional, wired device that supports eight units, switchable in two banks (1–4, 5–8), along with the standard "all lights on"/"all units off" options and brightness control. To reduce the button count, the brightness control only affects the most recent lamp switched, either on or off. This is fairly standard among most transmitter modules.

Sundowner Dusk/Dawn Controller (SD7233/SD533)

On the surface, this appears like the standard mini controller earlier, wired to the mains, with control for eight devices, along with "all lights on"/"all units off" and brightness control. However, it also includes a light sensor that will switch on a predetermined group of lights when it gets dark and turn them off when it's light again. These brightness settings can be tuned with a little trial and error, although with dusk and dawn changing throughout the year, this can't necessarily be used as a natural wake-up call.

Mini Timer (MT10U)

This device, shown in Figure 1-8, solves the dusk-'til-dawn problem by using a timer rather than a sensor. This allows you to control up to eight light or appliance modules but lets you preprogram only four of them, making them turn on or off (up to) twice a day. This allows you to mimic a "lived-in" feel for the house. Furthermore, it includes a randomize option, which will vary the programmed times by 30 minutes to give a "*human* lived-in" feel. This device can also double as an alarm clock.

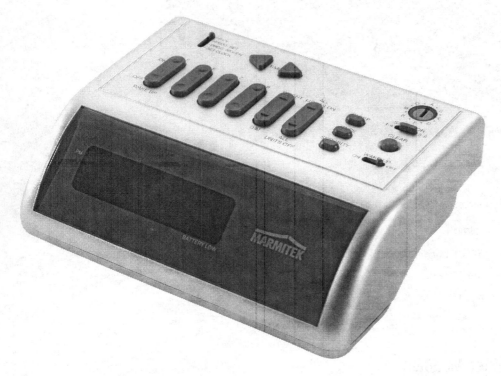

Figure 1-8. *The MT10U, 55 × 150 × 110mm*

Both this and the previous device alleviate the need for a computer server, because they can send out predetermined messages according to (simple) logic.

Maxi Controller (SC2800)

This device, although designed as part of a security system (MS9780), can also provide full wired control of all X10 devices in the house and is shown in Figure 1-9. Although it doesn't have any timing functionality, it does have a telephone socket that allows you to dial in from outside and switch lights on or off (by entering the unit code using a Touch-Tone phone, followed by either the * or # key, respectively).

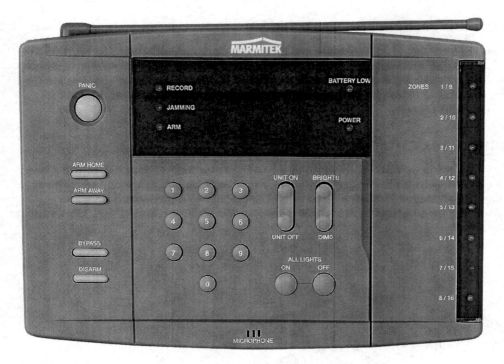

Figure 1-9. *The SC2800 provides easy access to your light switches via telephone*

Table 1-2 summarizes these desktop devices.

Table 1-2. *Desktop Controller X10 Modules*

Desktop Controller	Name
MC460	Mini Controller (4 × 2)
MT10U	Mini Timer
SC2800	Maxi Controller
SD7233/SD533	Sundowner Dusk/Dawn Controller (8)

Handheld Transmitter Modules

These modules work wirelessly and therefore require an RF-to-X10 gateway within range. Otherwise, they perform the same task as the tabletop transmitter modules, except they need batteries to power them.

Handheld RF Remote (HR10U)

These are comparatively cheap devices, capable of controlling all 16 devices in any given house code. They support brightness control but not "all lights on"/"all units off," and they have arranged the buttons in an on/off order, rather than the more geek-logical off/on.

One useful trait of this device is that it has a strip of card on the left side onto which you can write the names of the appliances that each button controls. Other than that, it's a fairly straightforward device that "does what it says on the tin."

There is an even smaller version containing just three device buttons called a Stick-a-Switch (SS13E, shown in Figure 1-10), which is also wireless and can therefore be placed on any wall. This allows you to control devices from the bathroom where mains-powered controllers would be illegal.

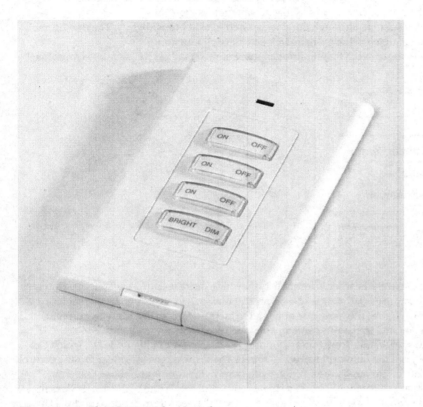

Figure 1-10. *The SS13E Stick-a-Switch*

Keyfob Remote (KR22E)

This, almost novelty, device allows you to control four successively numbered devices from your key ring using the "on," "off," "bright," and "dim" messages. It doesn't have a great range, and the batteries don't last very long.

EasyTouch Panel10 RF

This Marmitek device is one of the closest to being a cheap touch display. It is a battery-driven RF-to-X10 transmitter (just like the HR10U) but is operated by touching a screen. The screen, however, is merely an image behind a glass panel. That is why it's cheaper than the other solutions. Although this does prevent you from receiving any visual feedback from the devices, you can customize the image (by making one with GIMP and your printer) and control where on the touch panel the buttons appear; therefore, you can make this appear like a more expensive unit. Unlike the HR10U, which has a fixed set of 16 buttons, this can operate up to 30, providing enough space to control all your lights and other devices through Cosmic, part of the Minerva system (see Chapter 7), which lets you set timers, listen to news, and play your MP3 collection using only the basic set of X10 messages.

EasyTouch35 Universal Remote Control

This device's appearance is that of a traditional "all-in-one" infrared remote control, with separate menus for eight AV devices and the ability to learn the codes from other remotes. However, in addition to its infrared capabilities, it includes an RF transmitter to control X10 devices via an RF-to-X10 gateway such as the TM13.

As a standard IR remote, it works well enough, although the screen when backlit hums slightly. The touchscreen works well, and you can design the menu yourself using predefined icons for each function.

I'll cover universal remote controls in more detail later in this chapter. For the standard X10 wireless controllers, refer to Table 1-3.

Table 1-3. *Wireless Controllers for X10*

Wireless Controller	Name
EasyTouch35	Universal Remote Control
KR22E	Keyfob Remote
HR10U	Handheld RF Remote
SS13E	Stick-a-Switch

In-Wall Transmitter Modules

These appear to be like the wall switches I covered earlier insomuch as they hide inside existing wall outlets. However, these do not control any appliance directly. Instead, they solely send an X10 message to a specific device, such as a lamp or appliance module, relying on it to control the hardware attached to it. Therefore, to use these as automatic light switches, you need two devices, the in-wall transmitter and an appliance receiver.

One type of in-wall module is the MicroModule Transmitter Dimmer (TMD4, shown in Figure 1-11), which can command up to four different X10 units from the four switches wired into it. These messages include dimming control if you want to control lights or a simple on/off for appliances. People with large living rooms and those that enjoy mood lighting and multiple light sources may have four lights in a single room, and this is one of the few devices that lets you control all of them from a simple panel. Note, however, that each light still needs its own lamp module. Of course, it is not necessary for each switch to command an X10 device; it can simply place the message on the power lines and let the PC controller do something with it, such as change the volume on the stereo.

Figure 1-11. *The TMD4*

Motion Sensors

Most sensors on the market are passive infrared sensors (PIRs) and exist in both indoor and outdoor varieties, with the latter being commonly used as security lights that are mounted in the same area as the sensor. PIRs, like the EagleEye Motion Sensor (MS14), send an "on" message to specific but user-selectable X10 modules whenever motion is detected. Most models can also be configured to send "on" and "off" messages at dusk and dawn, respectively. Although some devices can send the message to more than one device (the PR511 and PSH01 spring to mind, both of which contain built-in floodlights), most only communicate to a single device, requiring a computer in your X10 setup to relay this message to other devices if required. You'll discover how later!

Gateways and Other Exotic Devices

A *gateway* is any device that allows communication data to flow through it, despite each side of the conversation having different protocols. In most technologies, a gateway performs a two-way function, converting the protocols in either direction. In an X10 gateway, there is generally only one direction, that is, *into* X10.

The primary device in this category is the TM13U, the RF-to-X10 gateway that I've touched upon already. One of these devices, shown in Figure 1-12, allows a wireless RF remote control to place messages onto the power lines for an X10 device to process. It never does the reverse. This device will listen for all RF messages coming from the same house code as is set on its front dial and retransmit them (using the same house code) to the mains line (provided that the socket is switched on). If the dial is set to P, however, it will respond to RF signals for all house codes but retransmit them on the original house code. This device generally has a hardwired address of 1.

Figure 1-12. *The TM13U, 122 × 52 × 33mm, or 224 × 52 × 22mm with aerial extended*

To transmit over two or more phases, you will need a coupler. This will listen for X10 signals on one phase of the mains and replicate it on another. This can either occur in single unit (like the TF678) or require a separate device for each phase that needs to be coupled (an FD10, shown in Figure 1-13).

Figure 1-13. *The FD10, an interesting filter/coupler module, looking very uninteresting*

Both of these coupler devices are, in fact, known as *filter/couplers*, meaning that instead of duplicating the X10 messages, they can filter them out entirely, thereby preventing the messages from leaking into your neighbors' houses. And by extension, they can prevent your neighbors' X10 devices from controlling yours.

A bridge is a device that functions as a go-between for two different protocols. In this context, the protocols invariably exist to bridge home automation systems such as from X10 to C-Bus or from X10 to UPB PulseWorx. Such devices are useful for upgrading systems piecemeal or for controlling very specific devices that don't exist on your system and/or for which no suitable software drivers exist. However, the cost involved in both the bridging device and the original module would have to be *very* special to make it worth the money in most cases.

This, and many other exotic devices, are covered in Table 1-4.

Table 1-4. *Miscellaneous X10 Controllers*

Miscellaneous Device	Name
FD10	DIN Filter and coupler
MS14	PIR-EagleEye Motion Sensor
PR511	PIR with flood light
PSH01	Power horn siren
TF678	Whole House filter
TM13UAH	RF-X10 Gateway, for all house codes

Computer Control

But far the most powerful and creative device available is a computer interface, such as the CM11, as shown in Figure 1-14. This is a transceiver that's able to pass messages from the power line to the computer and send messages back from the computer onto the power line. Unlike most X10 devices, the power socket on the CM11 is not controllable by X10 and instead is a simple through port. Consequently, if you want to control your computer with X10, you have two options.

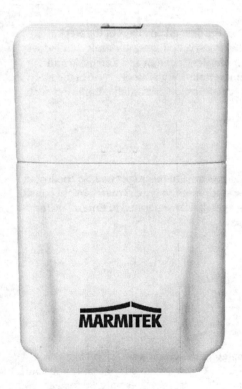

Figure 1-14. *The CM11EFL*

■ **Caution**   Be wary about putting the computer's power onto the normal house code, because you might accidentally switch it off when issuing an "all units off" message.

First, you could assign the computer an unused unit code and configure the computer to issue a shutdown command when it is seen on the power line. (I'll show you how shortly.) Second, you could use a separate appliance module and simply plug the computer into it. This is a workable although poor solution, since you're likely to have the machine plugged into an uninterruptible power supply unit (UPS).

In addition to being a controller, this device can also act as an event scheduler and message-relay system, even when not connected to a computer. Therefore, you can use the software (that is, the supplied Microsoft Windows version or a Linux equivalent, such as Heyu) to program the device and let it run stand-alone, since this programmed information now lives within its own EEPROM, which retains the data even if there is no power, allowing it to be moved from one place to another without reprogramming. (This also means it's possible to have a—slightly— automated house without a single computer!) However, you must keep a copy of the file and data that you uploaded to the CM11, since it is impossible to download it from the device.

■ **Caution**   When unplugging the CM11U from either the mains or the computer, always remove the serial cable from the device first, because stray noise from the cable can affect the internal memory and its settings.

The event scheduler allows you to send any X10 messages at any time of the day, on any days of the week, between any dates of the year. On its own, the device doesn't have the ability to vary the times randomly, but it does have a dusk and dawn setting that works after you've given it details of your physical location as a longitude and latitude. You can find your longitude/latitude from an atlas or (if we're being serious for a moment) one of the many geo sites on the Web. Your IP address is often accurate enough for these calculations and is available from sites such as the following:

```
http://api.hostip.info/get_html.php?position=true
http://whatismyipaddress.com
```

In CM11 parlance, the message-relay system is termed a *macro*. This allows an X10 message (such as "bedroom light on") to spawn additional custom messages to any, or all, of your other equipment. A typical macro might consist of "landing light to 50 percent," "bathroom light on," and so on. These messages can be separated in time, allowing a single "bathroom light on" message to become a short program such as this:

```
Bathroom light on
Stairs light to 50%
Wait 5 minutes
Bathroom light off
Wait 2 minutes
Stairs light off
```

So, in short, the CM11 can provide most of the functionality an automated house could want, albeit in a very static way. For your CM11 to dynamically process X10 messages, you'll need the computer on permanently and some software. Unfortunately, the software with which CM11 currently ships is for Microsoft Windows only. So instead, you can call on the community for software such as Heyu, which works as a replacement.

Heyu

Heyu is a simple command-line tool, available in most *nix systems (including most Linux distributions, BSD, and Mac OS X), capable of performing two-way communication with an X10 computer module and of programming the EEPROM with macros and scheduled events. You can also download it from the home page at www.heyu.org. This is not free software or open source as the OSI would consider it, but the source is available for free, and it is free to use.

Once installed, the software auto-configures itself when first run. This takes a few seconds and involves opening the serial port (/dev/ttyS0 by default) and verifying that the CM11 is truly plugged in and working correctly. The best way of doing this is to include Heyu in the startup sequence by running the following command:

```
heyu engine
```

This ensures that the Heyu background process is running, which allows incoming messages to be picked up, triggering external scripts. The engine parameter also starts the state machine inside Heyu, allowing it to remember the last setting for each lamp and appliance, which is useful since many devices (especially the cheaper ones) do not let you query their status. In a noncomputerized environment, this feedback loop is unnecessary since, as a human, you can see whether the light came on when you pressed the button, so you can see if you need to try again. A computer is not as talented. It is also good design practice for any computer interface to indicate the module's current state, making this feature more important. If you are likely to be using a lot of computer-based interfaces in your home (say, through a web page), then it can be worth upgrading to the two-way lamp and appliance modules covered earlier.

Configuration

The configuration is held within various files inside /etc/heyu, specifically x10.conf, which holds the serial device, default house code, aliases, scenes, and scripts. By default all log information is written to /var/log/heyu.

Aliases, as the name suggests, provide a human-friendly form of the house and unit codes for each device you want to set up in the x10.conf file along with whether the device is a lamp module (StdLM) or an appliance module (StdAM):

```
ALIAS  lounge e5   StdLM
ALIAS  stereo e6   StdAM
```

Once specified, the alias can be used within the configuration file and in the commands issued upon it. This abstraction reduces the number of changes necessary should you ever need to renumber your house appliances.

Scenes are Heyu's way of describing relay messages or macros. Each line contains a label name and a list of semicolon-separated commands:

```
SCENE  movie_mode  on tv; on stereo; dimb lounge 10;
```

The dim range in Heyu is between 1 and 22 and is supported by relative and absolute brightness change commands (dim and dimb, respectively). Note that if you change the Heyu configuration file while it's running, you must issue the following command to refresh the parameters:

```
heyu restart
```

Sending Messages

This is done simply with commands such as the following:

```
heyu turn studio on
heyu onstate studio
heyu bright lounge 5
heyu lightsoff _    # the underscore means current house code
```

which can be placed in larger shell scripts, called out from other languages, or triggered through a web site with CGI. Note that these are all blocking commands, so the rest of the script won't execute until the X10 messages have been sent—unless you begin the task in background mode, of course:

```
heyu turn studio on &
```

These commands can also be placed in your crontab, saving the need to upload changes to the CM11U's internal EEPROM:

```
export EDITOR=vi
crontab -e
```

Then as a sample line, add the following:

```
30 9 * * 1-5    /usr/bin/play /usr/share/sounds/alsa/Noise.wav
```

This adds an alarm call at 9:30 a.m. (when else!?) on every day of the month (the first wildcard) in every month of the year (second wildcard) when it's also a weekday (Monday=1, Friday=5).

If you want to add a random element, say within half an hour of 9:30, then you can use some simple bash to instead call this:

```
00 9 * * 1-5 sleep `echo $((RANDOM%60))m`; /usr/bin/play ↵
/usr/share/sounds/alsa/Noise.wav
```

Note that I've begun the delay 30 minutes earlier but created a random value that lasts up to 60 minutes.

Receiving Messages

Whenever a command is received, Heyu is able to launch an external script as specified in the configuration file. In many cases, this might be to switch on additional lights, acting like a scene or macro:

```
SCRIPT bedroom on :: /usr/local/bin/heyu turn bedside_light1_mine on
SCRIPT bedroom on :: /usr/local/bin/heyu turn bedside_light2_theirs on
```

Instead of controlling only lights, it could run an external script. This has the benefit of being editable by a user other than root, it doesn't require a heyu restart, and it provides a lot of flexibility that can't be squashed onto a single line. Code such as the following:

```
SCRIPT bedroom off :: ~steev/bin/housenight
```

will run a private script that switches off all the important lights and appliances in the house (remember that there is no "all *units* off" command), post something to your Twitter feed, and play a "Good night" sound effect:

```
#!/bin/bash

wavplayer default play ~steev/media/good-night-gorgeous.wav
tweet Good night all

/usr/local/bin/heyu turn studio_light off
/usr/local/bin/heyu turn kitchen_light off
/usr/local/bin/heyu turn lounge_light off
shutdown -h now
```

Alternatively, it can detect a message sent by a sensor transmitter that goes to no device at all but is relayed to several others:

```
SCRIPT pir_detect_msg on :: /usr/local/bin/heyu lightson _
```

Instead of controlling X10 devices, you can also control the PC itself. This example intercepts the messages from a single switch to control the volume of the PC to which the CM11 is connected:

```
SCRIPT E6 on :: /usr/local/minerva/bin/mixer default dec master 10
SCRIPT E6 off :: /usr/local/minerva/bin/mixer default inc master 10
```

These commands are run with the same user privileges as whoever issued the initial command:

```
heyu engine
```

This ensures the commands and devices (such as /dev/dsp) are available to this user. It is possible to build complex scripts and interactions solely using X10 messages. In Chapter 7, I'll discuss Cosmic.

Programming the EEPROM

All of the functionality of the CM11's EEPROM is available for programming through Heyu. You simply create a text file called /etc/heyu/x10.sched (there is a sample file in this directory also) with a suitable list of commands and type while the CM11U is connected:

```
heyu upload
```

The process will convert this text file into a suitable binary image and upload it to the device through the existing serial cable. Because it is impossible to retrieve this data from the CM11, you will want to ensure that you keep a backup of the x10.sched file or the resultant image for later use:

```
/etc/heyu/x10image
```

The full details of the x10.sched file format are available in the manual, including how to switch date formats to DMY from the default YMD. For now, I'll include some fragments of my own schedule by way of an example:

```
macro movies_on 0 dimb lounge 22; 0 on tv; 0 on stereo;
macro lounge_off 0 off lounge; 0 off lounge_table; 0 off tv; 0 off stereo;
timer  ...wt..    01/01-12/31 21:00 00:02  movies_on lounge_off
trigger e1 on movies_on
```

Z-Wave

Z-Wave was created by Zen-Sys, founded in 1999, as a proprietary protocol for controlling products wirelessly in the home automation space. In 2008 the company, and the technology, was taken over by Sigma Designs who still manufacture and supply the lions share of the chips. This has meant that all the manufacturers producing Z-Wave branded equipment must buy from Sigma (or their affiliate, Mitsumi) and all have to go through a testing and verification procedure to be allowed to brand their product as "Z-Wave." These vendors are part of the Z-Wave Alliance, and currently total 200 manufacturers with around 600 different products.

System Design

The communication channel used in Z-Wave is a 900MHz RF signal (which varies slightly according to your geographic location), transmitting around 40kbits/second. (Although newer devices with the 400-series chips can support up to 100kbs.) While the signal strength suffers the usual vagaries of walls and floors, each device has a range of up to 20–30 meters, and can be connected in a mesh formation, so that one device can repeat messages to the next, thereby extending the range. As well as sending messages between themselves, these devices also communicate with a hub, or primary controller, which is used to connect them to a wider network, either via a ethernet router, or computer. Typical controllers include the Tricklestar and Z Wave Aeon USB adapters, which requires a PC, and the VeraLitz Z Wave Controller which doesn't. There is also a RaZberry Z Wave controller which connects directly to the GPIO controller of your Raspberry Pi, if you wish to adopt that path.

When each new Z-Wave device is added to the system, it is paired with a nearby controller that determines the signal strength between them, which is then used in the routing algorithms. This makes it possible to send signals to devices that are placed underground and in garages, provided there is at least one device that is in range of it, and the rest of the network. However, with such a low data rate, it is easy to overload nodes if you try to force them into acting like repeaters.

For security, Z-Wave relies on this pairing arrangement, since buttons are pressed on each unit in a similar fashion to Bluetooth pairing to ensure each unit may talk to another. It is far from ideal, but given the comparative low uptake the chance of a man-in-the-middle attack is rather low.

Like X10, Z-Wave has a house code (which is called a Network ID), and a unit code (its Node ID) for addressing. These allow for 232 different nodes on a single network which, although slightly fewer than the number available with X10, is enough for the majority of houses, although it is not difficult to bridge between networks, should the need arise.

Z-Wave's biggest advantage has always been compatibility, since the interoperability labs at the Z-Wave Alliance ensured that virtually all devices could communicate with every other. This closed shop, however, ensured that no open source software could work. But that has now changed . . .

Bypassing NDAs

Because every member of the Z-Wave Allinace must sign an NDA and confidentiality agreement to access the formal specification and whitepapers, it was impossible for open source developers to build a true Z-Wave device—until hackers started to reverse engineer the protocols! There are now a couple of options.

Open Z-Wave

With such a direct and typically open source name, it's no surprise that this project has garnered a lot of attention. It comes in two main parts, the library, and the web-based configuration interface, which comes with its own mini web server. The library depends on `libudev`, which depending on your system may need to be explicitly installed. For example:

```
apt-get install libudev-dev
```

You can then build Open Z-Wave from sources in the traditional fashion:

```
svn checkout http://open-zwave.googlecode.com/svn/trunk/ open-zwave
cd open-zwave/cpp/build/linux/
make
```

The control panel, because of its web server, needs an up-to-date version of the httpd library and so is usually best to install it from source. Most of the problems occur when this step is omitted:

```
wget ftp://ftp.gnu.org/gnu/libmicrohttpd/libmicrohttpd-0.9.19.tar.gz
tar zxvf libmicrohttpd-0.9.19.tar.gz
cd libmicrohttpd-0.9.19
./configure
make
sudo make install
```

You can then grab the sources for the control panel:

```
svn checkout http://openzwave-control-panel.googlecode.com/svn/trunk/ openzwave-control-panel
```

and amend the configuration by uncommenting the three Linux-specific configuration entries around line 36. Then build normally with make, linking the web configuration directory to that of the Open Z-Wave library:

```
ln -s ../open-zwave/config/
```

and run it, specifying the port:

```
./ozwcp -d -p 13112
```

You can then browse to the page, enter your device name (or tick the USB box, for controllers attached in that way) and click "Initialize". By using the -d flag you will see the debug information on the console, which is always helpful in cases like this. You're now ready to talk to your house!

LinuxMCE

The LinuxMCE project has been gathering freely available Z-Wave information for a while now, and has dedicate part of their wiki into describing it:

```
http://wiki.linuxmce.org/index.php/ZWave
```

What's more, they have succeeded in implementing a version of the protocol:

```
http://svn.linuxmce.org/svn/branches/LinuxMCE-0810/src/ZWave/
```

Although this is, primarily, a media center project, you may find it introduces more dependencies that you might normal want, especially if installing it on smaller form PC, such as the Raspberry Pi. However, if your controller is not supported by Open Z-Wave and LinuxMCE is able to work with it, then you should smile and accept the overhead!

ZigBee

Sometimes (and unfairly) refered to as "the other Z protocol," ZigBee (http://www.zigbee.org) is a protocol that uses RF to communicate between devices at a range of between 10 and 100 meters. Unlike most other systems, there is no separate controller necessary, and all devices can become a coordinator of the network (ZC), a router (ZR) or a end point device (ZED).[5] In this way they are connected in a mesh formation, allowing the range to be naturally extended to other parts of the house. It also supports security with 128-bit keys and, with chips being available from many suppliers, they are comparatively cheap.

Politically speaking, ZigBee have an alliance (called, not unsurprisingly, the ZigBee Alliance), which provides a focal point for the specification, standards, and details of the 600+ products available from over 400 different companies. Because membership is open to all, the low barrier to entry has provided some innovative products such as AlertMe, LG's air conditioners, and energy monitors along with the usual range of buttons, lights, dimmers, and sensors.

Linux Software

By being more open than Z-Wave, with the specification being freely available, the range of software should have eclipsed Z-Wave. But didn't! This is because the ZigBee Alliance included a single clause that requires all licensees using the ZigBee mark to be members of the alliance. And membership of the alliance costs money. Loads of money! And clause 2c of the GPL (under which Linux kernel is written) states:

> *You must cause the whole of the work to be licensed at no charge to all third parties under the terms of this License.*

Therefore, it is not possible to include ZigBee in the kernel. Some projects have tried calling themselves Xbee to avoid this, and had short lives. Others (http://sourceforge.net/apps/trac/linux-zigbee) have moved away from ZigBee and toward other radio-based protocols, such as IPSO and 6LoWPAN.

Naturally, there is nothing preventing developers from working on libraries that are incorporated into the kernel by the end user, but this raises the barrier to entry somewhat. One such project is:

http://support.robotis.com/en/software/zigbee_sdk/zig2serial/linux.htm

It is a valiant effort but, like the others, destined to be deprecated unless the alliance introduces a zero-cost tier (like Bluetooth did), which allows the code to be included in the mainline kernel, and so reach mass adoption.

The Differences with Z-Wave

It seems that coders only need one common letter to start asking this question, as if it might be a fork or there's some juicy gossip associated with development politics. In fact, ZigBee is a similar protocol only insomuch as it uses RF to communicate from a hub to a set of similarly purposed devices. (And they both begin with "Z"!) But to say one is better than other is wrong, as they are intended for different purposes. The same questions that should be asked when considering whether to use X10 lighting or Hue, should be asked here as a larger question of "which is the best solution for me?"

For the most part, Z-Wave devices have better compatibility between themselves. As much as a closed shop might cause chagrin, it has ensured a set of devices that are happy to talk to each other—and being hardware, it's not as if one could easily make changes to the firmware. Seeing as we are able to communicate freely with both Z-Wave and ZigBee devices such philosophical standpoints are moot. Instead, it comes down to the use case. If you want devices from a number of different manufacturers, and you don't have the ability to pretest their compatibility, then

---

[5]Some devices marked a ZED's may not be able to work as a ZC or ZR because less functionality is required and so might have been built this way on purpose. The price may be a guide.

Z-Wave is likely to be the better choice. On the other hand, if there's only a subset of devices, or you plan on building your own then Zigbee is more likely to appeal. Especially given the Arduino XBee shield (`http://arduino.cc/en/Main/ArduinoXbeeShield`) and its successor (`http://arduino.cc/en/Main/ArduinoWirelessShield`) are still available.

Next, look at the physical space of your home. If, for example, you have lots of basement space or similar situations that need multiple units to allow the RF to "see around corners," then ZigBee is a better choice, because its better bandwidth can facilitate more messages being repeated in order to get the signal to its destination. The caveat here is if your traditional WiFi signal is unable to permeate the walls, then neither will ZigBee, as they operate on the same frequency and there'll be even more lost bandwidth as both devices try to coexist.

C-Bus

Although there are several well-known protocols for appliance control, X10 and Z-Wave are better known, with members of the knowledgeable public being aware of them, primarily because of their generally low barrier to entry. Within the HA community, however, it is the ownership of a Clipsal C-Bus system, which becomes the goal.[6]

About C-Bus

The C-Bus system was developed by an Australian company, Clipsal, as a means of controlling various light systems remotely. Clipsal's original intention wasn't in the field of HA but in stadium lighting rigs and commercial arena and conference centers. This meant the system had to support much longer cable runs than would be utilized in a home setup and a larger address space. It succeeded on both counts, with cable lengths of 1km being possible with 100 appliances on a subnet—with each subnet being capable of connections to another six through basic bridges or considerably more through the now available Ethernet bridges.

Differences Between X10 and C-Bus

C-Bus's primary difference is with its installation. Although X10 transmits its data along existing power cables, C-Bus devices are controlled by utilizing a proprietary protocol that travels along a separate Cat-5 cable. Consequently, such installations can be carried out only by qualified Clipsal-approved staff, pushing up the initial cost. However, once all the cables have been laid, one achieves the benefit of a near-zero level of maintenance since the interconnects will always exist and remain future-proof. It also provides two-way communication between the switch and a computer, making it trivial to query the state of the light dimmer or appliance. Furthermore, because the signal speed is not limited by the zero-crossings in the power line, all light changes happen instantaneously—a benefit that only those with many years of experience with X10 systems can truly appreciate.

To lower this initial overhead, Clipsal has recently introduced a wireless version of C-Bus, which eliminates the need for costly installations, so it is this subset of devices on which I'll concentrate. This optionally supports 128-bit encryption of its data stream, making it more secure than an (unfiltered) X10 wireless solution, although it's still hackable by the determined. Its wireless range is no better than the RF-X10 combinations covered previously, with a 5 to 20 meter range according to material. Unfortunately, there is a maximum of 30 devices on a C-Bus wireless subnet, making it less capable than an X10 system using two house codes. The generally adopted approach to C-Bus installations is that a wired version is used for the initial house configuration, with wireless being added later as a cheap upgrade path.

---

[6]C-Bus is used mostly in the United Kingdom and Australia, with the U.S. equivalent known as SquareD Clipsal. This is to avoid confusion with a similar technology called CEBus/EIA-600 utilizing the consumer electronics bus (CEBus).

For the geek, the primary difference is in the software because the protocol is closed, making Linux tools impossible. To reclaim this market, Clipsal has released an RPM containing a binary-only driver that is available for zero cost on its website.

■ **Note**   A Red Hat package manager (RPM) can be utilized on non–Red Hat platforms such as SUSE or converted using tools such as Alien. The biggest problem with drivers packaged in this way, however, is its level of compatibility with the Linux kernel. Any change in the driver API, or similar breakage between kernel version numbers, will render the driver (and therefore your C-Bus system) useless. In these situations, when there is no more open solution available, it is always best to keep a low-level legacy system available and be prepared to migrate other software away from the box when necessary.

Unlike X10, each C-Bus device contains a microprocessor that makes it possible to control other devices remotely, without a computer. This is provided by switching the device into one of its five modes, which break down roughly as follows:

- Normal, stand-alone, switch
- Basic peer-to-peer switch control
- Networked switch control
- Networked switch control, with remote
- Interfacing with a wired C-Bus install

The adscititious computer is of benefit to smaller HA installations and those concerned about complex lighting UI. But for those of us intending to control other devices, the inclusion of a PC is not an issue.

Devices

Like X10 devices, C-Bus has the ability to dim lights and control appliances that are attached to it. Where they differ is the ability of a C-Bus light switch to control one or more other devices straight out of the box and with minimal on-device configuration.

■ **Note**   I'll consider only the wireless devices here, for the reasons given previously.

Controlling Lights

There are two designs of light switch, Neo and Saturn, which fall in the 5850 and 5880 product ranges, respectively, and differ by their decorative styles only, although within each group you have the choice of two-, four-, six-, and eight-button versions. They are always paired, with the first two buttons controlling the dim function of the connected lightbulb. Each subsequent pair is required to transmit the button press information (wireless) to another device,[7] or devices. Because of the built-in microcontroller, these switches can be configured as a dimmer switch, an on/off

---

[7]Provided that they are configured in a networking mode.

pair, a remote trigger, or a scene trigger (the latter being the C-Bus term for macro programming, where several state changes can occur on several devices at the same time). Scene programming can also occur through the C-Bus Toolkit Software, although this is currently available only for Microsoft Windows.

There are several devices in each family, capable of various support loads and characteristics, but generally speaking a C-Bus dimmer will support incandescent and halogen lamps between 25W to 500W (up to 2A), along with fan motors (up to 2A).

These two series also provide basic switch units. These appear the same as their lamp-controlling counterparts, except that they lack the dim functionality. By way of compensation, they can support a much greater range of devices (up to 2KW, and 8A in places) including fluorescent lights.

■ **Note** There appear to be no in-wall units for sale, meaning you cannot use wireless C-Bus electronics with your own style of face plate.

Controlling Appliances

Like X10, C-Bus provides an appliance module that plugs into the wall and controls the flow of current to its corresponding socket. These are known as the 5812 series plug adapters and look like their X10 counterparts, with the exception that they, too, support dimming and switch versions.

Because every C-Bus device includes a microcontroller and the C-Bus protocol supports the remote programming of other devices, any of the light switches mentioned earlier can also be used to control an appliance switch by programming an "association" on the switch, equivalent to a Linux symbolic link.

Controllers

The Series Wireless remote control 5888 is the main device here. It is an RF transmitter (operating at 433.92 MHz) supporting ten devices up to 70 meters away (although 25 is more likely inside a building). Because of the unified design of all C-Bus modules, it is technically possible to control more than the allotted ten devices by using the remote to control one switch, which in turn controls another two through the use of a scene. Furthermore, no RF gateway is required to use this remote, since the C-Bus wireless network is already operating on RF. This also means that multiple remotes can control any individual device, and any individual button can control multiple devices.

Like X10, it also supports an "all off" message.

Gateways

With so much emphasis on the wireless network, it is sometimes necessary to revert to wires. This is where the Wireless Gateway C-Bus 5800 Series comes in. This is a necessary feature and the only way that the wired and wireless versions of C-Bus can be connected together. Also, through the use of software such as C-Bus Toolkit, it can be connected to a computer for remote, sequenced, and intelligent control. Consequently, this device is also necessary for a wireless-only network that needs to feature PC control because the 802.11 wireless protocol used by commercial routers is not suitable as a C-Bus wireless gateway.

Lighting Control

In addition to the general purpose appliance controlles that I've discussed, there are also a number of specific controllers for lighting. This is a recent development, but not a great surprise, since lighting is one of the major contributing factors in uptake for home automation. Most of us start with a controller light switch, after all. Given that lights are a specific case, it is therefore possible to add extra functionality to the communication protocols which would make no sense if it were a tradtional appliance, such as colour.

■ **Note**   Although many bulbs class themselves as WiFi, this is rarely the case because they communicate to a hub, which in turn talks to the network.

Hue

Designed by electronics giant Philips, this is the most prominent lighting-only solution at present. The basic starter kits provide a control hub and three bulbs, although the unit can support up to 50. This hub connects to both a wired ethernet port and a power socket. It then uses the ZigBee light link (wireless) protocol to talk directly to the bulbs.

Hue's biggest selling point is the color; or, rather, its range of colors. Each screw bulb supports a dynamic range of colours, selectable from a color wheel on the app. These colors may be picked from a photo, and programmed into a scene, so that the three lights are able to reflect the color scheme of your room, maybe by enhancing the colors present in your mantelpiece photograph, for example.

Configuration is automatic (as you'd expect for a consumer device) and the hub acquires its IP from your DHCP server, which serves a web page that redirects to the Hue online service where you can register your device and make a connection between the (online) account and your bridge. Once this has happened you can operate it remotely through the web site. This works through a polling protocol whereby, every half second, the Hue bridge makes a call to the Hue server to request any new commands, and update the server of the bridge's IP. You can verify that the Hue website can see your bridge by browsing to http://www.meethue.com/api/nupnp.

Alternatively, you can control Hue through your phone, with both iOS and Android devices currently supported.

For those of us working with open source, the reliance on an app is an occasional bind, although Phillips have just launched their API that allows you to talk directly to the hub to control the lights. This is available at http://developers.meethue.com/coreconcepts.html. After getting the IP of your bridge, you must set up a user by pressing the "link" button on top of the bridge and then, within 30 seconds, issue the command:

```
$ curl -H "Content-Type: application/json" -X POST -d '{"devicetype":"myhome"}'
http://192.168.0.27/api/
```

that returns a JSON object with a username, such as d7ae8b2151d50df1e61f380289f33bf, which should be used in all future requests.

You can then ask the bridge to search for lights on the system with:

```
$ curl http://192.168.0.27/api/d7ae8b2151d50df1e61f380289f33bf/lights
```

It will take a few moments for the scan to happen, before you can re-issue the command to get those available, returned in the form:

```
{"1":{"name": "Hue Lamp 1"}}
```

From here the fun begins as you can query the state:

```
$ curl http://192.168.0.27/api/d7ae8b2151d50df1e61f380289f33bf/lights/1

{
  "state": {
    "on": true,
    "bri": 254,
    "hue": 14922,
```

```json
    "sat": 144,
    "xy": [
      0.4595,
      0.4105
    ],
    "ct": 369,
    "alert": "none",
    "effect": "none",
    "colormode": "ct",
    "reachable": true
  },
  "type": "Extended color light",
  "name": "Hue Lamp 1",
  "modelid": "LCT001",
  "swversion": "65003148",
  "pointsymbol": {
    "1": "none",
    "2": "none",
    "3": "none",
    "4": "none",
    "5": "none",
    "6": "none",
    "7": "none",
    "8": "none"
  }
}
```

Change the color and brightness:

```
$ curl -X PUT -d '{"transitiontime":0, "bri":255, "hue":28000, "sat":200}'
http://192.168.0.27/api/d7ae8b2151d50df1e61f380289f33bf/lights/1/state
```

And lots more in addition. You should be aware that, true to its name, Hue uses the HSB color space, that is, Hue, Saturation, and Brightness, which allows it to emanate more natural whites and better mood shades of pastel. It also supports programmatic control through the CIE model (which maps colours on a chromaticity diagram, detailed at http://developers.meethue.com/coreconcepts.html#color_gets_more_complicated), which means that if you're used to the more traditional RGB notation, you will need to adjust your thinking or your code.

There are several web sites that can provide a visual representation of color conversion, such as http://www.workwithcolor.com/color-converter-01.htm. To convert the HSB values presented into Hue parameters you must:

- Multiply the Hue by 200 (technically it's by 182.04!)

- Rescale the percentages given for both brightness and saturation to values between 0 and 255

■ **Tip** Hue has a transition time between each state change operation. This provides a much smoother process than you can manage in code, and its use in long fades up or down is recommended.

There is also an open port on the bridge, 30000, to which you can `telnet` and issue commands directly such as `[Link,Touchlink]` However interesting the result, they don't offer any functionality that's not available already from the API so need not be discussed any further. Similarly, for more unofficial goodness you should visit everyhue.com.

■ **Note**   You can not change the color of Hue bulbs while they're switched off, although you can still issue "alerts" to bulb that will make them come on temporarily to indicate the arrival of mail, or the pressing of a door bell.

Insteon

Although capable of controlling more than just bulbs, it is with lighting that Insteon has found its mark. It has taken the X10 idea of passing all messages around on the power line, but extended it by providing a second "mesh" through its RF network. It has also improved on the X10 model by allowing every device to both receive and transmit messages, which means that every device is also a repeater, ensuring better coverage throughout the house.

■ **Note**   Although X10 and Insteon can work on the same power lines, Insteon will not repeat X10 signals as it does its own.

In fact, in most cases, Insteon is a better choice than X10—it's faster to react, has better data throughput, the device status can be queried in all cases, and all addresses are assigned uniquely at the factory so there's no issue with house codes or neighbour disputes. Where is does come lacking is in the range of devices available (something that is being remedied) and Linux software.

As with X10, you will need a special unit, such as a PowerLinc Modem[8], to allow your Linux machine, or Raspberry Pi, to communicate with an Insteon device. You will also need the appropriate USB driver (iplcd) and control software. And therein lies the problem! The only real contender in this space is at http://www.bobsplace.com/ilinks, but even that has ceased development work. Fortunately, the code survives and does work on most of the older devices. Otherwise you should look toward Mister House (misterhouse.sourceforge.net), as this contains an Insteon driver that is more up to date than the others available. Although it does mean installing more code than it necessary, it does have a better than average chance of working!

Lifx

Originally started as a kickstarter project in 2012 this comes under the heading of "one to watch." As supplied, the bulbs can be either set to master or slave. The master is given an IP address, and connects to a Wi-Fi network, and is able to distribute commands, in a mesh formation, to the slave bulbs. Current claims indicate that 9 slaves can be connected to each master. Smart phone control apps, and a hacker SDK, are expected around the same time as the bulbs and should available before the end of 2013.

Night Lights

By far the cheapest, and easier, automatic lights you can find. These have zero intelligence and comprise of a plug, a bulb, and a light sensor. When it's dark, they light up. When it's light, they switch off. It's that simple. However, despite the simplicity one need not ignore their benefits out of hand. They are, after all, incredibly cheap. Therefore, if you

---

[8]The older Power Line Controllers are not compatible with newer Insteon devices.

wanted to provide low level illumination for the landing, this is the most cost effective way of doing it. For those that insist *some* hackery takes place, you can look at replacing the bulb with a loop of electroluminescent wire (EL-wire), which will provide a Tron-esque feel to the house, guiding you between bedroom and bathroom.

Sheding Light

For most people, automatic lights are a good way of making the house seem lived in and, more importantly, occupied when you're away. However, with the ability to control their colour you can do more than just fade them up in the morning, to mimic sunrise, or fade them down at night. You can vary the tone of the light throughout the evening. The key term here is "blue light."

The bright screen on a tablet, or PC, is a bad thing, as it fools the brain into thinking it's still daytime, and therefore more difficult to go to sleep. By gradually lowering the brightness in the evening it can help a restful sleep. Or, to be more specific, lowering the brightness of the *blue* colour component can help. This is because the color blue reminds our million-year evolutionary process that the blue sky is still visible, and we should be alert.

There are a couple of options when it comes to automatically changing the color settings of your Linux monitor, f.lux and Redshift, and both work under X Window.

■ **Note**   With color-changing light bulbs, such as Hue, being readily available, there are expected to be scripts that implement blue light solutions in the near future.

---

f.lux

This is free (as in beer) software from Stereopsis and available from:

```
http://stereopsis.com/flux
```

in versions that come as executables for Windows, OS X, and Linux. However, unlike most free beer software, it is also available as source which, when working with Linux, is more easily installed and also available at the site:

```
wget http://secure.herf.org/flux/xflux.tgz
tar -xvzf xflux.tgz
sudo cp xflux /usr/local/bin
sudo chmod 755 /usr/local/bin/xflux
```

It can be run as a userland application by specifying your longitude (-g) and latitude (-l):

```
./xflux -l 51 -g 0
```

If you are unsure of these parameters, you can determine your location with one of the many online tools, such as http://itouchmap.com/latlong.html.

The program will then run in the background and use your geographic location to determine sunset, and then recolor your window manager as appropriate. It also has an option to disable itself for an hour, so that you can do any color-dependent work, such as photo manipulation, or even games.

Redshift

There is a fully open source equivalent to f.lux, called RedShift, available in most repositories. So in Debian, for example, you'd use apt with:

```
apt-get install redshift
```

This works in exactly the same way as f.lux, as a userland application accepting a longitude and latitude parameters and affecting the color of your monitor in the same way (although the specific colors used do vary slightly, so you might want to experiment with both to see if you get better sleep patterns with one or the other).

Because it doesn't run as a daemon, you should invoke it thus:

```
redshift -l 51:0 &
```

If you need to disable it temporarily, then you need to send a USR1 signal:

```
kill –USR1 1195
```

Where 1195 is the process ID, naturally, which can be retrieved either by executing:

```
echo $!
```

immediately after the redshift command, or by searching for it in the process list:

```
ps ax | grep redshift
```

Networked Devices

Although X10, Z-Wave, and C-Bus both provide a good means of sending simple controls to simple devices, more complex communication requires something better. More specifically, it requires something with more bandwidth. When the command is "play this song," it needs significantly more bandwidth. The most accessible way of supplying this is through a local Ethernet network, because it can send commands and data at high speeds without the distance limitations of USB, RS-232, or parallel cables. And, unlike X10, two-way communication is provided for free as part of the specification.

Ethernet Devices

There are many devices that support communication through Ethernet, either to control it or to supply it with data. Some can work on their own without additional hardware, such as personal video recorders (PVRs) and media enclosures. Both consist of a method of storing the media and the technology for playback. Others require a server to supply it with data. The functionality of the device, and its use within an automated home, is always improved by utilizing networked capabilities. This means you will need a server, of some kind, for most future appliances. This elicits the distinction of two necessary parts—a front end and a back end—connected by a local area network, be it wired or wireless.

The front end, or head unit, will generally consist of a device connected to a nearby HiFi or TV in order to play media located on a physically remote machine. Because such a unit is placed in the living room or bedroom, it should be small, silent, and attractive. Preferably, it should also be fairly cheap, because one front-end unit is needed for every room in the house that wants to participate in streamed media.

The back end, by contrast, is stored away from the main living areas (since it's generally a big PC with a noisy fan) but able to supply media streams to all the head units within the house via the network.

I'll cover various media-oriented head units in Chapter 3, although most of those shown could be re-created with a Linux machine running the appropriate software. However, the power usage, noise, and cost will generally be larger than a custom-built embedded device, even though many of those devices may be running Linux themselves! To connect the units, however, you need to know how to set up a network.

Networking Primer

To best utilize the devices here, you will need to configure a Linux machine as a suitable server. Most computer science books will begin their networking section by describing the OSI seven-layer model of networking . . . I won't! Instead, you'll learn only the necessary, practical steps of providing and configuring a suitable home network for automation.

■ **Note**   Each Linux example here, and throughout the book, is based around Debian and the packages within it. This is not advocacy on my part, merely practicality, because it's what I use. Some distributions may place the files in slightly different places or have slightly different names, but the principles are always the same, and the equivalents are easy to find.

Concepts

A home network is a way for each computer in the house to share a set of common resources such as printers, scanners, and storage space. In this sense, it's very much like an office network. Where the home differs is in the level of technology and, consequently, the expertise needed to run it. One of the main bugbears in office IT systems is the issue of security. With a home network, the relationships between the people using it are very much different, and social mores are brought to bear.

The standard network configuration has two parts—internal and external. The *internal* part is a network that connects all the house computers together, along with their peripherals, and makes them invisible to the outside world. These devices may be networked together through cables or wireless.

The *external* network is everything else! The big, wide Internet is generally unavailable the computers at home; it is available only by connecting to an ISP through a modem, broadband connection, 3G card, or similar device.

To connect these two sides of the network together, you need a router. Sometimes the router is a small box that comes as part of your DSL/cable/broadband package and automatically separates the internal and external traffic. Sometimes you'll need to buy one. They have one RJ-45 socket carrying the external network traffic, into which you plug the network cable from the broadband modem, and one or more outputs to the internal network.

Alternatively, you can use a PC with two network cards—one configured to talk to the external network and one for the internal. If you have a 3G card, then this acts like your externally configured network card.

With the router existing in both internal and external networks, it is able to automatically keep both sets of traffic separate and block any data or software you don't want moving between the two. Most routers are configured, by default, to allow all outgoing traffic but block all incoming traffic, except those on specific ports. The port is the route by which traffic protocols flow and is dereferenced by a number. All web pages, for example, are requested on port 80. So if your router is blocking incoming traffic on port 80, you won't be able to access your internal web server from outside your home's internal network.

Depending on the number of machines on your network, you might also need a switch that provides additional network sockets, into which you can plug more computers. Although it is unlikely that many people will fill eight sockets with computers, it is not uncommon to have non-computer devices that also use Ethernet to transmit data, thereby exhausting the available sockets.

Addressing

Every device on the network must have a unique address. There are two current forms of addressing, IPv4 and IPv6. IPv4 was the original form of describing addresses by means of a dotted quad, such as 89.16.172.66, and is used by virtually every machine and home device on the planet. IPv6 was introduced in 1998 by the Internet Engineering Task Force to overcome the various problems with IPv4, such as address exhaustion. However, its adoption is less than widespread, and many of the small, home-oriented devices do not use it, so I'll be concentrating on IPv4.

For a machine to have an address, it must be given one, either by a human or by a suitably configured computer. It cannot randomly generate one in case the address conflicts with another machine on the network or is one of the reserved addresses, such as 127.0.0.1. All the networked machines in the home should exist within a specific range of addresses, known as a *subnet*, and should be assigned to one of the private address ranges provided by the IPv4 specification. This not only stops conflicts with other existing sites on the Internet but also ensures the data within these networks is secure and invisible to machines outside the network, because all routers, switches, and gateways do not recommunicate any traffic with a private address range outside the local network. These private address ranges are 10.x.x.x,[9] 172.16-31.x.x, and 192.168.x.x, where x can mean any value between 0 and 255. For the purposes of demonstration, I will assign my subnet to the 192.168.1.x range, giving me 254[10] possible devices on the network. Most people use this for private networks because nearly all the routers sold for the home allocate addresses within this range. Also, most questions found on the various Internet forums will probably have answers detailed using the same addresses as you have.

Now knowing the address range of your network, you have to consider the individual addresses. The first one to assign is the router, which usually earns the 192.168.1.1 designation,[11] followed by the Linux server, which I will assign 192.168.1.2.

■ **Caution**   Configuring properties such as IP addresses requires you to be logged in as root, so tread carefully!

You can provide a Linux machine a static address either by using the tools in your desktop GUI or by configuring the /etc/network/interfaces file directly:

```
auto eth1
iface eth1 inet static
        address 192.168.1.2
        netmask 255.255.0.0
        broadcast 192.168.1.255
        network 192.168.1.0
```

This tells the system to use the network card assigned as eth1[12] for the static IPv4 address 192.168.1.2, with all the standard parameters.

---

[9] You might also see this listed as 10.0.0.0/8, with the 8 indicating that the first 8 of 32 binary digits within the address are fixed resulting in a range of over 16 million addresses between 10.0.0.0 through 10.255.255.255. Similarly, you might also see the following in use: 172.16.0.0/12 (providing a range of over 1 million addresses between 172.16.0.0 through 172.31.255.255) and 192.168.0.0/16 (providing a range of 65,536 addresses between 192.168.0.0 through 192.168.255.255).

[10] There are two addresses reserved for the subnet (0) and broadcast (255), thus reducing the total number from 256 to 254.

[11] Some routers can not be configured away from 192.168.1.1, so it's best to avoid using this number for anything else.

[12] Determine whether this is eth0 or eth1 by either checking the output of `dmesg | grep eth` or adding the alias `eth1 mynetcarddevice` to /etc/modules.

You *can* use this approach to assign static IPv4 addresses to every machine on your network—simply make note of which machine is given which number. However, this can become tiresome after a while, and many embedded devices don't allow such control over the configuration. Either case requires you to upgrade to DHCP.

DHCP stands for Dynamic Host Configuration Protocol and is a way of configuring the networking facilities of each client machine on the network. The software comes in two parts, a client and a server. The client says simply, "I'm a machine; where is the network?" by transmitting a message onto the cable for all machines to hear. The server listens for any and all of these messages and responds by returning all the configuration data that the sender should use for networking, such as its IPv4 address, domain name, and so on.

Configuring a DHCP client in Linux is easy and involves replacing the earlier section of the /etc/network/interfaces file with the following:

```
auto eth1
iface eth1 inet dhcp
```

Creating a DHCP server takes a little more work but can often be avoided as many network routers include one, although it's sometimes disabled by default.

To prepare one in Linux, you should first install the DHCP server software with a command such as this:

```
apt-get install dhcp3-server
```

You can then edit the /etc/dhcpd.conf file to assign addresses to each machine. Prior to editing, you may need to run this:

```
ln -s /etc/dhcp3/dhcpd.conf /etc/dhcpd.conf
ln -s /usr/sbin/dhcpd3 /usr/sbin/dhcpd
```

The addresses of each machine can be assigned by following these steps:

1. Giving it the next free number in a series, say 100–254. These are pooled addresses.

2. Looking at the MAC address of the network card that sent the message (all MACs are unique) and giving it a specific address based on that number.

3. Doing any combination of 1 and 2.

Because these pooled addresses are finite in number, they are never *given* to a machine. Instead, they are *leased*, and the DHCP client of each machine must rerequest the address if it's still using it after a certain amount of time. The software does this automatically behind the scenes. If you have a lot of visitors to your home (who'd rather use the Internet than talk with you!), then leasing addresses is the simplest way to go because each friend wouldn't need to have a static address that would require configuration.

Pooled addresses are configured like this:

```
subnet 192.168.1.0 netmask 255.255.255.0 {
  option routers        192.168.1.1;
  range 192.168.1.5 192.168.1.115;
}
```

Otherwise, the number of machines in your house is probably limited, so static addresses add very little work and make it quicker to troubleshoot since you know in advance what IP each computer should have. A typical configuration would appear like this:

```
host teddyspc {
    hardware ethernet 00:A1:68:8E:9E:AA;
    fixed-address 192.168.1.4;
}
```

This host section can be included within the subnet section shown previously to create exceptions in the pooling rule.

You can determine which leases have been granted by typing the following:

```
more /var/lib/dhcp3/dhcpd.leases
```

Many other options are available in the DHCP server, but these provide enough to get everything working. I'll cover the specific extra cases as appropriate.

Computer Names

My name is Steven, often shortened to Steev. My computer's name is 192.168.1.110, which is less easy to remember for nongeeks. Chances are there will be more nongeeks in your house than geeks who will want to refer to each computer by a name such as "Holly's computer" or "Angela's laptop." There are two strains of problem here: getting the computers in the house to have usable names and getting them to know the names of each computer outside the house on the Internet.

Computer names are usually distributed automatically around the local network, so they are not a problem, although it can sometimes take 30 seconds for the information to propagate to all machines. In case of problems, you can force-feed a mapping between IP addresses and computer names by adding a line like this:

```
192.168.1.110    mediapc
```

to the file located at /etc/hosts or C:\WINDOWS\SYSTEM32\DRIVERS\etc\hosts depending on whether you're working on Linux or Windows, respectively.

Converting Internet domain names into numbers is done through a type of server known as Domain Name System (DNS). This is a simple client/server process whereby a client provides a domain name, such as google.com, and the server returns the globally accessible IPv4 address of the computer. There are many of these servers throughout the world, arranged in a hierarchy. So, if your local DNS server doesn't know about a particular domain, it will ask its parent DNS server, and so on, all the way up to the master root zone server. All you need to do is configure your home machines to use the first DNS server in this chain, and the searches will happen automatically. If your ISP has provided you with a DNS server address, you can use this directly. Alternatively, if you are using a router, then this will often configure itself automatically by looking for a DNS server on the external part of the network (which only it can see) and then act as a DNS relay whereby it pretends to be a DNS server for internal network but instead passes all requests the ISP's DNS, before returning the results to you.

Having got an IP address of the DNS server (you'll use the 192.168.1.1 of the router in this example), you can use the DHCP server to distribute this information to each machine when it also requests an IP address of its own. Because the same DNS server is used for all local machines, this can be done by setting the global option at the top of the /etc/dhcpd.conf file:

```
option domain-name-servers 192.168.1.1;
```

Alternatively, if you are not using DHCP to provide the networking credentials, then you must revert to the same /etc/network/interfaces file in which you specified its static address and add the following:

```
dns-nameservers 192.168.1.1
```

Network Services

Having a machine on a working network is not enough to make one machine do something with another machine. Communication needs to take place. You've already seen two services in action (DHCP and DNS), and you're probably aware of others such as HTTP to access web sites and FTP to transfer files. For your machine to work like this, you need to install a server of some kind. The trick is to know what kind of server is needed for any particular task. I will introduce these servers as needed. The first that I'll show how to set up is a file-sharing server with the ability to provide files across the local network, allowing a music collection to be situated on one machine but playable by any other on the subnet.

▪ **Note** It is possible to make files from the internal network available externally, but I'll cover that later in this book.

The service that makes files available is called Samba, which allows files (and printers) to be shared between machines. Because it operates on a well-understood protocol (called SMB/CIFS), it can share these resources between different operating systems including Linux, Windows, and Mac OS X.[13]

It is installed in the usual way as your distribution, as shown here:

```
apt-get install samba
```

And it's configured by editing this file:

```
/etc/samba/smb.conf
```

This is used to specify which folders on the local machine are available to the other computers and under what conditions, such as passwords or read/write privileges. Because the machine in question is on a private address range, the files will be accessible only to local machines, so you can generally make all these folders publicly accessible because in this context "public" means everyone in the house. Unlike a corporate network, abuse of networking facilities in a home environment (usually by the kids!) can be covered by not providing them with any dinner!

There are many ways of configuring Samba to provide files, but the defaults are good for a home environment. I personally add sections to share various files in three specific ways. The first provides full access to my music and video files on my media server, such as //mediapc. These are mounted in a directory structure like this:

```
/media/mp3
/media/tv
/media/movies
```

and provided with the configuration section, like this:

```
[media]
comment = Media Server
path = /media
browseable = yes
public = yes
writable = no
read only = yes
guest ok = yes
```

---

[13] Version 10.2 and earlier.

This gives anyone at home, including visitors, a chance to listen to whatever band I've been enthusing about. It's public (meaning my visitors don't need a user account on my computer) and browsable (so it can be found on the network, without anyone knowing its exact name). However, it is made read-only, preventing visitors from accidentally (or maliciously, with rogue viruses perhaps) deleting the files.

They can see it from their Windows network neighborhood (or by typing \\mediapc\media) or from Linux (either by desktop or command line, with `smbmount //mediapc/media local_media_folder -o guest`[14]).

Next, I have a second share to the same location. This has a password, meaning that only I can add the latest DVD rips or music purchases to the system.

```
[media_incoming]
comment = Media Incoming
path = /media
browseable = no
public = no
writable = yes
read only = no
guest ok = no
```

The final share is my computer's DVD drive. This is almost unused in my house because I've had the time to rip all my CDs and DVDs into files on my local machine, but it is still occasionally useful. The default installation provides a suitable example on the method here:

```
[cdrom]
comment = Media server's DVD
writable = no
locking = no
path = /dvd
public = yes
preexec = /bin/mount /dvd
postexec = /bin/umount /dvd
```

The last two lines will automatically mount the disk when asked for and unmount it after it's been unused for a short period of time. The system is told how to handle the (un)mounting of /media/dvd with a suitable description in /etc/fstab:

```
/dev/scd0       /dvd    udf,iso9660 user,noauto     0       0
```

Depending on the range and login configurations on your network, you may want to set up specific Samba users. If you're a sysadmin by trade, setting up a centralized login database for all machines (Windows/Linux/Mac) might appear like a simple task. But for the rest of us, each machine will maintain its own set of usernames and passwords. Consequently, the Samba server has no way of knowing about these other machines or when their respective users decide to change their passwords. This makes it impossible for Samba to know what username/password combinations it should accept from this other machine. Therefore, it uses a separate set password table.

You simply need to type, as root, the following for each user who has password access to the particular Samba shared folders:

```
smbpasswd -a steev
```

---

[14] Which, unless the mount is in /etc/fstab, can only be unmounted by using umount directory as root.

For each user, you will be asked for the following:

```
New SMB password:
Retype new SMB password:
```

at which point you can either ask the family member for a password or assign them one—knowing that it can be changed only by root on this same machine. Once the user has logged in from a particular machine, however, the operating system will usually remember the credentials, so no one will be continually prompted for this information.

You should then restart the Samba service to make these changes visible to the world.

```
/etc/init.d/samba restart
```

This is all that's necessary to make the files available across your network. This allows you to use the various media-streaming devices, or head units, currently available.

CCTV Cameras

Although the perception of CCTV is grainy black-and-white footage attached to small TV screens, the reality is much removed, particularly as color CCTV is now very cheap and the images are often transmitted via Ethernet. And although the technology behind webcams and CCTV cameras are similar, it is not particularly easy to use cheap webcams as a suitable replacement for the more expensive CCTV cameras:

- Webcams use USB to transmit their data, which imposes a limit on the cable length to around 5 meters, without special extension cables

- Webcams don't work particularly well in low-light environments

- Webcams are not physically rugged, or waterproof, enough to live outside

So, although you might be able to get away with a webcam peering out of the window beside the PC during the daytime, you won't get much further than that. Instead, you'll need a specially designed camera, generally transmitting its images through a wireless network, so you can position the camera where it's needed—rather than whether you can run a cable to it.

■ **Note**   Several versions of CCTV camera are available that are wired for indoors only. The primary benefit that these have over traditional webcams is that they transmit their data across an IP network, meaning that they don't need to be directly attached to a PC.

Virtually every CCTV camera on the market requires a power cable (although a Power-over-Ethernet connection can often suffice), so regardless of whether you choose wired or wireless networking, you will have to run at least one cable to the camera's location. Apart from that, the main choice is for an indoors or outdoors mounting, the latter being more resilient to the weather. If you buy for indoors (such as a Y-cam) and later change your mind, you can usually place it in a wall mount unit (the Y-cam shell) and attach it underneath a soffit.

For indoor CCTV, used maybe as a baby monitor, there are cameras like the Panasonic Wireless IP camera (BLC-20), which has motion detection and a built-in web server so it doesn't need a PC to operate and can be viewed remotely provided the appropriate network ports are opened on the router. Its elder brother (BLC-131) also provides remote control of the camera with pan and tilt functionality.

When a camera is located inside but pointing outward, then it is best to look for those supporting some form of "night view mode." Those using a CMOS sensor are better in this regard because they can work at light levels down to 0.2 lux, whereas traditional CCDs (as used in webcams) are a mere 3 lux. Most CCD cameras that claim night mode usually implement it in software and do nothing that a good GIMP session couldn't fix, so opt for CMOS wherever possible.

For the most part, all CCTVs will work in the same way; it's a case of balancing specification and price for your budget. Consider the size of the images, FTP upload, web access, whether you get e-mail notifications on motion detection, and so on.

Wireless Cameras That Aren't

Many CCTV cameras on the market use the phrase *wireless* in a context that does not refer to WiFi. One such device is the XCAM2 Wireless Camera System. They actually use the industrial, scientific, and medical (ICM) wireless radio band to transmit their signals to a customized receiver, often for display on an attached monitor. These are therefore unsuitable for integrated home automation solutions, where the CCTV output needs to be viewed remotely.

However, if the particular receiver provides an output to RCA composite video, you can plug these into a TV card and record from that or use a hardware media recorder such as the Emprex ME-1. This limits you to one camera and prevents you from using the TV card (for recording or watching) while the CCTV is active. Of these, the second problem is easily solved by buying a second TV card. The former is more difficult.

If you need multiple cameras, then you will need to employ some additional control hardware, which could push the cost beyond that of an all-in-one IPCCTV camera. There are two approaches to the problem.

The first involves using several cameras but only one receiver. You can then use X10 to switch particular cameras on and off as required. The receiver will pick up the (only) signal now present and pass it to the TV card as before. This is the method suggested for the XCAM2, but it means you can't review all the cameras at a glance.

The second solution uses multiple receivers (and therefore more cost) and a TV switcher to select between the different inputs. Some of these will even combine all images into one. Switching these units will require the use, and programming, of a computer-based IR transmitter because most are not IP-controllable. (We'll look at IR control later.)

Custom Hardware

In many cases, it is not necessary to build your own CCTV configurations, because it's a known problem for which manufacturers have provided their own solutions. One such unit is a CCTV recorder/DVR, which usually comes with a CD rewriter and video out. This box will capture the feeds from multiple cameras and provide their output by S-video or composite, which can then be fed into a TV card, as before, for remote viewing and recording. Some versions are also supplied with an infrared remote control and network port.

Another alternative, if you'd like to keep everything PC-based, is a PCI card for real-time surveillance that can monitor four or more input channels from a single card, like the RW-1240R. The software and drivers for most of these, however, are currently Windows-based, so we don't dwell on it any further.

■ **Caution** Many of the stand-alone CCTV devices accept camera inputs from BNC video connectors, whereas the webcam-based ones use RCA.

Linux Software

Once the webcam image is available in a digital format, either through a USB driver or connected to the composite input of a TV card, the image can be processed or transmitted at will. Generally, the processing will occur through one of the standard video for Linux drivers (V4L), now in the second major version. This allows the data to be processed by any compatible software. Here are some examples:

> *xawtv*: An X window utility to play back and record video streams, including composite input and TV stations. It has some functionality for previewing many video streams at once, but because most (analog) cards have to retune between devices, the results are not real-time

> *camserv*: This provides its own web server whereby you can watch the video input in real time from any web browser, supporting the motion JPEG format. There is no sound support here, however

> *mencoder*: Part of the mplayer package, this provides a command-line interface to record the AV signal from a V4L channel

> *motion*: A small utility that incorporates motion detection so that you only need to record the feed (and therefore use up hard disk space) when there is something moving outside. The specific amount of movement is user configurable to prevent it wasting space on trees swaying in the wind or your cat walking across the view

Stand-Alone BitTorrent Clients

This is one of many "Linux-in-a-box" devices that have seen an upsurge in recent years, and no doubt there will be more to come. These, such as the Emprex NDS-100, take the place of a full-powered PC and provide functionality for BitTorrent and file and printer sharing. Essentially, it's the low-power functionality you'd want from an always-on machine, without the high-power hardware to run it. If you already have, or plan on using, your own home server for other things, then this will not save you much depending on the type of server used. A Mini-ITX box, for example, will have a similar power footprint and provide a better level of functionality.

Infrared Remote Control

For couch-potato living, nothing has the convenience of an infrared remote control. A small infrared LED in the handset flashes in a predetermined sequence, which an "eye" on the receiving device decodes to change the channel, increase the volume, and so on. IR remotes are so cheap that every device has once. That is the first problem because as the number of devices increases, the free space on the sofa proportionally decreases!

The second problem is line of sight, by which all IR remotes work. This means you have to point the remote at the device, within a moderate tolerance, for the signal to be received. But it's not always convenient to have the device placed in front of you; a projector, for example, will usually be behind you. If the TV audio is wired up to a HiFi, they may be in different places in the room, because of lack of space or power sockets. Or you might want to run cables from the DVD player into the bedroom or kitchen to continue a film uninterrupted. In each case, you may be unable to remotely control the device without moving yourself or the devices.

An occasional third problem with IR remote controls is with the receiving eye, which doesn't always see the signal. This third problem can often be solved by placing a piece of frosted glass or Scotch Magic Tape[15] over the "eye." This diffracts the incoming light from a greater range of angles, making it more sensitive. The first two problems need more involved hardware.

---

[15] See www.cleverandeasy.com/Multimedia/increase-operating-angle-of-infrared-remote-control.html.

All-in-One Remotes

There are so many combined all-in-one remotes that it's difficult to know which to get without trying them. Unfortunately, that is what you must generally do, because each one has some quirk or another that makes it unsuitable for your particular set of devices.

Although several varieties of "all-in-one" remotes exist, they are not created equally. You need to consider the specifics of each device you want to control because in the United Kingdom and Ireland, Sky Plus, for example, uses a slightly different IR protocol than normal, so unless your remote is specifically designed to handle it, you device will appear mute.

A number of learning remotes are available now, and these can prove a good investment. Another useful feature is a *macro*, which will store a number of commands in sequence. For example, a movie mode macro could switch the TV to DVD input, switch on and eject the DVD tray, and set the HiFi to accept a DVD input.

IR Relays

These devices overcome the line-of-sight problem by retransmitting IR signals from one place to another. They consist of both a transmitter (which watches for IR signals and relays them over the air) and a matched receiver (which replays the same IR message to the device). With a suitable transmission range, you can remotely control the downstairs TV from upstairs.

Sometimes it's possible to have multiple transmitters, one in the kitchen and one in the bedroom, say, that both send the signals to one place, allowing you to remotely control the TV from anywhere.

By the same token, it is sometimes possible to have multiple receivers, enabling an all-in-one remote to send commands from the bedroom to both the TV downstairs and the HiFi in the next room. However, this configuration is less common because, if you've installed an IR relay, the location of the equipment doesn't matter, so it is usually in the same physical location; therefore, you only need to mount one IR receiver, which sends the relayed signal to all devices at once. If the devices are fairly close to one another but the receiver can't see both devices, then it is usual to use a Y-splitter and two IR LEDs rather than buying another receiver unit.

Communication between the two transmitter and receiver is done through one of the ways outlined next.

Over the Aerial Cable

If your primary purpose is to relay IR controls for a TV, then you can get devices that embed the IR data onto the existing coaxial aerial cable, hiding it with similar results to X10. The Labgear MRX120 HandyLink, for example, provides such a solution. Naturally, this approach requires an aerial cable in each room, which there will be if your focus is TV control. If the aerial cables already exist, then scaling up is easy, because adding extra amplifiers is fairly cheap and is a simple plug-and-play affair. Without existing cables, however, this can be more trouble than it's worth, given the IR-RF-IR possibilities, but it can provide a solution where RF reception is especially poor.

In both cases, it is impossible to watch different channels in each room, even with Sky, because it's distributing a single signal from the tuner.

▓ **Note**   You may need an IR bypass kit when passing IR signals over coax cables because the messages get muddled when passing through distribution amplifiers.

IR-RF-IR Gateways

These devices relay IR data through the air, at the 433MHz radio frequency used by so much wireless equipment, before being replayed. For these devices, you have a choice between IR-only transmissions and TV senders.

An IR-only transmitter, such as the Powermid XL, is the simplest of these devices and will allow you to remotely control devices without installing cables or sockets. They are fairly cheap but pass only IR data, so the controlled device must be able to have an impact on you when you're in another room.

TV senders are the wireless versions of the over-the-aerial cables or old TV distribution systems, which involved an aerial amplifier and a separate aerial cable into each TV in the house. The TV sender takes a single input and transmits it to whichever receivers are listening, encoding whatever IR signals it also saw. There are many variants on the market, including those with SCART sockets (instead of the old-school coaxial aerial sockets) and RCA composite video. Even the cheaper models often have a "channel" switch on them, allowing multiple receiver-transmitter pairs to be used in the same house without the signals getting mixed up. And with these devices becoming more mainstream, some are almost as cheap as an IR-only transmitter, with the TV functionality becoming a free bonus feature.

IR Over IP

It is also possible to send data over your existing Ethernet cables, using devices such as the Keene IR Anywhere over IP (KIRA). This eliminates any distance or interference issues you might get from the other methods and also provides a way of remotely controlling IR devices from a computer, without needing to have the computer and its IR transmitter physically in range of the device.

Being IP-controlled also means that IR signals can be sent via the Internet. Although this is pointless in itself (because you can't derive any benefit from changing the TV channel when you're not sitting watching it), it does provide an off-the-shelf way of controlling IR-based devices from a remote computer. And if something can be controlled from a computer, then it can be controlled from anything connected to the computer, such as a web page or cron job.

Using KIRA to retransmit IR codes first requires that you teach it those codes in the first place. This is done by generating text files, using the software shown in Figure 1-15.

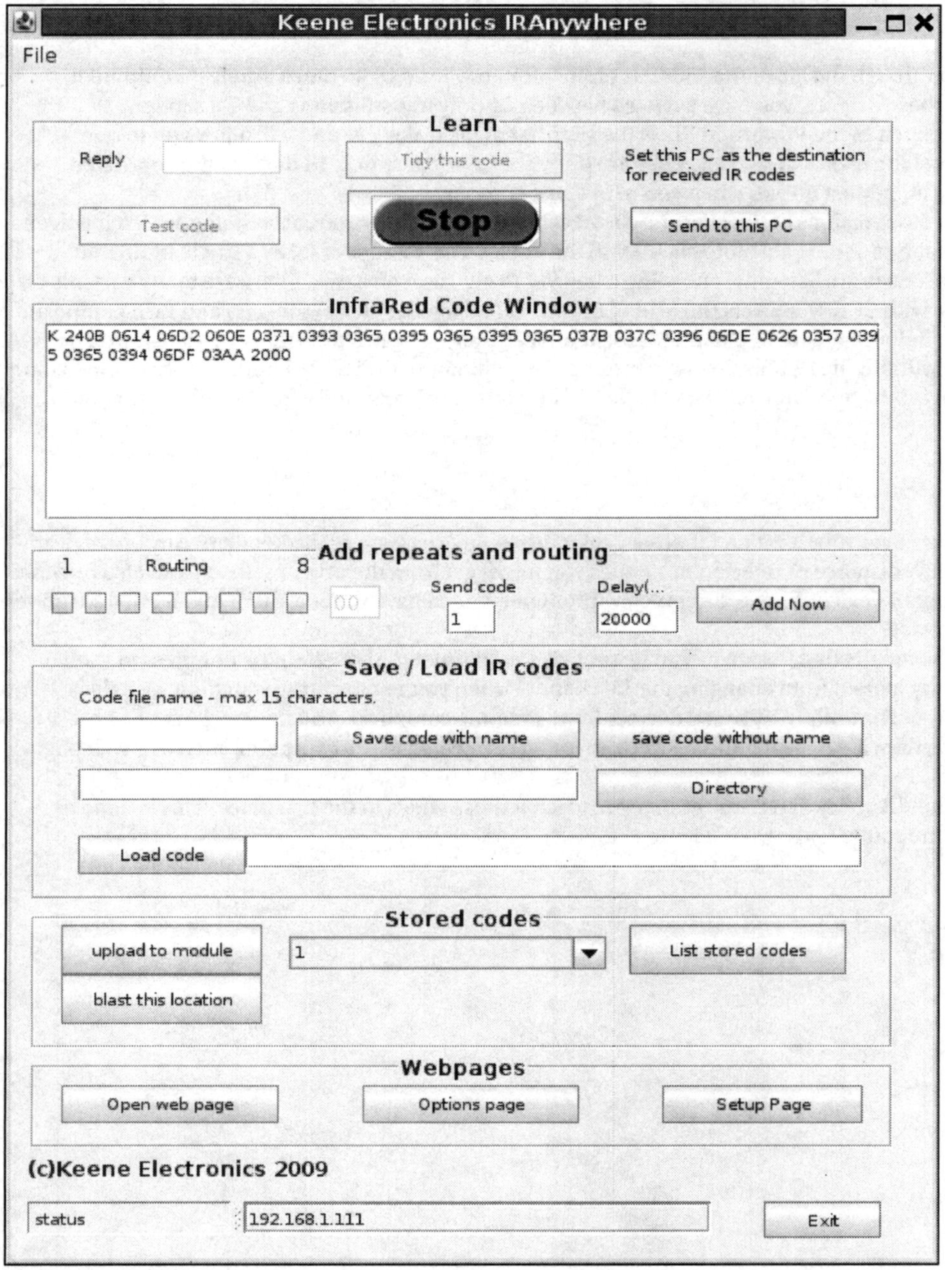

Figure 1-15. *Configuring KIRA*

This software is available from the Keene web site[16] and has been thoughtfully written in Java, making it Linux-friendly. After attaching KIRA to your network and after it's used your DHCP server to provide it with an IP address, you can add new commands. First you request that all the IR messages are sent to this machine, and then you press Learn before hitting the first key on your remote. This should present the code, such as the following, which can then be copied and pasted into a text file for later use:

```
K 240C 037F 0369 03AC 034D 0624 035A 0378 0382 0378 0381 0396 0366 0377
0382 0396 0365 0396 06E0 03AF 034C 072C 0353 0378 2000
```

I have used a directory hierarchy for each device so that the on/off button for my TV is in the directory ir/tv/codes/on. Since the same button performs both functions, I created a symlink between off and on. Those with bigger houses and more TVs might like to use a more descriptive name than TV.

Although KIRA has a web page, it isn't very configurable and limits you to four prestored IR codes. Fortunately, it also listens for commands sent on UDP ports 30303 and 65432. The former is for device discovery and configuration, so consequently the port cannot be changed. The latter is the IR control port, which processes all the basic commands to control the various IR devices within range. All responses to these commands are returned by UDP also, so you need to run two instances of the Swiss Army knife of network utility, netcat, to handle it.

Begin by creating two terminal windows, and start a UDP server in one of them by typing the following:

```
nc -u -l -p 30303
```

This will now listen on port 30303 for any UDP messages sent to it. Now, in the other window, send a message to KIRA (whose IP has been determined as 192.168.1.111 by the DHCP server) on the same port:

```
echo disD | nc -q 0  -u 192.168.1.111 30303
```

You should see the other window spring to life and report various stats about the device. If not, check that the ports are open and working with (that other Swiss Army knife of networking) netstat:

```
netstat -ntpl
```

With some averagely clever bash coding, you can achieve the same result with a script such as the following:

```
#!/bin/bash

TEMPFILE=`mktemp`
nc -u -l -p 30303 >$TEMPFILE &
PROCESS=$!
echo disD | nc -q 0  -u 192.168.1.111 30303

# Wait for a second so the output has finished writing
sleep 1

kill $PROCESS
cat $TEMPFILE

rm $TEMPFILE
```

---

[16] See www.keene.co.uk/electronics/multi.php?mycode=KIRA.

The process for sending IR messages is the same, except you need to switch onto the IR port. Here's an example:

```
cat ir/codes/tv/off | nc -q 0  -u 192.168.1.111 65432
```

The only response sent to port 65432 is ACK, which can be safely ignored. However, if you do decide to listen to port 65432 (and you have requested that all IR messages are forwarded to your PC), then you will see the key codes appear. These can be copied from the terminal window (instead of using the web interface) into your own configuration files. There is a supplied API document detailing each of the commands that each port handles. Note that by using your Linux machine to maintain the IR codes, you don't need to ever upload keycode files to one of the four slots on its web server.

■ **Note**   You can have several KIRA devices on your network, each transmitting messages to different devices, although for KIRA to receive messages and send them back to a PC, you must explicitly enable the functionality from its web interface and give it the IP address where `netcat`, or similar, will be listening.

IR Control

If you have a PC fairly close to the IR devices you want to control, it is easy to add a suitable USB-based transmitter or receiver to it. These can be either bought from places like RedRat or built from one of the circuit diagrams provided by the LIRC (Linux Infra-Red Remote Control), which also provides the software.

■ **Caution**   Most PCs attach USB ports directly to the motherboard, and if you make a mistake when building your own device, you could destroy it. Purchasing a separate PCI board with USB sockets should provide some protection from mishaps.

For IR transmission, you need to know the specific control codes of the device you want to control. If you have a standard TV or video, this data is usually available online (`http://lirc.sourceforge.net/remotes/`); otherwise, you will also need to purchase or build an IR receiver to teach LIRC the existing codes. Fortunately, if you took the earlier hint and bought a RedRat, you will have a receiver built in that, along with the supplied Windows software or LIRC, can be used to program the codes directly.

LIRC[17] is the Linux-standard method for reading and transmitting IR data. It comprises a standard daemon, `lircd`, and a set of tools to record the input messages and transmit them back again. It adopts a modular approach to support the wide variety of LIRC devices available. Reproducing an installation guide here would be foolhardy, but suffice to say there are three main types of supported control:

GPIO devices: These are generally supplied with TV cards, such as those from Hauppauge. The modules are usually compiled into the standard daemon build

Serial port device: This covers a wide range of different devices, including home-brew transmitters, and because they process serial data directly, they don't need any specific driver code. Typical circuits are available from the LIRC web site. If you're unsure about connecting your own electronics onto your PC motherboard, you can buy serial PCI cards, which offer a level of protection against rogue electronics

---

[17] `http://lirc.org`.

Kernel drivers: These, such as the RedRat3 device, require you to build LIRC from source and (in some cases) copy the new driver code into the LIRC directory. From here you can rebuild the setup (`data2setup.sh`) file and build as normal. These devices will make use of the `/dev/lircd` device, which should have `ugo+rw` privileges

Once built, the drivers can be configured and prepared according to the table at LIRC,[18] which also provides sample configuration files for the various devices that describe each button with a human-friendly name and the details of the IR signal to be sent. From here, you can add specific commands to be triggered upon the various button presses within the `.lircrc` file, which has a format typical of this:

```
begin
  prog = mythtv
  button = Rew
  config = Left
end
```

Each button on the remote is mapped to a function of the software (`prog`) in this fashion.

One of the big benefits in using RedRat, and LIRC in general, is its inclusion in many standard media players, mixers, and TV applications. Consequently, if this is your primary purpose of IR, then you have completed your media installation already since those commands can trigger something useful in the existing software!

LIRC also has a network mode whereby you can communicate with an LIRC daemon through a network socket, allowing an external application to act as if it were a local IR remote control. This is useful for testing and as a method of remotely a PC-based media player without writing new code.

For more specific applications, you will need to make use of `irexec`, as shown here:

```
begin
 prog = irexec
 button = ok
 config = /usr/bin/someprogram with arguments here
end
```

In this way, you can use an IR remote to interact with other arbitrary applications, including media players on other machines. Additionally, you can adopt the same ideas as Cosmic (mentioned earlier in this chapter and covered in more detail in Chapter 7) to develop a state-based control mechanism using very cheap IR transmitters.

Conclusion

Each device in your home should have the ability to be controlled remotely, either through the power lines (with X10 or C-Bus), with an Ethernet socket, or through basic Infrared. This is the first step of a two-stage process. The second is when you have a computer able to issue control messages to those devices. At that point, the devices can be used seamlessly from anywhere in the world. When the device doesn't support such functionality, you have to hack it. And that's where the geeky fun begins!

---

[18] `www.lirc.org/html/table.html`.

■ ■ ■

## CHAPTER 2

Appliance Hacking: Converting Existing Technology

There are three classical forms of hacking: software, hardware, and wetware (also known as *social engineering*). More recently, firmware hacking has become prominent because low-cost hardware utilizing embedded Linux has opened the door to software hackers unable to build hardware. It is hardware hacking, and its associated software, that I will cover in this chapter.

Software Hacks

For most developers, software is an easier hack, because the chance of breaking something irrevocably is much reduced compared to hacking hardware. In fact, when Steve Wozniak and Steve Jobs were building machines at the Homebrew Computer Club, they reasoned that for every one hacker who was interested in hardware, there were 100 who were keen on software, so they focused on the software capabilities of the Apple computer. A similar motif was true when Acorn built the BBC A and BBC B in 1981 as they worked hard on the software to make it suitable for learning in schools.

As history surely repeats, the Raspberry Pi used these ideals to provide a small machine where the software was the easily hackable part. They even paid homage to the original Acorn machines by naming the first two iterations of the Raspberry Pi Model A and B! Such has been the success of the Raspberry Pi that it has become difficult to ensure supply can meet demand. Consequently, it is sometimes necessary to scour eBay to find old second hand equipment to do the tasks better suited to the Raspberry Pi!

Linksys NSLU2

This old device, also known affectionately as "the Slug," is a small, embedded Linux device intended to function as a network addressable storage (NAS) device. You plug in power, a network cable, and (up to) two USB hard drives, and you're able to retrieve the data stored on it from any machine on the same network subnet using the Samba protocol.

The machine itself is silent, powered by an Intel XScale IXP420, and incorporates 32MB of SDRAM and 8MB of flash memory where the software is stored. Its low price point and openness of firmware makes it attractive to hackers wanting to add or change the software on the machine. The machine was officially discontinued in 2008 but is still available in various stores and online.

In its intended form, the Slug is a suitable machine when only a file server is needed, either to be a remote backup for desktop work (perhaps located under the stairs or in a loft) or to provide music to media players around the house. By changing its firmware, however, it can become the following:

- Web server (Apache, PHP, Perl, and Python are all supported)
- Mail server

- Printer server (the cost of a Slug can be less than the difference between a USB printer and its networked equivalent, although this is less of a difference than it once was)

- Media server (shared through Squeezebox Server, iTunes, or just Samba)

Before any software changes take place, you must first install an unrestricted version of Linux into the firmware of the device, which takes place through its built-in web interface. There are two main variations here: Unslung (which uses Optware packages) and SlugOS (formally called OpenSlug) based around OpenEmbedded.

Unslung

For basic improvements and a minimal of fuss, Unslung (`www.nslu2-linux.org/wiki/Unslung/HomePage`) is the preferred option because it installs over the top of the existing firmware and appears very similar to the end user, since it is based on the original Linksys code. This firmware provides extra functionality such as the ability to use FAT-formatted disks, which is necessary if you want to use an existing hard drive, as any disk used in the Slug needs to be specially formatted (to ext3) before use.

It is also possible to install extra software packages through Optware using commands like the following:

```
ipkg install apache
```

However, you need to be careful as they are installed to the internal flash memory, which can run out very quickly and therefore lead to an unbootable device. To prevent this, you need to move the operating system onto either one of the external drives (either a USB memory stick or an entire hard drive, depending on the scope and size of your intended additions) in a process known as "unslinging your Slug." Alternatively, you can perform a hardware hack to increase the memory.

Several hundred packages are available for an unslung Slug, including the following:

- BitTorrent clients

- Streamers for Xbox Media Server

- Apache web server

- Asterisk VoIP

- CUPS

- Git

- MySQL

- SSH

As you can see, most major packages are available, making this a very low-power machine, capable of providing most home tasks. However, they are all limited by the 2.4 kernel, so for more exotic hardware (like Bluetooth), you will need to adopt SlugOS.

SlugOS

SlugOS is a much larger endeavor and treats the Slug like any other piece of hardware, with a base operating system and separate packages for the main functionality, fitting in with the traditional Unix ideology of "do one thing and do it well." This also removes the Slug-specific functionality such as the web-based configuration tool and basic services such as Samba that you will consequently have to explicitly install.

If you are using the Slug as the basis for a much larger home automation server, then this provides greater scope in the upgrade path, because it gives you access to the many thousands of packages provided by the OpenEmbedded project on which SlugOS is based. But doing so requires that you devote some, or all, of one of your connected hard drives to the operating system, which is a process that requires you to install a small system into the flash memory and then bootstrap the operating system onto the hard drive. In doing so, SlugOS permits the use of a 2.6-based kernel as well as RAID and NFS functionality.

When using an external USB drive to hold the operating system, always use a hard drive (as opposed to a memory stick). This is because some applications (such as MySQL) create a lot of memory writes to the swap file, and because flash memory becomes unusable after about 100,000 writes, this can happen sooner rather than later. You could, alternatively, assign the swap file to a second (hard) drive, allowing the operating system to boot and run from a read-only memory stick.

Developing on the Slug

To write your own software for the Slug, you should start with SlugOS because this gives you access to the standard development tools, which run on the device allowing the code to be written, compiled, and tested on the Slug. This is known as *native development*. First you need to run the following command, along with the other standard build packages (all detailed at `www.nslu2-linux.org/wiki/HowTo/SlugOSNativeCompileEnvironment`), before developing your code as normal:

```
ipkg install slugos-native
```

Without a screen, however, you will not be able to use GUI debuggers such as `kdbg`, which can be a scary downgrade for some. It is perfectly possible to run the machine headless, however, as you can connect remotely through `ssh` or `telnet`. This is preferable because the speed of the machine makes a GUI approach impractical for large applications. You would more likely write and test your application for your desktop machine and then, when it's ready, cross-compile for the Slug.

Cross compilation is a process whereby a compiler running on machine A is able to produce code suitable for machine B. To do this, you need a new set of compilers, tools, headers, and libraries (known together as the *toolchain*) that are built purposely for the other architecture. These are stored separate from your existing development files since they would otherwise conflict with those running your machine. The compilation process then occurs as normal (through either `make` or a variant of `gcc`, such as `armeb-linux-gnu-gcc`) to produce a suitable executable file, or *elf* in Linux parlance.

The best introduction for the installation of these tools is at `www.nslu2-linux.org/wiki/DebianSlug/CrossCompiling`.

Note that if you're using only existing packages, compilation tools are not necessary in any form, and you can rely solely on the prebuilt packages.

Hacking Game Consoles

Game consoles are great for playing games. Old game console are great for playing old games—and hacking into Linux machines! As the previous generation of machines becomes cheap and technologically obsolete, old game consoles provide a good embedded platform for media players, web servers, control units, and the like because they always have suitable connectors for a TV and look natural in the living room. In this section, you will learn how these machines can be bent to your will, rather than specific uses for them.

It is not smooth sailing, alas, because the manufacturers do not make the compilers or development environments available to anyone outside the computer games industry, and even then it is only with strict nondisclosure agreements (NDAs).[1] Although this should be enough to satisfy an overzealous legal department,

---

[1] An NDA is a legal document formed by companies to prevent you from talking about their technology or ideas with anyone else.

they then build in security measures to make it difficult to run home-brew code on them by encrypting the disc format, BIOS, or executable. This in itself makes it an interesting problem for hackers. And because most manufacturers lose money on the console (knowing they'll recoup it on the games), the subversive hackers enjoy this process even more.

Despite the ever-decreasing circles of cost, it is not worth buying a new console for the sole purpose of hacking it into a Linux machine, but charity shops and online auctions can provide the hacker with the previous generation of hardware at a cost that makes the time and geek-cred worthwhile. (Even though it's an *easier* proposition to just use a Raspberry Pi!) With all technological challenges, however, the interest of those leading these console-hacking projects tends to wane as newer and more powerful machines become available or as the time benefits outweigh the cost of alternative equipment. Therefore, it is likely that some (or all!) of these projects might have fallen out of favor by the time you read this, as the Xbox 360 becomes old hat and the PlayStation 4 is the current console du jour.

Sega Dreamcast

The Dreamcast was a game console released in 1998 in the wake of the ill-fated Sega Saturn. It was the winner of an internal competition in Sega between two teams of engineers, led by IBM researcher Tatsuo Yamamoto and Sega hardware engineer Hideki Sato. The resulting console featured elements from both designs and was based around a 200MHz Hitachi SH4 RISC processor and the PowerVR2 graphics chip from VideoLogic, which is fast enough for video playback.

It also featured an optical GD-ROM drive, which supported a standard CD-ROM partition (on which the OS was included), as well as a proprietary format section for the game. The console also marked Microsoft's first exploration into the hardware arena by combining the Windows CE OS with its DirectX technology.

The console also included a visual memory unit (VMU), which in addition to being a basic memory cartridge also featured an 8-bit process, 48 ×32 pixel LCD screen, D-pad, and four basic buttons. It was intended to be used as an auxiliary play device, rather than a handheld console in itself, and needed to be plugged into a controller in order to function. It was a good idea (and one reused by Sony years later with its PocketStation device, which also featured IR control), but it was not powerful enough for any significant work, compared to the equivalent technology at that time.

Sega was also ahead of the curve by providing peripherals for the Dreamcast such as a mouse, keyboard, and Ethernet (known colloquially as a *broadband adapter*, or BBA). The latter two are considered essential for the installation and use of Linux.

LinuxDC (`http://linuxdc.sourceforge.net`) is an old—almost defunct—project that has recently seen a small spurt of new life. It is a reasonably complete distribution suitable for web browsing (with a BBA), movie playback, and emulation. This itself is a good hack, but there are also cables to provide two-way serial communication, either between the Dreamcast and a PC or between peripherals such as infrared (IR) transmitters and receivers. You can either build this cable yourself using one chip and three capacitors from the circuit shown at `http://mc.pp.se/dc/serifc.html` or purchase a similarly compatible cable, which is known as a *DC coders cable*.

There is also Dreamcast emulation software for Linux called LXDream, which provides a quick way to verify the working, or not, of various Dreamcast software hacks. You can find this at `www.lxdream.org`, which also provides all-important links to prebuilt disc image ISOs of LinuxDC, from `www.lxdream.org/wiki/index.php? title=Dreamcast_Linux`.

■ **Note**　Emulators such as LXDream require an image of the machine's original BIOS. Because these are usually still under copyright, they are not packaged with the emulator and must be extracted from a machine (that you legally own).

In addition to these, there are various pieces of stand-alone software that can be cross-compiled and uploaded via the serial DC coders cable to the Dreamcast. Some of these are shown on the pages at `http://mc.pp.se/dc`. This includes example source code for text, graphics, sound, and serial communications. By avoiding an operating system, you can make better use of the comparatively small 16MB of memory and 200MHz processor, at the expense of ease of development.

Sony PlayStation

Sony is now promoting its third generation of PlayStation console, imaginatively titled PlayStation 3 (PS3). It is still too new to make it financially viable to turn the whole machine into an home automation device (and since it's a very capable media playback device already), but you can install Linux on it if you want, provided you use firmware version 3.15 or earlier, or use OtherOS++.[2] (Note that the Slimline version of the PS3 does not support this.) For software engineers, it is a good platform to learn the CELL architecture, but because the kernel isn't optimized for this chip, the operating system is comparatively slow, meaning the same money and electricity could be put to better use with a standard PC. However, the newness of this machine means there are two older consoles being neglected that can be had for very little money.

PlayStation 1

The first PlayStation released in 1994 (now referred to as the PlayStation 1, to differentiate itself from the PlayStation brand) had a mere 2MB of RAM, a 33.8MHz CPU, and no memory management unit (MMU), meaning that only the uClinux kernel was suitable for porting, but even then converting the rest of the system was difficult. Only one installation seems to have existed, Runix (originally called PSXLinux), although this is now near impossible to find. This is no great loss because, unlike modern game consoles, it didn't have a hard drive, which limits its use as a Linux machine.

Instead of using existing Linux software, it is still possible to develop applications from scratch using Net Yaroze and utilizing the 128KB memory card for temporary storage. This comprises a black PlayStation, controllers, cables, software, and manuals for software development, and it was intended to get hobbyists into the field by providing a means of compiling software on a PC and uploading it through the serial cable—which was also used for debugging—to the PlayStation. The machine was sold via mail order and to universities but wasn't a big success. Ultimately, there aren't many of these devices available, so they're mostly traded between enthusiasts for excessive money. However, the speed of the machine makes it unsuitable for video playback,[3] and its lack of communication ports further limits its potential.

A much better use for the PlayStation 1 is not as a computer but as a CD player, especially the first versions. This is because the original console had a much-improved DAC inside it over later versions, giving it professional audio quality output when playing CDs. This model can be distinguished by the model number SCPH 100x and the separate audio and video RCA outputs.

PlayStation 2

Sony's second machine was released in 2000 and called the PlayStation 2 (you might detect a naming pattern here!), and it provided a significant increase in power over its predecessor. It had 32MB of RAM and contained separate chips for I/O, sound, and graphics, and it had a main CPU called the Emotion Engine (running at 294.9MHz or 299MHz depending on whether it was an original or later device). This made it a more realistic specification for Linux. Furthermore, an easy route for doing so was provided by Sony, which sold its own supplementary kit, called PS2 Linux. It provided the end user with a hard drive, a keyboard, mouse, an Ethernet adapter, and the necessary software and manuals to develop software. These kits are no longer sold or supported, but some are available from old stock and from secondhand dealers. Development is much easier on the eye if you ignore the TV output and use a monitor—you'll need one that does sync-on-green. The supplied distribution is ultimately based on an old version of Red Hat with a 2.2.*x* kernel, although newer versions now exist, along with Mozilla, XChat, and various lightweight GUI applications; utilities that make use of the USB ports such as printers and cameras; and the network port. The site has since been retired, although kits and software disks still surface on eBay occasionally. There is still some web content available through the Wayback Machine at http://web.archive.org/web/20130303202328/http://playstation2-linux.com.

Outside of the official Linux distribution, there is a wide selection of home-brew software, such as media players and emulators. You can download them as elfs from sites like http://sksapps.com or the old exploitstation.com site (now languishing at http://web.archive.org/web/20100712044012/http://www.exploitstation.com), or you can build them yourself on a PC using a set of cross-compilation tools and run from a disc, memory card, network, or USB memory stick.

---

[2]http://www.ps3devwiki.com
[3]The codecs now in use require more CPU power than the formats used in games of that time.

Persuading a PS2 to run nonapproved software is no longer difficult, because several software-only exploits have been discovered, along with the hardware hacks where a so-called modchip is physically soldered into the computer itself.

One soft hack is called the PS2 Independence Exploit, where a disc from a PlayStation 1 game is used to load a special file from the memory card, which in turn triggers a buffer overrun allowing unsigned code to run. This is explained in detail at http://sksapps.com/index.php?page=exploitinstaller.html.

Free McBoot (http://freemcboot.psx-scene.com) is a newer soft hack, which also allows you to run home-brew software by installing special software tied into the specific memory card. It also works on Slimline PS2s and most new machines (unlike the Independence Exploit), with the only currently known exceptions being those with a date code of 8c and 8d (BIOS Version v2.30).

Recent hacks and liberation efforts have resulted in a project called kernelloader (http://kernelloader.sourceforge.net/) which utilizes these methods to create a full Linux distribution on your PS2 (a Slim PS2 needs to boot from a Live DVD and not the network) at which point you can use the machine as normal.

In addition to the sites listed, several video-sharing web sites include visual tutorials describing the process. And, as always, you may be able to find suitable modchips for hardware hacking.

PlayStation Portable

There is one final PlayStation product to mention, as the PS3 is too new, and the PS Vita too underused, to be of concern to us! The PlayStationPortable (PSP) was released in 2004 and is based on the PS2. This is a handheld device and benefits the HA hackers with 802.11b WiFi connectivity. IrDA is also featured on the older PSP-1000 models, with the newer version (PSP Go) supporting Bluetooth. All have dual MIPS R4000 chips running at 333MHz[4] and 32MB of RAM, making them more than capable devices.

Like most consoles, however, the PSP has been designed to run only signed code created by Sony, thereby eliminating its ability to be a programmable computer in any real sense. And, like most consoles, hackers found ways of circumventing this, by exploiting an issue in the original 1.5 firmware. This ultimately led to a cat-and-mouse game of firmware upgrades by Sony to close these loopholes (and bribing users to upgrade by including new features like web browsers) as the hackers attempted to reopen them or work out ways of downgrading to 1.5 (without triggering the Trojan code that Sony had placed in the firmware, which would "brick" your machine) to use the old exploit.

A wide range of home-brew software is available for PSP including the YouTube viewer PSPTube and a control application for the Xbox Media Center; a good source is http://dl.qj.net/PSP/catid/106. However, one of the real benefits of this device is that you don't even need to hack it in order to install a web browser, as (from version 2.0) the NetFront Browser has been included by default, and from 3.90 it has included Skype for VoIP calls. Because most home automation equipment comes with a web server or one can be written fairly easily, a web browser is enough for a fairly high level of home control.

■ **Note**   If you plan on using custom or cracked firmware to run home-brew software, always do it early in the device's ownership life cycle. That way you won't lose any personal data if something does go wrong in the firmware update process.

Microsoft Xbox

Like the Sony PlayStation 3, Microsoft's current game console—the Xbox 360—is too new and expensive to be worth hacking into something else, although many people have worked on the problem and created the www.free60.org project in doing so, which is now capable of running homebrew code.

---

[4]Firmwares prior to 3.50 are underclocked at 222MHz.

The Xbox game console was introduced in 2001 and was probably the first time that many people considered the possibilities of using a (near-)standard PC connected to their standard TV. This was no doubt helped by the knowledge that Microsoft was using its Windows and DirectX technologies in the unit, both of which were well known, thus presenting a very low barrier to entry for the hackers.

As a unit, the Xbox is based around a 733MHz Pentium III chip with 64MB of RAM, along with a DVD-ROM and a 10GB hard drive—the only last-generation console to do so—by default. It also has Ethernet support and USB ports but with a proprietary form factor and wiring. This remonstrative oversight caused many companies to generate business plans based solely around the sale of Xbox USB converters, of which there are many!

As a physical unit it is quite large (320 ×100 ×260mm) and has a fairly noisy fan, although hardware hackers might be able to squeeze this down to laptop size and replace the fan with a silent one. In any case, you will certainly want to locate the machine away from your ears and the speaker system in use.

Running Linux

There is a perverse geek pleasure in running Linux on Microsoft's first flagship console. Furthermore, because we're coming in at the end of its life cycle, any breakages, void warranties, or bricked machines are less important to us than they would have been a few years ago. Also, the hacker community has had enough time to improve the hacking process so that even those scared of soldering irons can do it without fear. The primary site is `www.xbox-linux.org`.

■ **Note** Although all Xboxes are capable of running Linux, there are many issues with version 1.6 since the BIOS is no longer stored in a chip that can be (re)flashed. This chip, known as a *thin small outline package* (TSOP), is instead hardwired, *requiring* the use of an extra hardware modification chip loaded with the Cromwell Linux BIOS, and even then the output resolutions possible are much reduced (only composite and S-video with overscan, and up to 480p HDTV) because of the different graphics hardware in use. You can determine the version number with the chart at `www.xbox-linux.org/wiki/Xbox_Versions_HOWTO` (which may need to be access through its archived versions at `http://web.archive.org/web/20100728124622/ http://www.xbox-linux.org/wiki/Xbox_Versions_HOWTO`).

As is usual with console hacks, there is a hardware way to do it and a software way. The hardware way involves the purchase and soldering of a modchip; although their use has questionable legality,[5] this provides the most expansive scope for hacking as you can do the following:

- Increase the hard drive size (but less than 137GB is still recommended)

- Replace the DVD with another hard drive or DVD-RW

- Use all the disk space under Linux

After fitting the chip, you need to trick the Xbox into running code that allows you to make use of it. This is done through an exploit, such as the MechAssault Exploit, which uses broken code within the game and a well-crafted save game file, at which point you can transfer arbitrary data onto the Xbox (through the network) and run an application to flash the BIOS with it. The process is simple but fiddly, as you need adapter cables, the correct version of the game, and a separate machine. As mentioned, this is the only (relatively) safe way of introducing Xbox Linux to a version 1.6 machine.

The downside of a hardware hack is that the online components of Xbox games (in other words, Xbox Live) are unavailable, as Microsoft will ban anyone found using Linux on its machine.

---

[5]Some cite contravention of the DMCA/EUCD, and some cases have been dismissed.

The software hack involves most of the same steps, with the few added complications explained in detail at www.xbox-linux.org/wiki/Software_Method_HOWTO (or http://web.archive.org/web/20100728124622/http://www.xbox-linux.org/wiki/Xbox_Versions_HOWTO if the site is offline). Naturally, being software, the Linux install disappears on each reboot—your data remains, but you must reinstate the hack to boot Linux in order to access it.

There was once The Xbox Chocolate Project, where Xbox Linux users would help would-be users modify their machines. It is still going, but fewer volunteers are available. Asking at your local Linux User Group (aka LUG; see www.linux.org/groups for your local group) might be another idea.

The reason for hacking an Xbox is up to you. If you just want to make it play DVDs, then the Microsoft DVD Playback Kit is a better option, and it comes with its own IR remote control. As a set-top box, it might be a little noisy compared to the other solutions I've mentioned (and will mention) by today's standards. But as a secondary (or even primary) file server, web server, or even desktop machine, it has extremely positive geek credentials.

Xbox Media Center

Despite the name, there are more versions of Xbox Media Center (XBMC) running on non-Xbox platforms than there are on the Xbox, including versions for the Raspberry Pi and a Live CD, all available from www.xbmc.org! This is because the software can only be compiled using the Xbox development kit (XDK), which is made available only to licensed developers. And because Microsoft isn't happy with Linux developers writing open source software on its console, this is not available to hobbyists in any form. Consequently, the only native versions of XBMC running in the wild are those compiled by licensed developers and those versions that have leaked out from those developers. The legality of such versions is seriously suspect. In either case, you will still need a modified Xbox to run the code, as you would with Xbox Linux.

■ **Note**   If you do have access to the Xbox software, then you can use the IR remote control that is supplied with the Microsoft DVD Playback Kit with XBMC.

As software, XBMC contains a lot of top-end functionality and is still in active development. This includes an initiative to reduce the boot time, making it appear more like a set-top box and less like a computer running software—one goal to which all home automation devices should aspire.

Its functionality includes the ability to play back media of almost every format (coming from hard disks, optical media, network shares, online streams and feeds, and DAAP for iTunes), display photographs, run Python-written plug-ins (for weather reports and the like), and play games. It is also able to support the media with data services from IMDb (the Amazon-owned Internet Movie Database) and FreeDB (for CD track listings). For many, the main XBMC hackjoy concerns its skinnability, allowing anyone with a minimum of knowledge to create custom interfaces for the software.

Despite its prominence, there are several forks of XBMC: Boxee, with integration into social networking applications; MediaPortal, a Windows-centric version with PVR handling; Plex, which focuses on the Mac OS X and associated Apple platform-oriented functionality (such as the iTunes app store); and Voddler, which supports media streaming from its (commercial) video-on-demand site.

Hardware Hacks

The hacks in this category will involve changes you can make either to existing hardware or to new hardware you can easily build that controls, or is controlled by, an existing computer.

Linksys NSLU2

The existing NSLU2 unit (aka the Slug) requires no hardware hacks to make it run any of the custom Linux firmwares covered earlier. However, you can improve the unit with various hacks.

Always On

Like most consumer hardware, the Slug has an on/off button. For normal operation, this is fine. But for a home automation system, which is generally intended to work 24/7 (like the rest of the house), this can cause problems whenever there is a brief power outage, as the machine then needs to be manually switched back on. Also, if you are controlling the Slug's power remotely, maybe through a timed X10 appliance module or stand-alone timer, it won't fully turn on because it needs the button to be pressed.

In the first instance, there are obvious solutions here, such as putting the Slug onto a UPS or keeping it accessible so you can manually control it. However, these negate the benefits of it being cheap, hidden, and (importantly for HA) controllable.

You can solve this by invalidating your warranty by performing one of several hardware hacks to ensure the machine always switches on when the power is applied. These vary from using USB Y-cables in various configurations to soldering components to the board. All are detailed, with their relative merits online (`www.nslu2-linux.org/wiki/HowTo/ForcePowerAlwaysOn`).

Overclocking

Prior to 2006, all Slugs ran slower than necessary as their CPUs were clocked at 133MHz, despite the chip being designed to run at 266MHz. This technically meant the original versions were *under*clocked, which means the following hack is known as *de-underclocking*, rather than overclocking. If you log into your Slug (through `telnet` or `ssh`, depending on your firmware) and type the following:

```
cat /proc/cpuinfo
```

you'll see a BogoMIPS value, indicating the currently speed. If this is within 10 percent of the 133 value, then you can improve the speed by removing the resistor shown in Figure 2-1.

Figure 2-1. *The de-underclocking resistor (second from the bottom in the R84 stack). Image from* `http://www.nslu2-linux.org/gallery/hardware` *released under cc-by-sa*

61

You can remove it using nail clippers, a soldering iron, a saw, or any combination of the above. Just be sure to not to damage any other components.

Serial Port

You can use a standard serial port for two-way communication between many pieces of old technology such as joysticks, along with LCD text displays and other forms of home-brew electronics. It also provides a way of controlling the Slug through getty when other routes, such as the network, are failing.

There is already a serial port hidden away at J2 on the Slug motherboard. Alas, its control voltages are 0/+3.3v, and not the +/−12V necessary for the standard RS-232 serial port, which means you'll require a power-level converter. (However, strictly speaking, the standard requires hardware to differentiate between voltages in the range of +/− 3–15V.) Some converters can be purchased as a single chip (such as the MAX3232) or already included in some mobile phone data cables. You can find full details on the web site (www.nslu2-linux.org/wiki/HowTo/AddASerialPort).

There are also circuits available that allow you to connect an LCD character display (such as the HD44780) to the Slug with a minimum of effort, providing a basic (and very low-power) display to report the current media playing or the machine status. However, this also requires opening your Slug to make hardware adjustments.

LEGO Mindstorms

First released in 1998, LEGO Mindstorms was originally known as the Mindstorms Robotics Invention System (RIS) Kit and contained a control brick known as RCX to which you uploaded a program with infrared. The software would then run, control the various motors and sensors connected to the RCX brick, and communicate with others via IR. This naturally had the usual problems associated with IR as covered in Chapter 1 (primarily line of sight). There were two versions of RCX released, and both operated the IR at different carrier frequencies (although both RCX modules can transmit on either frequency) but were functionality identical.

The programming could be done in many languages, including cut-down versions of Java, C/C++, Lisp, and Forth, provided it was compiled into suitable code for the internal microcontroller, a Renesas H8/300. Because of its age, it is now available fairly cheaply, although the supplied IR transmitter has no support for any 64-bit operating systems and is losing support for newer 32-bit ones.

From RCX, LEGO moved to Mindstorms NXT in 2006. This increased the specification of the main brick by improving the processor (now a 32-bit ARM7/TDMI chip) and communications devices (it now included USB, Bluetooth, and an onboard 100 × 64 pixel LCD matrix). This upgrade in processor has necessitated a change in control software, but that is to be expected, and most of the RIS code has now been ported to NXT. The LEGO components also improved, as shown in Table 2-1.

Table 2-1. *LEGO Mindstorms Specifications*

Kit	Motors	TouchSensors	LightSensors	UltrasonicSensors	SoundSensors	ColorSensor
RIS	2	--	2	1	--	--
NXT	3*	1	1	1	1	--
NXT 2.0	3*	2	1	1	--	1
NXT Education	3*	2	1	1	1	--

* *These are servo motors, which internally monitor their position for greater positional accuracy.*

Since 2009, Mindstorms has been on its third iteration (NXT 2.0) and consists of the same RCX brick as NXT version 1.0, some alternative LEGO Technic bricks, and a change in sensor from sound to color. This was an odd change, as now all NXT 2.0 robots are deaf by default! This might have been a ploy to sell more add-on sensors, however, but for the wily hacker, these can be made much more cheaply using standard electronic components using instructions found on the Web or in various books, such as *Extreme NXT*.[6]

Where LEGO Mindstorms excels is its ability to rapidly prototype hardware that can be controlled by the computer, as well as remote sensors that can relay information back to it. This provides a method whereby the computer's state can be demonstrated by something in the real world. Similarly, it allows the real world to be understood, to some degree, by the computer.

Home automation is full of ideas, and not all of them have the staying power to enhance your living once their novelty has worn off. This makes LEGO perfect as a means of building proof-of-concept hardware before devoting time and money on PIC chips, motors, and cases that will be used for only one project. Here are some ideas:

- Create a robot that waves, or gestures, when an e-mail, private instant message, or phone call is received

- Use the LCD on the NXT processor block to relay information, such as weather

- Create a robot to open the fridge and bring beer into the living room[7]

- Create a Bluetooth gateway for sensors and devices around the house (for a cat flap or pressure mats)

The handling of each sensor and motor is very simple because it's just a matter of programming, using one of the available Linux environments, such as leJOS NXJ (Java for LEGO Mindstorms) or NXC (Not eXactly C). There are books and web articles abound on the subject, including this useful start point: http://www.eggwall.com/2011/08/lego-nxt-mindstorm-with-linux.html.

Arduino as an I/O Device

The Arduino and its many clones and variants are microcontroller boards that you can think of as grown-up LEGO—it provides a simple way of interfacing the real world with the computer, handling basic processing tasks on a chip (instead of in software), and working with hardware motors and sensors.

There are currently 16 forms of Arduino, based on a simple microcontroller, but the most popular development version is now the Arduino Diecimilanove based on the ATmega168 chip, although this is being superseded by the Arduino Uno using the ATmega328. It supports 14 digital pins that can be configured as either input or output and 6 analog inputs. The missing part here is analog *output*, which can be provided by using pulse width modulation (PWM[8]) on 6 of the 14 existing digital outputs or with additional electronics. Power can be provided by the USB port, by a power socket, or by connecting the wires from a battery clip to the board. An onboard jumper is used to switch between USB and external power sources.

To those used to large machines, the specification of the Arduino's chipset appears rather small:

- 14KB of available Flash memory (30KB on the ATMega328 versions), for software

- 2KB of Flash memory, used by the bootloader

- 1KB of SRAM memory (2KB on the ATMega328 versions), for data

- 512 bytes of EEPROM (1KB on the ATMega328 versions), for permanent data; acts like a mini hard disk

- 16MHz clock speed

---

[6] Formally called *Extreme NXT: Extending the LEGO MINDSTORMS NXT to the Next Level* (ISBN 978-1590598184).
[7] This is a difficult one to build, by the way, because the suction on most fridge doors is more powerful than the LEGO motors.
[8] PWM is where the digital output voltage is switched between high and low so that the average voltage, over time, is somewhere between the two. Not all hardware can be powered like this, however, but it is a cheap compromise.

Even the ATMega328, with double the memory capabilities, or even the ATMega2561 with 256KB, seems less than adequate, especially when compared to the Raspberry Pi. However, the tasks the Arduino will generally perform are very simple and usually in the realm of comparing various inputs and performing simple logic, so this specification is more than large enough. The complex tasks found in operating systems, like TCP/IP stacks, are not usually necessary since you can transmit requests to a connected PC for these tasks. And when they're not, the problem is generally solved in hardware by building the appropriate circuit and including the necessary driver software for that hardware component.

If you're experienced with other microcontrollers or PIC chips, the Arduino isn't different in any technical way to them, so you can continue to use whatever chips you have used previously. However, the Arduino offers many benefits to those less experienced with electronics:

- A C-based language and development environment, instead of assembler

- USB input/output control as standard

- A large community of hackers, publishing project designs and sharing tips

- Robust development boards that are less likely to blow up if you wrongly connect something

- A wide range of prebuilt, compatible circuit boards (called *shields*) to provide more complex functionality such as wireless communication. You'll see some examples later in the chapter in the "Arduino Hardware" section

- And, for the purists, open source hardware and architecture. This is an often overlooked point. Having the hardware open source allows clone makers, such as Seeeduino, to exist. Clones can be cheaper and more robust and can use surface-mount components while still remaining pin compatible with the Arduino and its assorted shields

The scope of possible projects is similar to that of the LEGO Mindstorms, although now the circuits can be very much smaller, involving more discrete components and wider functionality achieved through the aforementioned shields. Whereas a LEGO device might be able to beep or play a short sound to indicate the arrival of e-mail, the Arduino can use speech synthesis or full audio playback.

Installation and Setup

All Arduino software is written on a PC and transmitted to the board through USB. This is also used to receive any data the Arduino chooses to transmit, by default through /dev/ttyUSB0. (Remember to add your user into the dialout group so that /dev/ttyUSB0 is accessible.) The development can take place in any fashion you desire, but it is simplest with the Java-based IDE. Even if you adopt a command-line approach, the code will need to be compiled using the avr-gcc toolchain, which can be installed under Debian with this:

```
apt-get install gcc-avr avr-libc avrdude
```

Java, if uninstalled, will need an extra line, like this:

```
apt-get install openjdk-6-jre
```

From here, it's a simple matter of installing the IDE. This is provided as a single archive from the web site at http://arduino.cc/en/Main/Software. Extract this to an appropriate directory (root access is not required for any of these steps), and run ./arduino from the directory. You should then set up the appropriate USB device and type of Arduino (Tools ➤ Serial Port and Tools ➤ Board, respectively) before use.

You can begin a project by selecting File ➤ New from the menu. This creates what the Arduino IDE calls a *sketch*. This involves a subdirectory in the Arduino working folder and a primary source file. Other source files can be added into the sketch (through Sketch ➤ Add File) and will be automatically included into the project build. There is no Makefile equivalent here, and every file added to the sketch, even if it is a library file from another directory, is copied into the sketch directory. Note that despite the visual similarity to C code, all files are given the extension .pde for clarity.

■ **Note** You cannot create a sketch of a given name. Instead, you must create a blank new sketch and then select Save As as a separate step.

The build process itself is handled behind the scenes using avr-gcc, a cross-compilation toolchain for the Atmel AVR RISC processors, of which the ATmega168 is one. It creates a separate applet directory inside the sketch folder and copies all the header files into it, along with a concatenation of all the source files (ending in .pde). It is this (.cpp) source file that is then cross-compiled into hex for upload to the Arduino.

Arduino Software

The simplest circuit that most people build to test their setup is that of a flashing light. Pin 13 on the Arduino Diecimila board has a built-in resistor, allowing you to directly connect an LED to it and the 0v supply without damaging it. Some boards also have a surface-mount LED, so you don't even need that! The blink tutorial code, which can be loaded from the IDE (File ➤ Examples ➤ 01.Basic), is simply this:

```
int ledPin = 13;              // LED connected to digital pin 13

void setup()                  // run once, when the sketch starts
{
  pinMode(ledPin, OUTPUT);    // sets the digital pin as output
}

void loop()                   // run over and over again
{
  digitalWrite(ledPin, HIGH); // sets the LED on
  delay(1000);                // waits for a second
  digitalWrite(ledPin, LOW);  // sets the LED off
  delay(1000);                // waits for a second
}
```

It is easy to understand this code, with many of the usual C/C++/Java-ism being unnecessary:

- No header files are needed
- Main has been replaced by two functions: setup and loop
- There is no event loop or callbacks. You must read the pin states each time around a loop

If you are a classically trained developer who vehemently opposes the blocking function delay that's used here, then there are examples that demonstrate the use of the millis function to infer the timing without blocking.

For most complex software and libraries, you can, of course, reference header files, but remember that any additional source files added to the project will be *copied*. It is certainly possible to create your own libraries, but on such small-scale projects, it often proves to be a bigger time sink.

Reading Digital Inputs

These are the simplest circuit to build, because they consist of a single resistor and switch combination, as shown in Figure 2-2.

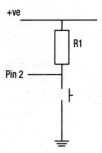

Figure 2-2. *Reading a digital switch on the Arduino*

In this configuration, pin 2 is used as an example and reports a 1 (high) voltage to the Arduino at all times the switch is open. This is because of the "pull-up" resistor, R1. Without it, the pin is effectively disconnected, so its voltage may fluctuate to any value between 0 and 5v, causing false readings. (Most of the time, however, it will float up to 1.) When the switch is closed, the pin is connected directly to the 0v ground rail, causing a 0 to be read. The Arduino code then watches for this change as follows:

```
int inputSwitchPin = 2;
int lastState = HIGH;

void setup() {
  Serial.begin(9600);
  pinMode(inputSwitchPin, INPUT);
}

void loop() {
  int pinState = digitalRead(inputSwitchPin);

  if (pinState != lastState) {
    Serial.println(pinState?"released":"pressed");
    lastState = pinState;
  }
}
```

This will work in some situations but not all, because hardware isn't that simple! Switches, being mechanical beasts, have a tendency to "bounce" between on and off a few times when they're pressed. If this switch were connected to a light, you probably wouldn't see it switch on and off, however, because the time involved is measured in milliseconds. But a computer is fast enough to spot it, so you need to program the code to ignore any state changes that occur within, say, 100 ms of each other.

```
int inputSwitchPin = 2;
int lastState;

long timeLastPressed;
long debouncePeriod = 100;
```

```
void setup() {
  Serial.begin(9600);
  pinMode(inputSwitchPin, INPUT);
  lastState = digitalRead(inputSwitchPin);
  timeLastPressed = millis();
}

void loop() {
  int pinState = digitalRead(inputSwitchPin);

  if (pinState != lastState && millis() - timeLastPressed > debouncePeriod) {
    Serial.println(pinState?"released":"pressed");
    timeLastPressed = millis();
    lastState = pinState;
  }
}
```

The switch I've used here is normally open and, as the name suggests, remains open (so that no current flows between the contacts) under normal circumstances and is closed when the switch is pressed. Some switches are marked as normally closed, in which case you simply reverse the output in the example.

It is also possible to use analog devices, such as a light sensor, to report a digital on/off input when you're are not concerned with the quantity involved. In this example, you might be interested in whether it is light outside but not how bright the light was. You can amend the circuit as shown in Figure 2-3.

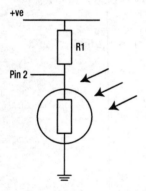

Figure 2-3. *Reading the light on the Arduino*

This circuit is known as a *potential divider circuit*, since the voltage (known formally as *potential*) is divided proportionally by the resistors placed across the supply rails. R2 is a light-dependent resistor (LDR), which has a very high resistance (like an open switch) when it is dark but acts almost like a closed switch (that is, low resistance) when it is light. (This is an oversimplification of the process but is enough to get things working.) The exact resistance of the LDR under these conditions is governed by the specific LDR, and not all manufacturers or suppliers provide this information, so you might have to experiment.

This basic circuit can be used to switch on lights when it gets dark (remembering to point the LDR away from the light in question!) and can be used to monitor people passing by the sensor because their shadow is usually enough to switch the LDR off. You can also get infrared transmitters and receivers that work in similar fashion, which can be placed on either side of a doorway or front gates, so you can get forewarning when someone is approaching your house.

■ **Note** When you're interested in the state change from off to on, this is known as a *rising edge trigger*. And changes from on to off are called *falling edge triggers*.

Reading Analog Inputs

These detect a continuous range of values. Unlike the digital pins, which can be used as either input or output, the analog pins on an Arduino are hardwired, so there is no need for initial configuration. This leaves you nothing to do except read their value:

```
int analogInputPin = 2;
int value = analogRead(analogInputPin);
```

The result of value will be in the range 0 to 1023 and represents the voltage on the pin, between 0 and 5v.

If you reuse circuit from Figure 2-3, feeding the input to an analog pin instead of a digital one, you can watch the range of values being output by using this:

```
Serial.print("LDR brightness = ");
Serial.println(value);
```

This allows you to determine the precise brightness of the light empirically. You will notice a lot of fluctuations with this data, so the best approach is to determine whether it's bright or dark enough to control the light, by having two limits and a dead band in the middle. That is, if the number drops from greater than X to less than X, then it's considered light, and if it increases from less than X+N to greater than X+N, then it's dark.

You can then add a variable resistor into the circuit to fine-tune this brightness, as shown in Figure 2-4.

In addition to light, you can also measure temperature (thermistors), distances (ultrasonic range finders), and rotary positions (by attaching a handle or wheel to the spindle of a potentiometer).

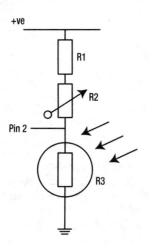

Figure 2-4. *Controlling the brightness at which the Arduino is controlled*

The method of reading analog inputs doesn't change if you use a different type of sensor. Indeed, there's a QM-NG1 gas sensor that could be replaced into the above circuit to give an audible warning if a leak is detected in the kitchen. Similarly, the MQ2 smoke detector could be used for a similar purpose. Both cases are traditionally confined to local warnings. But by passing the warning to your phone through a SMS alert (see Chapter 5 for details on how to send such messages) you can call a friend or neighbor to check for you, particularly as the alarms might not be audible outside the dwelling.

Sending Digital Outputs

This is as simple as it sounds and includes those cases in which you want to send nothing more than a simple on/off to something like a light switch or small motor. The code requires a simple setup and invocation like this:

```
int outputLightPin = 2;
pinMode(outputLightPin, OUTPUT);
//
digitalWrite(outputLightPin, bState ? TRUE : FALSE);
```

From here, it's all about the circuit.

Each pin on the Arduino is able to source current, up to around 40 milliamps. This is enough for most small loads such as lights, buffers, and some small motors. If your device uses no more than 300 milliamps, then you can draw this from the circuit board itself using the Arduino as a switch only with a circuit like that in Figure 2-5.

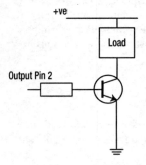

Figure 2-5. *A transistor switch circuit, allowing you to draw up to 300mA*

For anything larger, you will need to employ a relay and separate power source, as shown in Figure 2-6.

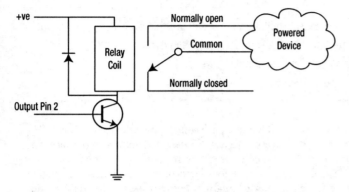

Figure 2-6. *Using a relay to control high power loads*

■ **Note** In reality, the Arduino is good for higher power loads up to 800 mA. But for dirty loads, such as motors, the 300 mA is probably more conservatively sensible.

Sending Analog Outputs

As mentioned previously, analog output is available on the basic Arduino only when using PWM. This is supported only on pins 3, 5, 6, 9, 10, 11, and 21.[9] The pulsing of the output pin to provide the output is handled automatically, including the setup, so you need only to write this:

```
analogWrite(analogWritePin, value); // value is between 0 and 255, inclusive
```

This will allow you to vary the brightness of LEDs and the volume of piezo-buzzers and speakers, but not a lot else. In reality, you won't need a lot else in home automation environs. Moving a motor to a specific position, for example, is better done with servo or stepper motors, and many other forms of positioning should be done through the use of feedback loops—switching the motor on to begin movement and switching it off when a sensor reveals it has gone far enough.

Creating Audio Outputs

This is one of the simplest forms of human-friendly feedback the Arduino can provide, because the circuit needs only a buzzer attached to a digital output pin. The code is a simple loop changing the output state between on and off 440 times a second, for example, to produce the A note above middle C.

The examples on the main Arduino site provide the necessary code to make it beep and play short tunes. For those looking for more advanced music control, there is Armstrong (www.bluedust.dontexist.com/armstrong), the Arduino music system, which provides a small melody processor allowing you to play the chimes of Big Ben with code like this:

```
ancInitialize(OUTPUT_LOCAL);
ancAssignChannelToPin(CHANNEL_OUTPUT_PIEZO_SPEAKER, piezoPin);

char *pChimesPhrase1 = "L3204edcL6403g";
char *pChimesPhrase2 = "L3204cedL6403g";
```

---

[9]Older boards using the ATmega8 support only pins 9, 10, and 11, whereas the newer Arduino Mega can support PWM on 12 of its pins.

```
char *pChimesPhrase3 = "L3204cdeL64c";
char *pChimesPhrase4 = "L3204ecdL6403g";
char *pChimesPhrase5 = "L3203g04deL64c";

// a quarter past
ampPlayString(CHANNEL_OUTPUT_PIEZO_SPEAKER, pChimesPhrase1);

// half past
ampPlayString(CHANNEL_OUTPUT_PIEZO_SPEAKER, pChimesPhrase2);
ampPlayString(CHANNEL_OUTPUT_PIEZO_SPEAKER, pChimesPhrase3);

// a quarter to

ampPlayString(CHANNEL_OUTPUT_PIEZO_SPEAKER, pChimesPhrase4);
ampPlayString(CHANNEL_OUTPUT_PIEZO_SPEAKER, pChimesPhrase5);
ampPlayString(CHANNEL_OUTPUT_PIEZO_SPEAKER, pChimesPhrase1);

// top of the hour
ampPlayString(CHANNEL_OUTPUT_PIEZO_SPEAKER, pChimesPhrase2);
ampPlayString(CHANNEL_OUTPUT_PIEZO_SPEAKER, pChimesPhrase3);
ampPlayString(CHANNEL_OUTPUT_PIEZO_SPEAKER, pChimesPhrase4);
ampPlayString(CHANNEL_OUTPUT_PIEZO_SPEAKER, pChimesPhrase5);
```

Using the various shields provides more complex audio output, including sample playback.

Communication with a PC

The basic Arduino allows bidirectional communication with a PC through its built-in USB port. This uses the same serial port that's used to upload the program in the first place. It must be set up first before data can be sent or received, both of which are supported with this method:

```
Serial.begin(9600);
```

The Arduino can read data from the PC only on a byte-by-byte basis, so you will need to read it within a loop using code like this:

```
int incomingData = Serial.read();
```

Note, however, that this function is blocking. That is, it will not return from the read function until there is data on the serial port. If your device responds only to messages, then this will work fine. However, it is more usual to place this at the start of your loop, surrounded with this:

```
if (Serial.available() > 0) { /* ... */ }
```

Writing data from the Arduino back to the PC, however, is easier since the size of the data is already known. This can be handled by the Serial.print or Serial.println function for quick and easy string messages. Or individual bytes can be written using Serial.write:

```
Serial.write(byteData);
```

This is useful for applications wanting to transfer a lot of data. But for testing and development, I find a simple ASCII-based protocol easier to work with, because a simple serial terminal allows me to send and receive messages in human-readable text. The Minerva feature, MINX (Minerva INput transfer), uses the delimiters <| and |> to surround control messages, allowing an Arduino to pass messages back to the PC so that further processing can take place, without affecting any other debugging or trace messages. I'll cover this fully in Chapter 7.

▪ **Note** Some models of Arduino, such as the Mega, have three additional serial ports addressable as Serial1, Serial2, and Serial3.

On the PC side of this transmit-receive equation, you have a much simpler job because everything in Linux is treated like a file. You can therefore issue this:

```
tail -f /dev/ttyUSB0
```

To see all the data that is sent back from the Arduino and introduce commands to the board, use this:

```
echo -n send data > /dev/ttyUSB0
```

It is from this that demonstrates the benefit of an ASCII-based protocol. In the simplest case, you can issue this:

```
Serial.print("1");
```

from the Arduino to switch the PC control program into an on state, with an equivalent for off. This makes the C program very simple:

```c
// USB script trigger
#include <stdio.h>

char *szUSBDevice = "/dev/ttyUSB0";
int main() {
char v;

FILE *fp = fopen(szUSBDevice, "r");
if (!fp) {
  printf("Failed to open USB...");
  return 1;
}

while(1) {
 if (fread(&v, 1, 1, fp)) {
   if (v == '1') {
      // button pressed
   } else if (v == '0') {
      // button released
   } else {
      printf("%c", v);
```

```
        fflush(stdout);
    }
  }
}

return 0;
}
```

This also includes the functionality to write noncontrol codes to `stdout`, which may be redirected to a log file. If you compile the previous program with g++ as `arduino_read`, you can start it as a process in the background, making it daemon-like for very little effort:

```
./arduino_read > logfile 2>&1 &
```

Arduino Hardware

For some complex applications, the ATmega168 chip on the Arduino board is not powerful enough to handle the task. So, in common with other computers, additional chips are necessary to ease the burden. In keeping with the modular design of the Arduino, these chips are built up into stand-alone boards with the necessary interfacing circuitry so that they can be directly mounted *on top* of the existing Arduino board. For this reason, they are known as *shields*. Most shields also include a pass-through so that other shields can be placed on top of it. There is then a separate software library that is used to control the device and that is copied into the `Arduino/hardware/libraries` directory.

■ **Note**   Not all shields are compatible with all models of Arduino.

There are many Arduino shields on the market, most with freely available specifications and circuit diagrams. Each shield has a specific task and includes the following problem domains.

Ethernet Networking

There is the Arduino Ethernet Shield that supports four concurrent connections, working in either client or server mode using TCP or UDP packets. It is based on the Wiznet W5100 chipset and uses digital pins 10–13 to communicate.

Wireless Control

Thanks to the exceptional work of Arduino hackers, there is now a WiFi shield available, capable of using the 802.11b and 802.11g protocols. The code at `http://arduino.cc/en/Main/ArduinoWiFiShield`, along with the WiFi shield library, provide WEP and WPA2 encryption along with an onboard SD micro slot. There are also examples to turn the unit into a web server.

As befits its status, the WiFi shield makes use of many pins to communicate between itself and the Arduino. Consequently, if you have an input/output heavy application, then look to the 4051 chip (`http://playground.arduino.cc/learning/4051`) to multiplex the outputs and expand its capabilities.

■ **Tip**   If the shield and Arduino refuse to talk, then shorting pins 3 and 7 might help.

Stepping outside of 802.11, the main alternative is the Xbee shield, which uses the ZigBee wireless protocol, meaning it is not directly compatible with existing WiFi connections but can act as a radio transmitter and receiver for basic scenarios and has an improved indoor range of about 30 meters. This is often a better choice for connecting sheds and outhouses to the house, for basic security measures.

Motors

The motor shield, from LadyAda, supports medium power control for DC, servo, and stepper motors. The total number of supported motors and the total power drain are governed by the specific motors themselves, but the quoted specs permit you two DC servos (on 5V) and up to four DC motors, two stepper motors, or one stepper and up to two DC motors. This shield does utilize a lot pins for control, and a lot of power, but can be used to lock cat flaps or build a robot.

Example: The Arduino Welcome Mat

With this knowledge, you can build a simple circuit, write some Arduino software, and add a Linux-side script to trigger a piece of speech whenever someone enters or leaves the house.

I'll show how to use the Arduino to monitor the state of a pressure mat (using a normally open switch) placed under a rug and transmit messages to the PC. The Arduino will also remember the current state, so once the switch inside the pressure mat has been stepped on, the house state is assumed to be "vacant" since people have left the house, and when the switch is closed again, the state changes to "occupied." The circuit is a simple switch, as shown in Figure 2-2. Naturally, you could write the same code on a Raspberry Pi, but there is no reason to waste so many CPU cycles unless you were also going to add a front door cam or other such feature.

■ **Note**　You can also use a pressure mat to determine whether you've gotten out of bed after your alarm has gone off, and you can use the act of leaving the bedroom as a means to stop the alarm from sounding.

The Arduino software is slightly more complex because you are looking for the case when the switch goes from the closed state to the open, as people might stand on the mat for a minute or more while they put on their coat. I have also included a timer here so that the house state doesn't change if a second rising edge (caused by someone else stepping on the mat) is detected within two seconds of the first. This is to allow several people to leave the house at once, without the state getting confused. Naturally, this doesn't solve the problem of only *some* occupants leaving the house, but it's a start!

```
int inputSwitchPin = 2;
int lastState;

long timeLastPressed;
long debouncePeriod = 100;

int houseState;
long doormatUnblockAt;
long doormatDelayPeriod = 2000;
int blockSteps;

void setup() {
  Serial.begin(9600);
  pinMode(inputSwitchPin, INPUT);     // declare pushbutton as input
  lastState = digitalRead(inputSwitchPin);
```

```
    timeLastPressed = millis();
    blockSteps = 0;
    houseState = 0;
}

void loop() {
  int pinState = digitalRead(inputSwitchPin);

  if (pinState != lastState && millis() - timeLastPressed > debouncePeriod) {
      if (pinState == 0) {  // i.e., pressed
        if (!blockSteps) {
          houseState = 1-houseState;
          blockSteps = 1;
          Serial.print(houseState?"1":"0");
        }
        doormatUnblockAt = millis() + doormatDelayPeriod;
      }
    timeLastPressed = millis();
    lastState = pinState;
  }

  if (millis() > doormatUnblockAt) {
    blockSteps = 0;
  }
}
```

Finally, the USB script trigger code shown previously is adapted to watch for the serial messages of 0 and 1:

```
if (v == '1') {
   system("enter_house.sh");
} else if (v == '0') {
   system("leave_house.sh");
... as before ...
```

which runs either the enter_house.sh script for entering:

```
say default welcome home
x10control default on lounge_light
```

or the leave_house.sh script for leaving as appropriate:

```
say default Goodbye

RAIN=`weatherstatus | head -n 1 | grep -i "[rain|shower]"`

if [ "$?" -eq 0 ]; then
    say default Remember your umbrella it might rain today.
    say default $RAIN
fi
```

In these code samples, I have used simplified commands without paths to demonstrate the process. The commands themselves are the abstractions that appear in the Minerva system, covered in Chapter 7.

This "house state" information could be extended to switch on security lights or redirect personal e-mails to a work account, for example. To connect the Arduino output to the rest of the system, you will either need to use a networking shield (either wired or wireless, depending your connection points) or need a local PC with one. The advantage of a PC (such as a Fit-PC2, notebook, or similarly small machine) is that it can be reused as a display and control panel. In this example, having a panel by the door displaying the tasks for the day and printing reminders about the weather can provide a suitable excuse for the extra expense.

The code can be further expanded by using personal knowledge of the habits of yourself, and your family. Consider, for example, the act of leaving your house and returning 10 seconds later to collect your gloves. On the one hand (no pun intended), you could add a warning for lower temperatures to the speech synthesize module. On the other, you could determine that anyone activating the pressure mat within 20 seconds is returning home (and not someone else leaving it) and so ignore the usual messages.

Furthermore, you could extend this period of grace allowing you to get to the car, only to realize you've forgotten your keys. At this point, you could automatically trigger an AlertMe device, which, when attached to the key, makes a beeping noise so you can easily find it when the pressure mat detects that you have returned.

■ **Note**   With minor modifications, you could employ two pressure mats (one inside and one outside) to more correctly determine the direction of travel.

Depending on the type of pressure mat used, you could also place one under a rug by the cat flap, as your pet's weight is normally enough to trigger it. This would allow you to interface it with a LEGO robot that could then feed the cat when they returned from their customary wander.

■ **Caution**   Most pressure mats cannot be cut to size because of their internal electronics.

Example: The Arduino Dictaphone

Most people make notes on the back of train tickets and shopping lists because the effort to switch on a computer or find the phone's notepad application is too much. By combining the interface-less environment of an Arduino and the audio functionality of a monitor-less PC, you can create a very simple voice recorder.

You start with the basic switch circuit, but you then replicate it three times—once for each of the record, play, and erase buttons, as shown in Figure 2-7.

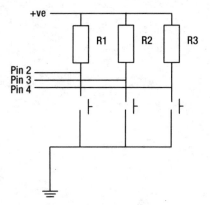

Figure 2-7. *Using three switches and inputs to control a voice recorder*

You can then adapt the similarly banal Arduino control program to check for three buttons instead of one, remembering to debounce each of them. There's also a slight change here; because you're using the record button to govern the length of the record, consequently it sends a start message when the button is pressed and a stop message on release.

```
int pinStates[3];
int lastStates[3];
long timesLastPressed[3];
int inputSwitchPins[3] = {2,3,4};

void setup() {
  Serial.begin(9600);
  for(int i=0;i<3;++i) {
    pinMode(inputSwitchPins[i], INPUT);
    lastState = digitalRead(inputSwitchPins[i]);
    timesLastPressed[i] = millis();
  }
}

void loop() {
  for(int i=0;i<3;++i) {
    int pinState = digitalRead(inputSwitchPins[i]);

    if (pinState != lastStates[i] &&
            millis() - timesLastPressed[i] > debouncePeriod) {
      switch(i) {
        case 0: // record
            Serial.print(pinState==0?"B":"E");
            break;
        case 1: // play
            if (pinState == 0) {
              Serial.print("P");
            }
            break;
        case 2: // delete
            if (pinState == 0) {
              Serial.print("D");
            }
            break;
      }
      timesLastPressed[i] = millis();
      lastStates[i] = pinState;
    }
  }
}
```

Notice that I have also extended the control codes. Instead of a simple 0 and 1, I now have B and E to begin and end the recording, P to play back the sounds, and D to delete them all. You can then adapt the PC-based C code as you did for the doormat to run one of three scripts you've written on the PC to control the sound card:

```
if (v == 'B') {
    system("vox_record.sh start");
} else if (v == 'E') {
    system("vox_record.sh stop");
} else if (v == 'P') {
    system("vox_play.sh");
} else if (v == 'D') {
    system("vox_delete.sh");
 ... as before ...
```

This might be to record the sound with vox_record.sh:

```
#!/bin/bash

LOGFILE=/var/log/voxrecordpid
DIR_INCOMING=/usr/local/media/voxrecord

if [ "$1" == "start" ]; then
  FILENAME=`mktemp -p $DIR_INCOMING`.wav
  arecord -f cd -t wav $FILENAME >/dev/null >/dev/null 2>&1 &
  PID=$!
  echo $PID >$LOGFILE
fi

if [ "$1" == "stop" ]; then
  PID=`cat $LOGFILE`
  kill $PID
  rm $LOGFILE
fi
```

or play back each sound in the directory with vox_play.sh:

```
#!/bin/bash

DIR_INCOMING=/usr/local/media/voxrecord

for F in "$DIR_INCOMING"/*.wav
do
    play $F
done
```

or even delete them all through vox_delete.sh:

```
#!/bin/bash

DIR_INCOMING=/usr/local/media/voxrecord

rm -f $DIR_INCOMING/*
```

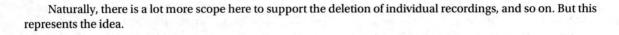

Naturally, there is a lot more scope here to support the deletion of individual recordings, and so on. But this represents the idea.

■ **Note**   The Minerva system abstracts these ideas out into Minx, which eliminates the need for separate executables for each Arduino application. Minerva will be covered in Chapter 7.

Example: Arduino Interfacing

For the most part, Arduino is capable of indicating its status only through an LED, or maybe a small LCD text display. The majority of the friendly home interfaces require larger screens, or speech output. For these, the Arduino generally makes a request to a larger machine somewhere else in the house. However, with the ever-growing range of shields on offer, and the introduction faster chips and more time to devote to more custom programming, other means of interfacing it now possible from a humble Arduino.

■ **Note**   Many of the advanced software hacks require precise timing by using Fast PWM, which is activated by setting the waveform generation mode bits to 011. Be aware that if the rest of your code uses this in its normal operation, you will need to reliquish control to the library, which might include disabling other shields that use it. Similarly, you may also need to also avoid the your normal poll-test-output loop in some cases.

Speech synthesis

The use of speech, covered more fully in Chapter 5, is a double-edged sword. On one hand, it's the most natural form of communication, that us humans have perfected over millennia. On the other, computerized speech still sounds like a bad 60s B-movie and is unable to convey the nuances present in language, when spoken by a person.

But it is cool!

The most natural way for an Arduino to speak arbitrary text strings is to use a shield such as GinSing (http://www.ginsingsound.com) or Voicebox (http://www.sparkfun.com/short/9799). Both are fairly equivalent in terms of ability and cost, with GinSing winning out slightly due to its higher-rated power amplifier, and improved 16 Khz playback rate. For those wanting a pre-built shield, it also wins out over the Sparkfun offering. However, the only test you need to run concerns the output—that is, which voice you prefer. Both are of the old school variety, so listen to examples from both sites and choose accordingly.

■ **Note**   There is one notable example of speech synthesis with an unsheilded Arduino, https://code.google.com/p/tinkerit/wiki/Cantarino, but this is primarily a tech demo, and it will take reasonable work to convert to anything else.

Sound production

This can range in scope from simple beeps, to sample playback. It cannot support multiple sound sources, however, because there is not enough processing power to manage real-time mixing of the sounds. If you like, there are some proof of concept that use multiple speakers, but they are rarely good enough. Or, you could buy two Arduinos, but at that point it's better to get a Raspberry Pi!

Individual beeps can be used as a simple acknowledge tone, to indicate that the system has carried out a particular task—a high pitched beep for "okay," and a lower tone for "error"—or to issue an alarm bell (think of the range of sounds an 80s computer game managed with a similar level of technology!) Its biggest, most obviously, benefit is that sound requires so little processing power, that you can run complex operations on the chip. We saw this in operation earlier with software-lead Armstrong, but you can also rely on hardware, and use the voice synthesis chips to generate multichannel audio.

Sample playback is obviously a better solution for audio feedback. Although beeps are sufferable, they are just that—sufferable! If you listen to any TV show or film, the beeps and chirps of the high tech equipment presented always have more color (or timbre) to the sound that a simple square wave. The beeps of R2D2 in *Star Wars* might sound basic, but if you analyze them you'll see they have great texture. So having samples to replace beeps is an obvious step up.

Also, sound samples can be used to represent anything. Including pre-recorded speech. This (as we'll see in Chapter 5) can be used in place of speech synthesis to create a more natural sounding house voice. Some people have taken Majel Barrett's voice, the computer from *Star Trek,* in this regard! So, as long as you only need prerecorded phrases, this provides a very nice interface.

■ **Tip** With the exception of news stories, most feedback systems can be quantified with predetermined error codes and messages. You might have to reword the message from "You have only N megabytes of free space on /dev/sda1" to "Your server is running low on disc space," but it is usually preferable.

The method for sample playback is a little more involved than making a simple beep. This is because to make a recognisable sample you have to change the output pin more often. Usually, an order of magnitude more often. For example, to play a square wave at 440Hz (the "A above middle C") you must change the output level of the pin from high to low 440 times a second. (This is 880 operations.) For a sample, you will often need a minimum of 11050 changes per second, with each level change requiring the additional time penalty of a memory access, and the use of an analog output. The Nyquist theorem indicates that to represent a sound of 1000Hz, you will need a sampling frequency of at least twice this, 2000Hz. As a guide, CDs have a playback frequency of 44,100Hz.

However, it is possible!

Two software-only solutions are at your disposal, both stem from the base code at http://playground.arduino.cc/Code/PCMAudio, which provides a fairly low-level solution of manipulating the PWM signal on pin 11. The expanded (i.e., high level) version of this library is at http://hlt.media.mit.edu/?p=1963 and lets you initiate playback with code such as:

```
#include <PCM.h>

const unsigned char sampleData[] PROGMEM = {
  126, 127, 128, 128, 128, 128, 128, 127, 128, 128, 128, 129, 129, 128, 127,
  ... lots more data here ...
};

void setup()
{
  startPlayback(sampleData, sizeof(sampleData));
}

void loop()
{
}
```

You will notice that playback always takes an array of sample data, rather than a filename. If you have a shield which lets you work with an SD card, or USB memory stick, then you can fashion playback from a file. Without it, however, you need to access it directly as raw data that involves processing the audio file offline, and producing a large array that can be read as such.

There are various code solutions to the problem of generating this array, although the output is nothing more than the 8-bit output levels of each sample in the sound. Typical packages include EncodeAudio (`https://github.com/damellis/EncodeAudio`) and wav2c, mplayer, and sox.

The limitations of this method are many but, on an unshielded Arduino, what do you expect!? Primarily, you need to store the data in its Flash memory (not RAM) that takes away from your program space. But still, you are limited to around 4 seconds of audio, in 8-bit, sampled at 8Khz.

To surpass these limitations you need two things: more memory, and a custom chip capable of faster playback. Fortunately, these problems go hand-in-hand, as you need a shield that supports external flash memory to handle the former, so makers of the latter have included it for free. The two workhorses in this area are the Sparkfun MP3 Player shield (`https://www.sparkfun.com/products/10628`) and Lady Ada's wave shield (`http://www.ladyada.net/make/waveshield`) which provides playback support for `.wav` files, up to 16-bit mono 22KHz samples, which is a marked improvement over the PCM examples we saw earlier. It also provides a small power amplifier, able to drive 1/8W 8 ohm speakers. This could be used for a talking clock, a kitchen-based stopwatch, or a virtual pet.

Before planning any projects however, you need to careful consult the specification of the hardware since the software libraries necessary for this task can be very large (because they include Flash access, as well as sample playback—the wave shield for example uses 10KB of memory) so you might not have room for all of your automation control logic. Or you might need to upgrade to a better chip.

■ **Note** The filesystem on Arduino-accessible flash memory generally uses 8.3 filenames, so it is not possible to prerecord speech for every word from the dictionary without an additional lookup table.

Display systems

If you need a full display, or high resolution graphics, then your Arduino will probably have to concede defeat to the Raspberry Pi. However, for many applications, this isn't necessary.

The simplest form of display to connect is an LCD, such as the SparkFun SerLCD (`https://www.sparkfun.com/products/9393`) that provides two lines of 16 characters, along with a back light. Such devices require no additional driver hardware, and the LCD library is provided as standard. The font is also held in the device, so messages can be display simply with

```
// initialize the library with the numbers of the interface pins
LiquidCrystal lcd(12, 11, 5, 4, 3, 2);

lcd.begin(16, 2);
lcd.print("hello, world!");
```

This is normally enough for warnings and basic messages, although you can always buffer and scroll messages along if need be.

If wiring is more interesting to you, then it is also possible to drive several LED matrix devices from a single Arduino, like this example `http://g33k.blogspot.co.uk/2010/02/arduino-56x8-scrolling-led-matrix.html`. This has the benefit of having per-LED control, and still be fairly low power. The next step up from here is to use a TV display, which the Arduino is capable of driving directly through the composite socket!

The TVout project (https://code.google.com/p/arduino-tvout) uses two resistors and a piece of wire to control a 128 x 96 pixel display on a standard TV set. It only supports black and white rendering, but has been used for small games, as well as more traditional applications. The processing overhead of generating the image is, naturally, high so the control logic needs to be fairly tight but it is still very possible to make useful reporting apps.

Joysticks for Input

Joysticks, particularly old ones, make wonderful input devices because they interface with the parallel port on most standard sound cards and are physically rugged. This enables the buttons to be reused, particularly as foot pedals, to control software. Indeed, this provides a very cheap way of adding a dictation module to your machine, without the need for an Arduino providing the input. In addition to triggering individual events on a Linux machine, such as requesting a weather report or the state of the machine, it can also feed messages to other applications. mplayer, for example, can operate in slave mode, allowing commands to be fed to it from the standard input or a named pipe. Similarly, the X Window TV-viewing software, xawtv, comes with xawtv-remote to change channel and volume (as per most remote controls), giving you capture on/off and screenshot facilities. This makes it possible to freeze frame magic shows to see how they do it!

You can read the joystick directly from /dev/js0, but it is usually better to use an abstraction, like the Simple DirectMedia Layer (SDL). This allows you to port the code elsewhere if necessary, avoid the vagaries that come with a reliance on the device hierarchy, and make it easier for others to add and adapt your code.

The code to read and process the joystick is a very simple loop of C code:

```
#include <SDL/SDL.h>

int main() {
    if (SDL_Init(SDL_INIT_JOYSTICK) < 0) {
        fprintf(stderr, "Couldn't initialize SDL: %s\n", SDL_GetError());
        exit(1);
    }

    SDL_JoystickEventState(SDL_ENABLE);
    SDL_Joystick *pJoystick = SDL_JoystickOpen(0);

    SDL_Event event;
    while(SDL_PollEvent(&event)) {
      switch(event.type) {
        case SDL_JOYBUTTONDOWN:
          // Use event.jbutton.which, event.jbutton.button, event.jbutton.state
          break;
      }
    }
    SDL_JoystickClose(pJoystick);

    return 0;
}
```

The button presses can naturally trigger software internally or make use of the Minerva Minx system I mentioned earlier to execute separate external scripts (Minerva is covered fully in Chapter 7).

Some joysticks can also be used as output devices, through an technique known as *force feedback*, available under Linux with libff. This functionality is provided through one of two drivers, HID driver (hid-lg2ff) or I-Force driver (iforce.ko), which cover a number of the force feedback devices on the market. Alas, not all of them are included, so it is best to check compatibility first (`http://sourceforge.net/apps/mediawiki/libff/index.php?title=SupportedDevices`). The use of force feedback is primarily for games, because the game causes a slight jolt of the device, through a small motor in the joystick, when the player is attacked or dies. The vibrate option on mobile phones and pagers works in the same way. There is very little scope for shaping the vibration in any advanced or meaningful way, and very few (if any) games in Linux support the library. However, `fftest` (from the ffutils project at `http://sourceforge.net/projects/libff/files/ffutils`) may be hacked to provide a small rumble when an e-mail arrives.

Other Input Controllers

Game development has never been a strong selling point to the Linux community; consequently, the libraries available (and the resultant quality of the games) have been few in number. This has led to a sporadic approach to the problem of device control. One good example of this is the separation between SDL (for good solid joystick processing, but with force feedback currently available only in an unstable SVN branch) and fflib (for force feedback). There is currently just one project that is attempting to close this divide, and it's called the Object Oriented Input System (OIS); you can find it at `http://sourceforge.net/projects/wgois/`.

OIS is planning on abstracting away all the device (and driver) specific elements of user input devices (including keyboard, mice, and joysticks) and providing a unified API to them. Although this is admirable for the games developers, it doesn't help us a great deal...except for the recent introduction of code that supports the Nintendo Wii's remote wand (aka the Wiimote). This peripheral operates through Bluetooth and can determine the area of the screen it's pointing at by imaging into its sensor the infrared LEDs held in a bar attached to the top or bottom of the screen. This can also determine its orientation and acceleration. This makes it a very suitable controller for complex applications running on a TV screen, where a mouse is not suitable but an equivalent means of control is needed.

There is also the CWiid tool, available in some distros by default, which provides a mouse driver wrapper, allowing unported mouse-based applications to be controlled by the Wiimote.

Hacking Laptops

The price of netbooks, with solid-state storage and preinstalled Linux software, are now so low that their cost isn't much greater than the top-of-the-range stand-alone photo frames. And as a bonus, you get a better processor, video playback, network connectivity (often wireless), and VoIP software. This makes the netbook an ideal home automation panel, with many uses.

Obviously, older laptops can also be used for hacking. Any that are lacking a hard drive, have dead batteries, or have broken keyboards are particularly good value because the cost of new parts makes them too expense to rebuild, and having a laptop reliant on a tethered power line is not such a problem for home automation users as it is for others.

Their use as a control panel is obvious, because the screen and keyboard halves can be folded flat and mounted to any wall or surface quite easily. Or, the keyboard base (with the lion's share of electronics) can be hidden away underneath a desk or worktable, with just the screen poking out. It can then be controlled with a joystick input or, more impressively, a touchscreen.

Touchscreens can be added retroactively to most laptops. They exist as a transparent membrane that fits over the screen and a PS/2 socket that mimics the behavior of a mouse delivering X and Y coordinates and left-button up and down messages. It should be noted that the software interface must be suitably programmed, since the membrane cannot detect the mouse position unless there is pressure on it (i.e., mouse over or hover events won't exist), and there is no input for a right mouse button. Fortunately, most web interfaces are generally suitable.

▧ **Note** The touchscreen membranes cannot be cut to the size of your laptop; they must be bought presized, so check carefully before purchasing, and remember that screen size is measured diagonally across the LCD screen itself, not the visible area.

Your Own Powered Devices

Even some hardened geeks balk at the idea of creating hacks with mains electricity.[10] But with a little care and attention, you can add control to any mains-powered device, such as water heaters, heaters, garage door motors, and so on. To do so requires a controllable relay system, accepting a control signal and closing, or opening, a set of contacts that allows current to flow from the plug to your unit. You can even wire them directly to standard consumer equipment (like modems and printers) to reboot or power cycle them. There are a few options in this area.

X10 Control

Building an entire X10 unit to control a motor, for example, is so far beyond the scope of this book that it wouldn't be fair to try. Instead, I will show an inline appliance module, such as the AM12W, which handles the dirty work of processing the X10 protocol and results in a set of closed contacts between two of its connections. It works in the same way as the AM12 you saw in Chapter 1 (although slightly cheaper), but instead of controlling the flow of current to a plug socket, it controls the flow between the mains and the X10 unit and between the unit and the device. Figure 2-8 shows this wiring.

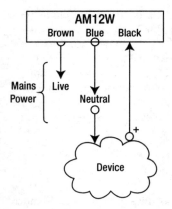

Figure 2-8. *Connecting an AM12W to a mains-powered device*

This works for any unit that is remotely controlled only through X10. To support a local switch (either in the on/off variety or a momentary push button), a better choice of module is the AD10. This also supports a manual override on the device, shown as the blue button in Figure 2-9.

---

[10] Since January 1, 2005, in England and Wales, the Building Regulations Part P specifies that only certified engineers can carry out this particular electrical installation work. If it not carried out by such a person, then the work must be certified upon completion. Other countries may have similar laws.

Figure 2-9. *The AD10 module*

Figure 2-10 shows the wiring; although both types of button are featured here, only one would be used in practice.

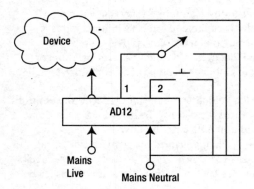

Figure 2-10. *Wiring an AD10 to a mains-powered device*

The main advantage of this module over the AM12W is that the switches used are standard electrical ones and not the (more expensive) X10 variety.

■ **Note**   All devices should be grounded accordingly, not as shown in the figures for clarity.

WiFi Control

With suitable electronics, you can connect a Raspberry Pi or Arduino to a WiFi board, and add some relays to control external devices. However, such hacking is not always necessary as some prebuilt devices already exist, which eliminate the need and worry of working with mains power.

One such device is the DIN Relay III (from http://www.digital-loggers.com/din.html), which is WiFi enabled and allows you to control up to eight devices, powered by either AC or DC, at once. This has natural benefits of scale if you have several devices located in a cupboard under the stairs for example. Even if your current house wiring isn't home run (to a single location) this device makes such a task more tempting, because it provides a centralized control system with very little expense.

Although it has a scripting language (which is wholly ignorable!) it does have scheduling and a built-in status LCD that is controllable, and need not display information about the status of the unit.

Low Voltage Control

For many applications having control over a 115/240V power line isn't necessary. This is because virtually all household devices work on a much lower voltage, usually 24V or less. This includes a number of more modern 24V light bulbs. Therefore, instead of controling the device at the plug you can bypass it, and switch the current flow between the exit of the power supply and the entrance to the circuit board.

■ **Note**   Some devices have dual power lines, such as a 3.3V and a 5V rail. In this case you will need a "double throw" relay so that both power circuits can be opened, or closed, at the same time.

This switching action can happen with any suitable relay. What determines a "suitable" relay is governed by the "contact ratings." This is how much current, at a specific voltage, a relay is capable of safely switching. If this is exceeded the relay could remain permanently on, or off, without any warning that it is doing so. These are always specified on the relays, or the switching units that use them. The National Electrical Manufacturers Association, or NEMA, have introduced a series of designations for both AC and DC, which indicate the type of current flow, and the maximum voltage.

You can build your WiFi Relay Switch using an Arduino, a relay, and the guidelines above for digital output control of an Arduino. For those looking for a prebuilt solution, http://www.relaypros.com/Relay/Relay/Wi-Fi_Relay, and http://www.relaycontrollers.com (along with many others) both provide suitable functionality.

Of course, it needn't be an Arduino controlling the relay as a Raspberry Pi, or any form of Microcontroller, can handle the task equally well. One famous case of this was "Feed Toby," by Nat Morris (http://www.natmorris.co.uk/feedtoby) who used a Micrcontroller to release food pellets to his pet dog, via Twitter. In this case a motor was used instead of a relay.

Conclusion

In the same way that you can build complex and evocative systems using a couple of well-chosen pieces of hardware, so can you build smart automation tools with a minimum of effort. By using alternate input devices, such as pressure mats and joysticks, you can change the way that you interface with your home. By adding alternate output devices, perhaps powered by old game consoles, you supply visuals to areas previously inaccessible to full-scale desktop PCs. And the introduction of robots and computerized welcome mats adds a level of previously unknown of coolness to your home.

■ ■ ■

## CHAPTER 3

Media Systems: Incorporating the TV and the HiFi

The most visible part in any home environment is the media system. Ever since real fireplaces fell out of fashion, the TV or stereo system has become the focal point of most living rooms. The TV and stereo system are also the devices with which we spend the most time interacting. It is therefore essential that you understand the possibilities of these devices.

As with all consumer electronics, the feature sets and prices change on a daily basis. Therefore, I'll concentrate primarily on the necessary features and inner workings of the machines without detailing specific makes and models because by the time you read this other machines will already be available.

The Data Chain

The simple act of "playing an album" changes significantly in the home automation field. Not only is the location of the media itself unconstrained, but it's also the place where you can listen to it. This has been exemplified recently with iTunes, which allows you to play music on several different computers, and with Spotify, which provides a music-streaming service allowing access to various music tracks from your home PC or mobile.[1] If your interest in music is casual, or chart-based, then these services are often enough. But many people have albums in their collection that are either rare or obscure enough to not appear on any commercial-led web site. Some people might prefer to have their music data stored on their own computers, lest the company go out of business, change the terms of service, or lose connectivity in some other fashion. When this is the case, we need to provide a way of getting the music from a hard disk to the human ear. This is the *data chain*.

There are four steps in this chain. The first step is the data itself. This is the directory structure of WAVs, MP3s, or OGGs that represent the music (or other media) in your collection. This data is then read by a server (which is the second step) before being distributed (the third step) to one or more speakers in the house. The fourth and final step is when the human gets to hear (or see) the media. This model still applies when playing music on a portable music player or desktop PC, although for a desktop PC all of the logical units are held within one physical box.

Extracting the Data

Often known as *ripping*, this is the process by which the media, usually stored on DVD or CD, is converted into a computer-friendly data format, ready for playback. Many pieces of software are available, so I'll cover these with an example only.

---

[1] Access through a mobile phone requires the paid-for premium service.

Compact Disc

A CD is the easiest and quickest format by far, because most of the constituent parts are available within Linux. A tool, such as abcde, can automatically do the following:

- Extract the audio as a WAV file

- Convert it to OGG Vorbis

- Determine the artist and album

- Download and apply the tags automatically

- Name the files accordingly

All that is then necessary is to copy the files to your filesystem. I personally always extract my CDs to a separate (local) folder for reasons of speed—it's faster to write locally and then copy en masse because it means that my server isn't dealing with lots of small write requests when I might want to stream something else. This also gives me an opportunity to manually change the files in case there's a problem, as sometimes happens when the album is longer than the standard 74 minutes.[2]

For mass ripping, you can write a short script that saves time by automatically opening and closing the CD drawer. It might not sound a lot, but the initial hurdle in extracting your music collection is psychological; the thought of swapping many hundreds of CDs and renaming and tagging each file is daunting. Because the audio is ripped at the speed of your CD or DVD drive (and not related to the duration of the album), you can extract a whole disc in about 5 to 10 minutes. And with the online track listings database (CDDB, which combines the start time and duration of each track into an ID for the disc as a whole), the tagging process is also automatic. Sometimes there are duplicate IDs, which requires manual intervention, but most of the discs can be processed automatically using the -N flag, as shown in the following script. The abcde script also supports arguments that allow you to specify the format of the filenames, if this is important to you, along with layout information for handling albums with multiple artists.

```
#!/bin/bash
while :
do
 echo Insert next disc...
 read x

 cdcd close
 abcde -N
 cdcd eject
done
```

DVD

With the more complex format of DVDs and the industry's perpetual insistence that encryption is necessary, the ripping of DVDs has an extra requirement,[3] namely, libdvdcss2. This is a library that circumvents the copy protection on encrypted discs, which most commercial movies use. Its legality is uncertain, so the major Linux distributions have erred on the side of caution by not including the package. Instead, the library must be downloaded separately, either from an alternative repository or from compiled source. Naturally, I must take the same "safe" approach and can only tell you how you might install it, if you find the files on a web site somewhere.

---

[2] You have to terminate the hung process and manually tag the file.
[3] You might also need the Win32 codecs package (w32codecs).

On Debian, for example, an extra repository is added by placing a single line in the /etc/apt/sources.list file:

```
deb http://www.debian-multimedia.org lenny main
```

This is followed by the following traditional process:

```
apt-get update
apt-get install libdvdcss2
```

Sometimes you have to download and install the package manually. That command line invocation would be as follows:

```
dpkg -i libdvdcss2_1.2.10-1_i386.deb
```

Alternatively, the source installation would be as per the INSTALL file, probably something like the trinity of this:

```
./configure
make
make install # as root
```

Once you can use VLC to play DVDs, you know the library is successfully installed and is consequently available to all the main media player applications, such as mplayer, totem, xine, and so on.

When ripping DVDs, you have to consider the amount of hard disk space that you want to devote to your collection, whether you want (or need) the DVD menus, and on what devices they are being played. Ultimately, there are two choices.

Rip As ISO

Rip As ISO makes a raw copy of the entire disc and stores it as a file. This is the easiest process to initiate, because you simply invoke the following:

```
dd if=/dev/dvd of=TheOffice-series1.iso bs=1024
```

This will generally require between 4GB and 8GB of space and includes all of the DVD menus, titles, chapters, and subtitles. Movie players such as VLC will be able to handle interactive components such as menus, but others won't. This is especially true of units that don't support the DVD logo because they won't have the CSS code as well as of smaller low-power devices such as MediaMVP. In the case of the latter, you can partially solve the problem by using VLC to remotely transcode the movies, but it still won't be able to handle the processing of the DVD menus.

As with all disk images, Linux is able to mount them to a directory so that they can be read and so that their files can be queried normally. This can be done automatically through the desktop or with the following:

```
mount -t udf -o loop TheOffice-series1.iso dvdimage
```

Note that you cannot mount the image to your usual DVD location (such as /dev/dvd) because that is a block device, and you can only mount images to a directory.

Rip As Movie Files

This method occupies the bulk of "DVD ripping" software, with many available versions for both the command line and the GUI. Although the GUI versions provide screenshots of the titles and chapters and an array of configurable options, they are (almost without exception) merely front ends to a set of standard back-end tools, such as mencoder. You can remove the resources and time utilized by this middleman by going straight to the metal.

UnDVD (http://sourceforge.net/projects/undvd/) is a Perl script that provides a simple command-line method to rip DVDs into their component titles, taking whichever language or subtitles you want at the same time. A typical invocation to rip the first three tracks, with English audio, might be as follows:

```
undvd -t 1,2,3 -a en
```

The number of tracks available can be determined with the associated tool, scandvd. Because most households will speak a common language, the necessity for the full ISO is reduced, making this a consistent process. The following script provides a full rip of the disc into its own subdirectory. It could even be triggered from a link on the household web page, for example.

```perl
#!/usr/bin/perl
my $language = "en";
my $subtitles = "off";
my $output = `lsdvd`;

$output =~ /Disc Title\:\s+(.*?)\n/s;

my $title = lc $1;
$title =~ s/\b(\w)/\U$1/g;
$title =~ s/_(\w)/ \U$1/g;

my $cmd = "undvd -t 1";

my $count = $output=~s/\nTitle\://g;
foreach(2..$count) {
  $cmd .= ",$_";
}

mkdir($title);
chdir($title);

$cmd .= " -a $language -s $subtitles -e 2";
system($cmd);

chdir("..");
```

Issues with Movies

With so many codecs and players available, it's inevitable that you will occasionally find one that has a problem, such as being unable to play the movie, crashing partway through, losing synchronization between video and audio, unable to fast-forward, and so on. Even the commercial offerings have these problems, so they're not unique to the open source community. In fact, because we work primarily with software-based solutions, we have a better deal, as the problems can be fixed fairly quickly. Here are some tips:

- Sometimes you can solve sync problems by pausing and unpausing the video.

- Movies that won't fast-forward often don't have a chunk index, which can be built when starting the movie with `mplayer -idx`.

- Other problems will usually need to be reencoded (or transcoded). This can be handled from the larger tools, such as VLC.

Blu-ray

Since its release in 2006, Blu-ray has been a thorn in the side for Linux and, more latterly, Raspberry Pi users. This is because no official software playback tools have been released, and the encryption methods used are more draconian. The first case exists because the licensing of applicable patents is controlled by One-Blue, which cannot (will not?) license to Linux developers. Consequently, the only way to play Blu-ray discs (BD) is to separate the decoding and playback parts and transcode the original disc into another format. We shall come to solutions, shortly.

The second case is more troublesome, especially because part of the Blu-ray design allows the encryption keys to be changed should one get compromised. To date, several keys have been published online, but no sooner than that happens, a set of new ones are introduced to keep the format closed. This demonstrates that the industry hasn't learned the equivalent lesson from the days of the suffragettes, and so we are stuck with this perpetual cat-and-mouse game for the foreseeable future.

The easiest answer is to forgo Blu-ray entirely. But, although it is easy to argue that there is little point in upgrading DVD films to their Blu-ray equivalents, new films often have quality and feature extras that make it worthwhile purchasing. And, for many, the fundamental view of ignoring all DRM-oriented media is impractical (especially as that also includes much online music and DVDs). Therefore, the pragmatic view is to transcode all BDs and file the physical copies somewhere safe.

Rip As ISO Files

In a word—don't! Because nothing plays them, they're only useful for creating an ISO that could be later ripped. Because you have to read the disc contents anyway, you're not saving time now. And because a BD can take around 25GB for a single layer (50GB for a dual layer), the cost of storage is significantly higher than for a DVD. If you're curious as to how much, a 1TB drive can hold 40 single-layer images. If the drive costs $100, then it's $2.50 for that image. Compared to a transcoded version, which comes in at around 5 cents, the difference is marked.

Rip As Movie Files

The most direct method for this is to exploit the "analog hole" (but in a digital sense, i.e., the "digital hole"). This requires a player with HDMI out and a graphics card with HDMI. The output of the first is fed into the input of the second, and recording is made in real time. Although this is guaranteed to work, we know of better solutions.

The primary candidate here is "MakeMKV," downloadable from the forum section of http://www.makemkv.com, and it is a pragmatic choice for ripping software. That is, it is neither free, nor open. But given the limited choice we shall use it. Fortunately, while it is in beta, the cost has been removed if you use the download key from http://www.makemkv.com/forum2/viewtopic.php?f=5&t=1053. Luckily, it's been in beta since 2010 and, although a new copy of the key will be released during the production of this book, it is hoped that a new beta key will allow the program to be used for free (as in beer).

Follow the instructions on the forum download page, and you can rip your BDs as if they were any other disc. Some people have noticed that if you type

```
touch tmp/eula_accepted
```

before running the make procedure, you can install the software without having to read and agree with the EULA.

Once in MKV format, you are free to transcode into any other format. This may be necessary because HD video requires an HD player, and some (older) media streaming boxes may not support it. Note, however, that an HD video requires an HD transcoder, so you'll need the later tools (such as Handbrake) as many of the older workhorse programs have not yet been upgraded to cope with it.

Cassette Tapes and Vinyl

Yes, really! There are many people with these beloved relics of technology who want to keep them alive electronically. These are the slowest form of media to rip because they must be done in real time.[4] The obvious way to do this is to connect the phono outputs from your deck (be it tape or record) into the line-in inputs of your sound card. You should have as few components in the signal chain as possible, so if your turntable has a preamplifier, so much the better. Otherwise, consider the relative merits of your sound card and deck, and let the higher-quality unit perform the preamp stage. Vinyl particularly *requires* a preamp stage with RIAA equalization to avoid a tinny sound.

Once you have the deck connected, find the loudest section of music, and monitor the levels in an audio-recording program, such as Audacity. It should be as loud as possible, without clipping. This ensures that you get the most out of the 16-bit resolution, the maximum possible dynamic range. This volume, however, should come from the preamp if possible, as a power amplifier will introduce noise.

To ensure maximum quality during recording, you need to take care of external hardware elements, too. So, don't use the microwave while recording because this can introduce electrical noise that might affect it, don't fiddle with the connectors, and so on. It is also a good idea to plug the deck into a high-quality UPS or power smoother to limit the amount of wow and flutter caused by fluctuations in mains voltage.

The same approach also works for cassettes, although most tape players have a built-in preamp, so you have no choice here.

There are currently some all-in-one units on the market that combine a tape or record deck with all the necessary amplifiers and converters necessary to provide you with a digital input over a USB cable. These are ideal for casual users, but because they are made to a price point, and not for quality, you won't get as good results as you will from a manual setup.

Once you have the recording digitized, it is then a matter of extracting the individual tracks from the file called side_1.wav and encoding them accordingly. There are some tools to do this automatically. Audacity has its own Silence Finder function (in the Analyze menu), which looks for suitably long gaps in the recording and places markers by them. You can then adjust these markers if necessary and select Export Multiple to save the data between these markers as individual files.

You can then encode them as appropriate. Here's an example:

```
#!/bin/bash
LIST="$(ls *.wav)"
for FILE in "$LIST"; do
 flac $FILE
done
```

or with the following:

```
oggenc $FILE
```

---

[4]It is technically possible to play tapes and records at higher speeds (using high-speed dubbing tape players or switching the record deck to 45 rpm) and compensate by pitch shifting in software. But isn't really worth the effort or loss in quality.

According to the music and your personal opinions of high-fidelity audio, you may choose to keep this music in one or more formats. The most direct is to keep only the OGG files, because they are suitable for casual around-the-house listening and some fairly involved critical listening. For more discerning audiophiles, Free Lossless Audio Codec (FLAC) provides the same quality as WAV but in a smaller footprint. Some people will keep the FLAC versions stored away on a separate (offline) hard drive while using the OGG files for everyday use. This allows the high-quality recordings to be reencoded at a later date when better-quality codecs become available, without needing to rerip the data.

True audiophiles would never be happy with a computer sound card and should never rip the music in the first place!

Storage

All data must be stored somewhere. In desktop computing, that's an internal hard drive. In home automation, we want that drive to be accessible everywhere else. This generally means that it must be on a network and controlled by a network service such as Samba.

Stand-Alone NAS Systems

Network addressable storage (NAS), to all intents and purposes, is a hard drive that connects to the outside world through a network cable and IP address instead of an IDE, SCSI, or SATA cable. There are two main advantages with this approach. This first is that by being naturally network-aware, you can use the files anywhere in the world with little to no additional configuration. This includes your office, your partner's office, the bedroom, or even a laptop in the garden or on the train, connected wirelessly. The second is that by being separate from the main computer, you can declutter your main work area by hiding the NAS drive in a cupboard or in the loft/attic. This has a security benefit: any burglar stealing your computer hasn't stolen your data as well.

Naturally, without a computer to control the hard drive, there has to be a driver somewhere in the data chain determining the disc format, capacity, and network connectivity. This can exist either in the NAS unit itself or from the server machine wanting to read the drive. Many different versions are available.

Hard Drive Considerations

The main selling factor of any NAS is its storage capability. Currently, anything less than 1TB is rare, which is fortunate as many older IDE drives had a limit of 137.4GB because of the 28-bit addressing mode of Logical Block Addressing (LBA). Avoid anything smaller than 137.4GB in case the manufacturer is using old hardware under the hood, even if it supports an external USB drive, as that will invariably be governed by the same limitation.

Alongside the argument for disk space is the concept of disk format. This is usually given as FAT, FAT32, NTFS, or ext2, and limits the maximum file size possible (as shown in Table 3-1). The format also governs your likelihood of being able to recover it if you need to mount the drive in another machine.

Table 3-1. *Filesystem Functionality*

Filesystem	Maximum File Size	Maximum Volume Size
FAT16	2GB	2GB
FAT32	4GB	2TiB or 8TiB*
NTFS	16EiB	16EiB
ext2/ext3	16GB to 2TiB	2TiB to 32TiB*
ZFS	16EiB	16EiB

Variation depends on cluster size when formatted.

So, clearly, if you want a NAS to store DVD images, you will need a filesystem that can support 4.7GB files. This usually means FAT-based systems are inadequate or that you will have to remove the DVD menus and reencode the movies into an alternative (and smaller) format.

The recover question is slightly more involved. If you ever have to remove the hard disk from its NAS mounting and place it in a standard PC to recover the data, you will need a PC that is able to read whatever filesystem is used by the NAS.

NTFS fares slightly better in the Linux compatibility stakes, but not much. Although it's possible to read NTFS partitions under Linux, writing back to them is considered dangerous, although there are two open source drivers (Captive NTFS and NTFS-3G) that do support it. Additionally, there is a commercial driver (NTFS for Linux, from Paragon) that solves the same problem. For basic recovery, a read-only disc is fine, although you won't be able to repair the disk without reformatting it, for the most part.

The natural solution is to use ext2 for any and all NAS drives, because this has the widest support in the Linux world. Many NAS devices now support this, so it can be worth spending a little more to get one because it ticks all the boxes. If your main desktop machine at home is Windows, then there are even ext2 recovery tools for Windows such as Linux Recovery from DiskInternals.

The type of data you're storing will determine the type of backup plan you need. When this is personal data, such as letters or photographs, then consider a NAS featuring built-in RAID functionality. These often autoconfigure themselves when a second drive is plugged in, so be warned if you insert a used drive thinking you'll gain extra space! Several types of RAID configuration are available, but the most common in this case is RAID-1, which uses a second drive to make identical copies of anything written to the first. It does this automatically and transparently from the user, so should either drive fail, the other can be used to recover the data. You should always remember, however, that RAID isn't a backup! It just makes it a bit less likely that you'll lose data to disk failure. It won't protect against corruption from controller failures, fire, flood, or theft.

■ **Note**   Using hardware RAID solutions is a double-edged sword for some system administrators. They work seamlessly and take no effort to set up and maintain. However, if the RAID system has a problem and uses a custom disk format, then it might be impossible to recover the data on the disk. You can solve this by buying two pieces of hardware and verifying that you can swap the disks without a problem before they are put into active service. Alternatively, you can check with the manufacturer that the disk format used either is known or comes with suitable software recovery tools.

Backing up data, such as DVD or music rips, doesn't (and shouldn't) require RAID—although having one does no harm. Because this type of data changes less frequently, you can make do with an external USB hard drive plugged into your desktop machine. You can then run the backup software of your choice (see Chapter 6 for some possibilities here) to copy only those files that have changed and then unplug and store the drive. This prolongs the life of the drive and is worth the extra effort.

As with all backups, they are useless unless tested regularly, so make sure that you do test them. Some people will test them by copying their backups to a new drive every 6 to 12 months. The cost is negligible, compared to the many hours spent ripping and organizing the data. Furthermore, the price per gigabyte comes down every year, allowing you store more data in a smaller form factor. If you are desperate for extra space, you can then reuse the older drive elsewhere in your system. Although tape backup systems are a favorite of most businesses, the cost and convenience of USB hard drives render them unnecessary for the home market.

■ **Note**   Hard drives either fail in the first few weeks or the day before you remember to back up. Therefore, when buying disks, always buy from different manufacturers and at different times, so if you get one disk from a bad batch (IBM Death Star, hang your head!), you minimize your chances of getting two.

Networking Considerations

For the most part, the network setup of a NAS is straightforward. Usually, it will acquire its own IP through DHCP and provide access to the disk through the services of CIFS/Samba. Sometimes you will need a Microsoft Windows machine to run the setup software, but this is becoming less common as configuration is done through a web page running on the NAS. The main warning here is to look out for machines that don't have a Samba service and instead rely on something such as ZFS.

ZFS is a filesystem that originated at Sun Microsystems and features on NAS systems such as the Netgear SC-101. But despite the ZFS specification and its use in larger commercial systems, it does not yet have a suitable kernel driver (because of license incompatibilities). It is currently only possible to run it in conjunction with the Filesystem in Userspace (FUSE) project or the supplied closed Windows drivers. Consequently, if only a ZFS service is provided (such as the aforementioned SC-101), it is necessary to install specific drivers on every device that wants to read data from the NAS. This makes it annoying for PC users and impossible for other hardware such as the Squeezebox.

Controlling a NAS through Windows Vista[5] can be problematic because some NAS systems use alternate authentication systems. This can be fixed with a registry hack here:

```
HKEY_LOCAL_MACHINE\SYSTEM\CurrentControlSet\Control\Lsa
```

by setting this:

```
LmCompatibilityLevel = 1
```

Extra Functionality

With many NAS drives being little more than embedded Linux machines, adding extra software is trivial . . . for the manufacturer. Typical applications include the following:

- Printer server

- BitTorrent client

- Backup support

- iTunes server

If you want to add your own software, then you are usually out of luck, unless you have one of the variants that has been already hacked, such as the NSLU2, or have a lot of time on your hands to discover the hack yourself! When planning a much larger home installation, you will probably only need a very basic NAS drive, because it's likely you'll soon upgrade to a custom Linux server that will support all the extra functionality you can possibly throw at it, with the NAS service being available for free.

When buying your first NAS, do not worry about the extra functionality but of the storage space it supports because you might not have enough free space left to warrant running a BitTorrent client on it, for example. So many NAS machines are available, at fairly cheap prices, that you don't need to be concerned about having everything in a single box. It is not uncommon to have one NAS with several terabytes of space for the primary media storage area for DVD and CD rips and another used as a secondary store and a function server. This second NAS then acts as a daily backup for your desktop PC and printer server. These roles allow you to power down one NAS (through X10, perhaps) for the times when it isn't needed.

---

[5] The same applies to Windows XP SP3, Windows 7, Windows 2003 Server, and Windows 2008 Server.

NAS with Media Playback

To some, this is simply a NAS with a TV-out socket on the back. To others, it constitutes a paradigm shift, because it allows you to treat the unit as if it were a portable VCR and video library rolled into one. As with everything, its value is governed by how you intend to use it.

One of the big selling points of these devices is that they can be moved from room to room, and even from house to house, without requiring a network. This makes it much easier to show your photographs and home videos to the ungeeked members of your family and friends because you can simply plug a media-enabled NAS device into any TV, and it will work. It is also a way of introducing (a small level) of control over what the kids are able to watch, because they'll be limited to the contents of the hardware.

■ **Note**   There are many applications that block content for kid-safe viewing. But as parenting books tell you (or, as any parent knows), you can't solve these problems entirely by technology because it is not really a technological problem.

If you want to expand your media beyond a single room, you will need a version that supports Ethernet, such as Freecom's MediaPlayer II or cineDISK NAS. These are combined NAS drives, supporting file sharing through Samba, and media streamers that play back files to a TV or HiFi. They have the benefit of being able to stream from a local disk, thereby eliminating any network latency and limiting the cost of separate media units such as the MediaMVP. Furthermore, by distributing your media between several of these devices, you won't lose everything if an unbacked-up hard drive fails. With minimal effort you can distribute the files to those machines that are more likely to play them, such as films in the living room, TV series in the bedroom, MP3s in the den, and cartoons in the kids' room. If you are separating media in this way, be mindful of potential storage upgrades. Some devices provide a USB port for an external hard drive or memory stick (although some cheaper machines intend this for memory sticks only and do not support large disk sizes), so place these machines in rooms that are likely to increase their disk footprint the most. From personal experience, the disks holding TV shows have filled up the quickest.

The problem with these type of devices, as with all embedded hardware, comes from their upgrade path, and not all companies will add or release new firmware with the latest codecs or fixes to old ones; many of the devices are too new to have a hacker community to help. Also, unlike the MVPMC, there is not usually a way to use an external transcoder in this situation.

Also, check the specification of each device carefully, because despite the name "NAS" appearing on the box, not all provide a network socket. Some manufacturers will claim it's "HD-ready" when what they mean is that it will decode the files . . . but is only capable of viewing it in standard definition. Also, many are supplied without a hard drive but will require one, even if you only intend to stream media through the network, such as with the Emprex Multimedia Player.

However, it is always worth keeping an eye on the market for these devices, and they will often provide new ideas that can be implemented in software, such as the "watch YouTube on your TV" feature.

Configuring a Linux Box

By far the most flexible NAS server is the one that you build for yourself. Any machine is suitable, as the processing power need not be great, so it can be an old laptop, Mini-ITX box, or NSLU2. The only requirement is that it has network compatibility. The optional features include USB ports (for additional drives) and a modern BIOS with 48-bit LBA so that it supports disks larger than 137.4GB. This does not just apply to internal disks; it's also necessary if you are using external USB hardware as they usually rely on the machine to control the disk.

As ever, it is not necessary to store all your media on the one machine nor is the one machine suitable only as a file server. If you are distributing your media across different physical disks, then it is preferable to store those that necessitate higher bit rates (such as movies) on internal drives and low-bit rate media (such as cartoons or music) on external drives or on slower servers.

Each machine needs to be set up as you saw in Chapter 1, but you need to take care with your naming convention if there are multiple servers or you're likely to move the units.

Preparing a Machine

As each machine is Linux-based, they will already have their own filesystems in place (including commercial devices that are based around the filesystems), so your only task here is to provide a place for your files.

For internal hard drives, always create a separate ext3 partition for your media. A separate partition is used so that it can be mounted separately (which makes for easier recovery in case of a crash or power outage), and ext3 provides a journaling filesystem. Also, because the media partition is likely to be the first one filled, your Linux machine will not run into problems if it finds that there's no more disk space left. Provide a mount point by adding a file to /etc/fstab:

```
/dev/sda7  /mnt/mediadisk  auto user,noauto   0      0
```

And create hard links from somewhere more convenient; I use a root folder on the server called /media:

```
ln /mnt/mediadisk/media/tv /media/tv
```

Note that I have not stored files in the root of the sda7 partition but, instead, inside the media/tv folder. This conventional directory structure will benefit me later, should the disk's purpose be extended to include extra functionality such as backups.

External USB hard drives work in the same way but with a different line in /etc/fstab:

```
/dev/sdb1         /mnt/usbdisk0  auto user,noauto      0        0
```

In both cases, the disks are not mounted automatically. This is a personal preference, because it *requires*—and requires *me*—to check the disks after a major power failure or crash, a step that others might ignore or skip, to the detriment of the filesystem.

The other change for external USB devices is that as the directories are on different physical disks, you are required to use a symlink instead:

```
ln -s /mnt/usbdisk0/media/tv /media/tv
```

One addition for these drives is to note which physical hard disk is used to store the content. This is for when a drive breaks, or is about to, and you need to remove the correct one. It is also helpful in those cases in which two USB drives have been mounted in the reverse order.

To do this, I simply change to the root directory of the drive in question and type the following:

```
touch THIS_IS_THE_SILVER_LACIE_500G_DRIVE
touch THIS_SHOULD_BE_MOUNTED_UNDER_SDB1
```

This demonstrates another reason for not polluting the root. If you've followed the tip about buying hard drives from different manufacturers, these names are easy to pick.

Preparing a Filesystem

Once the machines are ready, the media filesystem must be considered; you must think of it in global terms across every server and across the whole house. There are three elements to the storage chain to consider:

- The machine name
- The machine's physical location
- The shared folder names for the media stored on that machine

Taking these in order, the machine name will often be provided by the manufacturer, such as cineDISK. If you have the ability, rename it to cineDISK1, and add a sticky label to the back of the device indicating this. Always add an incrementing number to the devices if possible, because this will make scanning, backup, and maintenance scripts easier to write as each name is logically created, without arbitrary caveats.

You might want to name the device without any reference to the manufacturer, as in `media_nas1`. This is also fine, but it's recommended that you note to which device this refers. I use a single page on my home's internal wiki containing all the devices, model numbers, MAC addresses, firmware versions, web forums, and so on, of each piece of hardware connected to my network. I also use this to note the physical location of each machine.

The shared folder names should all follow a convention such as `media_movies`, `media_tv`, and so on. If you have kids and are providing them with access to the network, then providing separate folders such as `media_kids` might be an idea. The reason for splitting all the media into separate shared folders is that each can have distinct Samba access rights (each with or without passwords) and be unmounted on its own without affecting the rest of the system. It would be much harder work to control a directory of `media/movies` if only the root `media` folder was shared.

Preparing a Master Server

So far we have a number of servers, with lots of technical information and metadata. These names are *all* for the purpose of maintenance. No user would want, or should need, to know that the cartoons are on `media_nas2` in the spare bedroom, under `media_children`. Nor should a family member be interested that you've split the `movies` folder across two separate disks[6] because there were too many for the old drive. To this end, you should designate a master server. It can be one of the media servers or an entirely different machine. It is recommended that this master server be running the most prominent and important services in the house, one that also stays on 24/7. This allows it to be used as Node0, which you'll learn about in Chapter 4.

This Node0 machine then mounts each shared folder, from each server, into its own directory structure. And it is *this* directory structure that is shared so that each media-streaming device can access the media.

▒ **Note**   On first glance, it appears wasteful for NAS1 to connect to Node0, only to be connected back to NAS1, but to scale up effectively, provide all media in a unified environment, and support dynamic changes in the media architecture, this is the best way to do it.

The directory structure I use pulls together all the Samba shares like this:

```
/net/homenet/slug1/media_tv
```

and local disks like this:

```
/net/homenet/mediapc1/usb2/media/movies
```

into a hierarchy underneath `/net/homenet` as a number of links or Samba mounts. This becomes a self-documenting report for the media server layout of home. I then create a series of links under the `/net/media` directory to hide the structure:

```
ln -s /net/homenet/mediapc1/usb1/media/tv      /net/media/tv
ln -s /net/homenet/mediapc1/usb2/media/movies  /net/media/movies
ln -s /net/homenet/itx1/usb1/media/mp3         /net/media/music
ln -s /net/homenet/slug1/usb1/media/videos     /net/media/videos
```

---

[6] If you're a keen systems administrator, you can use Logical Volume Management (LVM) 2 to dynamically grow the size of partitions on your Linux system.

It's then a simple matter of adding Samba shares for each directory:

```
[media_tv]
 comment = Media (TV)
 path = /net/media/tv
 browseable = yes
 public = yes
 writable = no
 read only = yes
 guest ok = yes
```

As in Chapter 1, I create basic Samba shares that are read-only for the family and create separate ones for me that are password-protected and read-write.

Note also that I have used my home's subdomain (homenet) as a delimiter from the rest of the directory, instead of placing everything in /net. It allows me, as a software developer, to create my own subnet that isn't part of the general home automation network in case I need to do something risky or experimental!

Media Extenders

Once you have a file server providing access to your media, you then need some way of rendering the media, aurally or visually, to the world. This can involve stand-alone hardware, a Linux-based machine, or a combination of the two.

Stand-Alone Hardware

To fit into this category, the hardware must connect the network, use DHCP to determine its IP address, and then stream the data from a file server to a physically connected TV or speakers. These devices invariably use Samba as a file server, because the installation of specific drivers (such as ZFS) is not a real-world possibility.

Hauppauge MediaMVP

This device, despite dating from 2002, can stream music, standard-definition video, and pictures across the network and display them on a TV. The retail unit is fairly cheap, small, and silent, making it an ideal head unit. It comes with just three sockets: power, RJ-45 Ethernet, and SCART. (The U.S. version expands this last socket to S-Video, composite video, and stereo audio.)

To work, the MediaMVP needs three separate services:[7] DHCP, TFTP for the bootup procedure, and Samba for data as it has no storage facilities of its own. Out of the box, these services are provided by a piece of Windows software, which has a number of limitations such as a slow menu system. The machine also prevents you from viewing any video that isn't MPEG1 or MPEG2 encoded. This is because the video signal is decoded by a custom chip inside the MediaMVP that only supports these earlier codecs. Fortunately, the protocols used by the MediaMVP to boot up are standard, enabling you to use Linux as a server. You can then take this stage further by replacing the firmware that runs on the actual device, allowing it to connect to VLC to transcode your files to MPEG2 in real time.

---

[7] The word *server* is used in this context to denote a physical piece of hardware, whereas a *service* is for elements of software that provide access to data or resources on a server. Confusingly, the most common name for these services are things such as *e-mail server, web server,* and so on.

Creating a Server

The bootup procedure of the MediaMVP is twofold. First, it sends a DHCP request asking for an IP address of its own and the address of a TFTP server. Second, it uses this TFTP server to download the firmware, which is what ultimately runs on the MediaMVP to become a media device.

You begin by adding the configuration to /etc/dhcpd.conf:

```
group {
  next-server 192.168.1.2;          # IP address of your TFTP server

  host mvp {
      hardware ethernet 00:0d:fe:00:15:8D; # of the MediaMVP
      fixed-address 192.168.1.98;
      filename "dongle.bin";
  }
}
```

The address need not be fixed; however, I've adopted a convention on my network indicating that any machine on my subnet with an address under 100 is a "house device," such as a server or embedded hardware, and is not liable to change or move and therefore is always available. Everything 100 or greater is a computer that might be removed from the network or switched off at any time.

From here, control is passed to the TFTP server, so that the MediaMVP can request the firmware, given by the filename dongle.bin.

TFTP stands for Trivial File Transfer Protocol, which is a very much simplified version of the usual FTP often used to copy files between machines. It's installed as normal:

```
apt-get install atftpd
```

This will add the appropriate lines to /etc/inetd.conf and /etc/default/atftp, indicating the directory for file transfers (usually /var/lib/tftpboot). The primary distinction with TFTP from my point of view is that no username and passwords can be employed with TFTP. Although this might have made the programmer's original job very much simpler, it was at the expense of security, meaning that you should not open the TFTP port (UDP 69) to the world.

You can then copy the dongle.bin file to the /tftpboot folder and switch on the MediaMVP. From here, it is a simple matter to replace dongle.bin with one of the other firmwares available to the MediaMVP, such as MVPMC, to provide improved functionality, such as real-time video transcoding or connecting with MythTV.

MediaMVP Media Center

This is probably the most fully featured alternate firmware currently available; it's downloadable from http://www.mvpmc.org. It comprises a replacement dongle.bin and a configuration file. Because MediaMVP itself is running a small version of Linux, this configuration file is, conveniently, simply a script containing shell commands, which makes it very simple to make amendments to the firmware image without rebuilding it. At a bare minimum, it should contain commands to mount directories into the filesystem and invoke the main mvpmc program:

```
mkdir /media
mount.cifs "//192.168.1.110/media" /media -o user=mvp,pass=mvppass,rsize=34000;
mvpmc &
```

You can then add arguments to this command according to the extra functionality you want to introduce. I'll now cover some of them.

> ■ **Note** It is not also possible to use anonymous logins from the `mount.cifs` command within MediaMVP, so create a separate Linux account on the computer running the file server (192.168.1.110 in this example). Because this username/password is visible in the configuration file and this configuration file is visible to anyone with TFTP access, you should make doubly sure that it's not visible outside your network.

Weather Reports

This data is downloaded from the Yahoo! weather service and is rendered, with graphics, from one of the menu options onscreen. It needs to know where in the world you are located and that you have access to the Internet. For me, in London, this requires the following alternative line:

```
mvpmc --weather-location UKXX0085 &
```

You can determine this code by visiting http://weather.yahoo.com, searching for your town or city, and grabbing the RSS feed. This will direct you to a URL such as the following:

```
http://weather.yahooapis.com/forecastrss?p=UKXX0085&u=c
```

where you will notice the city code (p=UKXX0085) and the units (u=c), allowing you to present the data in either Celsius or Fahrenheit.

Video Transcoding

The biggest problem with hardware solutions is their lack of upgrade path. Although MediaMVP provided a means of changing the firmware, the MVP hardware didn't use a powerful enough processor to allow firmware that could decompress video in real time. Instead of converting all of your past DVD rips into a suitable format, it is instead possible to convert the format on the fly (known as *transcoding*) while you're watching them. This requires configuration of the MediaMVPMC and a transcoding server running VLC.

In the first instance, you need to add the appropriate arguments that tell MVPMC the address of the transcoding server.

```
mvpmc --vlc 192.168.1.110 --vlc-vopts dvd &
```

Naturally, as with every other server we've seen, the server involves only software and can exist on the same physical machine as the DHCP or TFTP server. However, because of the increased processing power necessary, you might want to run the transcoding software on a separate machine or your desktop. This allows you to have a small, low-power server running the main systems in your house, with the "big iron" being used only when necessary.

> ■ **Tip** The transcoding server only needs a CPU with reasonable specs, meaning that an old stripped-down P3 or P4 can be fast enough. Making use of your desktop is often a good idea, because the transcoding won't slow your work down as you'll be watching a film at that time!

Depending on the speed of your transcoding server, you might not be able to manage the highest-quality images. By amending the -vlc-vopts to either SVCD or VCD, you can reduce the resultant quality to that of the Super Video CD format, or standard Video CD format, respectively.

■ **Note**   The MediaMVP device itself only has hardware to output a standard-definition image. If you've been ripping your Blu-ray discs as HD files, then you will need to use VLC to transcode them into SD.

It is also recommended that you use the `--use-mplayer` command-line switch, which will switch to `mplayer` transcoding if VLC doesn't understand the file format properly.

The biggest caveat about using a transcoding server is that the filename being played by the MVPMC client software must be *exactly* the same as it appears to VLC running on the server. This can be arranged by the careful use of symlinks, as my media is mounted elsewhere on the disk and I have no desire to change it. I have therefore created a special folder in the root of my server with suitable links:

```
mkdir /mvpmc_media
ln -s /media/mp3 /mvpmc_media/mp3
ln -s /media/movies /mvpmc_media/movies
ln -s /media/videos /mvpmc_media/videos
```

I then replicated these on the MediaMVPMC by creating its own `mvpmc_media` directory and mounting the folders across the network:

```
mkdir /mediamount
mkdir /mvpmc_media
mount.cifs "//192.168.1.110/media" /mediamount -o user=mvp,pass=mvppass,rsize=34000;
ln -s /mediamount/videos /mvpmc_media/mp3
ln -s /mediamount/videos /mvpmc_media/movies
ln -s /mediamount/videos /mvpmc_media/videos
```

If you like, you can test your mount instructions by applying them dynamically while the MVPMC is running, as you can `telnet` into the MediaMVP hardware (username: root, no password) and issue commands directly.

This process has another benefit as the filesystem browser on the MVPMC is very literal; whereas a directory entitled `vids` might be good enough for the geek who created it, a more descriptive title such as `Music Videos`, replete with capitalization and spaces, would be appreciated by other home dwellers. Consequently, you can repeat the previous process using full names to achieve that goal without offending the sensibilities of your Linux naming conventions.

■ **Note**   Although DVD VOB files can be played on this system, the DVD menus are not supported.

Other Functionality

Other features available in MVPMC include the following:

- Access of data from MythTV or ReplayTV

- VNC Viewer

- Streaming live web radio

Their setup requirements are straightforward enough and covered in the online documentation and so I won't cover them here.

The Xtremer

This is one of several devices that plays back media files through a TV or HiFi system. Its low price point and inclusion of HDMI make it a good foray into media streamers. It is a good test unit because it supports media playback from its internal disk, an external drive, or the network—both wired and wireless. This makes it suitable for trying different configurations without buying additional boxes. In addition to music and movies, it also supports image previews, weather reports, and live streaming from YouTube, Picasa, and Flickr.

Squeezebox

This device was launched in 2003 and is one of several that acts like an audio-only version of the MediaMVP with a similar scope for "hackability." It also works on a client/server arrangement. The server in this case is a set of open source Perl scripts called SqueezeCenter (formerly SlimServer) running on Linux, Mac OS X, and Windows. This provides the clients with the audio data for your locally stored music and a way of connecting to external sources such as Internet radio or your MP3tunes music locker. It is also able to control the client machines by sending them commands. The server itself doesn't play audio, although you could run a software client on the same physical machine to transparently achieve the same result.

You then need one or more client machines (that is, head units) to play the music in a remote room, connected by either a wired or wireless network. This head unit can be as follows:

- Squeezebox Classic, with display and outputs to a HiFi amplifier

- Squeezebox Receiver, without display, controlled remotely

- Squeezebox Boom, with display, built-in amplifier, and speakers

- Transporter, reportedly a higher-quality playback engine

- A software client

With an appropriate remote control, you can link the Squeezebox instances together so that they all play the same music, providing a full, whole-house audio system.

Server Software

Installation under Linux is straightforward, and by using the software client, you can test the environment without purchasing any hardware. First, go to /etc/apt/sources.list, and add the following anywhere in the file:

```
deb http://debian.slimdevices.com stable main
```

Next, do this:

```
apt-get update
apt-get remove --purge slimserver    # in case of an old install
apt-get install squeezeboxserver
```

And, after ensuring that your music collection has the appropriate read and execute permissions set for the (new) SqueezeCenter user, you can connect to its web server (on port 9000) and configure the server.

Other Software

SoftSqueeze is a software emulation of the Squeezebox hardware and available from
http://softsqueeze.sourceforge.net; it supports Linux, Mac OS X, Windows, and most platforms with
a good Java implementation. This is good for testing a new server and for using as a standard media player; however,
because of its overzealousness at emulating the two-line LCD emulation, navigation is a little tiresome. However,
you can use the SqueezeCenter software—through its web interface—to control the playlist, if you like. Naturally, by
opening the appropriate ports, you can do this remotely.

Videobox (http://videobox.sf.net) is a means of using a (hardware) Squeezebox to pass its IR signals back
to the server so it can trigger external scripts and code. One example given is that of starting movie playback on the
server so that it can be viewed on-screen.

Emprex ME1

This modern device hails from 2007 and is one of several media playback devices now available. It claims to support
HD output but lacks an HDMI port; therefore, it provides its highest quality through upscale via YPbPr in 720p or
1080i. It can also function as an AV recorder, but only through composite inputs. Where this unit benefits most users
is in its low cost and local storage support. This can be with either IDE hard disks (or SATA disks, with more recent
versions, which also increases the storage space from 500GB to 750GB) or through USB, be they memory sticks or
USB hard drives.

As with much technology, utilizing the latest firmware is recommended; it now supports NTFS (the default
filesystem was the ill-chosen FAT32, which limits the maximum file size), and there have been stability issues with
the internal hard disk. Fortunately, an internal disk is optional on later firmwares, allowing you to use one attached
to USB.

Naturally, the device can also read movie files from the network, and you can also use it to remove movies
recorded on the ME1's local storage for archive elsewhere. This method is detailed on the (very) low-traffic web page
http://emprex-me1.blogspot.com along with their Google Groups lists.

Just Linux

The GNU/Linux operating system has appeared in so many distributions (aka *distros*) over the years that it's difficult
to keep up with them. Many people adopt one early in their careers and never change. When using a Linux machine
as the basis for a media player, these rules need to be reconsidered because what's good for the desktop isn't
necessarily good for media playback. Consequently, I'll consider the necessary benefits and features of a suitable
Linux distribution and only mention specifics as examples because, as in the case of hardware, the field moves too
quickly to give definitive "best" answers.

The Operating System

The OS comprises, in the truest sense, a kernel, its drivers, its modules, and its associated software. These components
are packaged in distributions to make them easy to install. Consequently, there are very few variables to consider
when choosing a suitable distribution.

First, and most obviously, you need to have access to a healthy supply of drivers built for the supplied kernel.
Hardware, especially in high-end fields such as graphics, requires high performance and specific drivers to ensure
that it is utilized effectively. Although most graphics cards don't have accelerated onboard video decompression,
they do have hardware acceleration for a lot of other features, which *will* show a marked improvement in performance
for video.

Second, you should consider the bootup time. xPUD, for example, takes around ten seconds, making it appear
like a true set-top box rather than a small computer. XBMC, as you saw in Chapter 2, is also in this range.

And, finally, the total size of the distribution needs to be determined. This is always the last consideration because it can be solved with very little effort, namely, with an extra few cents on a larger hard drive or solid-state memory card. The latter is preferable for most media streamer machines as you can boot quicker from them, they last longer (since more of the operations are memory reads, not memory writes, and have no moving parts), and they allow for a much smaller form factor. If you are building your own Linux machine specifically for media streaming, then make sure that it can support booting from compact flash or a USB memory stick.

The Software

A good media player distribution depends not primarily on the operating system but on the software. It is, after all, the software with which you will be interacting. Most media streamers start life as media players. These are completely wrong for a streamer. Consider the basic scenario—you have a media player on your desktop controlled by a mouse and keyboard while sitting on a chair and watching a monitor that is 2 to 3 feet away. Alas, most software is developed and tested on a desktop PC, where the subtle differences might be overlooked. Remember to consider the following:

> *The visuals*: You will be generally using the interface from a long distance away in a comfy chair. Therefore, the buttons and font need to be large and legible, placed on a screen that is uncluttered and moderately high contrast, with antialiasing.

> *The screen*: Unless you have the latest LCD technology in your living room, your TV will generally be of a much lower quality than your monitor, so small details (especially thin horizontal lines) will get lost or be indistinguishable on-screen.

> *Control*: Without exception, any home theater PC without a remote-control option is going to fail. No one will get out of that comfy chair to press buttons on the machine or will want a keyboard or mouse on their lap.

> *Navigable interface*: Going hand in hand with control, there must be a clean way of moving between menu options. Entering the server IP with a keyboard is only acceptable during initialization.

All of these points have been classified together as an approach known as the "10-foot user interface." This is not to say that these rules are golden or immutable, but spotting several contraventions to this in a single piece of software can be a clue that the project is not yet particularly mature and has been used little in the real world.

MythTV

Of all the Linux PVRs out there, the most famous is probably MythTV (http://www.mythtv.org). This consists of two parts—a back end (mythback) that allows you to record shows from a TV card into the local hard disk and a front end that plays back the media files from a mythback server. In this way, you can have a powerful single server containing many TV cards with the software coordinating the best way to record channels with them and a number of smaller front end units placed in the various rooms of the house all taking their data from the server. This also provides a way of streaming live TV around the house.

In addition to media playback, MythTV supports alternative skins and plug-in modules, allowing the front-end units to display the weather, show a photo gallery, play games, and surf the Web.

If you are looking for a PVR stand-alone form-factor, you can incorporate both mythback and mythfront into the same machine, provided that it is powerful enough. A TV card with hardware encoding (such as the newer Hauppauges) can help reduce the size and power of this machine, allowing you to get away with a fanless system.

The software approach to PVRs will always win out over hardware, because new features can be added more efficiently and vagaries in codecs can be catered for. I'll now briefly cover some examples.

Freevo

Freevo (`http://freevo.sourceforge.net`) is a play on the name of the infamous hardware PVR called TiVo.[8] It consists of an all-in-one approach, with video capture, recording, and playback existing within the same piece of software. (But under the hood it has a separate TV server section.) This makes it a closer relative to the Xtreamer type of device and especially suited more controlled installations.

Like MythTV (and most software PVRs, if I'm being honest), it can also support skinned interfaces and plug-ins, although most have been folded into `freevo1`, the stable version of the software, so any changes will require a bigger recompile than usual. This can make it more difficult for casual developers to make changes. These plug-ins include the usual array of weather reports, X10 control (through `heyu`), Skype, and Flickr.

It also has images for LiveCD versions (again, like most software PVRs, if we're honest) so you can test it without installation on your hardware.

Xbox Media Center

This is to remind those of you who skipped Chapter 2 to go back and read it! XBMC supports and runs on more non-Xbox platforms than it does on Xbox. It supports the usual array of plug-ins and has a LiveCD version.

The Video Disk Recorder Project

The project at `http://www.tvdr.de` is for the most hands-on developers, because it also includes a suggested hardware component. It is this hardware that is the main draw to this project because it is based on a DVB-S satellite receiver (its primary concern, because analog and digital TV are provided by plug-ins) and a custom-made remote-control unit using a PIC chip. Although this level of custom hardware is largely unnecessary in today's world, it works well and gives the users an extra reason to feel passionate about their VDR. It also uses a lower spec than most current systems. Software-wise, it has a decent (if slightly too small) interface that looks like the *Star Trek: The Next Generation* LCARS system and a much wider range of plug-ins than most PVRs, including games, e-mail, and web browsing.

Remote Control and UPnP

For the most part, media streamers and their ilk are very localized services. You might stream data across a network, but the controller and display are physically close. Even when you have an app to control the device (such as the WDRemote app, or one of the many VLC variants) it is only taking the place of the IR remote control you'd normally use. And you're still tying the streamer to its remote control. The evolutionary next step is to formally separate these units, and build open protocols that allow them to communicate, and for individual components that can be replaced at will. As you might guess, from the heading to this section, this is available with UPnP.

A Brief History of UPnP

Universal Plug 'n' Play (UPnP) began formally in December 2008 with the publication of the ISO/IEC 29341 standard covering networked appliance. The leading principle was that an UpnP-enabled device could be connected—and, importantly, configured—without any human intervention. This is made possible by removing the need for device drivers, moving the logic into protocols, and then having these protocols considered as stages, each having rules around the limits of each stage. The basic stack breaks down into six areas.

---

[8] It even inspired its own term, *tivoization*, to cover any device that runs using free software but prevents you from exercising your rights to modify and reuse it through hardware chicanery.

Networking Addressing

As covered in the Addressing section of Chapter 1, the network works best with dynamic IP addresses, distributed by DHCP. All UPnP devices use DHCP to determine its local address, and so the (short) time investment in preparing such a network is considered very worthwhile. In those cases in which such a service is not available, UPnP should fall back to a link-local address, which may not be in your intended range. (It will always be on a private intranet address, but can be a different one to the rest of your set-up, as the 169.254/16 range is preferred, meaning that the devices will not be visible.)

With routers providing this functionality out of the box, even casual dabblers in HA can be sure of a hassle-free UPnP experience. Naturally, when the UPnP device is a software device, the IP is provided by the host machine.

Discovery

In the same way that other services, such as Bluetooth, are able to discover compatible devices on its network, this works through the Simple Service Discovery Protocol (SSDP) and behaves like DHCP or DNS. Consequently, port 1900 is awash with traffic looking for these devices. It is unlikely that you would want (or need) discovery services outside of your local intranet, so there is no need to open this port to the wider world. Also, because this is a multicast request, you won't be able to use it over wifi because, by default, most wifi routers disable multicast.

Description

This is an XML file, returned over HTTP, describing the device as a whole. It doesn't control the device itself, but it explains how to do so. An example of this file would be as follows:

```
<?xml version="1.0" encoding="utf-8"?>
<root xmlns="urn:schemas-upnp-org:device-1-0">
  <specVersion>
    <major>1</major>
    <minor>0</minor>
  </specVersion>

  <device>
    <deviceType>urn:schemas-upnp-org:device:BinaryLight:1</deviceType>
    <friendlyName>Kitchen Lights</friendlyName>
    <manufacturer>OpenedHand</manufacturer>
    <modelName>Virtual Light</modelName>
    <UDN>uuid:cc93d8e6-6b8b-4f60-87ca-228c36b5b0e8</UDN>
    <serviceList>
      <service>
        <serviceType>urn:schemas-upnp-org:service:SwitchPower:1</serviceType>
        <serviceId>urn:upnp-org:serviceId:SwitchPower:1</serviceId>
        <SCPDURL>/SwitchPower1.xml</SCPDURL>
        <controlURL>/SwitchPower/Control</controlURL>
        <eventSubURL>/SwitchPower/Event</eventSubURL>
      </service>
    </serviceList>
  </device>
</root>
```

(from http://developer.gnome.org/gupnp/unstable/server-tutorial.html)

Control

Having described the controls to which this device will respond, it is then possible for remote controlling applications to send messages to the device. These are wrapped with the Simple Object Access Protocol (SOAP), meaning that you'll be looking at a lot of XML!

Event Notify

With the control layer being used to receive incoming messages, it only makes sense that the even notify layer is able to send them. This happens when a state on the device changes. The specifics of these events vary according to device, so when a "control point" first subscribes to the device, a list (again, in XML) is sent back, which details the events to which the control point can listen. It then makes a request to subscribe to these events, and so initiates a push mechanism between device and controller.

Presentation

Ultimately, there is a layer whereby two devices have agreed that the media at a specific URL wants to be played, and that it should be played on a specific device. No indication is given in the specification on which media formats should be supported by the presentation layer, and therefore which files are compatible. This is "by design," and it is something that the Digital Living Network Alliance has tackled. (For more on this, see later in this book.)

Because the presentation layer is separate from the control and server, the architecture provides us with one very sneaky built-in advantage! That is, it is easy to stream one signal to two different presentation components. On the surface, this provides a basic "whole-house audio" system, or a means to watch the same program in the living room and continue watching it in the kitchen. Indeed, this is possible. But because the presentation components do not need to match in terms of functionality, this means that you can have a UPnP-enabled TV in the lounge but only a set of suitable speakers in the kitchen. In this way you can continue to listen to the program without being distracted by the visuals—something that may be of benefit if you're working in the kitchen.

Authentication

This is the seventh layer in our six-layer stack. That is to say . . . there is no authentication! Although this exemplifies our decision to not open ports and to our use of local network addresses, it does introduce a problem. In this case, the problem is not a technical one but a management one. If anyone on your local network can access your media, can you trust the people on your network? For the most part, these are members of your family who (should) conform the social norms and coercions necessary to stop them abusing such access. However, you do only have a large grain control mechanism, that is, removing their network access entirely, should this fail.

There are extensions to UPnP (such as the Device Security Service, and UPnP-UP (User Profile) and protocols that are still not widely supported.

If you need authentication, however, and you can't be sure that your younger children won't take an interest in your certificate 15/18/X-rated films, then you might want to resort to Samba with password-protected areas for your media distribution. It is less well supported, and less flexible, than UPnP, but it would provide peace of mind.

High-Level Separation of UPnP

Given the stack-based arrangement of the internal protocols, it is no surprise that the end user is introduced to this concept, too, as there is a separation of functionality for the various parts of the system. This split is very natural and is comprised of:

- server—to provide media to other devices on the network
- controller—to start/stop the media, on any given device
- renderer—to display the media, be it video, pictures, or audio streams

This separation means that you can have any (or all) of the layers of functionality implemented on any given device. If they live on a single device, you have a standard media player. When the server is separated, you have the typical media streaming setup with the NAS playing the role of a server, while the streamer is a combined controller and renderer. When they're all separate, you can control any device from anywhere, using any media. This extends further, so that you can start watching a program on one device (or renderer), use the controller, and send a command to a different renderer to continue watching.

It also means you need to install three pieces of software.

Server

There are several options here and the choice is best determined by the size of the machine that will be running it.

Minidlna

For miniature needs, such as the Raspberry Pi, we have the aptly named minidlna. This is miniature in size and presence, but it provides the standard functionality of audio, video, subtitles, and pictures out of the box. The biggest drawback is its lack of transcoding but, for a Linux-based HA solution, where the media renderers are able to cope with almost any format, this is an unnecessary drain on CPU cycles.

It can be downloaded from `http://sourceforge.net/projects/minidlna/` or, for those using ArchLinux, retrieved as a package at `https://www.archlinux.org/packages/?name=minidlna`. Most of the other distros have yet to include it, so you will generally need to compile it. You will always need to include the development versions of the AV libraries on which it depends:

- libavcodec
- libavformat
- libavutil
- libexif

Additionally, depending on the versions, you might need to amend metadata.c to handle a change in the AV header files. Specifically, head to around line 715 and explicitly add:

```
#define AV_DICT_IGNORE_SUFFIX 2
```

so that it precedes the function definition:

```
#define AV_DICT_IGNORE_SUFFIX 2

sqlite_int64
GetVideoMetadata(const char * path, char * name)
{
```

109

Configuring the server requires you to edit the basic configuration file, to indicate the port, the appropriate locations of your media files, and the log files. This file is minidlna.conf and should be amended to begin:

```
# port for HTTP (descriptions, SOAP, media transfer) traffic
port=8200

# set this to the directory you want scanned.
media_dir=A,/net/media/mp3
media_dir=/net/media/movies

# set this if you would like to specify the directory where you want MiniDLNA to store its log file
log_dir=/var/log
```

Multiple media_dir lines are perfectly acceptable, and the "A" designation ensures that only Audio files are included. This is handy because some newer albums include digital tracks and music videos alongside their audio counterparts.

From here you can start the server as a daemon from a user account with:

```
minidlna -f minidlna.conf
```

At this point, it will scan the specified media directories for all your files, although the server will begin before scanning has completed. Consequently, some media players will need to be refreshed (or, in the worst case, restarted) to pick up files as the scanning procedure continues. It will also install an inode notifier into the kernel to automatically look for new files in the media directories, although any changes to the configuration file to introduce new media will require you to restart the daemon. There is a command to force such a refresh:

```
minidlna -R
```

although success with this option has been widely variable.

If you intend to include minidlna (or any other UPnP server) in your startup scripts in /etc/init.d, then include it at the end of the sequence, to ensure that filesystem services such as RAID are fully started.

The cache of media files is stored, by default, in /tmp. If you wish this to be more permanent, for example, between reboots, then add a line to the configuration file to this effect:

```
db_dir=/var/cache/minidlna
```

Although there is no web administration tool, you can retrieve basic stats by pointing your web browser to port 8200, or install webmin. In reality, however, little administration is needed as it is intended to be operated headless, with a controller such as VLC.

Rygel

As a media server, Rygel (https://live.gnome.org/Rygel) builds on the conceptual functionality of minidlna by incorporating its main omission—transcoding. Naturally, this requires a machine with higher performance than minidlna, but the software still retains its focus on being used on a headless box.

Like minidlna, Rygel can be run by a local user and is configured by specifying the URLs of your media:

```
# In ~/.config/rygel.conf
uris=/net/media/movies,/net/media/mp3
```

However, unlike minidlna, Rygel appears to wait until the whole directory has been scanned before beginning. So after executing:

```
rygel
```

there is plenty of time to get a coffee!

XBMC

Naturally, behemoth media systems such as XBMC can work as a server as well as a renderer. This is an ideal solution if you have one main media box, with the others considered as subordinate (or slave) units that are not accessed concurrently. When an XBMC server is feeding additional renderers it may not have enough processing power left over to power its own local renderer, along with the other requests made of it, so using separate slaves is a viable solution.

Sharing XBMC content to other devices is straightforward, and requires only that you enable it under the heading of "Share video and music libraries through UPnP." Depending on the version of XBMC, this is either under Settings ➤ Network ➤ Services (version 11, aka Eden), or Settings ➤ Services ➤ UPnP (version 12, aka Frodo). You can then discover the media from your controller as normal.

■ **Note** XBMC is a non-free package, so users of some distributions (such as Debian) will need to add additional repositories to use this through their standard package manager.

On the Raspberry Pi, XMBC can be installed by using either a custom installation (of which three currently exist), or by adding it as standard package of the Raspbian distribution (`www.raspbian.org/RaspbianXBMC`). The installers can be found at:

- `http://wiki.openelec.tv/index.php?title=Installing_OpenELEC_on_Raspberry_Pi`

- `www.raspbmc.com/wiki/user/os-x-linux-installation/`

- `http://xbian.org/download/`

with more information given in Chapter 9. Although this combination of XBMC and Raspberry Pi is not the most perfect match when partnered with anything connected to USB (e.g., external drives and especially DVDs), a lot of work is being done in this area, so improvements are anticipated with breath a-bated!

Renderers

Almost all traditional media players can be considered renders. Whereas originally they were limited to replaying media from the local drive, this slowly expanded to handling files across a network (through Samba) and now to UPnP. Space permits me the opportunity to briefly cover just a few of these.

VLC

As a stalwart of media playback, VLC has embraced almost every new technology. UPnP is no exception, and it is the easiest one to use when verifying a newly configured UPnP server.

First, head the Tools ➤ Preferences menu. From here, select "All" to get the full tree view of configuration options. You can then open the Playlist branch and tick the "Universal Play n Play" option in the "Services and Discovery" section. You have now enabled UPnP on VLC.

To play UPnP content, you need to select the Local Network branch, which then displays the various services available on the network that includes the UPnP. After a short while, the discovery messages will have been received and you can navigate the tree as normal.

Totem

Totem is the default media for many Linux distributions, and it provides UPnP without configuration on most of them courtesy of the Coherence plug-in and controller. To ensure that UPnP servers can be found, simply use the Edit ➤ Plugins menu item, and make sure that Coherence DLNA/UPnP client is enabled. It can then be used from the same drop-down list that houses "Playlists."

■ **Note**   Coherence is also available as a stand-alone application, capable of acting as a media server.

XBMC

When functioning as a media renderer, XBMC is doing as originally intended, playing back music and videos. No specific configuration is necessary for XBMC, so you can go directly to Video ➤ Files ➤ Add Video and browse to the UPnP server in question.

Real-Life Hardware

With UPnP underpinning the DLNA (see later in this book), and DLNA supported by many real-life manufacturers, it is comparatively easy to find UpnP-enabled hardware. This includes TVs from Sony, Samsung, and others, The Playstation 3, Xbox 360, as well as various smart phones.

Also, most PCs supplied with Windows 7 or Windows 8 will automatically be running a UPnP server, providing access to the users' media and that of the machine in general.

Control Points

Also known informally as controllers, control points browse the data on the server and command the renderer to display it. Other than the "one size fits all" approach taken with UPnP controllers, accessing media through control points has the benefit of automatically parsing the metadata so that you can browse your collection by genre, album, artist, or playlist automatically.

Control points fall into two main categories:

- Ones that communication with an existing player or controller

- Ones that require an intermediate server

In the first category, you have a swathe of iOS and Android control apps, such as XBMC Command, Remote for VLC, and so on. These sometimes require you to open specific HTTP ports on the server.

Others, such as jfcontrol (www.digitalsirup.com/jfcontrol/index.html) and the Minerva app, require an intermediary server on a wifi-connected machine. The control point then connects to the server, which formats the message appropriately before passing it on. Although not strictly a UPnP control point, they are often used to control them and so deserve mention here.

For the command line junkies, XBMC can be controlled with requests such as:

```
curl -i -X POST -H "Content-Type: application/json" -d '{"jsonrpc": "2.0", "method":
"Player.GetActivePlayers", "id": 1}' http://xbmc:www@192.168.0.21:8080/jsonrpc
```

that returns a list of which media streams (audio, video, picture) are playing. The URL breaks down, as normal, to [username]:www@[ipaddress]:[port]. Further commands can be found at `http://wiki.xbmc.org` and is highly recommended, as the structure has changed between v11 and v12 of XBMC.

Developing New UPnP Applications

With UPnP being such a far-reaching standard, it is tempting to convert your existing applications to utilize its functionality and to expand its reach into the many devices currently available. The scope of programming such applications is beyond the scope of this book, so instead I'll direct you to some resources that make the task easier.

GUPnP is a framework for building UPnP applications. It is pure in its intentions by providing only the framework elements, excluding any DLNA specifics, and requiring you to implement any of the high-level media server-like functionality (`http://gitorious.org/gupnp/pages/Home`).

dLeyna is a comparatively new project intended to provide umbrella services to UPnP applications, and is detailed at `https://01.org/dleyna`.

If you're interested in writing your own UPnP devices from scratch, without using middleware or helper libraries, then head over to `http://upnp.org` and access the basic specs from `http://upnp.org/specs/arch/UPnP-arch-DeviceArchitecture-v1.1.pdf`.

There is also good information to be found at `www.upnp-hacks.org/upnp.html`.

UPnP—The Closed Versions

Naturally, with any good technology, one (or more) companies will build their own proprietary versions on top. The two well-known ones are DLNA (Digital Living Network Alliance) and AirPlay.

DLNA

As a Sony initiative from 2003, this has been incorporated into a nonprofit trade organization and now features over 200 different member companies, each adding their own take. Consequently, there are over 9,000 different devices compliant with DLNA, making it one of the most pervasive media distribution technologies available, especially when counting the number of hardware devices that appeal to both hardened tech-geek and SWMBO.

Although there is a very close match between DLNA and UPnP for the protocols, their specification separates when it comes to rendering content, as DLNA introduces limits on what media can be distributed. These limits come in the form of file format, encoding, and screen resolutions. Whereas this ensures that any DLNA will "just work" and truly live up to the "zero configuration" dream of UpnP, however, because DLNA was begun many years ago, and movie codecs are changed and upgraded (comparatively) often, it means that many of the widely used formats today (such as MKV) are not supported by DLNA. To combat this, you can solve the problem on either the server or the renderer. From the server side, you can transcode the movie into an acceptable DLNA format before streaming it. Although this is expensive, it is possible to do in real time on most reasonably powerful desktop systems. (However, if multiple streams and/or a Raspberry Pi are involved, you might as well copy the file to a USB memory stick and walk with it to your device!) From the renderer side, many off-the-shelf media streamers will support formats not included in the specification, to eradicate the problems of compatibility and transcoding.

Depending on your point of view, DLNA is either "UPnP done wrong" or "UPnP done right." I shall leave that argument up to you!

DLNA follows the ideas of UPnP by separating the different media functions into types. In the case of DLNA, they are:

- Digital Media Server. A DMS acts like a NAS and stores content and makes it available to the other devices on the network.

- Digital Media Player. A DMP pulls content from the DMS for the purpose of playback and display.

- Digital Media Controller. A DMC enumerates the content on a DMS, and sends a "play" request to a media renderer.

- Digital Media Renderer. A DMR accepts content that is pushed to it, by a DMS, as instructed by a controller (DMC).

- Digital Media Printer. A DMPr is the DLNA equivalent of a self-glorified networked printer. It could be considered as a "write-only" DMR, working until the control of a DMC or DMP.

As with UPnP, some devices combine two or mor, pieces of functionality in the same physical box.

Most software-based UPnP devices are also DLNA compliant but haven't paid the licensing fees to be formally licensed as such.

AirPlay

Originally called AirTunes, back in 2004, this Apple-originated equivalent of UPnP and DLNA allows for media streaming between all compatible devices. However, being Apple, such streaming is only possible if you own an Apple device and software or one of the few third-party licensed products entering the market. Consequently, it has had little take-up in the Open Source world, and even projects such as ShairPort, which attempt to emulate an Airport express, have faltered.

The only benefit of AirPlay in an Linux-based house is to provide a closed network for the kids to access media. You can have an open UPnP environment for the master bedroom and living room (where viewing habits can be socially policed), and an AirPlay one for the kids.

Distribution

This is the third step of our data chain. Once we have our media data served and decoded, we are left with an AV signal ready to be plugged into a TV or HiFi. But we still have choices.

Local Processing versus Remote Processing

The equipment covered earlier is all locally processed. That is, we decode the data in a location that is physically connected to the TV or HiFi. This is usual, as it gives us greater fidelity and means that controlling the unit is much easier, but there are cases in which the processing is better done remotely and only the resultant AV signal is sent.

AV Distribution

The output from nearly all media playback devices is our first port of call. This usually comprises RCA phono sockets for stereo audio or composite video, S-Video, EIA interface, SCART, or something of that ilk. This carries a fairly low-power, analog signal over short distances to an amplifier—be it TV or HiFi. Because these signals always need a power amplifier, we call this *active distribution*.

Providing distribution in this manner requires various interconnects and many cables. There is no upper limit on the length of these cables, so extensions and distribution boxes are possible, allowing the same image to be viewed in multiple places. Naturally, being an analog signal, the audio (or picture) will become softer as you get farther away from the source. Only you can determine what quality loss is acceptable for you.

If you are wanting to distribute high-definition images around your house, then you currently have to consider the more expensive options, such as matrix switchers, because the current crop is focused around RCA sockets.

Switching

The cheapest piece of necessary equipment is an AV switch box, or AV source selector box. This provides multiple inputs for your various devices, DVD, PVR, VCR, and so on, and routes one of these to the TV output. Most equipment give you the option of using either S-Video, RCA, or SCART inputs. This naturally requires that the TV is always set to receive the input from the box, not its internal tuner. There are many switch boxes available, so the features to consider include:

> *Infrared remote control*: This is a necessity, really. Because this box takes the place of your TV channel changer, it must have the functionality you'd expect from the TV . . . which at a bare minimum is a remote control.

> *Active or passive devices*: Active units have a small amplifier in them and therefore need power. These ensure a strong signal but at the expense of a lower quality on the cheaper models, as their internal amplifier isn't as good as the ones on the DVD player or on a TV. Passive devices have no such amplification and are more likely to lack an IR remote.

> *Input connections*: Although some boxes provide S-Video, RCA, and SCART for each input, they might not be interconnected. That is, the RCA input socket might only be connected to the RCA output socket and not to the S-Video or SCART. Because you only have one output to the TV, this requires you to compensate for adapting your interconnects to the most common form factor and to convert every other input into the same type of plug (there are converters available in most electronics shops). You then use the equivalent output. This part of the specification isn't usually well documented, so check the shops return policy first.

> *Number of inputs*: Count the devices you have, add to this the number of devices you want to buy, and add two more for good measure! Once this limit has been exceeded, you have no real choice but to buy a bigger switch box. You can chain them, which is troublesome and lowers quality, or you can use a separate EXT input on the TV for each switch box, which is equally annoying but has fewer electronics in the signal chain.

The biggest omission on the entry-level switch boxes is the facility to switch between stereo audio and 5.1 surround. Consequently, you will need a separate set of cables from the 5.1 output of the DVD (controlling the 5.1 speakers) and the stereo output of the DVD connected to your switch box.

Splitting and Merging

Once you have the AV signal ready, you might want to split it so that the video part of the signal goes the TV, while the audio makes its way into the line-input on a HiFi. There are two main ways of achieving this. The first is the easy way and works if your TV has its own stereo-out sockets, as they can be connected from the TV to the HiFi directly without a problem. The other way is to split the signal coming out the switch box into two (or more) outputs—one for the TV and one for the HiFi. This approach means you won't be able to use the HiFi to amplify any stations selected using the TV's internal tuner, but this can be rectified by watching the TV solely through a receiver (such as a cable tuner or digibox) or VCR, which has been plugged into the switch box. This can be done in a variety of ways. The cheapest is the use two Y-cables (aka Y-adapters), one each for the left and right audio signals. These provide two identical outputs from one input and require no power. These work well when splitting audio signals but can be less than satisfactory when used on video signals because of impedance problems. If the quality isn't good enough, then you need a more involved splitter box.

A splitter box acts like its Y-cable counterpart but usually has an amplifier in it to stop signal degradation. This also allows it to provide more outputs for very little extra cost, allowing you to run a separate pair of cables into, say, the kitchen and dining room.

If neither of these is suitable, you can split the output after the amplifier stage by running multiple speaker cables.

Wiring Looms

Wiring looms carry a powerful signal (pun intended!) via cables to drive various passive speakers around your house. Consequently, we call this *passive distribution*. You should create one loom for each area of the house where the same audio content is likely to be heard, because local control here is more difficult (unless you get speakers with a volume control or want to hack one yourself). In a room layout as that shown in Figure 3-1, you have little privacy between the living room and the dining area, so these would be on the same loom, as would the kitchen because you probably want to pop in and out without missing the music or TV output. If an extension such as a sun room or den were added to the rear of the house, by contrast, it would be considered a separate area with a different lifestyle purpose and would not be on the same loom. Instead, any music in there should be provided over IP.

Figure 3-1. *A standard downstairs plan*

The first component in a wiring loom is the main power amplifier, taking its input from the switch box we covered previously. Normally, this will drive one set of speakers, although some amplifiers provide extra outputs for additional sets. It's rare to have more than two and even rarer to have more than a couple of rooms on the same loom, so you don't often need any more equipment.

In those cases in which you need more outputs, you can add a speaker control box into the chain. This takes a single speaker output and splits it into many. These additional speaker cables can be run into the other rooms and wired directly into other speakers without the need for power. This is the main advantage of this approach; namely, the cables are easier to run (the holes are smaller because there are no bulky plugs on the end), and there's no need for power sockets nearby, enabling you to add music to the bathroom where media players would not be practical or possible.

■ **Note**   Special waterproof speakers are necessary for bathroom use, which have sealed cones and baskets so they can cope with water and humidity. Various models exist, including flush-mounting ones that can be placed in the ceiling.

Provided that you use a reasonable quality of speaker cable, the signal will not dissipate over the distances involved.

■ **Note**   If you have two outputs on your amplifier but want to control three sets of speakers, then connect the control box to the second of the outputs and your primary speakers (on which you're more likely to do critical listening) on the first. There's no point in adding a step in the chain if you don't need to do so.

Wireless AV Distribution

Running cables is not difficult but should be done with care to avoid drilling through power cables, water, and gas pipes. With this in mind, there are a few pieces of hardware now available, such as the AV video senders you saw in Chapter 1, built to wirelessly distribute audio signals.

For the most part, they offer a solution of convenience, but landscape speakers, which are built to exist outside and made to look like rocks (for example), provide the only practical solution. They must also be powered from batteries.

Matrix Switchers

For most home applications, a standard switch box is enough to control your AV setup. If you have a Blu-ray player or other high-definition equipment, you will generally plug it straight into the TV using HDMI because this eliminates all other components from the signal chain. And, alas, none of the reasonably priced switch boxes I've seen support HDMI.[9]

Furthermore, if you want to distribute two of your input devices (such as PVR or DVD) to two different places, then you'll find that you can't, because the switch only provides a single output.

Both of these limitations can be overcome with matrix switchers. They have a broader range of inputs (often including VGA) and can send the input signal from any one of (say) eight inputs to any (or all) of the outputs, which often number four or more. This allows the most powerful AV control method possible, with all your hardware being located in a single place and the results carried by cable to each room in the house. Also, because this is professional-level equipment, it usually comes with a serial port, making it easy for a computer to control it directly.

Utilizing a matrix switcher in your setup is a big step, not just financially. To make full use of the device, you will need to keep your AV equipment in close proximity to the switcher. Furthermore, not only will you have the usual mess of cables entering the switcher, but you'll have an additional mess of cables leaving it—one set to every room. And, for the most part, matrix switchers are not small. Consequently, it is impractical to have them in the living room. Instead, you need to consider a room or a hidden cabinet into which the switcher and AV equipment can be placed. With the equipment now hidden away, the purchase of an IR relay or gateway to retransmit IR signals to the devices inside the cabinet is essential. It will be needed for the matrix switcher and may come as part of the package, so buy it second!

---

[9] There are a few HDMI switch boxes now appearing on the market, but these contain only HDMI switching such as the one shown at http://www.tvcables.co.uk/cgi-bin/tvcables/hdmi-matrix-switch-4x2.html. They are still hugely expensive, so realistically the choice now is either to have local processing of data or to distribute only a standard-definition version of the picture around the house.

The output connectors vary between matrix switchers. Some provide the output as an AV signal, such as S-Video or other domestic formats, making it very simple to connect other receivers into your home and have it work. Others are intended for hotels and conference centers and encode each input into a proprietary protocol so that the output can be transmitted over Ethernet. This case requires an additional receiver unit for each room, thus saving the effort of running specific AV cables around your house. And because the data is traveling over your existing Cat5 cables, you can usually send the IR control data back the same way, saving you on the IR relays that are so often necessary.

▨ **Note**   If the majority of your source media is stored on a hard drive, then you probably won't need a matrix switcher at all, as it can be transmitted by Cat5 to small Linux-based head units using software-streaming solutions such as VLC.

For those evil geniuses living in an underground volcano, a matrix switcher provides a mission-control room scenario for very little extra cost! After all, you can connect one set of outputs to a row of small, cheap TV sets and watch multiple sources at the same time.

Control

Having the ability to play music in every room is one thing. Being able to *control* music from every room is something else. This is the next step in the chain but one that is not always necessary. Look at the house layout in Figure 3-1 again. This needs no complex control systems because the living room is controlled locally, and the kitchen audio stream is usually switched on when you start preparing dinner and switched off once you've finished. Consequently, being forced to control the AV from the living room is not an issue.

Nor is it an effort to wire several rooms together (for example, the master bedroom, bathroom, and den) with a speaker control box and leave them on all the time. In this case, it is likely that although two of the three rooms may be unoccupied for most of the day, when one of them is in use, it is at the exclusion of the others, making it unnecessary to apply the cost or effort in providing separate controls for each room.

Local Control

Being able to control the device (such as a speaker or stereo amplifier) from the device itself is the most logical solution, and fortunately most head units provide this automatically. A local amplifier or set of powered (active) speakers, for example, will have a volume control on its front and a means to change the source input. Therefore, any distribution system using AV or Cat5 cables will have control built in.

To affect the volume of a passive speaker (maybe one fed from a remote speaker control box), you need an attenuator placed in series with the speaker. For low-power solutions, it is possible to mount a double logarithmic potentiometer directly into the speaker mountings. (You need logarithmic because this is the way volume works, and you want double for stereo volume control.) This won't give you particularly good fidelity, as the two tracks inside the device won't be well matched with each other and some frequencies made will be lost, but it will be cheap. For a better solution, there are custom attenuators that come in a basic wall unit and provide a better-looking control mechanism with improved quality. If your speakers are not wall-mounted, then you will have to run an extra set of cables either inside the wall cavity or in external tracks. Consequently, the cable runs from the speaker control box to the switch and then to the speaker. It is better to consider this approach before laying other cables. Apart from the bathroom (where such attenuators need to be waterproof), this method of control is usually impractical and better served with active head units or no form of local control at all.

Remote-Control Methods

Your house will come alive with the sound of music. Until you've lived with music in every room, you cannot imagine the difference that this makes. Being able to change the volume is nice, but not necessary, because each album is normalized to be consistent within itself. However, if you're randomizing the tracks, then the volume can vary wildly, necessitating a local volume control. And if you're introducing such functionality, you'll often want more involved local control to skip those random tracks you don't want to hear. Such functionality requires more hardware.

Direct Control

Standard HiFi equipment is invariably supplied with an IR remote, making it possible to place an IR relay receiver in each room and line up its transmitter with the receiver eye on the device. Small receivers can be mounted in-wall alongside, or instead of, a light switch and be powered by batteries. Adventurous developers can utilize a cheap all-in-one remote control and incorporate its workings, along with an IR relay and replacement switches, into their own wall unit.

Relay Control

Although few consumer products come with anything other than IR, this doesn't mean that you have to control it with IR, provided that there is something in between that understands both protocols.

Bluetooth, for example, is found on all current mobile phones, and although it is slightly power-hungry, there are many free or nearly free applications that interface with a suitably equipped PC. And because many people carry a phone on them at all times, this provides a very accessible way of providing control.

All Bluetooth communication requires a Bluetooth address. This looks like a MAC address from traditional network scenarios and can be discovered with the following:

```
hcitool scan
```

Note that there is a slight delay in scanning the area for devices, and a further delay is realizing when it has disappeared! So although this program *can* be used to determine when the Bluetooth signal is coming back into range (and therefore when you are returning home), it is best to perform a directed scan for a single phone using bluemon.

Bluetooth control apps come in two halves, one for the PC and one for the mobile. The mobile side is usually Java-based but, despite its "write once-run anywhere" mantra, usually needs a version specific to your phone because of the vagaries of mobile development. The messages sent are usually in a protocol that the receiving PC app can process. This is then configured to send a suitable IR signal to the device in question that might be to control the media player currently running on the PC or lock the desktop screen should the Bluetooth signal fall out of range.[10] Vectir provides such functionality for Windows users, while those in the Linux community can choose packages[11] such as Remuco, Amarok, or RemoteJ. There are other packages to permit file transfers between phones and PCs, such as obexftp, but these are suited to syncing applications and therefore are outside the scope of this book.

X10 provides a similar mechanism for relayed control. Utilizing a handheld transmitter module (such as the HR10U), you can send an X10 message (such as lamp E10 on) to the RF-to-X10 gateway, which places the data on the power lines. Your PC can then listen for this particular message and control the media player, either by retransmitting an IR signal or by affecting the PC-based software. I'll cover the specific mechanics of this when looking at Cosmic in Chapter 7, which supports a full range of additional functionality.

---

[10] This is one of the prestated aims of the bluemon package.

[11] A complete list would be impossible here, but alternatives include http://tuxmobil.org/bluetooth_cell_apps.html.

Server Control

All of the relay methods covered can also be used to control a server running software, such as a media player. Indeed, this is usually preferable, because it limits the number of places where a problem can occur and is often employed where most media is stored digitally on a hard disk.

When the server is providing the media to external locations, everything should be configured as a client/server. This provides a more distinct separation than before, where the music being played was controlled by the remote amplifier but the speaker volume was controlled locally. Adopting a full client/server approach has many benefits, not least because it unifies the system. Here, every message (such as "pause track" or "increase volume") is sent by the client using whatever protocol (X10 or Bluetooth) is suitable. The server then listens to all of these messages and translates them into the correct Linux commands. The effect of these commands can then be heard wherever its outputs are connected. Furthermore, when a full-scale PC is available for server processing, more complex protocols can be used.

A Web Interface

A traditional LAMP (Linux, Apache, MySQL, PHP/Perl) installation provides a good means of controlling your house by the most ubiquitous interface of modern times—the web browser. Almost every device, including game consoles, mobile phones, and in-wall touchscreens, have a web browser of some description built in.

Building or hacking your own touchscreen is no longer a problem either. You can start with the current range of notebooks and subnotebooks that include a touchscreen (such as the Eee PC T91) or retrofit one to an old laptop (such as the Acer Aspire or Dell Inspiron Mini). These kits comprise a touchscreen membrane that is attached externally to the monitor screen and a USB plug that causes the screen to act like an external mouse.

These machines are small and powerful enough to fit anywhere, including on your refrigerator, but you can reduce the footprint further by using an old phone (such as the Nokia 7710) and mounting it yourself.

The software is, naturally, Linux. Several slimmed-down distributions provide a browser as its only software, such as Webconverger. These are live systems that can form a compact flash and are known as *kiosk systems*. With zero installation and very short boot times, these are very good for occasional house terminals.

SMS

SMS is the short-message system available to all mobile phones as part of the standard infrastructure. It can be utilized by the smart home in two ways. The first is to connect a mobile phone to the Linux machine and interface to it using Gnokii, SMS Server Tools, or some similar software. This software now provides support for many phones, although originally it was only for Nokia phones. Gnokii provides two-way communication for SMS messages, allowing your PC to read and interpret them or send out reminders or status updates.

▨ **Note** Use a prepaid phone if possible when the majority of the communication is outbound, lest a software bug or cracker cause a lot of sent messages and a very large phone bill. This isn't always the best choice for inbound communication, however, as some operators (in Northern American, notably) charge for inbound SMS on prepaid phones as well!

A second method is to subscribe to an SMS service provider, such as mBlox, which will provide you with a phone number, login credentials, and an API; this allows two-way communication with any machine as if it were a mobile phone. You should check with the service provider whether it's possible to limit the amount spent on the account in case of problems.

The SMS solution has fallen out of favor in recent times with the cost of G3 web access coming down, but it still provides a fairly cheap means of control for families where older phones are passed down to the kids.

Conclusion

Although a home automation system has a lot of components, you've seen that none of them are particularly complex or outside the realm of a standard Linux machine. It is only your geek-lust that requires (nay, demands!) more equipment. But even then, a solid server is a bedrock, although as a home automation system grows, the inclusion of more custom hardware becomes less suitable. Even though the cost of DVD players and PVRs is coming down, the bulk/expense of replacing each piece of kit, in each room, is troublesome. Plus, you have no benefit of being able to share media around the house and will be continually asking, "Who had the *Star Wars* DVD last?" The target goal for most systems is to have a very powerful computer hidden away somewhere and a lot of smaller (low-power, low-cost) head units in the various rooms, able to play all types of media. The area containing this powerful computer is called Node Zero, and I'll cover that next.

CHAPTER 4

■ ■ ■

Home Is Home: The Physical Practicalities

Running your own home is a great feeling. Having it run from your own Linux server is even better. Just being able to tell people that your home page is quite literally your *home* page lifts your geek credentials one notch higher. But having a machine running 24/7 introduces a permanent noise from the fans and hard drives, blinking lights, and extra heat. Being able to control one machine from another requires cabling. In this chapter, I'll cover some of the basics about the physical practicalities of a home automation setup.

Node0

Node0 is the place in the house where all the cables end up, or are "home run." This means Cat5 Ethernet, AV cables, IR relays, and even X10 wireless transceivers might all live within a single location. It is also the entry point for the outside world, so modems and routers will also live here.

Function and Purpose

The idea of using a single Node0 is to keep everything out of the way of day-to-day living. This means that the server, no matter how big and noisy it might be, can be positioned where it least impacts those trying to sleep or study. It also allows the mass of cables and expensive hardware to be placed somewhere, perhaps locked up with a single key, to minimize careless accidents involving spilled drinks and young children.

Although this introduces a single point of failure (a big no-no in general systems administration), the risks involved at home are much fewer, and it doesn't impact the already present single point of failure, namely, the sole modem cable entering and leaving the house.

The server machine itself also exists to provide a central repository of all the house-related data and information, including the main web site and e-mail services, and an abstraction to the various media repositories that might exist on other machines. In this way, every nontechnical house dweller can connect to //server/media and be transparently connected to whatever hard disk (on whatever machine) happens to include it. This makes it possible to upgrade and move disks around as they become full, without fielding support calls from your family!

Having a primary server generally requires it to remain switched on 24/7. Centralizing the tasks to a single location and unifying all the services onto a single machine means that only the Node0 machine requires protection from power outages (via a UPS) or theft (via a strong lock). Indeed, the data most at risk is usually on stand-alone laptops, so I'll cover backup plans for them later, too.

Determining the Best Room

Even the humblest of abodes has several locations suitable as Node0. Most people choose the closet under the stairs (as it's central and therefore requires less wiring), but there's more to it than that! In fact, while reading the next section, you are expected to mentally move the server from one room to another as each problem or solution presents itself. Furthermore, in some cases, it's not physically possible to find one room that can solve all of the particular problems, in which case you may have to drop the offending feature or use a second server in a separate location.

Lawful Considerations

Laws vary according to country and change over time, so it is important to take the necessary advice and acquire any permissions before work is begun. In reality, this affects very few people, such as those who are building new structures on their land (such as sun rooms) or amending buildings that have been granted "graded" or "listed" status.

Necessary Considerations

The necessary considerations in this section cover the limits of particular pieces of hardware and their interconnects. Because the main server will need full unfettered access to all your equipment, these considerations are of primary importance.

X10 signals can dissipate and get swallowed whole by various devices placed around the house, as mentioned in Chapter 1. Moving the Computer-X10 gateway (CM11) to another socket can change its reach quite considerably, so a lot of testing is necessary. Alas, it might not be possible to place the device in any single location that allows the messages to make a complete circuit in both directions around the house. This would subsequently require two servers or two gateways.

Ethernet over Power (EoP; not to be confused with Power over Ethernet) is one way of adding two-way networking capabilities using the existing power lines, in the same way that X10 introduces appliance control. Like X10, it is at the mercy of other devices on the power line, so should parts of your home become inaccessible to WiFi, this approach should be tested also.

Broadband and cable modems can often enter the house only at a number of predetermined points, thereby limiting the rooms available. It is, however, rarely necessary to have your server connected locally to the modem unless your Linux machine is acting as the gateway to the rest of your home. In most cases, a good router can effectively separate the internal and external network traffic with enough control to make the use of a full-blown PC unnecessary.

WiFi signals, like X10, dissipate. Furthermore, because the frequency band used is common to many other protocols, this can cause the connection quality to worsen considerably or disappear altogether. These devices include some wireless access points (such as the United Kingdom's BT Homehub), wireless phones, TV senders, and microwave ovens. Furthermore, because they travel through the air, they're more susceptible to external influences outside of your control, such as neighbors. You can limit the effect of these other devices by doing the following:

- Switching the WiFi channel. Depending on the country, WiFi is split into either 14 (Japan) or 13 (everywhere else) distinct frequency bands with each channel occupying a group of 4 or 5 of these bands. This places channels at midpoints at channels 1, 6, and 11 (for the United States) and 1, 5, 9, and 13 in most other places.

- Adding more WiFi base stations to minimize the distance necessary for each signal to travel. When setting this up, set all units to the same SSID, and connect to the same section of wired Ethernet.

- Switching to wired versions of the offending devices. To determine the offending device, simply turn them off in sequence, and/or point a spectrum analyzer in each direction to determine the source of the transmissions.

- Jamming the signal of the offending device (particularly if it originates from someone else).

- Using directional transmitters.

When using AV distribution to introduce whole house audio, the cable that powers speakers or amplifiers from the main server can affect the location of the server, as every meter of cable increases the chance of external noise affecting the quality of the audio. Also, because this is an analog signal, it will become less powerful if it has to travel farther. Good-quality cable can minimize this.

Cat5 cable is the best method of getting fast Ethernet throughout the house because it is not susceptible to the external factors of WiFi or EoP. However, you will need to ensure that you can effectively reach the majority of the house from your Node0 location. Concrete and structural walls have to be considered since it might not be possible to run cables through them. You will also want to have as few network switches as possible en route between server and clients, so the loft or attic might not be the best solution, particularly if you plan on streaming a lot of video to the TV room downstairs.

Power is a necessary evil of the system, so any room must have enough power (and be connected to suitable fuses) to allow several hundred watts to be drawn by desktop computers, laptops, lights, and TVs. This is more of an issue for older houses.

Negative Effects

Computers, even Linux-based ones, aren't immune to everything, and some rooms are naturally more hostile to electronics than others.

Kitchens, conservatories, cellars, and utility rooms are more prone to moisture and humidity than elsewhere. The moisture can cause untold damage to a machine when (not if!) it gets inside the PC case and reacts with the electronics. It should be noted that although humidity isn't a particular problem for the machine in itself, it will make it sticky, causing it to become a magnet for dust particles that in turn can clog up one of the PC's fans (there are usually three on most desktop machines: CPU, PSU, and graphics card). The dust can also settle in the various gaps between circuit boards, such as the PCI/AGP cards, making them inoperable.

Furthermore, the dust can carry moisture, which, in combination with that present in the water vapor, can cause the various components to rust and degrade, leading to short circuits and general damage. Relative humidity of 45 to 60 percent is generally accepted to be a suitable range, which can be measured with a hygrometer.

■ **Note** Problems with humidity also occur when there are brusque changes in temperature, such as when a machine is brought in from the cold. In this case, leave it to naturally reach room temperature before switching on.

Temperature can affect computers to the same detriment as moisture but in different ways. Although most machines can survive cold temperatures (certainly colder than most humans would be happy living in!), they are not as happy with hot temperatures—as the number of fans present will testify—and computers will often automatically shut down if the onboard temperature sensors exceed their limits. This can often eliminate the utility room, and sometimes the loft or attic, as a suitable location.

Because the only moving parts in a PC (other than the fans) are the hard disks, it can be necessary to consider their operating temperature. This can vary between drives but is around the 5- to 55-degree Celsius range.

Human Considerations

The computer is moving into your living space, not vice versa, so once you know the physical limits of your chosen location, you can consider the lifestyle impact of a machine living there. The antisocial elements of PC behavior include noise, lights, and heat.

The noise from a standard desktop PC comes from its various fans and the clicking and whirring of the hard disk. Although the fans produce a constant hum that soon disappears into the ambient background noise of your home, the disks make noise occasionally and can be more annoying. If you are used to sleeping in the same room as a PC, then you will appreciate that the fan often becomes a comforting bedfellow, whereby it later becomes difficult to sleep without its companionship.

The noise from a hard disk, although slight, has an interesting dual property. Although you (or your partner) might be disturbed by the noises coming from a hard disk somewhere within the house, it can provide a very good audible alert system should you suddenly hear the (normally) quiet hard disks suddenly fire up in the middle of the night.

As you'll see later when looking at server types, some machines are fanless (thereby eliminating most of the noise), and some can work from solid-state devices instead of hard disks (which eliminate *all* noise). Naturally, the positioning and/or soundproofing of Node0 might make the concept of noise a moot (mute?) point!

The lights on most PCs are the simplest form of output interface available. The standard front plate contains lights for power and hard disk activity, whereas the reverse has the equivalent for network activity, along with the other visible light sources on the motherboard shining through the rear cooling holes. There are similar lights on external hard disks, modems, and routers. The former lights give Node0 a distinct glow of cybercool (usually because more technology comes with blue LEDs nowadays!), whereas the latter creates an annoying flicker that, in the dead of night, is visible in the next room. Although all of these lights can be hidden by black tape, it is usually preferable to hide the units inside a box, cupboard, or drawer so that the diagnostics lights can be reviewed when needed.

In addition to being affected by heat, computers (particularly desktop ones) *produce* heat. And having one on 24/7 can raise the room temperature by 1 or 2 degrees. You will consequently have to consider the other home heating elements and consider whether placing Node0 on the ground floor of your house and allowing the heat to rise[1] can provide any reasonable savings on your bills. The downside of this excess heat is that it might get very uncomfortable to work on the machines in Node0 if they're in an enclosed space that is heating up by the second. Consequently, install only low-energy or fluorescent lights here to prevent it from heating up any further when you're working on it.

Determining the Best Room

Given the previous possibilities, most people will consider one of the following rooms:

- *Living room*: By being physical close to the TV and primary stereo system, the living room provides good access for all the media elements of an HA installation. This eliminates the need for IR transmitters and a lot of extra cabling. It's easily accessible if you plan on using physical DVDs, and if the server is connected directly to the TV and stereo, you get the highest-possible-quality AV. On the downside, however, having your server here can be intrusive to family life (particularly when you are tweaking physical connectors), and you can't use any server that needs a fan since the noise will often obscure the quieter music and dialogue in films and TV dramas.

- *Bedroom*: This is the first and last place you spend each day, so having the machine on hand, displaying news, videos, e-mails, and so on, can be highly optimal, if slightly unnerving at times. It also has many of the benefits of the living room, as the (master) bedroom is normally home to the second most important TV in the house. Consequently, it can suffer the same problems with noise, in addition to those associated with randomly blinking lights in the night and increased heat.[2]

---

[1]Technically, hot air is less dense, causing it to rise.

[2]It is often recommended that the bedroom be around two degrees cooler than other rooms in the house to help your body get to sleep easier.

- *Under the stairs*: This is nicely hidden from view and enclosed, meaning that most noise and light pollution is hidden and therefore acceptable. It is also central to the house, meaning you have shorter cables for the wired protocols (Cat5, X10, audio, and so on) and less chance of interference for the wireless ones. However, in most cases it is difficult to see how and where to get cables (especially power) into and out of the cupboard under the stairs without it being obvious. Additionally, it is usually a very small space, making it prone to temperature rises and difficult to work in—for both the machine and for you when carrying out Node0 maintenance.

- *Loft or attic*: This is a nice, hidden, and secure location that is highly unlikely to be burgled! It's also very easy to drop cables into all rooms on the upper floor. (But conversely, it's less easy for those rooms on the ground floor, unless you decide to run a large trunking all the way down through the ground floor's ceiling.) As mentioned earlier, getting a suitable amount of power to the loft might be tricky, as could temperature control.

Building the Rack

The equipment found in a home automation rack is wide and varied and consequently doesn't usually come in the correct form factor (of pizza-box-sized units) to fit into a rack. But although you might not use a rack in the traditional sense, you should consider some kind of stacking mechanism for your equipment. After all, you should be able to access every piece of kit on an individual basis, because you won't want to unplug and slide out the router, modem, and switch just to plug in some new toy in the USB socket on the back of the PC!

■ **Note**   You can ensure good access by not filling the entire Node0 space with technology. This also ensures there's space left for new kit as you acquire them.

If you have access to a nearby kitchen DIY store, you can sometimes find drawers and cupboards that can swing through 90 degrees as the door is opened, which can be misappropriated as a good rack mount. Alternatively, if there is a partition wall between the Node0 room and the next, you could mount an access hatch (similar to a kitchen-serving hatch) between the two. For the theatrical readers, you could hide this behind a painting with a secret hinge!

The equipment typically found in a Node0 rack may include the following:

- Modem

- Router

- Wireless router

- Home alarm system

- Phone exchange

- Network switch

- Main server PC or Raspberry Pi (low power 24/7)

- Media server PC (loaded with TV capture cards)

- Monitor, keyboard, and mouse (connected to servers through KVM switch)

- External hard drives (easier to replace/upgrade than internal and less likely to head crash)

- Audio power amplifier

- TV aerial booster

This connects to the rest of the house via a combination of Cat5 Ethernet cable, Power Line communications, WiFi, and AV cables where the data is picked up by the following:

- Media-playing head boxes
- Additional speakers
- Secondary audio amplifiers
- Personal laptops and desktop PCs
- Secondary TVs, using aerial input

Servers

To be a truly effective smart automated home, you will need a server that's on 24/7. Although many of the devices you've seen (such as the CM11U in Chapter 1) can be programmed to work offline, you only get a sense of power when there is something ready, willing, and able to make decisions at any time of the day or night. And a timed light switch doesn't count.

There are so many cool and interesting technologies in a home environment that it's very easy for the ideas to run away from themselves and for you start to place orders for the biggest and most powerful servers that you can't afford! In reality, there is no need to have only one server, provided there is only one in overall charge.

Server Capacity

The capacity of a server breaks down into three areas:

- CPU processing power
- Disk space
- Bandwidth capabilities

I'll cover these in order.

CPU Power

With a few exceptions, home automation software takes very little power. All of the standard tasks, such as web servers, e-mail, alarm clocks, SMS processing, message routine, and music playback require virtually no processing, and the lowliest Mini-ITX is capable of handling everything without breaking a silicon sweat.

Transcoding media from one format (such as the high-definition DVD rip stored on your server) into another (a smaller version suitable for low-end hardware such as the MVP or for playback on your portable device) is significantly more processor-heavy. Consequently, it is not uncommon to have two main servers, each one dedicated to these two main tasks.

Disk Space

Again, most of the HA tasks don't require lots of hard disk space, so if your operating system fits (and they're approaching 1 GB in size these days), then the extra 25 MB required for the control software is not going to break the bank. Only the media server requires extra space, and for this you'll need as much space as you can afford. External USB drivers are an excellent way of cheaply (and conveniently) increasing disk space, and they're fast enough to stream movies to the server and then across the network.

You might consider a separate file server whose sole job is to provide files for the rest of the house. In this way, it can be stored in a physically secure location (hidden out of sight, perhaps in the loft or attic) to prevent precious data from being accidentally destroyed or stolen. Securing the server in a solid rack also helps prevent against theft, because no one can easily walk off with a Backblaze Pod (`http://blog.backblaze.com/2009/09/01/petabytes-on-a-budget-how-to-build-cheap-cloud-storage/`)!

Bandwidth Capabilities

This is generally a nonquestion, as the current crop of network cards are all support at least 100 Mbs (with most suporpting 1000 Mbps without batting a silicon eyelid), which is fast enough to distribute several movie streams around the house. The modem speed will usually limit your external streaming capabilities, but so will many other factors such as broadband contention in your area, current network traffic, and the target machine and its LAN.

Unlike corporate servers, most home servers can suffice with only one network port since a decent stand-alone router can perform most of the necessary filtering and configuration tasks that often need two Ethernet sockets. However, any future upgrades to your machine (such as moving the firewall software to the server) or changes in family (introducing a separate restricted intranet for the kids) will need a second port.

Also note that there is no longer any cost benefit of buying hubs over network switches, so a switch should be the only choice because it allows the full 100 Mb to every port, and therefore every machine, on the network. You should route all network cables back to a single switch located physically next to your Node0 server to minimize maintenance. In a standard three- or four-bedroom house, this switch should have at least 16 ports.

Server Extensibility

In the corporate world, improving the facilities of a server generally means more memory or more disk space. To us, it also includes new hardware. Although not all HA applications or servers require new hardware, it is best to consider what else the server might handle.

TV cards are obvious, because a high-powered server could record from several TV stations at once or transcode a channel into a head unit–friendly format for streaming. Projects such as PromiseTV (`www.promise.tv`) take this to an extreme, but it's a viable option.

Similarly, additional sound cards can provide extra scope to functionality. Although the setup in Linux can be slightly painful, having two sound cards allows you to directly control the audio in other rooms. This can remove the necessity of having local control panels, since you can use any device that connects to the computer, such as a web browser, phone, or HR10U connected through Cosmic. Furthermore, remember that each sound card has inputs as well as outputs. This allows you to build a large-scale baby monitor for each room in the house. If you have a voice recognition system (covered in Chapter 5), then you have instant control in each room. There have been projects in the past to coax 6.1-supported sound cards to into three separate stereo ones, but they have not been maintained as well recently.

Types of Server

Naturally enough, given the title of this book, the server will be running Linux. It is not by luck that Linux is able to run on virtually any device, so it's no longer a question of hardware compatibility, but one of compromise between physical size, power consumption, and CPU power. There is nothing ultimately special about the hardware. Off-the-shelf machines are fine. You will be familiar with most (if not all) of the devices listed here. We need to consider their specific relative merits in the HA sphere. In most cases, the server will always have a mouse, keyboard, and monitor attached (unlike those in the business centers) to allow for simpler software maintenance—and if the server is located somewhere accessible, the monitor can display a web page presenting the current "house report status" for virtually zero processing cycles. When these peripherals are not to be connected permanently, you may need to adjust the BIOS to allow the machine to boot without them. This is especially true of desktop machines that will beep three times when no monitor is present and often issue the infamous "No keyboard connected – Press F1 to continue" error.

Rack Mount

These can be bought in many variants including those with redundant or dual power supplies and quad processors being the standard rather than the exception. Consequently, these power houses of processing can handle the transcoding needs of several users simultaneously, with enough cycles to spare to handle all the other services (web, e-mail, and so on) without affecting any other user. They are the industry standard for commercial applications for a reason because they can handle any load, for any length of time, and can run happily for many years without change.

Unfortunately, they are suitable for home use only if you can place them away from the living areas since they usually have large noisy fans inside and give off a lot of heat. Although the noise can be muted by placing the machine in a cupboard, you can't generally achieve the same result by replacing components with low-noise equivalents, as they're generally not of the standard PC design.

The heat is also something you will need to effectively dispose of. Air conditioning is standard in offices but not at home where the same effect is generally achieved by opening a window. Running a rack server at home will often need some kind of extractor fan at the very least.

The non-PC-ness will also hit home when considering its upgrade status. You will not be able to fit a PCI TV card into many rack machines because the connection form factor and size will be prohibitive. You will also need to buy a physical rack, or half-rack, in which to mount the unit. These are designed and priced at commercial installations, and although you will always need some kind of mounting for all the equipment mentioned earlier, there are cheaper ways of doing it with DIY shelving.

Desktop PC

This is the most popular choice, for all the obvious reasons: they are understandable, common, cheap, and built for home use. They can also be upgraded easily with additional cards, and replacements for worn-out (or too noisy) parts are available in your local bricks-and-mortar store. The current range of machines is fast enough to perform transcoding for a couple of media head units around the house, as well as handle all the other standard tasks.

Unfortunately, the home machine is intended to be used as a home machine, that is, for a few hours in the evening to check e-mail and play games. Using it as a server, running 24/7, can strain the physical components of the machine (fans and discs mostly) and increase the risk of breaking the machine's integrity. Unlike racks, these machines are built to a price point, not a quality factor, and so will use components that allow the price to hit that magic 299 figure, or whatever. Consequently, these components might have a lower tolerance for temperature variances (which will happen if the machine is working all day) or have a lower mean time between failures (MTBF). When the machine is continually accessing data, either from memory or from a hard disk, the chance of this happening will naturally increase.

My personal setup uses a desktop PC as the media transcoding server, which runs most of the time. I bought higher in the price range than I would for a traditional desktop machine, with quieter-than-standard fans and better components. I also bought spares for the fans at the same time so that if I needed to replace the moving parts of the machine, I would have some available. RAM chips (which are, admittedly, also likely to go bad over time) are usually available for many years after a machine's release, whereas the particular size of CPU fan isn't. This is because any server that lasts several years will outlive the current design of processors and motherboards, making spares for these components very difficult to come by. I also admit that when (not if) these components finally die, I will probably be unable to buy replacements and so will have to endure the pain of setting up an entirely new machine.

Mini-ITX

The Mini-ITX is a family of machines based around the 170 ×170mm ITX motherboard. Within this specification, there are a number of different options with varying processors, graphics chips, and cooling methodologies. This includes many machines that are fanless, relying only on the heat sink for cooling. This makes them more energy efficient than their desktop counterparts and suitable for placing in more communal areas, such as the living room where they are often used as media players.

Like desktop machines, there are a wide range of configurable options with ITX machines including TV (S-Video) and DVI output, compact flash (CF) adapters for diskless operation, wireless networking, and so on. They also have standard PCI ports for other cards. This configurability is both their manacle and demonic charm, because the workability of any particular device isn't necessarily known when you buy the machine. Although any ITX is powerful enough to run all the basic services of an HA setup, most machines cannot transcode media fast enough, and the older ones cannot play back modern formats (such as DivX, which has a fairly high CPU requirement). Furthermore, there are some issues with outputs, other than SVGA, being supported by the Linux drivers, making it an issue for using them as a head box for anything other than projectors. New combinations of ITX are released on a regularly basis, along with updated drivers, so always check with your dealer for support, along with the current web forums.

The other configuration consideration with the ITX machine is the case, since it's not supplied with the machine and you have to buy it separately. Furthermore, as space is such a premium here, you should buy any and all peripherals you intend to keep inside the case at this time. You should not expect to be able to update, or add to, the components and still have it fit within the same case. Even a 3mm gap between components can be the difference between a nice working system and one that overheats. So, consider whether you want a hard drive or CF card and whether a (slimline) DVD player would be necessary at the start.

■ **Note** Always buy the case from the same dealer as the machine so you can ensure they will fit together. These cases are considerably more expensive that desktop cases and therefore a costly mistake.

Naturally, with so many cases to choose from, you have every chance of getting just the size you want. They come in four basic variants, with most HA servers being a cube or rack, while the ITX motherboards used in media units often choose book.

- Book, around 70 × 270 × 320mm, with up to two drive bays; not all support PCI cards
- Cube, around 180 × 220 × 280mm, with up to four drive bays and usually a PCI card
- Rack, a 1U (482.6 × 44.45 × 381), with up to four drive bays and up to two PCI cards
- Vehicle, variable around 210 × 254 × 56mm, with one or two drive bays and occasionally one PCI card

A vehicle mount case is used for mounting in harsh environments, such as a car or garage, where it can be used as a kids entertainment center or web terminal. All four come in a variety of sizes, with the drive bays being either 2.5 inch or 3.5 inch. It should be note that not all ITX cases are compatible with all types of motherboards. In the ITX world, one size certainly does not fit all. So, check and recheck your specification.

ITX has begat two younger brothers, the Pico-ITX with a 100 × 72mm motherboard and the Nano-ITX at 120 × 120mm. Although the size reduction isn't worth the price increase if you still have to buy a larger case to fit a DVD drive, this size of machine can be hid virtually anywhere, making it good for media head units or for running control panels in the kitchen.

Mini-PC

The Mini-PC is a high-power, prebuilt PC in a box that has a very small form factor (often around 80 × 50 × 30mm) and usually a similarly low-power footprint. This causes them to be sometimes termed GreenPCs, but whereas Mini-PC often has a low-power footprint, a GreenPC *must* have one, as should its manufacturing process. Typical machines of this type include the Zonbu, Intense PC, and Fit-PC3.

Functionally, they are a cross between laptops (because they're prebuilt and therefore can't be upgraded, and the OS really needs to be preinstalled to ensure a complete set of drivers), desktop machines (with a high machine spec and single network port), and Mini-ITX machines (which look nice when placed under TVs, for use as head units). Consequently, many people will use them as more client-focused machines for web browsing and media playback.

But, as I've mentioned previously, the CPU required for most of your HA tasks is so minimal that these are perfectly suited to it. They also make good secondary servers in cases where the building itself doesn't allow for a single machine in Node0 to reach the entire house, as can be the case with X10 messages and wireless communication. Furthermore, because the power usage of these devices is often 10 watts or less, they are efficient and add very little overhead to an existing setup.

The specifications of these machines differ wildly, because many include custom hardware to improve on the apparent capabilities. The Fit-PC2, for example, includes only a low-powered Atom processing but is able to play back HD 1080p H.264 video by incorporating hardware acceleration.[3]

The biggest downside with these machines, however, is the lack of bravado when demonstrating your HA setup to friends. After showing how you can e-mail your light switch, send a text message to your video, and have your own home web server, opening a cupboard to show a small box that fits inside your hand is often a letdown for the male ego!

Custom Embedded

This group features both system-on-a-chip (SoC) machines and single-board computers (SBCs), of which there are many, including the Mini-ITX machines you saw earlier and the NSLU2 from Chapter 2. There are as many combinations of devices as there are uses for machines, so each needs to be considered on its own merits as the various components one often considers standard on a PC, such as a keyboard, mouse, and monitor, are not available on all SBCs such as the Gumstick.[4]

Also, some machines, such as the NSLU2, can have issues with seemingly normal peripherals, like USB hubs, and refuse to work with them. Consequently, these types of device are usually better suited to client machines in confined areas of the house, rather than servers, because the server will be running a wide range of software where *any* annoyances of hardware incompatibility will generally outweigh the benefits of size.

Raspberry Pi

Although the Raspberry Pi is conceptually no different to any of the custom embedded devices you might have discovered form the section above, it is not quite the same. Primarily, the fame and market acceptance of the Pi has ensured a solid user base which other platforms can't manage. Having now reached critical mass in the marketplace means that any problems you might find will have be solved by more than one person, and will have (at least) one web page, or forum thread, dedicated to the solution.

This mass of users has also meant that the main physical problem of using a Pi as a server has be solved—the case! It is possible to buy several different types and styles of case from the various sites on the Internet. This includes the list at `http://elinux.org/RPi_Cases` that also details some you can build from LEGO, wood, and with 3D printers.

Power Consumption

For many, home automation is likely to be the first time you need to consider the total cost of ownership (TCO) of a machine by factoring in its power usage. This can be computed empirically by using an electricity usage monitor, like Kill-A-Watt (`www.p3international.com/products/special/P4400/P4400-CE.html`). Such a device can be plugged

---

[3] The drivers for this are closed source but available for Linux.
[4] These incredible small machines measure less than a stick of chewing gum. See `www.gumstix.com`.

into the wall on one side and the computer on the other to determine the power it's using at any particular time. This will vary depending on whether it's in the following states:

- Idle

- Playing optical media

- Processing media (playback, recording, and transcoding all differ)

- Being used as a desktop machine

Knowing this information can help you calculate its running cost by multiplying the wattage shown by 8.76 (the number of hours in a year, divided by 1,000) to produce the number of kilowatt-hours. This is then multiplied by the cost per kilowatt-hour, which is generally shown on your electricity bill, to produce its TCO.

■ **Note**   You can even tweet your home's power usage with the simple hack known as Tweet-a-Watt, from www.ladyada.net/make/tweetawatt. There are also alternate solutions such as Owl, AlertMe, Wattson, and Enistic.

Unless the server manufacturer gives you its full power consumption data (remember that this varies according to task), you can only make a guess at its TCO. Table 4-1 shows some approximate numbers. They have been culled from various empirical tests, although only their relative values should be considered and only then as a guide.

Table 4-1. *Approximate Power Consumption*

Device	Approximate Wattage Used
Desktop machine	60–250
Desktop machine (sleep)	1–5
Laptop machine	15–50
Mini-PC	6–10
Mini-ITX[5]	8–20
Raspberry Pi (Model B)	1.65
Raspberry Pi (Model A)	0.715
RPi (B) with HDMI and USB drive	2.0–2.45
RPi (B) with HDMI and WiFi	2.175–2.4
CRT monitor	80
LCD monitor	35
DVD/CD-ROM (desktop)	20
DVD/CD-ROM (laptop)	5
Hard disk (desktop)	14
Hard disk (laptop)	4
USB-powered devices	2 (each)

---

[5]You can find a more complete power calculator for Mini-ITX machines at www.mini-box.com/site/mb/Power_MB.htm.

To calculate the cost of each device you need to know the cost per kilowatt hour that your utility company charges you, and plug it into the formula:

```
Total_cost = (Wattage_of_device × hours_used × kilowatt_hour_charge) ÷ 1000
```

To reduce consumption costs, you can do several small things for both the computer and the other home hardware connected to it.

First, switch it off. This applies primarily to consumer electronics such as monitors and TVs, whose power consumption in standby is almost as high as it is in normal mode, and it is sometimes said that 16 percent of your annual energy bill is spent on appliances in standby mode. Various products on the market detect standby mode either by monitoring the drop in power usage or by catching the IR signal to switch off the TV and consequently isolate all power to the device. In this mode it is, however, impossible to switch it back on automatically. You can manage this automatically using X10 or C-Bus. Remember that when switching the device back on, you might also need to send an IR signal if the appliance returns to a standby mode, instead of switching on fully.

Second, stop hard drives spinning. This reduces their consumption from 7W to around 1W, depending on device. You can achieve this with the hdparm tool by configuring it like this:

```
# /etc/hdparm.conf
/dev/sda {
  spindown_time = 60 # this means 5 minutes, since each spindown unit is 5 seconds
}
```

▓ **Note**   This is reported to work only when the BIOS supports AHCI. In all other cases SATA drives should be controlled with the sg3-utils package.

From a longevity point of view, however, hard disks should not be continually spun up and then down since the ball bearings will grind more and eventually wear out. Furthermore, the cost of getting them to spin back up is very high, so you really need to have kept them spun down for around 20 minutes to make the savings worthwhile.

Switch into standby, suspend to RAM, or hibernate to disk mode, each saving progressively more power than the previous one. The Advanced Power Management (APM) daemon and tools handle the process itself, while the sleepd daemon can be to used to trigger the APM tools automatically upon certain conditions, such as lack of activity or input.

Use alternative components. With the green lobby influencing most companies, you can buy more power-efficient devices than ever before. Better power supplies[6] can provide efficiencies in excess of 80 percent on moderate loads (90W), less powerful graphics cards use less power generally speaking (and often don't need fans), LCDs monitors are more efficient than CRTs, and the power usage in CPUs can vary wildly, so consider replacing them.

Unplug any unused devices, such as the CD drive used once for installation (but never again), USB units, and so on. This can be extended by using external hard disks throughout your system (with the exception of the boot device), which can be powered down via X10 after unmounting.

Make use of more solid-state discs and/or laptop hardware where possible. Both are intended to work from batteries and therefore have more suitable CPUs and hardware inside them. For the primary control server, these are perfectly adequate.

Use virtual machines (running on VMware, for example) instead of using a completely separate machine. This can offer real benefits when a particular device requires a specific version or operating system. The extra power used in processing the virtual is far behind that of a physical machine.

---

[6]The 80 Plus project, www.80plus.org, aims to promote manufacturers whose power supplies have a better than 80 percent efficiency rating. The average for a PSU is around 60 percent.

Reducing the load is something that should be considered in as many cases as possible because, although you might save only a watt, over the course of a year this can add up to a reasonable savings.

Server Coordination

Having multiple servers to control your house is fine. But if they're all switched on all the time, your electricity bill will increase disproportionately to the benefit gained. This also doesn't consider the case where the various machines can't communicate because the master server is offline.

Coordinating how to switch specific machines on and off to save power is an easy problem ... for a human. But it's incredibly difficult for a machine for automate! You would need to know what services are running on which machines, what dependencies exist on other hardware, and so on. This information would need to be synchronized among all machines in case one went offline (because of power outages or loss of network connectivity).

Consequently, it is better to not try or to do one of the following:

- Have human-designated time cycles for each machine

- Expect a larger than usual electricity bill

When running a separate media server to transcode streams to the MVPMC, for example, you will know that the machine needs to be on from 6 p.m. each weekday and all weekend, for example. If the machine is also in charge of recording TV programs, you will have write custom code to prevent it from switching off during one of those recordings.

The inverse timetable is true of a machine intended to be a download server, when you only want it to be leeching your bandwidth during the early hours of the morning when you're not likely to be web surfing or working from home.

Although it is possible for a machine to self-terminate (through the Linux command shutdown -h now), you can't generally force it to wake up at a specific time. Therefore, you will always need one machine (such as the lowest-power device you have) that remains on 24/7 to coordinate all the others.

Having a machine switch on automatically requires a technology called Wake on LAN (WOL). WOL is enabled on many machines (although sometimes defaulted to off in the BIOS) whereby the motherboard watches for a specially formatted network message containing a "magic packet" sent directly to the machine in question. Since there is no IP address for a machine that is powered down, the MAC address must always be used. (It's labeled as HWaddr from an ifconfig command.)

The command and package to initiate this magic is as follows:

```
etherwake 00:1d:33:a5:63:16
```

Note that this works only from a "soft" power down and needs power available to it, along with that of any routers between the sending machine and the target. That's an important point to remember during a power cut! Also, note that the Raspberry Pi doesn't have a soft power down option—it's without a on/off switch, so it's either on or off. However, it has such a low current draw that it isn't worth worrying about.

▓ **Note** Sometimes a password is required for a WOL command to be accepted. This is set in the BIOS of the particular machine and passed as an argument to etherwake.

Switching particular machines off is easier, because it's something most desktop users do every day, so I'll spend little time on it here. In its traditional invocations, you can initiate a shutdown with a single command, with a given delay from the issue of the command to the action with any console alert message you choose. You can also countermand any unenacted shutdown command with the -c flag.

All shutdown commands must be carried out by that machine's root user, and because root is disallowed from connecting to a machine through ssh by default, it is not always obvious how to shut down a remote machine.

The standard method is to use sudo, letting a nonprivileged user connect to the machine and then upgrading themselves to root temporarily to shut down the machine with the following:

```
sudo shutdown -h now
```

Although a password is generally required for sudo, this can be waived by amending the /etc/sudoers file with a line such as this:

```
steev localhost=NOPASSWD: /sbin/shutdown
```

This can be automated further by issuing the command from a script that relies on a little-used feature of ssh, namely, the ability to log in, execute a command, and then quit:

```
ssh steev@myhomemachine.homelinux.net 'sudo shutdown -h now'
```

Because the shutdown command was created at a time when all users worked on the console, the alert message is generally invisible to most house users, so you might like to create a shutdown script that uses speech synthesis or music to indicate that the server is being switched off. However, as reboots and shutdowns in Linux are rare and you're probably in the next room to your "users," this is less important.

Shutting down any Windows machines on your network may be more difficult, since the method for doing so is less well defined. A command such as the following:

```
net rpc shutdown -I 192.168.1.100 -U windows_username%their_password
```

can work in many instances but is dependent on firewalls, file-sharing options, and even the version of Windows.

Given these commands to start up and shut down most machines in your home, you can effectively coordinate them to ensure the best power usage scenarios for your needs using a simple crontab on your primary server.

UPS

An uninterruptable power supply (UPS) is an essential piece of kit for anyone relying on moderate- to high-cost technology. And because your house is now a high-cost peripheral to that high-cost technology, it becomes important part in your HA setup—not just to eliminate the effects of short-term power dropouts and blackouts but also to prevent the damage caused by surges.

Most UPS units work on the same principle; that is, a device looking like an oversize multigang power strip connects the mains and a battery together to provide consistent power to four or more sockets. In the cheaper and most commonly seen devices, the device monitors the mains supply and, if it fails or drops below a specified threshold, switches to the battery. The second type of UPS supplies the output from the battery at all times and uses the mains power to keep the battery charged. The shape of the output waveform varies too and is usually governed by the cost of the device. The output of the cheaper devices is usually a square wave, while more expensive ones have a sinusoidal wave form. This doesn't matter much for computers but can provide a difference when powering an audiophile record player, as mentioned in Chapter 3. Whenever a power drop is noticed, an alarm will sound and repeat the audible warning periodically. When the battery reaches a critically low level, the shutdown procedure will be initiated via the USB (or serial) cable so that the machine(s) connected to the UPS can close down safely. Each unit comes rated for a different VAs, indicating how much you can draw from it when it is disconnected from the mains. You will usually need a higher VA than the wattage. The required VA is the watts divided by the power factor of the connected device(s). The temporal duration of protection ranges from a few minutes to quarter of an hour, depending on what machines are connected to it and the tasks running on those machines. You can refer to Table 4-1 for a rough guide. For a buying, always get as high a power rating as possible.

■ **Note**   With most UPS units, the power sockets will be divided between those that are powered in the event of an outage and those that aren't. All sockets are generally protected against surges.

Given, say, four powered sockets, you have to decide what devices will use it. Naturally, your server should be a given. That's followed by the home's internal router or switch so that a "shutting down" message can be sent and processed by the other machines on a UPS. (This is for the computers benefit only, since any human will have noticed the lights going out and will instantly panic knowing they haven't hit the Save button on their application.) You may also want to keep the broadband router on the UPS also so that a warning message (via e-mail, for example) can be sent. This is usually a minor consideration, but if you work remotely with the machine, this will prompt you to ease up on any processor-heavy tasks so that the UPS can last for longer.

■ **Note**   When the UPS is first installed, test it with the circuit breaker but not by pulling the plug out, which can introduce a floating ground that is dangerous to electronic equipment.

The discussion of multiple servers reappears here, as it can be beneficial to have a low-power master server on the UPS, with the media-transcoding machine on its own UPS, to preserve the longevity of the main server and even finish recording that vital episode of *Doctor Who* you might have normally missed during the power cut!

If both servers are fairly high power and you have only one UPS, then it is usually worth consolidating both into one box to limit the power drain on the unit.

You might also consider keeping one powered socket for a monitor, perhaps connected to the second media server UPS unit. If you keep it turned off, it'll draw very little power from the UPS, but in the event of a problem, you are able to *see* the machine running through its shutdown procedure, and you can ensure that its closedown routine is working effectively. Without this, you will either have to trust the UPS software daemon is working or keep a laptop handy with a fully charged battery.

■ **Tip**   You can ensure your laptop is fully charged by using the crontab to switch on an X10 module for at least an hour every night.

Once the hardware UPS is in place, you then need a way to detect that the power has gone and so begin the shutdown procedure.

Most UPS units come with a USB cable (sometimes with a proprietary connector on one end, so don't lose it!) that allows a PC to query the state of the unit. Those that don't have one are not generally worth buying. Granted, they are cheaper, and your data is probably safe with the journaling filesystem you've already installed, but the extra cost and peace of mind knowing you'll get a clean shutdown is worth it.

■ **Note**   It is possible to mimic the shutdown functionality of a UPS by using `heyu` to monitor the power lines and, if it sees two (or more) lights going off at the same time, trigger a shutdown. But this method is liable to false positives and doesn't work during daylight hours.

Three primary packages are available to handle a UPS, all of which conflict if used together. They are `apcupsd`, `nut-hal-drivers`, and `nut`. I'll cover the latter because it is the most recent, flexible, and actively developed.

First, perform a traditional installation:

```
apt-get install nut
```

The setup procedure then involves creating four configuration files in your /etc/nut directory:

```
# /etc/nut/ups.conf
[apc]
    driver = usbhid-ups
    port = auto
```

This references the appropriate driver for your UPS unit,[7] which I have called apc here:

```
# /etc/nut/upsd.conf
ACL all 0.0.0.0/0
ACL localhost 127.0.0.1/32
ACCEPT localhost
REJECT all
```

This indicates that only the local machine should react to UPS messages, which eliminates hackers spoofing a UPS failure and causing your machine to switch off. Then set up a basic user that has access to daemon by doing this:

```
# /etc/nut/upsd.users
[local_mon]
    password = mypasswordhere
    allowfrom = localhost
    upsmon master
```

You can then configure the daemon by specifying its process commands:

```
# /etc/nut/upsmon.conf
MONITOR apc@localhost 1 local_mon mypasswordhere master
POWERDOWNFLAG /etc/killpower
SHUTDOWNCMD "/sbin/shutdown -h now"
```

You can set up multiple users if you will be monitoring the UPS from alternate machines, but it's not necessary, as you'll probably create a web page holding this information.

You can then fix the permissions for the files (as there's a password in there you'd probably rather the world didn't see):

```
sudo chown root:nut /etc/nut/*
sudo chmod 640 /etc/nut/*
```

and start the daemon running, like so:

```
upsdrvctl start
/etc/init.d/nut start
```

---

[7]The compatibility list is available at www.networkupstools.org/compat/stable.html.

This can be made to start at every boot by editing the /etc/default/nut file. You can then query the state of a given UPS and check that it's working by issuing the following command, where apc is the name given earlier:

```
upsc apc
```

The output is something like this:

```
battery.charge: 100
battery.charge.low: 10
battery.charge.warning: 50
battery.date: not set
battery.mfr.date: 2009/01/21
battery.runtime: 705
battery.runtime.low: 120
battery.type: PbAc
battery.voltage: 13.5
battery.voltage.nominal: 12.0
driver.name: usbhid-ups
driver.parameter.pollfreq: 30
driver.parameter.pollinterval: 2
driver.parameter.port: auto
driver.version: 2.2.2
driver.version.data: APC HID 0.92
driver.version.internal: 0.33
input.transfer.high: 266
input.transfer.low: 180
input.voltage: 242.0
input.voltage.nominal: 230
ups.beeper.status: enabled
ups.delay.shutdown: 20
ups.delay.start: 30
ups.firmware: 829.D2 .I
ups.firmware.aux: D2
ups.load: 49
ups.mfr: APC
ups.mfr.date: 2009/01/21
ups.model: Back-UPS ES 700
ups.productid: 0002
ups.serial: 5B0904T46000
ups.status: OL
ups.timer.reboot: 0
ups.timer.shutdown: -1
ups.vendorid: 051d
```

It is possible to have several UPS units controlled by a single server. This is usually beneficial because it allows your master server to handle all the system administration tasks, giving a single point of entry to the home network, which can be hardened as appropriate.

Having gotten the machine to shut down, you need a way of making it start up again once the power is back on full time. This becomes a hardware problem, and success is governed by whether there is an option in the BIOS to start up on power or similar. In the case of the NSLU2, you can physically hack the circuit board to perform the same task. It is also theoretically possible to hack the switch in a standard PC in a similar fashion, but it's not recommended.

The WOL trick covered earlier generally doesn't work across the Internet because it is a Wake on *LAN* feature. And even if your machine isn't behind a router or modem that filters out such packets, something else generally will be. If it's vital for your home machine to be powered for as long as possible and your machine cannot be made to boot when the power is connected, then you can employ an NSLU (hacked as shown in Chapter 2) as a bootstrap to issue WOL commands to your various server machines.

Backups

There are only two important things to say about backups:

- Do them.

- Test them.

Everything else is mere details.

The first detail is whether these should be held on-site, that is, at home, or off-site in a remote location, such as a colocated server or hired virtual machine. In an ideal world, you would adopt both. Keeping them off-site helps minimize loss caused by local problems, while on-site backups are useful for data that you cannot possibly store elsewhere, such as configuration scripts and network plans that you'd need to rebuild the HA system should there be major failure.

The next detail is what data actually *needs* to be backed up. Again, in an ideal world, that would include everything on every machine in the house. In reality, you have to consider the cost of replacing the data and the time necessary to perform the backup. This usually boils down to anything that you've personally created, such as the following:

- Photographs

- Letters

- Program code

- Artwork

- Digital video

- Music

Each member of the family will have their own list that they will be responsible for. You, as the HA administrator, will also want to back up the server configurations.

From here you can decide on the technology needed to carry out this task. Programmers will already be aware of source control tools, such as Subversion (`http://subversion.tigris.org/`) or Git (`http://www.git-scm.org`), and will be advocating their use. For the uninitiated, these tools don't just keep a copy of the latest version; they keep data to recreate copies of *all* the versions you've ever created, allowing you to go back in time to see what you wrote last week and why that does (or doesn't) work! For the most part, it's a good choice for code and system configurations because, as a developer, you have the mind-set necessary to perform the necessary update-merge-commit cycle at every juncture. However, with some coaxing, most family members will become au fait with it. Accessing the files requires a Subversion client, and there are several to choose from (such as TortoiseSVN or SmartSVN) that also have versions for Windows, eliminating that support headache. This also gives family members the ability to access their files from outside the home with no extra effort or software. On the downside, however, you will have to educate the family that word processing documents are usually stored in a binary format and, as such, are next-to-impossible to merge together if they change the same file at home and at school. Nor is it particularly efficient to use source control for large files that change often, such as raw Adobe Photoshop images.

■ **Note** Subversion stores its own work files inside the current directory, meaning they will each be littered with .svn folders. This is only a mild nuisance for end users but can cause bigger problems when they appear in system configuration folders such as /etc.

To make a direct copy of one set of files from one directory to another, you can probably use cp at the end of each day. However, this will wastefully copy files that haven't changed, and so rsync was born. rsync is a very old copy and backup program but is still a venerable workhorse. I make backups of my code directory, for example, with this single line:

```
rsync -a code steev@remote-backup-host.com:~/backup/daily
```

I recover them (for testing[8]) with this:

```
rsync -a steev@remote-backup-host.com:~/backup/daily code
```

The options here perform a recursive update, while maintaining all symlinks, permissions, and user settings and is the most typical in home situations. The manual pages detail other possibilities.

rsync does have two problems, however. The first is that it's available primarily for Unix-oriented platforms. Versions are available for Windows (such as DeltaCopy and the version with Cygwin), but they take a little while to set up and can be tricky.

The second issue is that it requires a password to be interactively given in order to log in to the remote site. This is a nuisance and prevents any kind of automatic backup. For a remote site to allow a user to connect without a password, they must first establish an alternative form of trust—in this case, the exchange of public keys. To copy from machine A to machine B, B must have a copy of A's public key. To copy from machine B to machine A, A must have a copy of B's public key. In our case, machine A is at home with our files, while B is a remote machine for backup.

So, our home machine must generate a key for the user who'll be doing the copying.

```
ssh-keygen -t rsa
```

which by default can be found in ~/.ssh/id_rsa.pub. This is then copied to the remote machine (perhaps using a password-directed rsync) and appended to the list of authorized keys that the remote user will accept:

```
cat id_rsa.pub >> ~/.ssh/authorized_keys
```

Once this is done, you should be able to rsync without a password:

```
rsync -a --bwlimit=100 steev@remote-backup-host.com:~/backup/daily code
```

Note that this limits the bandwidth (with the bwlimit argument) to 100 kilobytes per second so that other applications can make use of the Internet, since rsync and ssh are rather greedy when teamed up together.

One potential administration problem that can exist here is for the home user to be refused a connection because the address from which they're connecting does not match the one used in the key. This can happen when the hostname is something simply like linuxbox1 but appears to the remote machine as netpc-london-isproute-isp.com or something equally unhelpful. The target machine, by comparison, will usually have a fixed name because it must be addressable from the outside world. Because the home machine name might change (at the whim of the ISP), the easiest solution is to reverse all the instructions given here! That is, use the remote server to connect *to* the

---

[8]All backups are useless unless they're tested, remember!

home server, generate a key for the *remote* server only, and reverse the arguments to the rsync command so that the remote server pulls the data from the home machine in order to perform the backup. It is curious to note that it is the direction of the connection that requires the authentication, not the direction of the copy process.

■ **Note**   The root user cannot, by default, connect through ssh. Although it is possible to override this, it is not recommended, so create a new user, create the ssh key for them, and use their crontab to initiate the daily backup.

Although this solves the problems for Linux and MacOS users, there still needs to be a solution for Windows. If you can afford the time, preparing rsync on Windows can be worthwhile. Alternatively, you might want to instill best practices into the family by introducing a manual backup solution that requires them to do *something* to back up their work. This is one area in which Subversion scores higher, because the workflow encourages this automatically. What can be done instead is to create a writable SMB shared area on the network that is accessible to everyone, and it is their responsibility to add their files to it every night before bed. You can then use rsync to back up this network folder remotely. There are several free and shareware utilities for Windows that provide the copy-based backup necessary for the first step.

Of course, everything I've said assumes that you're storing your data at home. In most cases that will be true, but it is now easier than ever to buy space on a remote server (through Amazon's S3, for example, with a virtual machine), which means you never need to back up. Of course, backups are still being done (by the automated tools and support staff at the server provider), but they're transparent to you.[9]

In the cases of external storage, you would only want to store data that was fairly small in size since streaming a full movie from a remote server would be unwatchable, and having to wait until it had downloaded would be equally annoying and defeat the purpose. These situations are beneficial in some cases because they mean no personal data is ever stored at home. So if a burglar steals your laptop, you haven't lost the novel you've been working on.

Some people prefer to protect their private data in public, by using services such as Dropbox.com, Flickr, Google Docs, Google Drive (perhaps through the Grive client), and YouTube. The situation is the same as earlier with the exception that, being free services, there are fewer warranties about loss of data. Indeed, Google Mail has a personal storage limit of just over 10GB, which allows you to back up your data by saving them as attachments in your mail account! Or by using gmailfs.

There is also the possibility of backing up the physical items in your home, namely, your media. Although the importance in CDs and DVDs is in the packaging, it is possible to save the contents by ripping them (as we covered in Chapter 3) onto external hard disks and placing the drives themselves in storage, either held with friends, with family, or in a professional safe. You could probably arrange a pairing scheme with suitably technical friends who will store your collection of discs in return for you keeping theirs. The same pairing idea works if you both rsync your media to each other during quiet periods of network traffic, such as during the night, for example.

Hiding Your Home

Having a home connected to the Internet provides a way of consuming your media when away from home, remotely configuring your machines, and checking that you did indeed turn the lights off. It also provides great bragging rights! However, having it connected in this is naturally a concern for some. Even with the technical security issues I'll be covering in Chapter 5, there's some extra scope for hiding your automated home in much the same way as you'd put a blanket over the valuables in the car when you park it.

One way is to set up two domain names for your home machine. The first should be considered the public site, which provides a smoke screen, and may contain a web site and blog featuring your cat! By being the default web site, this will be used whenever the IP address is used alone. (I'll cover the method when discussing virtual hosts in

---

[9]As a paranoid geek, I would personally make my own backups periodically, in addition to those made by someone else.

Chapter 5.) You can then additionally set up a second domain with access to your home automation web pages. You will still secure these pages, naturally, but this is a good first step.

Although registering domain names is easy enough, it is not necessarily the best option when dealing with home machines, because your IP might change when a DHCP lease is not renewed at the whim of the ISP, and you'd have to wait another 24 hours for the DNS information to repropagate through the various DNS servers. Although this is unlikely, even if you decide to power down the server every night, better solutions are available by using dynamic DNS. The method assigns an arbitrary subdomain, from a known primary domain, to a given IP. Because subdomains do not need to be propagated by DNS before they can be used, they have a more immediate effect and can be registered for very little money—in most cases, zero.

One such service is available from dyndns.org. After registering (also free!), you can create your own subdomain and point it to your home server. This subdomain can extend from one of several primary domains, such as homelinux.net, mine.nu, or dnsalias.com. The T&C requires that you update this record periodically to ensure it's still active, but this can be done automatically with appropriate routers or through a package such as ddclient. This should be run periodically, either in daemon mode or from crontab, to keep their records up to date. The configuration simply requires your login credentials for DynDNS and the subdomain names you want to update.

```
# /etc/ddclient.conf

daemon=600
use=web, web=checkip.dyndns.com/, web-skip='IP Address'
login=your-username
password=your-password
protocol=dyndns2
server=members.dyndns.org
my.homelinux.net
```

Because this is a DNS record, only the name is registered. It's still up to you to support the services. But this is what you want, because it allows you to run your own servers for e-mail, the Web, SSH, and so on.

You can hide behind more curtains by providing access only through an external proxy—a proxy the existence and login of which is known only to you. The first step is to prepare the hosts.allow file with the following:

```
sshd: LOCAL myhidden.privateserver.com
```

and add the paranoid inverse to hosts.deny:

```
sshd: ALL
```

As you can guess, when used in combination, this limits all SSH connections to those originating from the local (192.168.x.x) network and those on an external server that might be a colocated server, work machine, or shell account.

■ **Note** These rules can apply to all protocols, not just SSH, by changing sshd to ALL in the previous examples.

This approach is not without risk, however, because should your server become inaccessible for any reason, you will be able to connect to it (and therefore solve the problem) only from the specified machines, which might be difficult if you are on vacation.

■ **Note** If your private server supports multiple domains, the name that is specified here to sshd must be the canonical one.

You can extend this idea by controlling your house through an alternate protocol, such as Simple Object Access Protocol (SOAP), from a remote server, although this does open up two potential points of attack.

Adding to Your Home

The simplest way to incorporate automation into your home is through wireless—or at the least, automation that uses no *new* wiring. This second approach covers a surprisingly large amount of ground, including networking through WiFi and Ethernet over Power, appliance control (with X10 over the existing power cables), and media distribution (with TV senders.)

But even then, with so many devices occupying the 2.4GHz range, there will be a limit to what is possible and how far it can be expanded. So, naturally, a wired approach will begin to win favor, which will require some drilling of holes and running of cables.

In all the advice that follows, remember that you must always plan ahead, thinking about what each room will have in it, what it could have in it next year, and how it will be used. Running cables is a time-consuming process and not something that wants to be repeated, so it's better to lay too many and have unused sockets than it is to run out when you attempt to plug in a new gadget and find that you first need to buy an expanded unit. Cable is, after all, comparatively cheap when compared to the cost of installation or maintenance. Having two cables is a also useful redundancy measure in all the following examples, if you have the space to include them.

General Considerations

Except in very esoteric cases, Node0 will always be at the center of your HA installation. Even if it is not physically close to the center of the house, all cables should be run into it. This is known as a *star configuration*.

The process of running cables from one location to another is known as *pulling cables*, since it involves the act of pulling them through one set of holes to another. When you're adding to an existing home, you will generally need to drill holes in the ceilings and pull cables down through wall-mounted trunking, as shown in Figure 4-1. With self-builds, you may have the opportunity to place the cables inside the walls themselves, making them invisible except for the wall plate beside the skirting board. Of course, if you're doing some major redecorating, then you might decide it's worth removing the wall and replastering to make the cabling invisible.

Figure 4-1. *Trunking to hide the cables and a volute to (try to) hide the join*

Whichever approach you take, it's best to pull all the cables at the same time: audio, Cat5, and coaxial. If necessary, buy four drums of network cable so you can pull multiple Cat5 cables through at the same time. This will save a lot of effort.

■ **Note** If you are planning a projector in any room, then you will generally need to run cables within the ceiling itself, which involves lifting the floorboards of the room above. When this is likely, do it earlier because you won't want to do it later and might live without a projector; plus, you can take the opportunity to lay a lot more cables in the same space than you would normally.

Remember that all cables have different flexibilities, so when pulling them, it is best to be as careful as possible, as if they were all fragile. Cat5 cables, as a guide, are generally stiffer than stereo AV, so try not to bend or kink the cable as you pull it through, and do so in a slow methodical manner. Don't jerk the cable, because this causes friction on the sheath. You might find it beneficial to use a length of drainpipe, or exposed trunking, to provide a channel in which cables can move and sit. The use of drainpipe also ensures there are as few corners as possible, with sharp corners being the worst offenders.

There is no trick to the act of pulling cables, although doing so with a partner will more than halve the time taken. You should gather them in bunches and tie the ends together with string that is twice as long as the cables. Tie the cable ends to the string middle, which allows you to pull them through en masse. You will then be left with half the string running alongside the cable and both ends of string visible. (One end of the run will have half the string, and the other will have a small amount, but that's OK.) With this method, you can leave the string in place and tie it to new cables for pulling, should you need to add new cables.

■ **Note** You will always need to add new cables.

Next I have two words about documentation—do some! It is best to label everything: cables, conduits, plugs, sockets, everything. This is also true of your living room and TV installations because your VCR, PVR, DVD, and TV will generally all sport identical black plugs! Use several bands of colored tape at each end to distinguish them, such as red-red-green-blue. (Begin labeling using the color nearest the cable end.) You should document these color codes as you go and reference them by taking photographs of the setup depicting the cables, connections, and wiring inside each box. Although they do not make for very interesting viewing, they will become essential if you ever need to change or repair anything.

Wired Network

Every room in the house should have at least two Cat5 cables running to it, directly from Node0. The living room should have at least four, as should the master bedroom. If you're lucky enough to have a separate TV room, then so should this. You should also have two Cat5 in the attic or loft if possible because this provides a very secure location for your personal storage devices. If you have enough space between the wall joists and the patience, running two Cat5 cables to every light switch is also a good piece of planning for the future. Determining the number of necessary sockets is usually calculated by doubling the number you think you need. And then doubling it again! In short, you can never have too many ports.

■ **Note**   Buy (or borrow) an IDC tool to bed down the Cat5 cables into their sockets. It will ease the process and, with so many sockets to do, pay for itself in time.

Having dual sockets isn't just for redundancy, as mentioned earlier, but for many other practicalities such as debugging, since any unit plugged into Cat5 may (will?!) go wrong at some point in the future. The easiest way to solve this is to sit down next to the device in question with a laptop to diagnose the problem. Having a second Cat5 socket makes this easier, because you're not reliant on wireless, and it lets you double-check the network socket at the same time.

Cat5 should also be wired in abundance because it can usefully be applied to non-networking problems. That is, the cable can be reused to provide power with a Power over Ethernet system, supply HDMI signals,[10] or provide electricity to low-powered wall units such as tablet machines. This is why I suggested Cat5 to the light switches earlier, because you can replace the old switches with high-tech touch panels with significantly more configuration possibilities. There is also the possibility of upgrading your X10 modules to C-Bus, if that's the route you want to take, using Cat5 cables.

In addition to power, Cat5 sockets can be fitted with cheap adapters to make them compatible with ISDN or standard landline telephones, should you want to extend your standard phones in this way.

If you can see the potential for a lot of Cat5 reappropriation, then it is worthwhile to upgrade from two ports to four ports in each room. In this way, you can keep two of them as traditional network sockets, which can always be extended further by adding a network switch to one of them, and give the other two alternate uses such as phones or power.

The location for the Cat5 sockets will often be governed by the wall into which you're placing them. This is usually near the corners, which is good aesthetically speaking if you're using external wall trunking. It's also practical since you'll want to place them close to the power sockets in each room so that devices using both sockets can run shorter (and therefore, tidier) cables. These devices typically include media head units, printers, laptops, and touchscreens.

■ **Note**   Keep a reasonable distance between the network cable and power cable to minimize electrical noise. This is naturally true of any type of data cable.

---

[10]You with need two cables for this, with Cat6 being recommended over Cat5 because HDMI is very picky about the timing of its signals.

If you read the hardware catalogs, you will see two types of Cat5 cable listed: solid core and stranded, with the solid cores being used for in-wall installations and the stranded variety being used for patch cables, as it's more flexible. In reality, however, making your own patch cables is rarely done because they're so cheap and more trouble than they're worth.

■ **Note**   Pull the longest cable runs first from the drum. What's left will suffice for shorter runs between machines and routers.

Once the cables are laid, you should terminate on each end with a socket, such as the one shown in Figure 4-2.

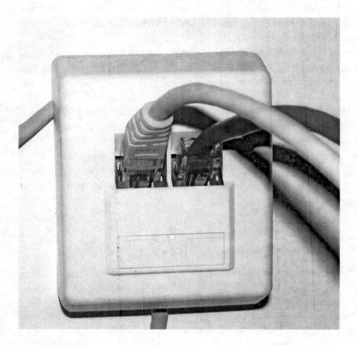

Figure 4-2. *A typical network point. I needed to make a separate hole in this one to eliminate a sharp cable bend*

You can then use patch cables to connect from the socket to the device. (Connecting an in-wall cable directly to a plug is asking for trouble, as it's likely to move and be pulled more often, which can break the plug connection at the other end.)

In my installation, the cables running from each socket are color-coded as follows:

- *Blue*: Any cable that goes from a wall socket to a switch or router

- *Gray*: For connecting devices—computers, media units, and so on—in the local area

- *Red*: Temporary devices, such as laptops

You might decide on a different color scheme, but the idea still stands because it lets you know whether the cable can be safely removed if you need to rewire or borrow a cable.

Wireless Points

Wireless is an addition to a wired network, not a replacement for it, so the WiFi routers and repeaters should exist to provide access primarily in those places where a wired network isn't already available. This often includes the kitchen, porch, and shed. Additionally, having wireless access in the main living spaces makes it easier to move around when the communal areas get too busy or noisy to work in. Consequently, placing an access point in rooms at the back of the house may be preferable. It doesn't need to be located in Node0, because it is wireless; therefore, provided it is connected to the wired network at some point, you will be fine. As noted earlier, there will be some instances when Node0 cannot physically provide WiFi coverage to the necessary areas of the house.

The position of the access point, however, is not an obvious choice since its range is affected by interference and obstructions, as well as distance. And these can only be determined empirically. Begin by placing the access point near the ceiling in a central part of the house, because this will give the best "line-of-sight" connection to most of the building, and then test the signal strength. You can buy specific devices for this, but unless you can borrow one, it's cheaper and no more difficult to walk around the house with a laptop.

WiFi signals are lost by two methods, absorption and reflection, and although walls cannot be avoided in a home, partition walls have less absorption effects than structural ones made of brick. Shiny surfaces, including glass, mirrors, and metal should also be avoided because the reflection of the signal introduces more internal protocol collisions and therefore less bandwidth and more dropped connections.

I've mentioned some of the devices operating in the WiFi 2.4GHz range, such as TV senders, cordless phones, microwave ovens, and baby monitors, which can also create interference, but you should not forget that other electrical devices, such as motors, fan heaters, and fluorescent lighting, can also have a negative affect.

Instead of WiFi, you can achieve pseudowireless connectivity by using Ethernet over Power to limit these problems. There are several EoP devices on the market (such as the MicroLink dLAN) where each unit plugs into both the wall socket and a networked device. Since this uses the same idea as X10, whereby a signal is hidden on the mains supply, it is susceptible to the same noise and interference.

Audio Cabling

Chapter 3 covered the idea of remote processing, whereby the music is decoded on a PC and the resultant signal is fed over standard audio cables to other speakers or amplifiers. The process of adding this wiring is fairly simple, since the cables are fewer in number, thinner, and more flexible than Cat5, which requires smaller holes and less mounting at each end. A standard stereo pair consists of only four wires, with two connectors at each end for left and right. You can use any connector you prefer, but phono sockets are good enough quality, easy to mount, and cheap.

The face gang plates for AV are more expensive than you'd expect, especially when compared to the cost of the (more complex) Cat5 sockets, but they usually come with extra sockets for SVGA monitors and composite video. With a drill, however, you can build your own using a standard blank facing plate, as shown in Figure 4-3.

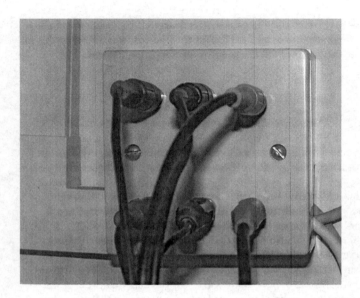

Figure 4-3. *An AV connection for stereo and composite video. The top row sends the local AV signal upstairs, and the bottom row receives an AV signal to downstairs. Note the trunking on the left and the exit for network cables on the right, which is simply passed through from the trunking*

The type and quality of the audio cable are an important decision, although not as important as audiophiles would make you believe! These cables are likely to be several meters long and used with some fairly standard connectors, so any cable greater than 42 strand is usually wasted. In fact, for some units, such as those placed in the kitchen, the extra ambient noise in the environment will render any critical listening impossible. In these cases, you could do as well with simple bell wire. In all cases, it's worth getting shielded stereo cable since it is bound into pairs, with a mark on one of them, making it obvious at each end which cable is intended to be ground.

The other side of audio cabling is the connection of a passive speaker distribution system, where the output to one set of speakers is routed to several others, without additional amplifiers. The same rules apply as stated earlier. You can also reuse the color-coding idea of network cables and use one color for powered cables (which enter and leave the amplifier) and a different one that distributes the signal to other speakers. You can see this in Figure 4-4, where you'll also note the black line on the white cable, indicating ground.

Figure 4-4. *The speaker distribution bay. This model also support push-button switches to turn each speaker pair on or off (not shown)*

If you can ensure that the cables won't move much, you can take the cables directly from the speaker switch box into the wall and along to the speaker, without using separate connectors as I did for the phonos. You would do this for better fidelity, which you can improve by soldering the cable directly to the speaker terminals themselves.

Other Access Points?

With Cat5 being such a ubiquitous method of cabling, there are fewer demands on the range of cabling that there once was. But they're still worth considering.

Telephones, for example, can make use of Cat5 sockets with an inexpensive adapter, so there is no need to wire for them explicitly, particularly with the increased uptake of mobile and VoIP, so add phone-only sockets only if you think you'll need them.

Infrared signals can be sent over wireless (but this adds to the already overcrowded spectrum) and through cables with IR distribution amplifiers (necessary to stop the already weak signal from dissipating further). But it is generally better sent over Cat5, using gateway devices like the Keene IR Anywhere, from Chapter 1.

Depending on the scale of you CCTV installation, you might also need to run separate cables for each camera back to the camera switching device. You can find information about these in Chapter 1.

Power is always an issue in HA installations, because there's never enough where you need it. Unless you are able to self-build, you won't have a choice as to where the sockets are or how many you have. You can always cheat the issue by converting any existing sockets into multigang units or by adding a spur from an upstairs light to provide a couple of sockets in the loft. This not only gives you the opportunity of adding a small secure filesystem in the loft, but it means you can use the space to store X10 DIN Rail devices where they are out of the way and don't add the heat in Node0 itself.

■ **Note**   Don't pack DIN rails too closely to each other because the heat can induce problems in operation. The recommended minimum separation is 20mm.

Additional power conduits are also useful for lighting driveways and powering electric garage doors. In the former case, you need only a low-power (around 12v) supply, which can also be used for water fountains, flood lights, outdoor Christmas trees, cameras, and PIRs. They can also help power sensors, such as the VAL-1 vehicle alerts that indicate when a car is approaching the garage or driveway. You can even install two to correctly determine the direction of travel, as we suggested for the Arduino door mat in Chapter 2.

■ **Note**   If your electric garage doors take ten seconds to open, for example, but your sensor is only in range when you're five seconds away from the door, you will need to employ a custom RF gateway circuit to trigger the door earlier.

There are also the high-powered devices, such as the garage doors, and mains sockets in a shed or garage for power tools. These are generally coated in rubber for isolation against the elements. In all cases, consult an electrician and the laws of your country before installing electrical equipment outside!

■ **Note**   You could also use the driveway sensors to switch on the porch light, ready for your arrival.

Conclusion

There is clearly more to a home network installation than a few cables and a network card. By carefully considering all the possible functions of the home ahead of time, you can ensure you run enough cables, of the right type, to each room in the house. Even then, you might still run out. Also, by aggregating as much of the technology in one place as possible, you create a central hub called Node0. This physical proximity allows you to place IR transmitters and control cables between devices and ensure that everything can be controlled from a single area. Again, plan the purpose and features of this area so that everything fits in and (importantly) has a method to access the machine's panels, plugs, sockets, and power.

CHAPTER 5

■ ■ ■

Communication: Humans Talk. Computers Talk

It is often said that language is the invention that makes all others possible. Within the world of technology, language is the protocol that makes all others live. Writing software for a stand-alone machine is all very nice, but when it manages to interface with the outside world, interface with another program across a network, or control an external piece of hardware, it seems so much more satisfying. Controlling even the simplest of robots with a computer is infinitely more impressive to the layperson (and many geeks!) than the demonstration of an optimized implementation of marching cubes.[1]

I have already covered a number of devices in Chapter 1 that are able to talk with external hardware, and I'll now discuss human-computer communication and demonstrate how we can interact with one machine or piece of software and have it control another one somewhere else. This includes the use of e-mail, SMS, and web pages. However, the onset of new technology is relentless, and with devices such as the iPhone offering a broadband[2] experience, the typical role of a mobile phone (as a device for voice calls, SMS, or e-mail) is very much reduced.

Why Comms?

There are four methods of communication within the technology arena:

- Computer-to-computer

- Human-to-human

- Computer-to-human

- Human-to-computer

These are all important to us for different reasons. The first was covered in Chapter 1 and allows devices to be controlled automatically according to some time- or logic-based programming.

Human-to-human communications are those that take place every day but can now be facilitated by technology. Before the advent of the telephone, our only form of real-time communication was face-to-face. Now we have e-mail, Internet relay chat (IRC), instant messaging (IM), and SMS to perform the same task. All remove the "face" element.

We have also streamlined our existing communication mediums. Telephones, which were once low quality and hardwired to a physical location, are now mobile. Through Voice over IP (VoIP) technology, you can make use of

---

[1] The marching cubes algorithm represents a method of extracting a polygonal mesh from voxel space and was a feature of the 1987 SIGGRAPH conference.
[2] Broadband in its truest sense of "always on" and with no connection to its actual transfer speed. However, iPhone users can enable tethering and use the mobile broadband share dock when at home to make use of their local WiFi router.

the (near) free cost of the Internet to provide financial savings and, when combined with mobile technology, facilitate the amusing situation in which using a mobile phone is used to order pizza online through a web page!

When we talk of computer-to-human communication, we are looking at reports and information about the house that the computer sends to us, as appropriate. In the simplest of cases, this might be the daily wakeup call or an e-mail containing the day's TV schedule. In more complex scenarios, it could be a full report of the computers in the house and how they are performing.[3]

And, finally, human-to-computer communication takes place most often and involves us telling the machine what we want to do via e-mail, SMS, or a web page. To be a truly smart and automated house, this list would include haptic interfaces. We don't need to issue an explicit command to tell the computer what to do; it knows what to do by studying the environment. For example, the computer would know to switch on the lights when the front door has been opened; shortly afterward, the inside doormat sensor will close because it had realized that someone is entering the house. You've already built similar haptic functionality in Chapter 2, so I'll cover explicit communications in this chapter.

IP Telephony

IP telephony or VoIP communications are commonplace and an expected feature of any smart home. For most, however, a VoIP installation will be a private one, existing only on personal laptops or desktop machines as a result of the personal nature of phone communication. But it can be used in combination with voice recognition to provide an intriguing (albeit error-prone) means of data input and a way to add an internal home intercom system.

Skype

In the same way that *Hoover* has become synonymous with vacuum cleaner and *Google* now is a verb meaning to search, *Skype* is the byword for VoIP. Begun in 2003 and released as freeware, Skype has provided clients for Linux, Mac, and Windows, each with varying degrees of functionality and with all versions allowing you to make free calls to other Skype users and subsidized voice calls to mobile numbers and landlines, like any standard phone. Most allow you to log in with the same account from several different locations, meaning that you can install Skype onto each terminal in the house with the same house-oriented phone number so that you can send and receive calls from any room in the house. With additional hardware, you can adopt a hands-free approach, moving between rooms during the conversation, such as to check on dinner, for example, returning you to the roaming possibilities that have existed since the introduction of cordless phones in the 1980s!

Asterisk

Asterisk is another software-based phone solution that also includes support for VoIP, mobile, and landline calls. Its benefit to us is that it is free software in the truest sense of the word and can support many protocols, because it is a full private branch exchange (PBX) and can support highly configurable call forwarding, voice mail, conferencing, and phone menus (so you can implement your own "Press 1 to turn your lights on" system!). As with Skype, you will need a service-providing gateway to connect the IP-based protocols to the phone network in general. This is a paid-for service and can be bought from many places, including Skype itself with its own Skype-to-Asterisk module. As an alternative, FXO interfaces are available which let you interface SIP to PSTN. You'll still have to buy the FXO interface (for around $15), but you won't need to purchase from anyone other than your phone provider.

The simplest way to install the mass of code that is Asterisk is currently through FreePBX, but even that is only worth the time if you have a large enough house to make shouting an impossibility or you're keen users of the phone, as you can get more solid communication through e-mail or the web (now both available on most phones) or SMS.

---

[3] If you have several machines, software such as Nagios can automatically monitor services and applications, sending messages and updating web pages on failure.

E-mail

E-mail is now the lifeblood of personal and professional life the world over. It is very easy to send and receive messages from anyone at any time—too easy, in fact, as the state of most spam folders will testify! But it is here to stay, so we can add e-mail to the list of protocols our house will support, allowing us to send messages to our video, light switches, or TV, and for our house to send messages back.

Preparing E-mail in Linux

The travel path of an e-mail is the same everywhere and consists of three parts:

- *Mail transfer agent (MTA)*: The MTA is also known as the *e-mail server* and is the software that communicates with other MTAs over the Simple Mail Transfer Protocol (SMTP) to route the e-mail messages it receives to the correct recipient, noting the destination address and passing it to the server on that machine.

- *Mail retrieval*: This is the method by which e-mail is transferred from the mail server and onto the client. The transfer of this data occurs through either Post Office Protocol (POP) or Internet Message Access Protocol (IMAP). In our case, these will be on the same machine because we'll run our own MTA, but they needn't be as we could also download our Google Mail to our local machine for processing, as I'll cover in Chapter 6.

- *Mail user agent (MUA)*: This is the client software used to actually read the e-mail as well as send it. This includes large GUI applications such as Thunderbird, web mail solutions such as AtMail, and smaller console-based ones such as Mutt.

Although corporate drones will bleat incessantly about the benefits of Exchange as an MTA (http://en.wikipedia.org/wiki/Comparison_of_mail_servers), you have four primary e-mail servers to choose from and many more MUAs than simply Outlook. Furthermore, because of the design of Linux (and Unix-like systems in general), you can automatically process incoming mail with great flexibility and issue noninteractive commands to send replies.

Each MTA has benefits and features the others don't. The big four—Exim, qmail, Postfix, and Sendmail—each has its own advocates and detractors. I personally use Exim because it has a guided install and "just worked" afterward. For alternate opinions, there is a wiki page covering the latest versions of these packages, along with some commercial offerings. I'll wait here while you install one of them.

Sending E-mail

After installing the server and testing it by sending yourself (and a second user) an e-mail or two, you can begin the short task of writing an automatic send script. This is the easiest thing to do with Linux and involves the `mail` command, which sends e-mail with any number of additional headers and settings. Here, you need only an abstraction script such as the following:

```
#!/bin/bash

SUBJECT=$1; shift
TOADDR=$1; shift
MSG=$*

echo "$MSG" | mail -s "$SUBJECT" "$TOADDR"
```

which can be called with this:

```
xmitemail "Hello" "steev@workaddress.com" "I bet you didn't think this would work!"
```

This command will send the simplistic e-mail shown and can be either invoked by typing it on the command line triggering it from a daily crontab or run as a consequence of some other household event. For example, someone coming through the front door (using the Arduino door mat from Chapter 2) could issue such as e-mail, or it could be sent as a warning when one of the hard disks get too full.

I have subverted the original interface to `mail` here, because it will be more usual for users to invoke the command in the manner shown earlier. However, there will be times when you want to revert to the original usage of `mail` by allowing the script to accept any input from STDIN. This requires the three-line replacement shown here to usurp MSG:

```
if [ $# -eq 0 ]; then
  while  read LINE ; do
    MSG="$MSG""^M""$LINE"
  done
else
  MSG=$*
fi
```

Note the ^M character, which is entered into editors like `vi` with Ctrl+V followed by Ctrl+M. Now the message can now be fed in from a file, like this:

```
cat filename | xmitemail "Here's the file" "steev@myworkaddress.com"
```

In Chapter 7, you'll learn how to extend this functionality to support a basic address book and multiple receivers.

Autoprocessing E-mails

Accepting e-mails on behalf of a program, instead of a human user, can be summed up in one word: Procmail.[4] Procmail was a project begun in 1990 by Stephen R. van den Berg to control the delivery of e-mail messages, and although some consider it a dead project, this makes it a stable project and one that's unlikely to break or introduce new complications any time soon!

Procmail is triggered by the e-mail server (an MTA, such as Exim) by passing each message for further processing to each of a series of *recipes*. If none of these recipes lays claim to the message, it is delivered as normal.

I'll begin by creating a simple example whereby you can e-mail your bedroom light switch. So, create a user with the following, and fill in all the necessary user details:

```
adduser bedroom
```

Then, create a `.procmailrc` file (note the dot!) in their home directory, and add the following recipe code:

```
:0
* ^From steev
* ^Subject: light on
|heyu turn bedroom_light on
```

---

[4] In the interests of objectiveness, I'll also admit that `maildrop` and `dovecat` exist and perform similar tasks.

This requires that the sender is steev[5] and that the subject is "light on" before it runs the heyu command to control the light. Both conditions must be met. You can, and should, extend these arguments to include the full e-mail address (to prevent any steev from having control over the light) and perhaps a regular expression to make the subject line case insensitive. But before we continue, I'll break down those elements.

Each recipe consists of three parts:

- *Mode*: This is generally :0 but can also include instructions for locking (so that the recipe cannot be run multiple times simultaneously) by appending another colon, with the name of a lock file (for example, :0:mylock).

- *Conditions*: Zero or more lines (beginning with an asterisk) indicating how the e-mail must appear for processing to occur. This also supports regular expressions. Because *every* condition must be satisfied in an AND logical fashion, you can accept all mail by not including any condition lines.

- *Action*: The final line indicates whether the message should be forwarded to another e-mail account (with ! forwarded@othermail.com), passed to a script or program (| command arguments), or merely copied to a file (the name of the file, without prefix characters). To support multiple actions, you will need to perform some heavy magic (involving multiple recipes, :0c modes, or branch handling; see http://partmaps.org/era/procmail/mini-faq.html#recipe-block for more information).

Each recipe is evaluated in order until it finds one that fulfills all conditions, at which point it stops. You can verify the input to Procmail by using the formail tool as part of the action in a catchall recipe:

```
:0
|formail >> ~steev/procmail-log
```

You can review this in real time by opening a separate terminal window, typing the following, and watching the mail messages appear:

```
tail -f ~steev/procmail-log
```

You can also use this technique when debugging Procmail-invoked scripts by taking a copy of a sent e-mail and redirecting it to the script's input. You can also debug Procmail scripts by using the LOGFILE directive. Here's an example:

```
LOGFILE=$HOME/procmail.logfile
```

The .procmailrc script itself also has some of the functionality of a standard bash script, so you can also prepare the PATH variables for the commands and preprocess the mail to extract the subject line, like this:

```
PATH=/usr/bin:/usr/local/bin:/usr/local/minerva/bin
SUBJECT=`formail -zxSubject:`
```

■ **Note** Some installations also require you to create a .forward file containing the single line "|/usr/bin/procmail" (with quotes) in order to trigger Procmail. This is when Procmail is not your local mail delivery agent.

---

[5] Obviously, adapt this to the e-mail address you will be using to test.

You could now create a separate recipe for switching the light off again, and it would be as simple as you'd expect. However, for improved flexibility, I'll show how to run a separate script that looks also at the body of the e-mail and processes the message as a whole so that you can include commands to dim or raise the light level. Begin by passing the subject as an argument[6] and e-mail content (header and body) into STDIN, which is launched from a new recipe:

```
:0
* ^From - steev.*
* ^Subject: light
|~steev/lightcontrol $SUBJECT
```

You then use the `lightcontrol` script to concatenate the body into one long string, separated by spaces, instead of newlines:

```perl
#!/usr/bin/perl

# Skip the header, i.e. any non-empty line
while(<STDIN>) {
  last if /^\s*$/;
}

my $body = "";
my $separator = "";

# Begin the message with the subject line, if it exists
if (defined $ARGV[0]) {
  $body = $ARGV[0];
  $separator = " ";
}

# Then concatenate all other lines
while(<STDIN>) {
  chomp;
  if ($_ !~/^\s*$/) {
    $body .= $separator;
    $body .= $_;
    $separator = " ";
  }
}
```

You can then process the $body to control the lights themselves, with either straight comparisons (meaning the text must include the command and *only* the command) or simple regular expressions to allow it to appear anywhere, as with the "dim" example.

```perl
if ($body eq "light on") {
  system("heyu turn e3 on");
} elseif ($body eq "light off") {
  system("heyu turn e3 off");
} elseif ($body =~ /light dim (\d+)/) {
  system("heyu dimb e3 $1");
}
```

---

[6] Although I could parse it from the header while in the main script, I do it by way of a demonstration.

■ **Note**   Remember that all scripts must be given the execute attribute.

With these simple rules, you can now create user accounts (and consequently e-mail addresses) for each of the rooms in your house and add scripts to control the lights, appliances, and teakettles, as you see fit.

■ **Note**   You can extend the dictation program we created in Chapter 2 by using the voice recognition macro to start (and stop) recording.

You can also use a house@ e-mail address to process more complex tasks, such as waiting for a message that reads "coming home" and then waiting one hour (or however long your commute is) before switching on the teakettle just ahead of time, as well as the porch and living room lights. This creates a welcoming sight, without wasting any electricity. Or you could place the .procmailrc scripts on your own e-mail account to watch for messages from your girlfriend (that are so important they must be replied to immediately, of course!) or on threads that include the words *free* and *beer*, in that order! To stop Procmail from processing this mail and discarding it, you must "clone" the message before passing it to the recipe by adding a c to the first line. The following example demonstrates this by making a vocal announcement on receipt of such a mail and sending the original to the inbox:

```
:0c
* ^From- steev.*
|/usr/bin/play /media/voices/messages/youve-got-mail.wav
```

Security Issues

As a plain-text method of data transfer, e-mail is often likened to the sending of a postcard rather than a letter, because its contents (in theory) can be read by any delivery server en route. It is also a public protocol, allowing anyone in the world to send a message to your server. These two elements combined make it difficult to ensure that no one else is going to try to e-mail your light switches.

I have taken some basic precautions here, including the following:

- Nondisclosure of the e-mail address or format

- A strict command format (an e-mail signature will cause the parse to fail in most cases)

- No acknowledgment of correct, or incorrect, messages

- Restricting the sender (albeit primitively)

Again, we've adopted security through obscurity. But, even so, there is still the possibility for hackers to create mischief. If you are intending to use e-mail as a primary conduit, then it is worth the time and effort to secure it properly by installing GnuPG, generating certificates for all of your e-mail accounts, and validating the sender using their public keys. This does mean that new users cannot control the house without first having their key manually acknowledged by the system administrator. The only time that this method breaks down is when you're unable to get to a registered e-mail account (when you're on vacation, for example) and you need to send a command from a temporary address. This is a rare case, however, and it is hoped that anything that serious would be dealt with through an SSH connection, or you'd have a suitable spare e-mail account configured for such an emergency.

For a quicker installation and one that works anywhere, you can have a cyclic list of passwords held on the server, and the e-mail must declare the first one on that list to be given access. Once you've been validated, the command is carried out, and the list cycles around, with the first element being pushed to the bottom:

```
tail -n +2 list >tempfile
head -n 1 list >>tempfile
mv tempfile list
```

In this way, anyone watching you type the e-mail or monitoring your traffic only gets access to an old password. Naturally, both methods can be combined.

Voice

The use of voice for interactive control is a goal for many people, especially when asking about home automation. I personally blame the talking computer on *Star Trek*! But all communication requires two parts, a speaker and a listener, and the fluidity of natural language makes both these tasks difficult. However, good progress has been made in both fields.

Understanding a vocal input is a two-part problem. The first involves understanding the words that have actually been said, which relates to voice recognition software. The second requires the computer to understand the *meaning* of those words and how they should be interpreted. The commands to do something with this information, such as switching on a light, are the easy bit. Because the intention is to control items in your house, rather than dictate e-mails or letters, the meaning can be governed by a set of rules that you create. So, each command must begin with computer, for example, to be followed with the name of a device (bedroom lights), followed by a command specific to that device (switch on). Again, I blame *Star Trek*!

For those with a multilingual household, there is the additional consideration of the target language. A phrase such as "the bedroom light is on" might translate into the equivalent of "the light in the bedroom is on." This means that any code like this will need to be changed on a language-by-language basis:

```
$message = "the $room light is $state";
```

This is a problem in the real world of software localization, but not here! This is because social contracts exist whereby a family will generally speak the same language to the computer at home, even if they don't when they're in public.

By contrast, generating voice output is a comparatively simple task ... but only because it's been done for us! There are three methods: vocal phonemes, sampled voices, and combinations of the two. I'll cover these shortly.

The Software for Voice Recognition

This part of the problem is rather poorly supported by Linux currently, which is not surprising. To understand even the simplest phrases, you need an acoustic model to generate representations of the sounds themselves in a statistical fashion (often as part of the initial training with a specific speaker) and a language model to consider the probabilities of what words and sounds are likely to follow another (to limit the processing necessary when analyzing speech), both of which are language-specific.

Most of the native Linux software is either old and incomplete, impossible to compile, or commercial. Even the high-grade solutions, such as Sphinx (http://cmusphinx.org), require so many levels of installation and training that no one is really sure if it works!

The commercial offerings have the problem of scarcity, with few to none of the supposedly available software sporting a "buy here" page. This absence even includes ViaVoice from IBM, which was once free but withdrawn in 2002. Even older software that once existed as commercial Linux software has transformed into Windows-only packages.

It is indeed a strange state of affairs when the easiest method of processing vocal commands under Linux is through Windows! This can either take the approach of running a virtual machine (through either Wine or VMware Server) or using a native Windows machine.

The virtualization approach has a few problems because of incongruities between the virtual and real sound cards, but software such as ViaVoice or Dragon Naturally Speaking can often be coaxed into working after a while. If the software is to be run on your server, which it usually is, then you are also adding the dependency of X Windows to it, increasing its processing load.

Consequently, the most efficient way is to employ a separate Windows machine running the previously mentioned software. Or, as you've already paid the "Windows tax," use the software built in to Vista, and download the Windows Speech Recognition Macros module. With tablet machines and subnotebooks beginning to include voice recognition software in their later versions, it may be soon possible to find a (closed source) library in a Linux machine in the near future.

Although it's important to have a good recognition algorithm, it is more important to have access to its results. In most Windows software, this is never a high priority. It is more usual for them to adopt the "We'll give you all the functionality we think you'll need in one package," whereas Linux uses the "Here are lots of tools we think you'll need; you can work out how to produce the functionality " method. Consequently, you will need to experiment with the software before purchase. The solution given here covers the use of the software built into Windows Vista.

Begin by training the speech recognition system in Vista; then work through the tutorial, and install Windows Speech Recognition Macros, downloadable from the Microsoft web site (`www.microsoft.com/downloads/details.aspx?FamilyID=fad62198-220c-4717-b044-829ae4f7c125&displaylang=en`). You next need to program a series of macros for the commands you want to use, such as "lights on" and "lights off." Each macro will trigger a command; in our case, this will be `wget` to trick Apache into running the necessary code on our server. Figure 5-1 shows the macro configuration panel.

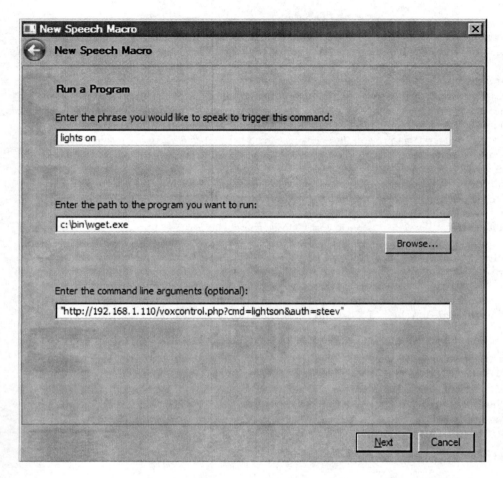

Figure 5-1. *Preparing a voice macro under Vista. (Used with permission from Microsoft.)*

Naturally, the `auth` keyword is a misnomer, as anyone (from anywhere) could request the same page and trigger the command. However, by using the machine's local IP address, the request will never leave your intranet, and by locking the Windows machine down, no one else could discover the secret key.[7] So, once again, you're vulnerable only to those with physical access to the machines (also known as your family, which has access to the light switch itself)!

From here, the server code is trivial and expected:

```php
<?php

$cmd = $_GET['cmd'];

if ($cmd == "lightson") {
    system("heyu turn bedroom_light on");
}
```

---

[7] You can also set up a virtual host to respond only to machines on your intranet so that any requests from outside would be unable to access this file.

```
else if ($cmd == "lightsoff") {
    system("heyu turn bedroom_light off");
}
?>
```

You can then work on abstracting and extending this at will. In Chapter 7 you'll integrate this into a general-purpose message system.

▓ **Note**   Before investing heavily in voice recognition software, ensure that it can distinguish between whatever different voices can control the system, because a lot of software can listen only to a single, preselected voice as its primary purpose is dictation and not voice recognition.

Note that most software of this type doesn't provide access to the words you've actually spoken; the computer just thinks that there's a higher probability of it being *this* one than *that* one. Although this gives you fewer opportunities for error, it also prevents the use of any analog or scaled commands, such as "dim to 72%."

From iOS

Something that has partially solved the problem of voice recognition is the cloud. By moving the processing into a remote device means that you can perform recognition by using more powerful algorithms than would traditionally be available on a hand-held machine, albeit at the expense of requiring yourself to be online, and finding yourself at the mercy of a (traditionally) nonopen technology. The most famous example of this has been Siri.

Released in 2010 as a standalone app, Siri has since been incorporated into the iPhone 4s and has been a staple feature of versions since iOS 5 on both iPhone and iPad. In its traditional mode of operation what happens is:

- Siri records your voice from the microphone

- Your iOS device uploads a rendering of it to their servers at guzzoni.apple.com

- The guzzoni server processes the voice, and works out the request

- The guzzoni server returns a command packet to your iOS device

As you can see, two parts of the chain require an iOS device. However, with tinkering (and software such as SiriProxy) you can circumvent half of this process. The operation then becomes:

- Siri records your voice from the microphone

- Your iOS device uploads a rendering of it to your server

- Your server passes the request to guzzoni.apple.com

- The guzzoni server processes the voice, and works out the request

- The guzzoni server return a command packet to your server

- Your server can then process any arbitrary command, using the text string that was recognized

- Your server passes a result string (with optional image) to the iOS device

As you can see, there is a fairly traditional proxy metaphor taking place here, with your server acting as a go between for the iOS device the guzzoni server so that it is able to step into the middle of the process, to perform custom commands.

Note that the iOS portion of the route is still obligatory as the guzzoni server will only talk to the authenticated iOS devices. The proxy manages it by regenerating it from your original iOS device ID (UDID).

Traditionally, you will only be able to run the SiriProxy from within your local network, as you wouldn't want random strangers connecting to an exposed port on your router. It is possible, however, to use a VPN to connect to your internal network, although that scope is beyond our space here.

For this to work you need the software at https://github.com/plamoni/SiriProxy

There is an install script and videos available, with the processes listed at https://gist.github.com/plamoni/1428474

Given how new the software is, I can only recommend you use the up-to-date instructions and bug fixes listed in that gist file.

Writing a Plug-In

Given that the proxy is written in Ruby, it makes sense that the plug-ins are also. Because there is virtually no code involved, it isn't difficult to do. And there is nothing to stop your from calling out to another shell script.

```ruby
require 'cora'
require 'siri_objects'
require 'pp'

class SiriProxy::Plugin::ControlLights < SiriProxy::Plugin
    def initialize(config)
        # standard initialization
    end

    listen_for /computer light (on|off)/i do |light_state|
        state = `homedevice default #{light_state} bedroom_light`
        say state
        request_completed
    end
end
```

There is additional functionality provided by the library, such as a basic state system, so you and detect whether the word "next" references the next piece of music or the next news item. You can also provide visual feedback, such as for the weather, by adding content through SiriAddViews, and send_object, and a model "ask" command so you can get clarification on the most recent command.

■ **Note**　Once you have created your own plugin, don't forget to add it to the config.yml file.

From Android

The best equivalent to Siri, for Android, is S Voice from Samsung. It works in an identical manner to Siri (using the Vlingo servers, instead), although in this case it requires a valid Galaxy S III phone ID to connect and make use of the service. At the time of writing, however, the only hack for this has been voicetalk.apk, which requires a rooted phone, and consequently this is not recommended.

Remote Voice Control

There are definite advantages to being able to use your voice in several different rooms of the house. However, this adds new complexity as you must do one of the following:

- *Run a microphone from every room in the house back to the computer*: You can purchase small audio mixers that will combine the inputs from multiple microphones quite cheaply. The most natural place is near light sockets and bulbs, as there's already a cable running nearby. However, you will need to shield their cables to avoid mains hum. Some jurisdictions will also require you (legally) to have a minimum distance between power cables and nonpower cables. In Australia, for example, this distance is 300mm. You should be safe and check the local laws for your country before proceding.

- *Have a separate computer in each room, and process the data locally*: This gives you the highest level of control as multiple people can talk to the server simultaneously, and the server is only processing request data, not audio data. This is more expensive, however, and requires that you're able to hide a (small) PC in each room.

In each case, the acoustics of each room will differ, so you might need to record your voice from difference places in the room.

■ **Note**   Using the Siri hack is only useful for a hand-held voice control solution, because Siri requires you to press a button in order to activate it. Indeed, this is a major block to much software that doesn't begin recording on a "trigger" or initial "key" phrase or word.

In old films, before the days of boom mics, microphones were hidden inside large props such as radios or telephones so that they could be positioned close enough to the actors to pick up their voices without extraneous noise. You can do the same on a smaller scale by mounting microphones (or even PCs!) inside a chair or under a table. The main consideration is then how you get the cables (for power and data) tp run back to the voice machine. If you're starting a home automation project from scratch or are decorating, then you have the option of pulling up floor boards and running cables underneath. Such decisions are not to be taken lightly, however, particularly because maintenance is very costly!

■ **Note**   Old Bluetooth headsets and hands-free units were both expensive and bulky. They are now, however, much cheaper and can provide a sneaky way of adding wireless remote microphones throughout the house for capturing voice commands or security monitoring.

For me, however, the second option is preferable because having a separate voice recognition machine isn't as bad as it sounds. Okay, so there's a high cost involved and extra power issues, but because the machine has nothing else to do, it can exist without keyboard, mouse, or monitor and sit quietly, untouched, for many years without maintenance. Also, with the low-cost notebooks available, you can place (read: hide) one in two or more rooms with their own microphones, thereby eliminating most of the problems of audio acoustics that you would otherwise encounter, along with the ponderings on how to wire microphones and their preamplifiers between rooms. The cost of the low-end machines preinstalled with Vista, which includes voice recognition software, is now not much more than the cost of a software license for some of the other packages. I hope those developers will soon realize this and the market they're missing before this book's second edition!

Speech Synthesis

This is the easy part of the problem, because the hard work has already been done for us, with one of the pacakages available.

Festival

The daddy in this field is a package called Festival (`http://www.cstr.ed.ac.uk/projects/festival/`). Festival began in 2004 from the Centre for Speech Technology Research (CSTR) at the University of Edinburgh where it still resides, although recent functionality has been provided by many sources, including Carnegie Melon University, because of its open source license. It generates words through a complex system of phonemes and prosodics and is able to handle the nuances of different languages by manipulating these dynamically with language-specific code, handled by Festival's built-in Scheme interpreter.

The basic install of Festival is available with most distributions, albeit with a limited set of voices. A quick study of `/usr/share/festival` will show you how many. These can be sampled by running Festival and using the interactive prompt:

```
$ festival
Festival Speech Synthesis System 1.96:beta July 2004
Copyright (C) University of Edinburgh, 1996-2004. All rights reserved.
For details type `(festival_warranty)`
festival> (SayText "Hello automation")
#<Utterance 0xb6a8eff8>
festival> (voice_lp_diphone)
lp_diphone
festival> (SayText "Hello automation")
#<Utterance 0xb6c56ec8>
festival> (quit)
```

The brackets notation is because of the Scheme interpreter that's processing the commands, and the `lp_diphone` reference is an alternative Italian female "voice" that's often supplied by default. Before you go any further, write a short script to simplify the speaking process (apologies for the obvious English bias):

```
#!/bin/bash

SPEAKER=/usr/share/festival/voices/english/$1
if [ -d $SPEAKER ]; then
  VOX=\(voice_$1\)
fi

shift
echo "$VOX (SayText \"" $* "\")" | festival --pipe
```

You can then call the following:

```
say default Hello automation
```

or the following to more easily switch to an alternate voice:

```
say kal_diphone Hello automation
```

For better voices, you need to look further afield at MBROLA.

MBROLA is a (currently) binary-only back end to Festival that provides alternate voices to Festival, without needing to upgrade the Festival package itself. The install for the base MBROLA code, through Debian on an Intel-based system, is as follows:

```
wget http://tcts.fpms.ac.be/synthesis/mbrola/bin/pclinux/mbrola3.0.1h_i386.deb
sudo dpkg -i mbrola3.0.1h_i386.deb
```

You then need to download new voice data to make use of this code. Several voices are available to us here, but the three main U.S.-centric ones are of primary interest here. I'll demonstrate an install of us1, with us2 and us3 requiring the obvious changes to the URL:[8]

```
wget -c http://tcts.fpms.ac.be/synthesis/mbrola/dba/us1/us1-980512.zip
wget -c http://www.festvox.org/packed/festival/latest/festvox_us1.tar.gz

unzip -x us1-980512.zip
tar xvf festvox_us1.tar.gz
```

The data can then be copied into the appropriate place, according to your distribution:

```
# these require root privileges
mkdir -p /usr/share/festival/voices/english/us1_mbrola/
mv us1 /usr/share/festival/voices/english/us1_mbrola/
mv festival/lib/voices/english/us1_mbrola/* /usr/share/festival/voices/english/us1_mbrola/
```

Of course, other distributions may package this for you, thus saving the work.

You now have an alternate voice that, if installed correctly, can be proven with the Festival command (voice.list) (with the brackets). It should now show us1_mbrola as a suitable voice, so you can test it with the following:

```
say us1_mbrola Hello automation
```

When you're happy you've found a voice you like, you can make it the default by setting VOX in the previous script:

```
VOX=\(voice_us1_mbrola\)
```

Having access to separate voices is good as people respond differently to different voices, according to the situation. The female voice, psychologists tell us, is good for information, issuing help, and reporting text, whereas humans respond better to commands given by a male voice. Within a household, you might have messages intended for different people spoken with different voices. If the listener knows the voice that's theirs, it's possible (through a auditory quirk known as the *cocktail party effect*) for them to isolate their voice among a lot of other auxiliary noise, including other spoken commands.

The default voice (usually kal_diphone or ked_diphone) is raspy enough that it works well as the final alarm call of the morning. However, ensure that guests know you're using it, because being woken up by something that's the cross between Stephen Hawking and a Dalek is quite disconcerting.

As well as simple phrases, you can ask Festival to read files to you either through the following:

```
say default `cat filename`
```

---

[8] Detailed in full at http://ubuntuforums.org/showthread.php?t=751169 if you'd rather copy and paste.

or through the following, which is more elegant:

```
festival --tts filename
```

Although only text files are directly supported, there are a number of tools such as html2txt (can be used in conjunction with pdftohtml) to allow most documents to be read to you, maybe as part of your alarm call or while you're cooking dinner and unable to read from a screen.

■ **Note**   Try to keep vocal utterances as short as possible, splitting longer phrases up into separate calls to Festival, as long paragraphs often cause the voice to slow down and become unintelligible.

It is also possible to build your own voices for Festival. Although the process is too involved and complex to discuss here, details are available through Carnegie Mellon's FestVox project (http://festvox.org). If you want a custom voice, it's easier to record one as an audio sample.

■ **Note**   Naturally, there are also commercial speech synthesis packages available, which is something that most open source devotees forget. One such example is available from http://cepstral.com. This web site also provides dynamic example voices.

Espeak

Festival is not the only game in town. If you don't like the voice of Festival, or just enjoy a change, then the espeak package can provide an alternative solution. Like Festival, it is capable of speaking in many languages and uses phonemes to convert between text and speech. However, unlike its bigger brother, it is much smaller in size (helpful for the Raspberry Pi) and uses only formant synthesis that results in a voice that is more robotic sounding to many ears. Usage is straightforward:

```
espeak "This is my other voice"
```

(the quotes are important)
    And:

```
espeak -f weather_report.txt
```

These commands can be supplemented with other options that provide basic control over the pitch and speed of the voice. It also has various voice files to provide regional accents, but these are a novelty and useful only to provide a slight variation in tonality, and not for more complex interfaces.

Flite

For really small Linux systems, such as the Raspberry Pi, you may get better mileage from Flite, which is comprised of a single executable and no data files. As you might expect, this is the most robotic sounding of the tools covered here, but it is perfectly suited to low-power ARM processors. The usage pattern follows espeak:

```
flite "My quotes are also necessary"
flite -f another_file.txt
```

It is currently only suitable for the English language.

Piecemeal Samples

Most automated train announcements are comprised of individual vocal snippets that are then rearranged into order by a computer. This provides a great range of possible phrases using a comparatively small set of original samples. With careful trimming of the sound files, they can sound very humanistic. The problem with this approach is that it is impossible to introduce hitherto unknown phrases into its lexicon. If you are using a human voice as an alarm clock, for example, you will know in advance every phrase and part-phrase that could be uttered. In the case of error reports from a software package, you probably won't, particularly when it comes to filenames and user input. In these cases, you will probably have to acknowledge when the samples don't exist and revert to Festival.

To create a vocal alarm clock, for example, you first need to consider the samples you will need. This can be as expansive as you're prepared to record for. Many countries have their own speaking clock service, accessible by telephone, that quote the time in 10-second intervals with many recording an entire 24-hour clock with each specific phrase. You also need to consider how grammatically exact you'd like to be. Does the phrase "1 second*s*" annoy you? If so, you'll need a specific sample for that. You also need to consider personal preferences, such as whether "15 minutes past" sounds better to your ears than "a quarter past," and so on.

Personally, I have a list of standard clock phrases that I consider important:

- "the time is"
- "p.m."
- "a.m."
- "midnight"
- "o'clock"
- "a quarter past"
- "half past"
- "a quarter to"

All the other times can be comprised of the following phrases:

- "minutes past"
- "minutes to"
- "past"
- "to"

and the numbers 1 through 20, 30, 40, 50, and 60, the latter being needed for the occasional leap second when my pedantic geek friends come to visit! I also add specific samples for the following to remain grammatically correct:

- "1 minute past"
- "1 minute to"

I can then retrieve the time with the following and piece them together with code:

```
HOURS=`date +%I`
MINS=`date +%M`
```

The 100-line script is left as an exercise for you![9]

Although the programming is comparatively simple, the record processing is not so. You need to get your voice talent to record a few samples of the whole phrase to get a feeling for the rhythm patterns in their speech. You should then sample all the words[10] and trim the individual phrases to leave no dead space at the start, while still leaving a suitable gap at the end that matches the speakers' rhythm when a second word is concatenated directly to the end. Having them say sample phrases first gives you an idea on their pacing so that in some cases you can ask them to leave a longer pause than normal after each item. With this in mind, ask them to read a longer list than you actually need. So for a number list ending at 60, ask them for 61. Unless they're experienced actors, humans naturally drop their voice when reading the last element in a list, which sounds unnatural when it is suffixed with another digit.

This whole process can take several hours for recording, rerecording, and editing. But it is worth having a personalized alarm clock for a distant partner or as a quirky 22nd-century gadget. If you record other phrases at the same time (such as "Good morning," "Good night," or "Oy, get out of my house!"), you can trigger the samples at other times and for other reasons.

On the Arduino

Playback of the samples is straightforward on all Linux machines, including the Raspberry Pi. But even this seemingly simple task is a lot for the Arduino to handle. It is possible. But it does require you to do a little more work and, in all cases, will only ever manage a single file playing at once.

Software Solutions

With just an Arduino and a speaker it is possible to playback samples of a recorded voice. Given the output levels on the Arduino, it can manage a reasonable volume without an amplifier—scoring above the humble Pi!

To achieve this minor miracle of engineering, you will need to be aware of the limitations:

- A maximum playback frequency of 8KHz, meaning the highest frequency sound which can be accurately portrayed is 4KHz (this is the Nyquist limit)

- The standard memory will allow for only four seconds of sample data

- You will have to preformat the samples into a suitable format, so no dynamic samples (or real-time update) are possible

- While using the sample player, the Arduinos duty cycle for PWM is directly manipulated in order to provide the 8KHz sample rate. This means that no other analogue output will be possible.

If these limitations have yet to dissuade you, then suitable code and samples (pardon the pun) are available from `http://hlt.media.mit.edu/?p=1963`.

However, with such a short sample memory, you will either need to use an external memory shield, or utilize it as more basic clock than detailed above. Or maybe use it as a virtual dog.

Hardware Solutions

One of the great benefits of the Raspberry Pi is that the chips are fast enough to handle sample playback out of the box. It is, after all, a true computer. However, in those cases in which a micro-controller is the preferred solution, it is always possible to add a "wave shield" to permit the playback of samples from an attached SD card. This will handle a maximum bandwidth of sounds that are monaural 16-bit waves at 22 Khz.

---

[9] The vocal time script is available in the Minerva package as `vtime`.
[10] Audacity is the still de facto standard for audio sampling and editing in Linux, in my opinion.

Although the cost of the shield is expensive, it scores over the software version by being able to handle 16-bit waveforms, and work without an amplifier circuit, as there's one built it. Also, depending on the amount of audio you might have, the built-in SD slot gives you more space than a vanilla Arduino.

Web Access

By far the most influential of all communication methods in the 20th and 21st centuries has been the World Wide Web. Also known as the Web, the interwebs,[11] the Internet (as a whole), and a series of tubes, the HTTP protocol is so ubiquitous that it now appears on the most lowly of handheld and mobile devices. This in itself makes it incredibly valuable, because you do not have to consider the technical issues around other protocols, specific code to manipulate them, or customized applications for each handheld device on the market. Using it control our house means that you, quite literally, have a *home* page.

The Web, like everything you've seen, works with both client and server components. The client is more commonly known as the *web browser*, running on an arbitrary machine somewhere in the world, while the server processes requests from the web browser and is located on the home server machine. These requests are generally for static HTML web pages, but they can be scripts—written in virtually any language—to dynamically generate a page or run software locally. The server runs under a user such as www-data, depending on distribution, meaning that any local processing will be done under the jurisdiction of this user, which may require that some software will require the appropriate permissions to access the necessary devices. This is often true of the audio device (for speech and music playback) and the serial ports (for X10 control).

When producing a set of requirements for the web server, you must distinguish between what processing is to be done on the client and what's on the server. As an example, if you think that it'd be a good idea to play MP3s from a web page, it's important to know whether your intention is to listen to your music collection while at work or to organize a playlist while at home (perhaps during a party), where you can hear the server's audio output but not necessarily access it physically.

Building a Web Server

The web server of choice for so much of the open source community is Apache. Currently at version 2, this project originated in 1992 and was called a "patchy" web server, because of its ad hoc development processes in the early years. It has since flourished into one of the most-used pieces of software in the world, running about 50 percent of all web sites on the Internet.

The power of Apache comes from its flexibility with modules. This allows an efficient and secure core able to enlist the functionality of supplementary code that can be loaded and unloaded at will. Naturally, each module provides another opportunity to open unintentional security holes, so we'll install only the modules you need. For these primary purposes, you need only the basic server and a scripting language. The Debian packages are installed with the following:

```
apt-get install apache2 libapache2-mod-php5
```

Other distributions are similarly named. Once it's installed, you can point your browser to localhost where you should see the "congratulations" web page, stored by default in /var/www, thus proving the web server works. You can then test the scripting module by creating a page called test.php containing the following:

```
<?php
echo phpInfo();
?>
```

---

[11] Flames in an e-mail to /dev/null, please!

Generally, the installation of these modules will also correctly configure them so that .php files are associated with the execution of the PHP module. If this is not apparent, you can enable the module with this:

```
a2enmod php5
```

In the very unlikely event of these not working, a log is kept in /var/log/apache2/error.log. A lot of important traffic relies on a working web server, so it is worth the time to ensure it's stable.

Virtual Sites

It is possible for one web server to serve web pages for more than one site, even if they are on the same IP address. This has been available since version 1.1 of the HTTP protocol (supported by all main browsers), which included the domain name into the request, as well as the IP address. In the home environment it's quite uncommon, but it is useful because it allows you to split the incoming web traffic into two parts to divert the curious. You can have one site for general access by friends and family, containing a blog with photographs of your dog and children, and a second for HA control.

You can begin by setting up two domains, perhaps through Dyndns.org as you saw in Chapter 4, and making two distinct directories:

```
mkdir -p /var/www/sites/homepublic
mkdir -p /var/www/sites/homecontrol
```

You then create two configuration files, one for each site. Follow the convention here of prefixing each site with a number. This allows you to name your publicly accessible as 000-public, meaning it will served first in the case of any web configuration problems, or the site is accessed with only an IP address. Dropping back to the public site in this fashion has less scope for damage, but it makes it impossible to use the HA control web site to correct the problem. Most errors of this type, however, are fixable only through SSH, so they aren't a problem.

These two files are /etc/apache2/sites-available/000-default containing the following:

```
<VirtualHost *:80>
    ServerName mypublicpresence.homelinux.org

    ServerAdmin webmaster@localhost

    DocumentRoot /var/www/sites/homepublic/

    <Directory /var/www/sites/homepublic>
        Options Indexes FollowSymLinks MultiViews
        AllowOverride AuthConfig
        Order allow,deny
        allow from all
        deny from none
    </Directory>

</VirtualHost>
```

and /etc/apache2/sites-available/001-control containing the same thing but with homepublic replaced with homecontrol and an alternate ServerName. They are then enabled manually, and the web server is restarted with the trinity of the following, run as root:

```
a2ensite 000-default
a2ensite 001-control
apache2ctl graceful
```

You now have access to two virtual sites that can be prepared accordingly, with modules and software that you'll discover later. But even with this basic level of configuration, you can explicitly deny users from known bad IP addresses by adding whitespace-separated dotted quads on the deny line, instead of the phrase none. Or, more preferably, you allow only from those addresses you know to be safe, such as work, school, or family homes using the same format. The latter is more complex because home users are often assigned a dynamic IP address by their ISP, especially those relatives with dial-up connections. Consequently, you generally need to protect the site using a separate username and password.

Secure Server

With the Web being a naturally open protocol and the home machine being a traditional secure environment, providing a way for secure access to your home and its data is a must. You can provide this with basic authorization that places specific files called .htaccess in each directory. These are read by the web server to govern access that does the following:

- Makes it easy to add and change user access rights

- Can be changed on a per-directory basis, without needing to be root

- Requires no rebooting between changes

One downside of this method, over changing the configuration files directly, is that these files are read on *every* access, making the service slower. In the case of a private web server, this is unlikely to be noticeable, however. More important, the username and password are sent across the wire in plain text when connecting, despite being present in an encrypted form on disk. Furthermore, they are stored (and are accessible) as plain text from any script running from inside this area. Consequently, it is recommended only for web servers that are inaccessible from outside your home network.

To enable basic authentication, you need two things: a password file and an access file. The password file is traditionally called .htpasswd and exists on the filesystem in a location that is accessible to Apache (that is, the www-data user) but not the files that Apache serves (not those underneath /var/www). You create the file and your first user like this:

```
htpasswd -c /etc/apache2/.htpasswd steev
```

You are then prompted for a password that is encrypted and added to the file. This password is for accessing the web site only. It need not match the password for the user, if they share a name, and in fact you can allow users to access the web site who don't have a Linux account at all.

You must then indicate which directories are to be protected by including an .htaccess file, as shown here, inside them:

```
AuthType Basic
AuthUserFile "/etc/apache2/.htpasswd"
AuthName "Enter your username and password."
require valid-user
```

You would generally protect the entire directory in this way, with any per-user control happening through code such as this:

```
if ($_SERVER['PHP_AUTH_USER']  == "steev") {
    // allow this
}
```

Add any per-file control with a change to `.htaccess` thusly:

```
<Files private_file.php>
  require valid-user
</Files>
```

Note, however, that although you don't need to restart Apache for these changes to take place (because you're not changing `apache2.conf` or its partners), you *do* need to ensure the following appears within those directory directives that use this authentication system:

```
AllowOverride AuthConfig
```

This is because most examples will default the previous line to the following, which does not support the feature:

```
AllowOverride None
```

You can also create groups of users by adding lines to the `.htpasswd` file:

```
FamilyGroup: mum dad sister
HouseOwnersGroup: mum dad
```

And you can amend the requirements line `.htaccess` to this:

```
Require group HouseOwnersGroup
```

When accessing these authorized-only web pages, you will be presented with a dialog box requesting your username and password. This naturally makes the page appear more difficult to bookmark. In fact, it isn't! The HTTP specification allows both of these to be passed as part of the URL.

```
http://myusername:mypassword@myprivatesite.homelinux.org
```

Although this is a security flaw, it must be remembered that the authorization credentials are already passed in plain text, so it does not open any *new* holes; it merely lowers the barrier to entry for script kiddies. Provided that the bookmark isn't stored on any publicly accessible machine, you are no worse off.

■ **Note**   Be aware that some media players will display the full URL (including login credentials) when streaming music from such a site.

A much-improved form of security is through Secure Sockets Layer (SSL). This is where two sites (the client and server) will communicate only once they have established that a proven secure connection exists by the exchange of certificates. These certificates prove that the server claiming to be `minervahome.net`, for example, really is the server located at `minervahome.net`. This certificate of authenticity, as it were, is issued by a higher authority who's reliability you can trust. And this authority is verified by an even higher authority, and so on. At the top of this hierarchy are companies such as VeriSign, whose entire worth is based on the fact they can never be confused with anyone else. Acquiring these certificates of trust costs money and is generally reserved for businesses, although home users are not explicitly excluded. However, you can always get around this requirement by generating a certificate that you sign yourself. This doesn't provide the full security package, but it provides secure access to your data that can't be seen by anyone else on the network.

From a technical level, SSL is an extension of the HTTP protocol that ensures that usernames and passwords cannot be monitored by packet sniffers watching the traffic to your home machine. However, because the security handshaking takes place before the domain name, only one virtual site may use SSL.[12] In our case, this would be our private house control web site.

The self-signed authentication certificate is valid for a certain number of days and applied to the web server on boot-up. To stop this certificate being copied and used on another web server (thus eliminating its purpose as a security mechanism), you will have to type a passphrase (a longer form of password, which should at least 20 characters and contain several words, to avoid basic dictionary attacks) when creating the certificate and at any time it is used, converted, or applied to a web server. Longer phrases are naturally better, but should you forget the phrase, you will have to revoke that certificate and issue a new one.

SSL self-signed certificates are generated with several (rather opaque) commands. There are many examples on the Web detailing these in varying degrees of detail. For our purposes, you care not about the why, merely the how. So, as root, begin with this:

```
cd /etc/apache2
mkdir ssl
cd ssl
```

and issue the following commands, filling in the prompts as requested:

```
openssl genrsa -des3 -out server.key 1024
openssl rsa -in server.key -out server.pem
openssl req -new -key server.key -out server.csr
openssl x509 -req -days 30 -in server.csr -signkey server.key -out server.crt
chmod 600 *
```

You can then add an SSL host to your available sites list by cloning the existing 001-control version and wrapping it with the following:

```
<IfModule mod_ssl.c>
<VirtualHost _default_:443>

# Normal configuration data goes here...

SSLEngine on
SSLCertificateFile    server.pem
SSLCertificateKeyFile server.key
BrowserMatch ".*MSIE.*" \
  nokeepalive ssl-unclean-shutdown \
  downgrade-1.0 force-response-1.0

</VirtualHost>
</IfModule>
```

You should then restart the web server with this:

```
a2enmod ssl
a2ensite 002-control-ssl
apache2ctl graceful
```

---

[12] There are solutions to the contrary detailed on the Internet, but they are too complex to be discussed here.

If all has gone well, you'll be asked for your passphrase, and the site will be available only when HTTPS is used.

■ **Note**   The process of setting up and configuring SSL is rife with possibilities for error, from differences between key and certificate (often when the location and domain information is entered) to broken SSL protocols to old certificates being used in preference to the new ones. Consequently, incorporate SSL only when you have some time and good access to the various Internet message boards!

To ensure that your users always use the SSL version of your web site, you can introduce some simple rules to the configuration by rewriting any HTTP request as an HTTPS one. This uses the famed mod_rewrite module and can be introduced with the virtual host configuration file like this:

```
<Directory /var/www/sites/homeprivate>
    Options Indexes FollowSymLinks MultiViews
    AllowOverride AuthConfig
    Order allow,deny
    allow from all
    deny from none

    RewriteEngine On
    RewriteCond %{SERVER_PORT} 80
    RewriteRule ^(.*)$ https://myprivatesite.homelinux.org/$1 [R,L]

</Directory>
```

You must then enable the module and restart:

```
a2enmod rewrite
/etc/init.d/apache2 restart
```

As an extra layer of protection, it is not unusual to utilize the "security through obscurity" approach. This means that you make it difficult for someone to accidentally stumble upon your server. For example, you could have the real home directory inside a child directory, descended from the root, which has no links to it. This would use a more obscure name, not housecontrol, and act like a first-layer password. Since you can't query a web server to determine which files are available to download, it is possible to access this area only if you know that it exists and its name. If you choose an arbitrary randomized name like bswalxwibs, you can always bookmark it on physical secure machines.

Naturally, this should always be used *in addition* to the standard security methods, not *instead* of. If you have registered a domain like MyMegaCoolAutomatedHouse.com, then it is likely that someone will find it and may be able to use the Whois directory to get your real-world address[13] (unless you've remembered to shield it).

---

[13] Thieves use a similar idea by pressing the home button on satnavs to drive to their victim's house while they're busy filing a police report on their recently stolen car.

Controlling the Machine

Although Apache is capable of running scripts dynamically when web pages are requested, they are done so as the user under which Apache runs. Depending on your configuration, this is usually the www-data or nobody user. Confirm this by including the following whoami.php script on your web server and then loading it in a browser:

```
<?php
system("whoami");
?>
```

Consider this user carefully. Because all system calls made by the server (on behalf of the user accessing the web page) will happen as www-data, there are further considerations to the code being run:

- This user probably has more access to your file system than you expect. No longer does someone need a user account on the Linux machine to read the filesystem; they can do so through the web page if there are security issues with the software or its configuration.

- Also, the permissions will be different, not just for the necessary configuration files but the access rights to devices, such as the CD-ROM or sound card. If you allow a web page to control your CD-ROM, for example, then /dev/cdrom must have read-write access granted for the www-data user. Because this is a little specific, it is more usual to grant read-write permission to an audio group and add user www-data to that group. Note that you have to restart the Apache server whenever such a change to their user's group is made. The same is true for access to /dev/dsp.

- The path used to determine the location of named executables will be significantly different from that of your normal user that you have tested with. This means you should explicitly use the path in all commands issued.

- The environment variables will also be different. You may need to set these up manually by logging in as the Apache user (for example, rlogin www-data@localhost) and setting up the environment accordingly. You can also use this approach to confirm that your permissions are correctly set by running the commands manually. This also allows you to create any configuration files that might be necessary.

- Finally, remember that most system commands are blocking. That is, they don't return until they've finished their task. So, when the task is being called from inside a web page, the user will be at a blank web page (with the "waiting" cursor) until the page has completed. Consequently, any output or error codes from the command cannot be shown on the page. Instead, you will have to write your software so that:

  - Your command executes asynchronously, using shell_exec("cmd &") or similar.

  - You can update the error or output status through Ajax.

  - You can retrieve error states through a secondary command, issued after an asynchronously command invocation.

None of these are unsolved problems, but it is an extra layer of complexity for those wanting to write their own home automation web applications.

Media Access

One common piece of functionality is to provide access to your music collection from outside home, such as from the office. Several Apache modules are available to handle this; one of them is mod_musicindex (http://freshmeat.net/projects/musicindex/, also available in the libapache2-mod-musicindex package). Although capable of being used to list general-purpose directories (as it does for its own online documentation), it is capable of rendering music-specific icons to let you download and/or stream this music anywhere in the world and create playlists interactively for the current folder and all the subdirectories underneath it.

To prepare an online portal for your music, first create a directory inside your web directory:

```
mkdir music
```

Then create an .htaccess file inside, granting permissions to whichever users you see fit. These permissions apply to this directory and every one underneath it, unless superseded by another .htaccess file. Because your music collection is likely to be stored outside of the web root, you must add a symlink to it:

```
ln -s /net/media/mp3 mp3
```

This also highlights the reason you created a separate media directory in the root—it eliminates the need for web-specific files polluting the directory structure of our nonweb media file hierarchy. You can then add the appropriate configuration lines to your virtual site configuration file, such as 001-homecontrol:

```
<Directory /var/www/sites/homecontrol/media>
  Options Indexes FollowSymLinks MultiViews
  MusicIndex On +Stream +Download +Search -Rss -Tarball
  MusicSortOrder filename album disc track artist title filetype filename
  MusicFields title artist album length bitrate
  MusicPageTitle Media Jukebox
  MusicDefaultCss musicindex.css
</Directory>
```

Then reload the Apache configuration in the usual way. This provides a functional but less than beautiful page, such as that shown in Figure 5-2.

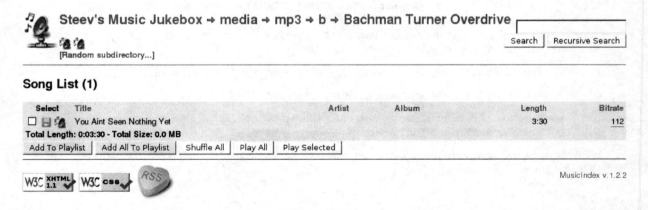

Figure 5-2. *An example of music index and your music being available anywhere*

Playback on the client side is a simple matter of installing a network-friendly media player, such as VLC. When your browser first encounters an unknown type (such as mp3 or m3u), it will ask for a suitable application to launch. If possible, you want to set this up so that each new song is queued in the media playlist, instead of launching a separate instance of the player. This is known as *enqueuing*.

Some browsers (such as Firefox) are often supplied with media plug-ins that take control of all media and attempt to play the media in the browser itself. This is generally undesirable, so by using the File Types menu option, you can remove this association and apply it manually.

An alternative package with similar scope is smb2www. As the name suggests, this provides access to all your Samba-related shares from across the Web. This has the advantage of being incredibly flexible and eliminates the need for specific symlinks to each folder you want to share but at the expense of opening a *lot* of your personal network to the outside world. Although I have this installed, I keep it switched off by default and switch it on (by entering through an SSH session) only when needed, that is, when I need to access a Windows machine that doesn't allow remote connection. When your server is often under a heavy load, that is, when it's used as a media server, then smb2www has the benefit of not requiring a reboot after changing its configuration. The new configuration is available immediately after editing the file:

```
vi /etc/smb2www/smb2www.conf
```

or using the following:

```
dpkg-reconfigure smb2www
```

SMS

The lowest common denominator in bidirectional wireless communication is undoubtedly the Short Message Service (SMS), or text message. This protocol exists as part of the mobile phone network infrastructure, making it zero cost for the provider and therefore low cost to the consumer, with many networks providing free text messages as part of their monthly package deals. Despite the rise of mobile Internet, the SMS remains a well-used protocol, especially among the young, for communication. To make use of SMS within your home, you can use one of two approaches to send and receive messages. The first and most obvious way is to perform all the processing with a secondary mobile phone connected to the computer. There is also the second method whereby a telecoms company provides you with a pseudomobile number that acts in same way as a physical phone, except you use it with an API rather than a keypad. In some cases this API is as simple as an SMTP gateway. In both cases, there are command-line tools to handle the telecoms data, so the method you choose comes down to financial preference.

■ **Note** Some hardware devices will control power lines on receipt of a mobile phone call (like the GSM Remote Control Switch; see www.gsm-auto.com), but their functionality is limited and often more expensive than the home-brew equivalent.

Processing with a Phone

This is the quickest way to experiment with a SMS-controlled home because most people have (at least) one old phone at home or one from a partner that can be borrowed for testing. Even without an existing device, the cost of a simple pay-as-you-go device is not that great. You will also need a valid subscriber identity module (SIM) card and a connecting cable to your computer. A number of phone shops (and even supermarkets) sell SIM cards containing very low credit and are ideal starting points if you don't have a second card of your own.

Most mobile phone packages come in one of two varieties, each with particular merits in the HA field.

- Contract deals are cheap to begin with, because the cost of a (new) phone is subsidized but expensive to maintain. Unless you convert all your all e-mail to text messages, it is unlikely you will ever make full use of the "free SMS for life" deals to make it worth the money you pay out every month on the subscription.

- Pay-as-you-go deals provide a comparatively cheap barrier to entry, as the bulk of the cost is up front; running costs are virtually nil. This is more true if you have a surplus phone from, say, a previous upgrade. The price of individual messages will be higher (than free!), but because most HA installations send very few messages, this is a worthwhile tradeoff. If your software goes haywire and issues too many messages, however, you will quickly exhaust your credit, causing further (and potentially more vital) communications to be lost.

■ **Note** The quality or age of the phone isn't important because it will be permanently plugged into a PC at home and unlikely to suffer the abuse of daily life.

The specific make of phone will depend on the software used. There are a couple of open source projects here, with most supporting the majority of functionality present on the Nokia devices, along with some Sony Ericsson handsets. Our basic requirements from a software point of view is that you should be able to send and receive messages to our phone. Access to the phones address book is useful but not necessary, as that can be better represented in software. It should also work as a command-line tool.

Gnokii (www.gnokii.org) has been the leading software in this field for a while, and its technology has spawned several forks over the years. Its name presents the fact that the majority of supported devices are Nokia-based, although devices do work with a standard cable. (See http://wiki.gnokii.org/index.php/Config for a list of known good devices.) For others, you may have more luck using the Bluetooth driver.

The setup, provided you have a compatible phone, involves a simple configuration file such as the following:

```
[global]
port = /dev/ttyACM0
model = AT
connection = serial
```

where the port can be determined by dmesg after plugging in your phone, although some others are chosen according the make and model of your phone. (Determine this from the web site at http://wiki.gnokii.org/index.php/Config.) Once it's plugged in, you can issue the following to determine that the connection is working:

```
gnokii --identify
```

Even though the phone might be able to communicate with Gnokii, the available functionality can vary. So, don't make critical changes your phone (such as writing data into the address book) without a suitable backup.[14]

The easiest functionality to test and demonstrate is that of sending a text message. This is also the most widely supported.

```
echo "This is a test message" | gnokii --sendsms myphonenumber
```

---

[14] Gnokii is able to provide this backup for you with gnokii --getphonebook ME 1 end --vcard >myphonebook.vcf.

The receiving of messages is no more involved, depending on what you want to do. To simply retrieve all of your messages, you can execute the following:

```
gnokii --getsms ME 1 end
```

This writes every SMS from your internal phone memory to the screen, where it could also be redirected into a file or parsed. There is a built-in parser, which will format text messages into that of an e-mail and append it in your inbox.

```
gnokii --getsms ME 1 end -a /var/mail/steev
```

Because this is an issued command, using received messages to control home devices takes a little work but is feasible, as you need to poll the phone periodically. An implementation would first require you need to keep a count of the messages you have in the inbox. This is not directly available, as the command reports all messages from every inbox:

```
$ gnokii --showsmsfolderstatus
GNOKII Version 0.6.26
No. Name                        Id #Msg
================================================
  0 Internal memory             ME   92
  1 SIM card                    SM    0
```

However, because we'd be parsing each message anyway, it isn't any more difficult and doesn't matter that you might also download the same message you sent out previously. So, you get the number of total messages, like this:

```
#!/usr/bin/perl

my $status = `gnokii --showsmsfolderstatus 2>/dev/null`;
$status=~/ME\s+(\d+)/;
my $count=$1;
```

After retrieving the last total (held in whatever temporary or log file you decide to use), you can recall only the new messages and then process them accordingly:

```
for(my $msg=$lastCount;$msg<=$count;++$msg) {
  my $txt = `gnokii --getsms ME $msg $msg 2>/dev/null`;
  if ($txt=~/Inbox Message/) {
    $txt=~/Date\/time\:(.*?)\n.*?Sender\:(.*?)Msg.*?\n.*?Text\:\n(.*)/;

    my $date = $1;
    my $sender = $2;
    my $message = $3;

    # process here...
  }
}
```

Using messages to control other devices requires us to create a standard format and stick to it. The core elements in an SMS—and indeed, any message—are, from address to address and message. You can use the *from* address to validate the user and the message to execute commands on the local machine. The case study for message systems comes in Chapter 7.

■ **Note**   It is possible to connect two phones to one machine. This allows you to use one that transmits standard messages with your daily schedule or reminders and a second for any emergency "house alert" messages that need to get through. In this way, should the first run out of credit, you will still receive the high-priority messages.

It is also possible to use the mobile as a display device by using --setlogo to control the text and/or graphic used in the phone's logo. This might report basic status information about your e-mail, weather, or RSS feeds.

You could also use the voice-dialing capabilities to call another phone so that you're able to listen in to the sound of the house (like a high-tech, remote, baby monitor) through this:

```
gnokii --dialvoice 12345678
```

For this to work, you'd need to keep the phone's microphone accessible (that is, not in a cupboard inside Node0) or wire an external mic to the phone. This can be extended as a personal "dial-a-disc" service, where the audio output of your computer is wired to the microphone in the mobile, and you can request music through a text message, which is then played back in the form of a voice call. It's not practical, however, unless you have free (or very cheap) voice calls.

The use of mobile for SMS is declining because newer phones contain broadband and usable web browsers as standard. The web interface has more control and flexibility than an SMS message could ever hope to have. But to equip all members of the family with one is a costly rollout, and you have no fallback method should your shiny new phone get sat on by an elephant! However, as a consequence, fewer new phones are likely to have SMS drivers because the development work would be appreciated by a comparatively smaller demographic. That is where the next solution comes in . . .

Custom Numbers and APIs

Having one (or more) mobile phones attached to your PC isn't the most cost-efficient way of handling messages. After all, all messages are entered into a phone, processed by the mobile networks' computer systems, and converted back for display on a phone. It stands to reason that there must be a way of connecting to these computer systems directly to send and receive messages.

There is!

A number of companies, such as IntelliSoftware (www.intellisoftware.co.uk) and Txtlocal (www.txtlocal.co.uk), offer an SMS gateway service that provides access to the mobile network through an API that lets you send and receive messages from any computer with Internet access. Their cost structure is that of a pay-as-you-go phone, with a setup charge (usually zero) and a per-message fee. This is usually cheaper than a pay-as-you-go phone because you don't need to have a custom number (which is the expensive bit!), and it eliminates the cost of your initial phone purchase. And because it's a web service, you can have as many different ones (for high- and low-priority messages, for example) as you like without running out of USB ports. There is still the problem of running out of credit during hectic periods, but you can usually provide a credit card number that will automatically top off your balance in these situations (which is dangerous, in my opinion!), or you can sign up (often with free trials) to many SMS gateway services to provide separate channels of communication, providing built-in redundancy to reduce failover.

Sending Messages

This is the easiest part to get working, because both of the services mentioned (which I'll use as an example) provide an API that takes a basic HTTP request and translates it into a text message. My code for mxsms-intelli, for example, is as follows:

```
#!/usr/bin/php
<?php
include 'IntelliSMS.php';

array_shift($argv);      // ignore program name

$type = array_shift($argv);
$toAddr = array_shift($argv);
$message = implode(" ", $argv);

$fromAddr = "MinervaHome";

$objIntelliSMS = new IntelliSMS();
$objIntelliSMS->Username = 'MyUserName';
$objIntelliSMS->Password = 'MyPassword';
$objIntelliSMS->MaxConCatMsgs = 1;

$result = $objIntelliSMS->SendMessage($toAddr, $message, $fromAddr);
?>
```

And that, believe it or not, is all the code that's necessary! You invoke it as suspected with the following:

```
mxsms-intelli sms 012345678 This stuff really works
```

Although text messages can be extended over several packets, I have limited the maximum here to 1, in case of excessive output from a runaway application. Naturally, the clever formatting is hidden inside the library, which is similar to that use in the Txtlocal version, exposed here:

```
#!/usr/bin/php
<?php
array_shift($argv);      // ignore program name

$type = array_shift($argv);
$toAddr = array_shift($argv);
$message = implode(" ", $argv);

$fromAddr = "MinervaHome";

# Things get different now...
$uname = ' MyUserName';
$pword = 'MyPassword';

$message = urlencode($message);
```

```
$data = "uname=".$uname."&pword=".$pword."&message=".$message."&from=".
$fromAddr."&selectednums=".$toAddr."&info=1&test=0";

$ch = curl_init('http://www.txtlocal.com/sendsmspost.php');
curl_setopt($ch, CURLOPT_POST, true);
curl_setopt($ch, CURLOPT_POSTFIELDS, $data);
curl_setopt($ch, CURLOPT_RETURNTRANSFER, true);
$result = curl_exec($ch);
curl_close($ch);
?>
```

The prologue to each piece of code is intentionally identical. This allows you to use either service interchangeably, maybe on a round-robin basis, according to whether you have credit or are sending a high- or low-priority message. By writing two differently named scripts, you can then either switch between them manually by issuing the following or have a separate script called mxsms that determines which transport to use:

```
ln -s mxsms-intelli mxsms
```

I have passed a $type parameter into this code so that SMS, for example, can become sms-high, as mentioned earlier. This can also be used to change the $fromAddr, which appears on your phone when you receive the message. It is limited to 11 characters, but since it is customizable, it could become part of your message, maybe to indicate the following:

- The priority of the message

- The service provider used

- The number of credits left

- The first 11 letters of the message

Each provider has a slightly different API, with different functionality, but as far as the end result is concerned, they can all be used the same way.

Some of the applications of SMS include sending daily weather reports, news feeds, or lottery results to your phone—or reporting when other house dwellers have arrived or left for work (so you can phone and encourage them otherwise).

■ **Note** The SMS protocol, as available to consumers, does not guarantee that the message will arrive or that it will arrive promptly. Most do, but it is possible (as most of us have experienced firsthand) for them to be delayed by hours, or even days, and sometimes they never appear at all. You should therefore have nothing critical—such as life-support machines—reliant on these messages.

There are two other types of message you may want to send, WAP and binary. A WAP message is a single-credit SMS message that includes a piece of text and a URL, which can be opened using the phone itself (which may incur a cost on that device). This can be used for more complex statistical information, where the executive summary is in the text, with the URL linking to a prebuilt graph that is uploaded to your WAP server at the same time.

The binary message is 140 octets of geeky goodness but because of its size is limited to sending small logos (which can also represent server performance graphs!) or ringtones.

Sending multiple messages to a group of users is possible through most, if not all, SMS gateway APIs, but their administration is usually through the Web. And because you have a fully empowered Linux box controlling your environment, you might as well store the addresses on your machine and send multiple messages that way. The cost is the same, and the time difference is generally negligible. I'll expand the mxsms script in Chapter 7.

Receiving Messages

This is no more difficult than sending messages, but it does require some extra steps—and, if you'd like your own custom number, more cost. In either case, the SMS gateway company receives a message on your behalf and then passes it onto you via an alternate commonly agreed protocol so that you can do something specific with it. Depending on the company, service level, and API, you might be able to do the following:

- Forward the text message as an e-mail

- Request a web page with the sender and message as arguments

- Send an autoresponse

- Forward to another (mobile) number

The two of interest here are the e-mail and web page handlers. In either case, the text-based format of SMS means that parsers are generally trivial to write.

Sending the message from a phone can happen in a couple of ways. The cheapest way is to share a number with other users. In this case, you will send a message, which includes your username, to the number supplied by your SMS gateway. The gateway then looks up the given user with a target machine and issues a request. The format of this message might be as follows:

```
username+your message here
```

or as follows:

```
username your message here
```

or even as follows:

```
null your message here
```

In the latter case (as adopted by Txtlocal), the gateway looks up the phone number from which you're sending the request and ties it to your account information, before passing the message on. It is also up to the gateway whether this username (or null) is included in the message.

■ **Tip** Choose a short username if possible to save SMS characters! You can save repeatedly writing your username if you save a version in your drafts folder and copy it out each time.

Alternatively, you can purchase a specific number for our own use. In that case, you don't have to include the username in the message anymore. This route usually incurs a setup fee. For those with even more money, you can buy a special short code (between four and six digits) that is an alias to the longer form of the number. These are usually used for businesses, however, and are priced accordingly. They might be easier to remember, but you only really need them when your phone has died, making your address book inaccessible. In which case, carrying a written copy of the number is cheaper!

So, once the message has arrived, you must process it. In the case of e-mail, you can use Procmail as you saw earlier to process the following into something useful with a simple regular expression:

```
##You have a new message from 012345678 saying Null This is my test.
```

Note that the word Null is a symptom of the free protocol and the specific provider, as mentioned earlier.

The web page request is the easier method, because the SMS gateway invokes a predetermined URL containing all the necessary parameters. Each company has a different format, so it is a good idea to create a script called echo.php for testing purposes.

```php
<?php
$rt.= "Get:\n";
$rt.= print_r($_GET, TRUE);

$rt.= "Post:\n";
$rt.= print_r($_POST, TRUE);

file_put_contents( '/tmp/log.txt', $rt, FILE_APPEND );
?>
```

Because the SMS gateway ignores all output from the web pages it requests, you'll never see this data, which is why you've redirected its output into a log file. You can have a rolling update of this file with the following:

```
tail -f /tmp/log.txt
```

Then send a text message and have it redirected to echo.php, and you'll see exactly what arguments are supplied. Using the earlier examples, IntelliSoftware provides the following:

```
Get:
Array
(
)
Post:
Array
(
    [from] => 012345678
    [text] => This is my last test tonight
    [msgid] => 50011005000001624552
    [type] => 1
)
```

Txtlocal gives this:

```
Get:
Array
(
)
Post:
Array
```

```
(
    [sender] => 012345678
    [content] => Null Wow this might work, you know!
    [inNumber] => 447786202240
    [submit] => Submit
    [network] => UNKNOWN
    [email] => none
    [keyword] => NULL
    [comments] => Wow this might work, you know!
)
```

Both contain enough information to let you switch your lights on with a text message. The code is trivial as follows:

```php
if ($_POST['from'] == "012345678") {
  if ($_POST['text'] == "bedroom on") {
    system("/usr/local/bin/heyu turn bedroom_light on");
  } else if ($_POST['text'] == "bedroom off") {
    system("/usr/local/bin/heyu turn bedroom_light off");
  }
}
```

To eliminate the sending of fiddly text messages (and perhaps save money), you can test future permutations of this script with a simple web page. Using the simpler format, you can write code such as the following:

```html
<form action="echo.php" method="POST">
 <input name="from" value="phone num">
 <input name="text" value="your message here">
 <input name="msgid" value="" type="hidden">
 <input name="type" value="1" type="hidden">
 <input type="submit" value="Send Fake SMS">
</form>
```

Because this is on an open web server, there are some security issues. You can eliminate one by having the phone number verified by a piece of code on the server (*never* validate credentials on the client). You can further limit another issue (although not eliminate it) by changing your simply named echo.php script to iuytvaevew.php, employing security through obscurity so that it is not accidentally found. Some providers will call your web page using HTTPS, which is the best solution and worth the extra time in setting up a specific username and password for them.

You can rebalance the concepts of security and accessibility by allowing multiple phones to access the house, by creating a white list of mobile phone numbers, and by adding to this list explicitly. Or you could ban any access to your page from an IP that isn't similarly approved and known to be your gateway provider. If you were likely to be communicating a lot through SMS, you could automatically add new phone numbers to a pending list of preapproved devices, which in turns sends a notification message to the SMS administrator, where they can issue a special command to add them onto the list.

If your facilities allow, having a physical mobile phone connected through Gnokii may be useful in emergencies when you have no Internet connectivity and you want to be informed that the automatic power cycling of the router (with a AW12 perhaps, as mentioned in Chapter 1) is in progress.

Conclusion

With so many ways of communicating into and out of a system, you must begin with a solid framework. My method is to separate the input systems from the processing, allowing any input mechanism (mobile phone, e-mails, or web interface) to generate a command in a known common format that can be processed by a single script. In a similar way, all messages are sent to a single script that then formats the message in a particular format, suitable for the given communication channel. You can also add an automatic process on receipt of any, or all, of these messages. So, once you have code to control a video, light switch, or alarm clock, you can process them in any order to either e-mail your video, SMS your light switch, speak to your alarm clock, or any combination of these.

CHAPTER 6

■ ■ ■

Data Sources: Making Homes Smart

Although being able to e-mail your light switch is very interesting and infinitely cooler than programming yet another version of "Hello, World," it never feels like an *automatic* house. After all, you as a human are controlling it. By providing your house with information about the real world, it is then able to make decisions for itself. This is the distinction between an automated home and a smart home.

Why Data Is Important

For years, the mantra "Content is king" has been repeated in every field of technology. Although most of the data in your home automation environment so far has been generated from your own private living patterns, there is still a small (but significant) amount of data that you haven't generated, such as TV schedules. I'll now cover this data to see what's available and how you can (legally) make use of it.

Legalities

All data is copyrighted. Whether it is a table of rainfall over the past 20 years or the listing for tonight's TV schedule, any information that has been compiled by a human is afforded a copyright. The exception is when data has been generated by a computer program, in which case the source data is copyrighted by the individual who created it, and the copyright to the compiled version is held by the person who facilitated the computer to generate it, usually the person who paid for the machine. Unfortunately, all useful data falls into the first category. Even when the data is made publicly available, such as on a web site, or when it appears to be self-evident (such as the top ten music singles), the data still has a copyright attached to it, which requires you to have permission to use it.[1] Depending on jurisdiction, copyright will traditionally lapse 50 or 75 years after the death of the last surviving author. However, with the introduction of new laws, such as the Sonny Bono Copyright Term Extension Act, even these lengthy periods may be extended. In this field, the data becomes useless before it becomes available, which is unfortunate.

Fortunately, there are provisions for private use and study in most countries that allow you to process this data for your own personal use. Unfortunately, this does not include redistributing the data to others or manipulating the data into another format. This, from a purely technical and legal point of view, means that you can't do the following:

- Provide the data to others in your household. They have to download it themselves. This includes reproducing the information on a home page or distributing a TV or radio signal to other machines.

- Improve the format of the data and provide it to others who are technically unable to do the same. This includes parsing the data from one web site to show it in a more compact format at home.

---

[1] IANAL: I am not a lawyer, and all standard disclaimers apply here!

189

There is even a questionable legality in some areas over whether you are allowed to provide tools that improve or change the format of existing (copyrighted) data. Fortunately, most companies turn a blind eye to this area, as they do for the internal distribution of data to members of your household—not that they'd know, or be able to prove it, if you did.

The larger issue has to do with improvements to the data, as most data is either too raw or too complex to be useful. Let's take a web site containing the weather forecast as an example; the raw data might include only the string "rain, 25," which would need to be parsed into a nice icon and a temperature bar to be user-friendly. A complex report could include a friendly set of graphics on the original site but make the original data set unavailable to anyone else who either tries to load the report from another site through deep linking or tries to reference the source table data used to build the image.

Screen Scraping

This is the process whereby a web page is downloaded by a command-line tool, such as wget or cURL, and then processed by an HTML parser so that individual elements can be read and extracted from it. This is the most legally suspect and most troublesome method of processing information.

It is the most suspect because you are downloading copyrighted content from a site in a manner that is against the site's terms and conditions—so much so that, until fairly recently, one famous weather site labeled its images as please_dont_scrape_this_use_the_api.gif!

Scraping is troublesome because it is very difficult to accurately parse a web page for *content*. It is very easy to parse the page on a technical level because the language is computer-based, and parsers already exist. It is also very easy for a user to parse the rendered page for the data, because the human eye will naturally seek out the information it desires. But knowing that the information is in the top-left corner of the screen is a very difficult thing for a machine to assess. Instead, most scrapers will work on a principle of blocking. This is where the information is known to exist in a particular block, determined beforehand by a programmer, and the parser blindly copies data from that block. For example, it will go to the web page, find the third table, look in the fifth column and second row, and read the data from the first paragraph tag. This is time-consuming to determine but easy to parse. It is troublesome because any breakages in the HTML format itself (either introduced intentionally by the developers or introduced accidentally because of changes in advertising[2]) will require the script to be modified or rewritten.

Because of the number of different languages and libraries available to the would-be screen-scraper and the infinite number of (as yet undetermined) formats into which you'd like to convert the data, there isn't really a database of known web sites with matching scraping code. To compile such a database would be a massive undertaking. However, if you're unable to program suitable scraping code, it might be best to seek out local groups or those communities based around the web site in question, such as TV fan pages. Any home will generally have a large number of data sources, and trying to maintain scrapers for each source will be time-consuming if you attempt it alone.

The mechanics of scraping are best explained with an example. In this case, I'll use Perl and the WWW::Mechanize and HTML::TokeParser modules. Begin by installing them in any way suitable for your distribution. I personally use the CPAN module, which generally autoconfigures itself on invocation of the cpan command. Additional mirrors can be added by adding to the URL list like this:

```
o conf urllist push ftp://ftp-mirror.internap.com/pub/CPAN/
o conf commit
```

This is then followed by the installation of the modules themselves:

```
perl -MCPAN -e 'install WWW::Mechanize'
perl -MCPAN -e 'install HTML::TokeParser'
```

---

[2] And although the Web exists as a free resource for information, someone will be paying for advertising space to offset the production costs.

Lest I advocate scraping a page of a litigious company, I will provide an example using my own Minerva site to retrieve the most recent story from the news page at http://www.minervahome.net/news.htm.

Begin by loading the page in a web browser to get a feel for the page layout and to see where the target information is located. Also, review other pages to see whether there's any commonality that can be exploited. You can do this by reviewing the source (as either a whole page or with a "view source selection" option) or enlisting the help of Firebug[3] to highlight the tables and subcomponents within the table.

Then look for any "low-hanging fruit." These are the easily solved parts of a problem, so you might find the desired text inside a specially named div element or included inside a table with a particular id attribute. Many professionally designed web sites do this to make redesigns quicker and unwittingly help the scraper.

If there are no distinguishing features around the text, look to the elements surrounding it . . . and the elements surrounding those. Work outward until you find something unique enough to be of interest or you reach the root html node. If you've found nothing unique, then you will have to describe the data with code such as "in the first row and second column of the third table."

Once you are able to describe the location of the data in human terms, you can start writing the code! The process involves a mechanized agent that is able to load the web page and traverse links and a stream processor that skips over the HTML tags. You begin the scraping with a fairly common loading block like this:

```perl
#!/usr/bin/perl -w
use strict;
use WWW::Mechanize;
use HTML::TokeParser;

my $agent = WWW::Mechanize->new();
$agent->get("http://www.minervahome.net/news.htm");

my $stream = HTML::TokeParser->new(\$agent->{content});
```

Given the $stream, you can now skip to the fourth table, for example, by jumping over four of the opening table tags using the following:

```perl
foreach(1..4) {
    $stream->get_tag("table");
}
```

Notice that get_tag positions the stream point immediately after the opening tag given, in this case table. Consequently, the stream point is now inside the fourth table. Because our data is on the first row, you don't need to worry about skipping the tr tag, so you can jump straight into the second column with this:

```perl
$stream->get_tag("td");
$stream->get_tag("td");
```

as skipping the td tag will automatically skip the preceding tr. The stream is now positioned exactly where you want it. The HTML structure of this block is as follows:

```html
<a href="url">Main title</a></td>
<td valign="top">
Main story text
```

---

[3]Firebug is an extension to Firefox that allows web developers (and curious geeks) full access to the inner workings of the web pages that appear in the browser.

So far, I have been using get_tag to skip elements, but it also sports a return value, containing the contents of the tag. So, you'd retrieve the information from the anchor with the following, which, by its nature, can return multiple tags:

```
my @link = $stream->get_tag("a");
```

Because you know there is only one in this particular HTML, it is $link[0] that is of interest. Inside this is another array containing the following:

```
$link[0][0] # tag
$link[0][1] # attributes
$link[0][2] # attribute sequence
$link[0][3] # text
```

Therefore, you can extract the link information with the following:

```
my $href = $link[0][1]{href};
```

And because get_tag only retrieves the information about the tag, you must return to the stream to extract all the data between this <a> and the </a>:

```
my $storyHeadline = $stream->get_trimmed_text("/a");
```

From here, you can see that you need to skip the next opening td tag and get the story text between it and the next closing td tag:

```
$stream->get_tag("td");
print $stream->get_trimmed_text("/td");
```

Because you are only getting the first story from the page, your scraping is done. If you wanted to get the first two stories, for example, you'd need to correctly skip the remainder of this table, or row, before repeating the parse loop again.

Naturally, if this web page changes in any way, the code won't work!

This admittedly simple approach can fail when Javascript is used to control the web page content or layout. Most commonly, this occurs when the page uses AJAX calls for pagination. In this case, the *next* button loads some data dynamically from the server (with Javascript) and rewrites the contents of the appropriate <div> element. You are unlikely to encounter such pages with the data sources that benefit home automation solutions, as none of the examples presented here do so. However, if you do uncover one (supermarkets, for example, do this a lot), then you need to upgrade to a headless browser solution, such as Casper and PhantomJS, which allows you to programmatically click buttons on the page and invoke those AJAX requests. A new technology that also aims to simplify this process is "Copy as cURL," covered at https://twitter.com/ChromiumDev/status/317183238026186752.

Fortunately, this game of cat and mouse between the web developers and the screen scrapers often comes to a pleasant end. For us! Tired with redesigning their sites every week and in an attempt to connect with the Web 2.0 and mashup communities on the Web, many companies are providing APIs to access their data. And, like most good APIs, they remain stable between versions.

Data Through APIs

An API is the way that a programmer can interact with the operating system underneath it. In the web world, an API governs how your scripts can retrieve (and sometimes change) the data on a web server. These break down into several broad groups:

- *Basic file access*: These files are dispensed via a web server with a filename formatted according to some predetermined rules. To get the UK TV listings for BBC1 in three days' time, for example, you can use the URL `http://www.bleb.org/tv/data/listings/3/bbc1.xml`. In the truest sense of the word, these are not APIs but REST requests. However, unlike static files, the same request can produce different data according to the time or location from where they're requested.

- *Public queries*: These can exist in many forms, including basic file requests, but they are usually based on Simple Object Access Protocol (SOAP) objects or XML over HTTP. This allows function calls, using strongly typed parameters, to be sent to the server with similarly complex replies returned using XML or JSON.

- *Private queries*: These require the software developer to sign up for a developer API key. These, like the ones for Amazon, are embedded into your code so that the server API can authenticate the user and monitor your usage patterns, thereby eliminating most DoS attacks.

There is no consistent legalese to these implementations. Just because a site uses publicly accessible files doesn't necessarily mean that you can redistribute their data. Again, you must check their terms of service (TOS), which are not always obviously displayed.

In the case of private queries, the TOS will be displayed beforehand, and you will be required to agree to the terms before a key is assigned to you. These terms will typically limit you to a specific number of accesses per day or within a particular time frame. Usually these limits can be increased with the exchange of currency.

If you are looking for APIs with which to experiment, then a good starting point is `http://www.programmableweb.com/apis`.

Distribution

Unless it is explicitly stated otherwise, any data that you generate is considered a derived work of the original copyrighted version. I have merely demonstrated methods by which this data can be obtained (and obtained for personal use only). After all, in most cases, the copyright holders have given their permission for the data to be used on the sites in question but not redistributed beyond that. The letter of the law includes redistribution inside your home, but in most cases (where the home server is private and unavailable to the outside world), it becomes a moot point.

Public Data

In this section, I'll cover data that is available to the public. It is not necessarily available in the public domain, however, so you must still adhere to all of the rules of legality mentioned previously. Within each section I'll cover some example data that will be useful to your smart home, examine how to access and process it, and talk about ideas of the ways in which public data can be incorporated privately at home.

TV Guides

With so many TV stations in so many countries, building a general-purpose data store for all the TV channels (let alone their programs) in the world is a massive undertaking. In the United Kingdom, you have Andrew Flegg to thank for handling all the digital, analog, and primary satellite stations in England, Scotland, Wales, and Northern Ireland.

The data presented on this site comes from daily scrapes of the broadcasters' own web sites, along with traditional data feeds, so it is accurate and timely. It is also legal, as permission has been granted to the site for its inclusion.

■ **Note** Curiously, the data for the UK's ITV companies are not available. This includes ITV, ITV2, ITV3, and ITV4. This is because ITV doesn't want its data shared on other web sites, although it has no objection to using other TV schedule data on its own site! This might be because of the purely commercial aspect of its business. However, until ITV changes its rules (or the petition takes effect), no geek following these instructions will be able to determine what's on ITV, which in turn will limit ITV's advertising revenues, causing them to have shot themselves in the proverbial foot!

The data itself is available as a web page on the site or as XML files that can be downloaded to your PC and processed at your leisure. The URLs for each XML file follow a strict format so that you can automate the process. The root URL is `http://www.bleb.org/tv/data/listings` and is followed by this:

- The day offset, between -1 (yesterday) and 6 (next week)
- The station name

Therefore, you can find today's BBC1 schedule here:

```
http://www.bleb.org/tv/data/listings/0/bbc1.xml
```

And tomorrow's TMF guide is here:

```
http://www.bleb.org/tv/data/listings/1/tmf.xml
```

The format is XMLTV and very easy to parse with a suitable library or even XSLT. With this data in a local usable format, you can then search the descriptions for films starring your favorite actors, be alerted to new series, or check for musicians appearing within talk shows or programs outside your usual sphere. These results can be piped into any file, such as a web page or e-mail, for review.

Despite its free nature, Bleb does have a couple of restrictions of its own, but the only requirements are that you don't repeatedly ask for data from the server by including a two-second gap between requests and that you include the program name that's making these requests along with an e-mail.

Minerva includes an example of this in action; I cover this in Chapter 7. There are many other examples, such as executables for Windows, Flash code, and the WhensItOn code found here:

```
http://ccgi.useyourhead.force9.co.uk/
```

This alphabetically sorts the entire week's TV schedule so that you can see at what time the show is on and when it's repeated.

Train Times

Like the TV schedules, obtaining complete timetables for every train around the world is a thankless and impossible task. But fortunately, like TV, the rail journeys of interest are generally based in one country, so you need to find only one suitable data source for your area.

Any search engine will return several different data sources for this information, depending on your country, so you need to spend a little time looking at each one to determine which have APIs (that are usable) or, failing that, which can be scraped with the least amount of effort. Most people who use trains regularly have a routine, and they know the timetables, so the web sites of most interest are those that report the live information, including late trains and cancellations.

In England, the foremost site is Live Departure Boards (`www.nationalrail.co.uk/times_fares/ldb/`), which provides reasonably accurate information about most trains on the U.K. network. It doesn't include an API, unfortunately, but it is very easy to scrape for the current train times and also comes with a Twitter feed detailing the station closures and the overrunning of engineering works. It also has the advantage of using a basic GET request to retrieve the times of all the trains between two named stations, making it easier to bookmark. One journey I make on occasion is between St. Pancras and Luton Airport. On reviewing the site, I can see that the URL incorporates both of these locations in the form:

```
http://ojp.nationalrail.co.uk/service/timesandfares/STP/LTN/today/0630/dep
```

So, this could be scraped in the same way as we saw earlier. However, a study of the site's source code reveals that there's an AJAX request that populates the page at:

```
http://ojp.nationalrail.co.uk/en/s/ldb/liveTrainsJson
```

This page can be controlled by amending the parameters (`?liveTrainsFrom=STP&liveTrainsTo=LTN`) and can be incorporated into code[4] for `whattrain.php` like this:

```
$url = "http://ojp.nationalrail.co.uk/en/s/ldb/liveTrainsJson?\
    departing=true&liveTrainsFrom=$fromCode&liveTrainsTo=$toCode&serviceId=";
$contents = getContents($url, "ldb_${fromCode}_${toCode}", 5*60);
```

As a simple request, this uses only GET, and so can accessed simply through cURL, or directly in the browser, which makes for simple and direct testing. You can also save the output into a temporary, local, file for offline testing. This resultant output from the URL provides a JSON object containing the next few trains to depart. No historical data from before midnight today is available, however.

It is also worth noting that the getContents method here involves a temporary file, which avoids downloading the data again if a subsequent query is made within five minutes of the previous one. This may need changing according to your needs. From here, we only need to decode the JSON:

```
$trainTimes = json_decode($contents);
$trains = $trainTimes->{'trains'};
```

which in turn allows you to read the information for each train:

```
foreach($trains as $entry) {
   $expectedTime = $entry[1];
   $destination = $entry[2];
   $status = $entry[3];
   $platform = $entry[4];
   $arrivalTime = $expectedTime;

   if (preg_match('/((\d+):0?(\d+))/', $status, $matches)) {
      $expectedTime = $matches[0];
   }
}
```

---

[4]This is screen-scraping Perl code, which may have broken by the time you read this. The relative pitfalls and considerations of this approach were covered earlier in the chapter.

This web site has been used, in part, because enough information is present to make automatic value judgments when it comes to catching the train. For example, knowing that it takes 35 minutes to travel from work to St. Pancras, you can exclude any train leaving in that window. Furthermore, by adding a grace period, you can limit the output to trains that will leave within ten minutes of you arriving at the station:

```
my $graceMinutes = $minutesAway - $timeToStation;
if ($graceMinutes >= $graceThreshold && $graceMinutes < $maxGracePeriod) {
    print "Get the $expectedTime to $destination from platform $platform.";
    print "There is $graceMinutes minutes grace.\n";
}
```

This code can naturally be extended to swap the source and destination locations so that the return journey can be similarly considered. This could happen by looking at the time of day, for example.

■ **Tip** Output each piece of data on a separate line, making it easier for other tools to extract the information. Or use a low-level structured format, like JSON, which has processing modules for most languages.

You now have a way of knowing which are the next trains to leave. This could be incorporated into a daily news feed, recited by a speech synthesizer while making breakfast, added to a personal aggregator page, or used to control the alarm clock. (The method for this will be discussed later.)

Road Traffic

With the whole world and his dog being in love with satellite navigation systems, the role of web-based traffic reports has become less useful in recent years. And with the cost coming down every year, it's unlikely to gain a resurgence any time soon. However, if you have a choice of just one gadget—a SatNav or a web-capable handheld PC—the latter can still win out with one of the live traffic web sites.

The United Kingdom has sites such as Frixo (`www.frixo.com`) that report traffic speed on all major roads and integrate Google Maps so you can see the various hotspots. It also seems like they have thought of the HA market, because much of the data is easily accessible, with clear labels for the road speeds between each motorway junction, with the roadwork locations, and with travel news.

Weather

Sourcing weather data can occur from three sources: an online provider, a personal weather station, or by looking out of the window! I will consider only the first two in the following sections.

Forecasts

Although there appear to be many online weather forecasts available on the Web, most stem from the Weather Channel's own `Weather.com`. This site provides a web plug-in (`www.weather.com/services/downloads`), mobile apps, and a native desktop application (Windows-only, alas) to access its data, but currently there's nothing more open than that in the way of an API. Fortunately, many of the companies that have bought licenses to this data provide access to it for the visitors to *their* web site and with fewer restrictions. Yahoo! Weather, for example, has data in an XML format that works well but requires a style sheet to convert it into anything usable.

Like the train times you've just seen, each site presents what it feels is the best tradeoff between information and clarity. Consequently, some weather reports comprise only one-line daily commentaries, while others have an hourly breakdown, with temperatures, wind speed, and windchill factors. Pick one with the detail you appreciate and, as mentioned previously, is available with an API or can easily be scraped.

In this example, I'll use the Yahoo! reports. This is an XML file that changes as often as the weather (literally!) and can be downloaded according to your region. This can be determined by going through the Yahoo! weather site as a human and noting the arguments in the URL. For London, this is UKXX0085, which enables the forecast feed to be downloaded with this:

```
#!/bin/bash
LOGFILE=/var/log/minerva/cache/weather.xml
wget -q http://weather.yahooapis.com/forecastrss?p=UKXX0085 -O $LOGFILE
```

You can then process this with XML using a style sheet and xsltproc:

```
RESULT_INFO=/var/log/minerva/cache/weather_info.txt
rm $RESULT_INFO
xsltproc /usr/local/minerva/bin/weather/makedata.xsl $LOGFILE > $RESULT_INFO
```

This converts a typical XML like this:

```
<?xml version="1.0" encoding="UTF-8" standalone="yes" ?>
<rss xmlns:yweather="http://xml.weather.yahoo.com/ns/rss/1.0"
xmlns:geo="http://www.w3.org/2003/01/geo/wgs84_pos#" version="2.0">

<channel>
  <title>Weather - London, UK</title>
  <language>en-us</language>
  <yweather:location city="Luton" region=""   country="UK"/>
  <yweather:units temperature="F" distance="mi" pressure="in" speed="mph"/>
  <yweather:wind chill="26"   direction="50"   speed="10" />
  <yweather:atmosphere humidity="93" visibility="3.73" pressure="30.65" rising="1"/>
  <yweather:astronomy sunrise="7:50 am"   sunset="4:38 pm"/>
  <image>
    <title>Weather</title>
    <width>142</width>
    <height>18</height>
    <url>http://todays_weather_chart.gif</url>
  </image>
  <item>
    <yweather:forecast day="Tue" date="26 Jan 2010" low="30" high="36"
      text="Mostly Cloudy" code="27" />
    <yweather:forecast day="Wed" date="27 Jan 2010" low="26" high="35"
      text="Partly Cloudy" code="30" />
    <guid isPermaLink="false">UKXX0085_2010_01_26_4_20_GMT</guid>
  </item>
</channel>
</rss>
```

into text like this:

```
day:Tuesday
description:Mostly Cloudy
low:30
high:36
end:

day:Wednesday
description:Partly Cloudy
low:26
high:35
end:
```

That is perfect for speech output, status reports, or e-mail. The makedata.xsl file, however, is a little more fulsome:

```
<?xml version="1.0" encoding="utf-8"?>

<xsl:stylesheet version="1.0"
        xmlns:xsl="http://www.w3.org/1999/XSL/Transform"
        xmlns:scripts="http://www.bluedust.com/sayweather"
        xmlns:msxsl="urn:schemas-microsoft-com:xslt"
        xmlns:yweather="http://xml.weather.yahoo.com/ns/rss/1.0">

<xsl:output method="text" encoding="utf-8" media-type="text/plain"/>

  <xsl:template match="/">
    <xsl:apply-templates select="rss"/>
    <xsl:apply-templates select="channel"/>
  </xsl:template>

  <xsl:template match="channel">
     <xsl:apply-templates select="item"/>
  </xsl:template>

  <xsl:template match="item">
     <xsl:apply-templates select="yweather:forecast"/>
  </xsl:template>

  <xsl:template match="yweather:forecast">
     <xsl:text>day:</xsl:text>

     <xsl:if test="@day = 'Mon'">
        <xsl:text>Monday</xsl:text>
     </xsl:if>
     <xsl:if test="@day = 'Tue'">
        <xsl:text>Tuesday</xsl:text>
     </xsl:if>
```

```xml
        <xsl:if test="@day = 'Wed'">
           <xsl:text>Wednesday</xsl:text>
        </xsl:if>
        <xsl:if test="@day = 'Thu'">
           <xsl:text>Thursday</xsl:text>
        </xsl:if>
        <xsl:if test="@day = 'Fri'">
           <xsl:text>Friday</xsl:text>
        </xsl:if>
        <xsl:if test="@day = 'Sat'">
           <xsl:text>Saturday</xsl:text>
        </xsl:if>
        <xsl:if test="@day = 'Sun'">
           <xsl:text>Sunday</xsl:text>
        </xsl:if>

        <xsl:text>
description:</xsl:text>
        <xsl:value-of select="@text"/>
        <xsl:text>
low:</xsl:text>
        <xsl:value-of select="@low"/>
        <xsl:text>
high:</xsl:text>
        <xsl:value-of select="@high"/>
        <xsl:text>
end:

</xsl:text>
     </xsl:template>

</xsl:stylesheet>
```

In several places, you will note the strange carriage returns included to produce a friendlier output file.

Because of the CPU time involved in querying these APIs, you download and process them with a script (like the one shown previously) and store its output in a separate file. In this way, you can schedule the weather update script once at 4 a.m. and be happy that the data will be immediately available if/when you query it. The weatherstatus script then becomes as follows:

```bash
#!/bin/bash
RESULT_INFO=/var/log/minerva/cache/weather_info.txt
if [ -f $RESULT_INFO]; then
   cat $RESULT_INFO
   exit 0;
else
   echo "No weather data is currently available"
   exit 1;
fi
```

This allows you to pipe the text into speech-synthesized alarm calls, web reports, SMS messages, and so on. There are a couple of common rules here, which should be adopted wherever possible in this and other types of data feed:

- Use one line for each piece of data to ease subsequent processing

- Remove the old status file first, because erroneous out-of-date information is worse than none at all

- Don't store time stamps; the file has those already

- Don't include graphic links, not all mediums support them

In the case of weather reports, you might take exception to the last rule, because it's nice to have visual images for each of the weather states. In this case, it is easier to adopt two different XML files, targeting the appropriate medium. Minerva does this by having a `makedata.xsl` for the full report and a simpler `sayit.xsl` that generates sparse text for voice and SMS.

Local Reporting

Most gadget and electronic shops sell simple weather stations for home use. These show the temperature, humidity, and atmospheric pressure. All of these, with some practice, can predict the next day's weather for your specific locale and provide the most accurate forecast possible, unless you live next door to the national weather center!

Unfortunately, most of these devices provide no way for it to interface with a computer and therefore with the rest of the world. There are some devices, however, and some free software called `wview` (`www.wviewweather.com`) to connect with it. This software is a collection of daemons and tools to read the archive data from a compatible weather station. If the station reports real-time information only, then the software will use an SQL database to create the archive. You can then query this as shown previously to generate your personal weather reports.

■ **Note** If temperature is your only concern, there are several computer-based temperature data loggers on the market that let you monitor the inside and/or outside temperature of your home. Many of these can communicate with a PC through the standard serial port.

Radio

Radio has been the poor cousin of TV for so long that many people forget it was once our most important medium, vital to the war effort in many countries. And it's not yet dead![5] Nowhere else can you get legally free music, band interviews, news, and dramas all streamed (often without ads—take that, Spotify!) directly to your ears. Furthermore, this content is professionally edited and chosen so that it matches the time of day (or night) at which it's broadcast. Writing a piece of intelligent software to automatically pick some nighttime music is unlikely to choose as well as your local radio DJ.

From a technological standpoint, radio is available for free with many TV cards and has simple software to scan for stations with `fmscan` and tune them in using `fm`. They usually have to be installed separately from the TV tuning software, however:

```
apt-get install fmtools
```

---

[5]However, amusingly, the web site for my local BBC radio station omits its transmission frequency.

Knowing the frequencies of the various stations can be achieved by researching your local radio listing magazines (often bundled with the TV guide) or checking the web site for the radio regulatory body in your country, such as the Federal Communications Commission (FCC) in the United States (search for stations using the form at `http://www.fcc.gov/encyclopedia/fm-query-broadcast-station-search`) or Ofcom in the United Kingdom. In the case of the latter, I was granted permission to take its closed-format Excel spreadsheet of radio frequencies (downloadable in various formats from `http://stakeholders.ofcom.org.uk/broadcasting/guidance/tech-guidance/tech_parameters/`) and generate an open version (`www.minervahome.net/pub/data/fmstations.xml`) in RadioXML format. From here, you can use a simple XSLT sheet to extract a list of stations, which in turn can tune the radio and set the volume with a command like the following:

```
fm 88.6 75%
```

When this information is not available, you need to search the FM range—usually 87.5[6] to 108.0 MHz—for usable stations. There is an automatic tool for this, fortunately, with an extra parameter indicating how strong the signal has to be for it to be considered "in tune":

```
fmscan -t 10 >fmstations
```

I have used 10 percent here, because my area is particularly bad for radio reception, with most stations appearing around 12.5 percent. You redirect this into a file because the `fmscan` process is quite lengthy, and you might want to reformat the data later. You can list the various stations and frequencies with the following:

```
cat fmstations | tr ^M \\n\\r | perl -lane 'print $_ if /\d\:\s\d/'
```

or order them according to strength:

```
cat fmstations | tr ^M \\n\\r | perl -lane 'print $_ if /\d\:\s\d/' | awk -F : ↵
'{ printf( "%s %s \n", $2, $1) }'| sort -r | head
```

In both cases, the `^M` symbol is entered by pressing Ctrl+V followed by Ctrl+M.

You will notice that some stations appear several times in the list, at 88.4 and 88.6, for example. Simply pick one that sounds the cleanest, or check with the station call sign.

Having gotten the frequencies, you can begin the search for program guides online to seek out interesting shows. These must invariably be screen-scraped from a web page that's found by searching for the station's own site. A term such as the following:

```
radio 88.6 MHz uk
```

generally returns good results, provided you replace uk with your own country. You can find the main BBC stations, for example, at `www.bbc.co.uk/programmes`.

There are also some prerecorded news reports available as MP3, which can be downloaded or played with standard Linux tools. Here's an example:

```
mplayer http://skyscape.sky.com/skynewsradio/RADIO/news.mp3
```

---

[6]The Japanese band has a lower limit of 76MHz.

CD Data

When playing a CD, there are often two pieces of information you'd like to keep: the track name and a scan of the cover art. The former is more readily available and incorporated into most ripping software, while the latter isn't (although a lot of new media center–based software is including it).

What happens to determine the track names is that the start position and length of each song on the CD is determined and used to compute a single "fingerprint" number by way of a hashing algorithm. Because every CD in production has a different number of songs and each song has a different length, this number should be unique. (In reality, it's *almost* unique because some duplicates exist, but it's close enough.) This number is then compared against a database of known albums[7] to retrieve the list of track names, which have been entered manually by human volunteers around the world. These track names and titles are then added to the ID tag of the MP3 or OGG file by the ripping software for later reference.

If you are using the CD itself, as opposed to a ripped version, then this information has to be retrieved manually each time you want to know what's playing. A part-time solution can be employed by using the cdcd package, which allows you to retrieve the number of the disc, the name, its tracks, and their durations.

```
cdcd tracks
```

The previous example will produce output that begins like this:

```
Trying CDDB server http://www.freedb.org:80/cgi-bin/cddb.cgi
Connection established.
Retrieving information on 2f107813.
CDDB query error: cannot parseAlbum name:
Total tracks:   19      Disc length:    70:18

Track  Length      Title
-------------------------------------------------------------------------
  1:    > [ 3:52.70]
  2:      [ 3:48.53]
  3:      [ 3:02.07]
  4:      [ 4:09.60]
  5:      [ 3:55.00]
```

Although this lets you see the current track (indicated by the >), it is no more useful than what's provided by any other media player. However, if you've installed the abcde ripper, you will have also already (and automagically) installed the cddb-tool components, which will perform the CD hashing function and the database queries for you. Consequently, you can determine the disc ID, its name, and the names of each track with a small amount of script code:

```
ID=`cd-discid /dev/dvd`
TITLE=`cddb-tool query http://freedb.freedb.org/~cddb/cddb.cgi 6 $(app) $(host) $ID`
```

The app and host parameters refer to the application name and the host name of the current machine. Although their contents are considered mandatory, they are not vital and are included only as a courtesy to the developers so they can track which applications are using the database. The magic number 6 refers to the protocol in use. From this string, you can extract the genre:

```
GENRE=`echo $TITLE | cut -d ' ' -f 2`
```

---

[7]This was originally stored at CDDB but more recently at FreeDB.

and the disc's ID and name:

```
DISC_ID=`echo $TITLE | cut -d ' ' -f 3`
DISC_TITLE=`echo $TITLE | cut -d ' ' -f 4-`
```

Using the disc ID and genre, you can determine a unique track listing (since the genre is used to distinguish between collisions in hash numbers) for the disc in question, which allows you to retrieve a parsable list of tracks with this:

```
cddb-tool read http://freedb.freedb.org/~cddb/cddb.cgi 6 $(app) $(host) ↵
$GENRE $DISC_ID
```

The disc title, year, and true genre are also available from this output.[8]

A more complex form of data to retrieve is that of the album's cover art. This is something that rippers, especially text-based ones, don't do and is something of a hit-and-miss affair in the open source world. This is, again, because of the lack of available data sources. Apple owns a music store, where the covers are used to sell the music and are downloaded with the purchase of the album. If you rip the music yourself, you have no such option.

One graphical tool that can help here is albumart. You can download this package from www.unrealvoodoo.org/hiteck/projects/albumart and install it with the following:

```
dpkg -i albumart_1.6.6-1_all.deb
```

This uses the ID tags inside the MP3 file to perform a search on various web sites, such as Buy.com, Walmart.com, and Yahoo! The method is little more than screen scraping, but provided the files are reasonably well named, the results are good enough and include very few false positives. When it has a problem determining the correct image, however, it errs on the side of caution and assigns nothing, waiting for you to manually click Set as Cover, which can take some time to correct. Once it has grabbed the art files, it names them folder.jpg in the appropriate directory, where it is picked up and used by most operating systems and media players. As a bonus, however, because the album art package uses the ID tags from the file, not the CD fingerprint, it can be used to find images for music that you've already ripped.

■ **Note** Unlike track listings, the cover art is still copyrighted material, so no independent developer has attempted to streamline this process with their own database.

Correctly finding album covers without any IDs or metadata can be incredibly hard work. There is a two-stage process available should this occur. The first part involves the determination of tags by looking at the audio properties of a song to determine the title and the artist. MusicBrainz is the major (free) contender in this field. Then, once you have an ID tag, you can retrieve the image as normal. These steps have been combined in software like Jaikoz, which also functions as a mass-metadata editing package that may be of use to those who have already ripped your music, without such data.

---

[8]There is one main unsolved problem with this approach. That is, if there are two discs with the same fingerprint or two database entries for the same disc, it is impossible to automatically pick the correct one. Consequently, a human needs to untangle the mess by selecting one of the options.

News

Any data that changes is new, and therefore news, making it an ideal candidate for real-time access. Making a personalized news channel is something most aggregators are doing through the use of RSS feeds and custom widgets. The soon to be retired iGoogle (`www.google.com/ig`), for example, also includes integration with its Google Mail and Calendar services, making this a disturbingly useful home page when viewed *as* a home page, but its enclosed nature makes it difficult to utilize this as a data input for a home. Instead, I'll cover methods to retrieve typical news items as individual data elements, which can be incorporated in a manner befitting ourselves. This splits into two types: push and pull.

Reported Stories: Push

The introduction of push-based media can be traced either to 24-hour rolling news (by Arthur W. Arundel in 1961) or to RSS[9] feeds, depending on your circumstances. Both formats appear to push the information in real time, as soon as it's received, to the viewer. In reality, both work by having the viewer continually pull data from the stream, silently ignoring anything that hasn't changed. In the case of TV, each pull consists of a new image and occurs several times a second. RSS happens significantly less frequently but is the one of interest here.

RSS Feeds

RSS is an XML-based file format for metadata. It describes a number of pieces of information that are updated frequently. This might include the reference to a blog post, the next train to leave platform 9¾ from King's Cross, the current stories on a news web site, and so on. In each case, every change is recorded in the RSS file, along with the all-important time stamp, enabling RSS readers to determine any updates to the data mentioned within it. The software that generates these RSS feeds may also remove references to previous stories once they become irrelevant or too old. However, old is defined by the author.

This de facto standard allows you to use common libraries to parse the RSS feeds and extract the information quite simply. One such library is the PHP-based MagpieRSS (`http://magpierss.sourceforge.net`), which also supports an alternative to RSS called Atom feeds and incorporates a data cache. This second feature makes your code simpler as you can request all the data from the RSS feed, without a concern for the most recent, because the library has cached the older stories automatically.

You utilize MagpieRSS in PHP by beginning with the usual code:

```
require_once 'rss_fetch.inc';
```

Then you request a feed from a given URL:

```
$rss = fetch_rss($url);
```

Naturally, this URL must reference an RSS file (such as `www.thebeercrate.com/rss_feed.xml`) and not the page that it describes (which would be `www.thebeercrate.com`). It is usually indicated by an orange button with white radio waves or simply an icon stating "RSS-XML." In all cases, the RSS file appears on the same page whose data you want to read. You can the process the stories with a simple loop such as the following:

```
$maxItems = 10;
$lastItem = count($rss->items);
```

---

[9] RSS currently stands for Really Simple Syndication, but its long and interesting history means that it wasn't always so simple.

```
if ($lastItem > $maxItems) {
    $lastItem = $maxItems;
}

for($i=0;$i < $maxItems;++$i) { /* process items here */ }
```

As new stories are added, they do so at the beginning of the file. Should you want to capture everything, it is consequently important to start at the end of the item list, as they will disappear sooner from the feed.

As mentioned earlier, the RSS contains only metadata, usually the title, description, and link to the full data. You can retrieve these from each item through the data members:

```
$rss->items[$i]['link'];
$rss->items[$i]['title'];
$rss->items[$i]['description'];
```

They can then be used to build up the information in the manner you want. For example, to recreate the information on your own home page, you would write the following:

```
$html .= "<a href=".$rss->items[$i]['link'].">".$rss->items[$i]['title']."</a>";
$html .= "<p>".$rss->items[$i]['description']."</p>";
```

Or you could use a speech synthesizer to read each title:

```
system("say default "+$rss->items[$i]['description']);
```

You can then use an Arduino that responds to sudden noises such as a clap or hand waving by a sensor (using a potential divider circuit from Chapter 2, with a microphone and LDR, respectively) to trigger the full story.

You can also add further logic, so if the story's title includes particular key words, such as *NASA*, you can send the information directly to your phone.

```
if (stristr($rss->items[$i]['title'], "nasa"))
    system("sendsms myphone "+$rss->items[$i]['description']);
```

This can be particularly useful for receiving up-to-minute sports results, lottery numbers, or voting information from the glut of reality TV shows still doing the rounds the world over. Even if it requires a little intelligent pruning to reduce the pertinent information into 140 octets (in the United States) or 160 characters (in Europe, RSA, and Oceania), which is the maximum length of a single unconcatenated text message, it will be generally cheaper than signing up for the paid-for services that provide the same results.

Retrieving Data: Pull

This encompasses any data that is purposefully requested when it is needed. One typical example is the weather or financial information that you might present at the end of the news bulletin. In these cases, although the information can be kept up-to-date in real time by simulating a push technology, few people need this level of granularity—once a day is enough. For this example, you will use the data retrieved from an online API to produce your own currency reports. This can be later extended to generate currency conversion tables to aid your holiday financing since home automation, as we've seen, doesn't stop at the front door. Even when you're abroad, you can make use of public data sources to keep a check on your spending by performing currency conversion.

Currency Conversion

Although there are many conversion sites available, they are highly variable in their offerings. Some require signup and an application ID. Some introduce adverts into the data stream. And some just plain ole don't work! Because Google provides conversion functionality for free as part of its search engine, there's no reason to be using anything else. So, we can extract the data from a request such as:

```
http://www.google.com/ig/calculator?hl=en&q=100EUR=?USD
```

which returns a JSON literal in the form of:

```
{lhs: "100 Euros",rhs: "134.14 U.S. dollars",error: "",icc: true}
```

It is therefore easy to see how an app can be built to provide a handy conversion chart, in both directions.

```php
<?php

$amount = "1";
$fromCurrency = "GBP";
$toCurrency = "EUR";

$url = "http://www.google.com/ig/calculator?hl=en&q=$amount${fromCurrency}=?$toCurrency";

$rawdata = file_get_contents($url);

$data = explode('"', $rawdata);
$data = explode(' ', $data['3']);

$conversionRate = $data[0];

for($i=1; $i<=20; ++$i) {
    print "$i $fromCurrency\t= " . number_format($i * $conversionRate, 2) . " $toCurrency \t";
    print "$i $toCurrency\t= " . number_format($i / $conversionRate, 2) . " $fromCurrency \t";
    print "\n";
}

?>
```

Of course, you may not be as lazy as I am in using the explode method, and you may prefer to formally decode the JSON!

With the rates at the time of writing, this produces:

```
1 GBP = 1.16 EUR        1 EUR = 0.86 GBP
2 GBP = 2.32 EUR        2 EUR = 1.72 GBP
3 GBP = 3.48 EUR        3 EUR = 2.59 GBP
4 GBP = 4.64 EUR        4 EUR = 3.45 GBP
5 GBP = 5.80 EUR        5 EUR = 4.31 GBP
6 GBP = 6.96 EUR        6 EUR = 5.17 GBP
7 GBP = 8.12 EUR        7 EUR = 6.03 GBP
8 GBP = 9.28 EUR        8 EUR = 6.89 GBP
9 GBP = 10.44 EUR       9 EUR = 7.76 GBP
```

```
10 GBP = 11.60 EUR          10 EUR = 8.62 GBP
11 GBP = 12.76 EUR          11 EUR = 9.48 GBP
12 GBP = 13.92 EUR          12 EUR = 10.34 GBP
13 GBP = 15.08 EUR          13 EUR = 11.20 GBP
14 GBP = 16.24 EUR          14 EUR = 12.07 GBP
15 GBP = 17.40 EUR          15 EUR = 12.93 GBP
16 GBP = 18.56 EUR          16 EUR = 13.79 GBP
17 GBP = 19.73 EUR          17 EUR = 14.65 GBP
18 GBP = 20.89 EUR          18 EUR = 15.51 GBP
19 GBP = 22.05 EUR          19 EUR = 16.38 GBP
20 GBP = 23.13 EUR          20 EUR = 17.30 GBP
```

From here, you can start expanding this into your HA setup by writing the data into a web page on your home server with an "I spent this" button, to keep track of how much you spent while abroad. Or add an "I lent money to ... " button that connects to your contact list, so you can both settle up later in your native currency. As a tool, it is no better than any of the other conversion apps or websites you might find, but when it is able to connect to your TODO list on the same server, reminding you to pay someone back, or to revisit the bureau de change, the benefits become clear.

In all cases, you write the current data into a regularly updated log file, as you did with the weather status, for the same reasons—that is, to prevent continually abusing someone elses servers. However, with the financial markets changing more rapidly, you might want to update this file several times a day.

Other Public Sources

Many other organizations provide data services to the public; so many, in fact, that it would be impossible to list them all here. Google, Amazon, and bit.ly all provide content to the public. Although a lot of it is interesting, such as the comparison of European fuel prices, most data has limited application in a smart home environment.

Typical starting places include:

```
http://www.google.co.uk/publicdata
http://aws.amazon.com/publicdatasets/
https://bitly.com/bundles/hmason/1
```

With third-party data source scrapers and sharers looking to become an ecosystem in its own right, it's no surprise that people have been thinking about standardizing it, so that different scrapes can interact with a shared meta-level API. The first foray into this is by:

```
http://import.io
```

This is a new technology that should be available to the public by the time this book gets to press, so hopefully it will provide a boon to those looking to discover and utlize more home automation data sets.

Private Data

Most of us have personal data on computers that are not owned or controlled by us. Even though the more concerned of us[10] try to minimize this at every turn, it is often not possible or convenient to do so. Furthermore, there are (now) many casual Linux users who are solely desktop-based and aren't interested in running their own remote servers and will gladly store their contact information, diary, and e-mail on another computer. The convenience is

---

[10]"Concerned" is the politically correct way of saying "paranoid."

undeniable—having your data available from any machine in the world (with a network connection) provides a truly location-less digital lifestyle. But your home is not, generally, location-less. Therefore, you need to consider what type of useful information about yourself is held on other computers and how to access it.

Calendar

Groupware applications are one of the areas in which Linux desktop software has been particularly weak. Google has entered this arena with its own solution, Google Calendar, which links into your e-mail, allowing daily reminders to be sent to your inbox as well as to the calendars of other people and groups.

Calendar events that occur within the next 24 hours can also be queried by SMS, and new ones can be added by sending a message to GVENT (48368). Currently, this functionality is available only to U.S. users but is a free HA feature for those it does affect.

The information within the calendar is yours and available in several different ways. First, and most simply, it can be embedded into any web page as an iframe:

```
<iframe src="http://www.google.com/calendar/embed?src=my_email_address ↵
%40gmail.com&ctz=Europe/London" style="border: 0" width="800" height="600" ↵
frameborder="0" scrolling="no"></iframe>
```

This shows the current calendar and allows to you edit *existing* events. However, you will need to refresh the page manually for edits to become visible, and *new* events cannot be added without venturing into the Google Calendar page.

The *apparent* security hole that this public URL opens is avoided, because you must already be signed into your Google account for this to work; otherwise, the login page is shown.

Alternatively, if you want your calendar to be visible without signing into your Google account, then you can generate a private key that makes your calendar data available to anyone that knows this key. The key is presented as a secret URL.

To discover this URL, go the Settings link at the top right of your Google Calendar account, and choose Calendars. This will open a list of calendars that you can edit and those you can't. Naturally, you can't choose to expose the details of the read-only variants. So, select your own personal calendar, and scroll down to the section entitled Private Address. The three icons on the right side, labeled XML, ICAL, and HTML, provide a URL to retrieve the data for your calendar in the format specified. A typical HTML link looks like this:

```
http://www.google.com/calendar/embed?src=my_email_address ↵
%40gmail.com&ctz=Europe/London&pvttk=5f93e4d926ce3dd2a91669da470e98c5
```

The XML version is as follows:

```
http://www.google.com/calendar/feeds/my_email_address ↵
%40gmail.com/private-5f93e4d926ce3dd2a91669da470e98c5/basic
```

The ICAL version uses a slightly different format:

```
http://www.google.com/calendar/ical/my_email_address ↵
%40gmail.com/private-5f93e4d926ce3dd2a91669da470e98c5/basic.ics
```

The latter two are of greater use to us, since they can be viewed (but not edited) in whatever software you choose.

If you're not comfortable with the XML processing language XSLT, then a simple PHP loop can be written to parse the ICAL file, like this:

```
$regex = "/BEGIN:VEVENT.*?DTSTART:[^:]*:([^\s]*).*?SUMMARY:([^\n]*) ↵
.*?END:VEVENT/is";
preg_match_all($regex, $contents, $matches, PREG_SET_ORDER);

for($i=0;$i<sizeof($matches);++$i) {
    // $matches[$i][1] holds the entire ICAL event
    // $matches[$i][1] holds the time
    // $matches[$i][2] holds the summary
}
```

The date format in ICAL can be stored in one of three formats:

- Local time

- Local time with time zone

- UTC time

You need not worry about which version is used, as you can use the existing PHP library functions, such as this:

```
$prettyDate = strftime("%A %d %b %Y.", strtotime($matches[$i][1]));
```

■ **Note**   Be warned that the XML version of your data includes back references to your calendar, which include your private key.

Naturally, other online calendar applications exist, offering similar functionality. This version is included as a guide. But having gotten your data onto your own machine, you can trigger your own e-mail notifications, send SMS messages to countries currently unsupported by Google, or automatically load the local florist's web page when the words *grandma* and *birthday* appear.

Accessing Webmail through POP3

Most of today's workforce considers e-mail on the move as a standard feature of office life. But for the home user, e-mail falls into one of two categories:

- It is something that is sent to their machine and collected by their local client (often an old version of Outlook Express); consequently, it's unavailable elsewhere.

- It is a web-based facility, provided by Yahoo!, Hotmail, or Google, and can be accessed only through a web browser.

Although both statements are (partially) correct, it does hide extra functionality that can be provided very cheaply. In the first case, you can provide your own e-mail server (as I covered in Chapter 5) and add a webmail component using software such as AtMail. This allows your home machine to continue being in charge of all your mail, except that you don't need to be at home to use it.

Alternatively, you can use getmail to receive your webmail messages through an alternate (that is, non-web) protocol. First, you need to ensure that your webmail provider supports POP3 access. This isn't always easy to find or determine, because the use of POP3 means you will no longer see the ads on their web pages. But when it is available, it is usually found in the settings part of the service. All of the major companies provide this service, although not all are free.

- Hotmail provides POP3 access by default, making it unnecessary to switch on, and after many years of including this only on its subscription service, now Hotmail provides it for free. The server is currently at pop3.live.com.

- Google Mail was the first to provide free POP3 access to e-mail, from pop.gmail.com. Although now most accounts are enabled by default, some older ones aren't. You therefore need to select Settings and Forwarding and POP/IMAP. From here you can enable it for all mail or any newly received mail.

- Yahoo! provides POP3 access and forwarding to their e-mail only through its Yahoo! Plus paid-for service. A cheat is available on some services (although not Yahoo!) where you forward all your mail to another service (such as Hotmail or Gmail) where free POP services are available!

Previously, there was a project to process HTML mail directly, eliminating the need to pay for POP3 services. This included the now defunct http://httpmail.sourceforge.net. Such measures are (fortunately) no longer necessary.

Once you know the server on which your e-mail lives, you can download it. This can be either for reading locally, for backup purposes, or for processing commands sent in e-mails. Although most e-mail software can process POP3 servers, I use getmail.

```
apt-get install getmail4
```

I have this configured so that each e-mail account is downloaded to a separate file. I'll demonstrate with an example, beginning with the directory structure:

```
mkdir ~/.getmail
mkdir ~/externalmail
touch  ~/externalmail/gmail.mbox
touch  ~/externalmail/hotmail.mbox
touch  ~/externalmail/yahoo.mbox
```

and then a separate configuration file is created for each server called ~/.getmail/getmail.gmail, which reads as follows:

```
 [retriever]
type = SimplePOP3SSLRetriever
server = pop.gmail.com
username = my_email_address@gmail.com
password = my_password

[destination]
type = Mboxrd
path = ~/externalmail/gmail.mbox

[options]
verbose = 2
message_log = ~/.getmail/error.log
```

If you'd prefer for them to go into your traditional Linux mail box, then you can change the path to the following:

```
path = /var/mail/steev
```

You can then retrieve them like this and watch the system download the e-mails:

```
getmail -r getmail.gmail
```

Some services, notably Google Mail, do not allow you to download all your e-mails at once if there are a lot of them. Therefore, you need to reinvoke the command. This helps support the bandwidth of both machines.

▦ **Tip** If you have only one external e-mail account, then calling your configuration file `getmailrc` allows you to omit the filename arguments.

You can then view these mails in the client of your choice. Here's an example:

```
mutt -f ~/externalmail/gmail.mbox
```

Make sure you let `getmail` finish retrieving the e-mails; otherwise, you will get two copies of each mail in your inbox.

If you are intending to process these e-mails with `procmail`, as you saw in Chapter 5, then you need to write the incoming e-mail not to the inbox but to `procmail` itself. This is done by configuring the destination thusly:

```
[destination]
type = MDA_external
path = /usr/bin/procmail
unixfrom = True
```

Twitter

The phenomenon that is Twitter has allowed the general public to morph into self-styled microcelebrities as they embrace a mechanism of simple broadcast communication from one individual to a set of many "followers." Although communications generally remain public, it is possible to create a list of users so that members of the same family can follow each other in private. This can be done by selecting "Protect my Tweets" in the account settings page.

One thing that Twitter has succeeded in doing better than most social sites is that it has not deviated from its original microblogging ideals, meaning that the APIs to query and control the feeds have remained consistent. This makes it easy for you (or your house) to tweet information to your feeds or for the house to process them and take some sort of action based on it. In all cases, however, you will have to manually sign up for an account on behalf of your house. The only change in the last few years has been to strengthen security by requiring the use of OAuth.

Posting Tweets with OAuth

The Twitter API uses an HTTP request to upload a new tweet, with the primary implementation being through `TwitterOAuth`, the library from `https://github.com/abraham/twitteroauth`.

```
$auth = getTwitterDetails($user);
$connection = new TwitterOAuth($auth->ckey, $auth->csecret, $auth->oatoken, $auth->oasecret);
$content = $connection->get('account/verify_credentials');

$connection->post('statuses/update', array('status' => $all));
```

This example uses PHP, but any language with a binding for OAuth works in the same way. You need only to fill in your login credentials, and you can tweet from the command line.

The $auth structure is as simple as it looks, and filled from the contents of a configuration file with code such as:

```
function getTwitterDetails($user) {
    $contents = @file("twitter.conf");

        $oauth = new OAuthDetails();
        $oauth->ckey = trim($contents[0]);
        $oauth->csecret = trim($contents[1]);
        $oauth->oatoken = trim($contents[2]);
        $oauth->oasecret = trim($contents[3]);

    return $oauth;
}
```

with the only complication of getting the values of those secret and token values. Luckily, this is standard practise, and if you've worked with OAuth before there'll be no alarms and no surprises. If you haven't, read on . . .

There are several different ways of accessing the Twitter API, but for our purposes, the solution we want is termed as "Just want to access the API from your own account . . . ". This is explained at https://dev.twitter.com/docs/auth/tokens-devtwittercom.

From here you can create a Twitter application, which is necessary because it is your script (i.e., an application) that communicates with the Twitter API, not the user. This provides you with a consumer key and a consumer secret, ckey and csecret. With these you are able to talk to Twitter through its API.

To be able to post, or read, messages on behalf of a user, they need to authenticate themselves with your application on behalf of Twitter. This requires the user to get the oatoken and oasecret. After creating the application keys, the Twitter web page has a section called "Your Access Token", which provides a one-click solution to getting this data. Add it to the configuration file, so that getTwitterDetails can parse it, and you are now able to programmatically send tweets.

Reading Tweets with OAuth

In the same way that tweets can be written with a simple HTTP request, so can they be read. The documentation includes URLs to retrieve details of your timeline, that of your friends, along with retweets, and so on. The calls return all the information available regarding the selected tweets with full information on the poster (such as their name, image, and followers count), message, and the in-reply data (featuring status, user, and screen name). This is more than you'll generally need, but it's a good idea in API design to never lose information if possible—it's easier to filter out than it is to add back in. You can use this code to follow tweets when offline by using the computer to intercept suitably formatted tweets and sending them on with SMS transmit code. We saw one such application of this in Chapter 2, with the automatic dog feeder.

Reading Tweets with RSS

The very nature of Twitter lends itself to existing RSS technology, making customized parsers unnecessary. The URL for the user @apress would be as follows:

```
https://api.twitter.com/1/statuses/user_timeline.rss?screen_name=apress
```

which could be retrieved and processed with XSLT or combined with the feeds from each family member into one for display on a house notice board. The results here are less verbose than their cURL counterparts, making it easier to process, at the expense of less contextual information.

Facebook

Although Twitter has adopted a broadcast mechanism, Facebook has continued to focus on the facilitation of a personal network with whom you share data. For HA, you are probably more interested in sharing information with friends than strangers, so this can be the better solution. However, writing an app that uses Facebook has a higher barrier to entry with comparatively little gain. It does, by way of compensation, provide a preexisting login mechanism and is a web site that many people check more often than their e-mail, so information can be disseminated faster. However, Facebook does change its API periodically, so what works one day might not work the next, and you have to keep on top of it. If you are using Facebook as a means of allowing several people to control or view the status of your home, it is probably easier to use your own home page, with a set of access rights, as you saw in Chapter 5.

If you're still sold on the idea of a Facebook, then you should install the Developer application and create your own app key with it. This will enable your application to authenticate the users who will use it, either from within Facebook or on sites other than Facebook through Facebook Connect. (A good basic tutorial is available at www.scribd.com/doc/22257416/Building-with-Facebook-Social-Dev-Camp-Chicago-2009.) To keep it private among your family, simply add their ID as *developers*. If you want to share information with your children, getting them to accept you as a Facebook friend can be more difficult, however! In this case, you might have to convince them to create a second account, used solely for your benefit. Facebook doesn't allow you to send messages to users who haven't installed the app (or are included in the list of developers), so this requires careful management.

The technical component is much simpler, by comparison, because Facebook provides standard code that can be copied to a directory on your web server and used whenever your app is invoked from within Facebook. It is then up to you to check the ID of the user working with your app to determine what functionality they are entitled to and generate web pages accordingly. You can find a lot of useful beginning information on Facebook's own page at http://developers.facebook.com.

Automation

With this information, you have to consider how it will be used by the house. This requires development of a most personal nature. After all, if you are working shifts, then my code to control the lights according to the times of sunrise and sunset will be of little use to you. Instead, I will present various possibilities and let you decide on how best to combine them.

Timed Events

Life is controlled by time. So, having a mechanism to affect the house at certain times is very desirable. Because a computer's life is also controlled by time, there are procedures already in place to make this task trivial for us.

Periodic Control with Cron Jobs

These take their name from the *chron*ological job scheduler of Unix-like operating systems, which automatically executes a command at given times throughout the year. There is a file, known as the *crontab*, which has a fine level of granular control regarding these jobs, and separate files exist for each user. You can edit this file belonging to the current user (calling export EDITOR=vi first if necessary) with the following:

```
crontab -e
```

There is also a –u option that allows root to edit the crontab of other users. A typical file might begin with the following:

```
# m    h  dom mon dow  command
00     7   *   *   1-5  /usr/local/minerva/etc/alarm 1
10,15  7   *   *   1-5  /usr/local/minerva/etc/alarm 2
*/5    *   *   *   *    /usr/local/bin/getmail --quiet
```

The # line is a comment and acts as a reminder of the columns; minutes, hours, day of month (from 1 to 31), month (1 to 12, or named by abbreviation), day of week (0 to 7, with Sunday being both 0 and 7), and the command to be executed. Each column supports the use of wildcards (* means any), inclusive ranges (1–5), comma-delimited sequences (occurring at 10 and 15 only), and periodic (*/5 indicates every five minutes in this example). The cron program will invoke the command if, and only if, all conditions can be met.

Typical uses might be as follows:

- An alarm clock, triggering messages, weather reports, or news when waking up

- Retrieving e-mail for one or more accounts, at different rates

- Initiating backups of local data, e-mail, or projects

- Controlling lights while on holiday

- Controlling lights to switch on, gradually, when waking up

- Real-life reminders for birthdays, anniversaries, Mother's Day, and so on

Because these occur under the auspices of the user (that is, owner) of the crontab, suitably permissions must exist for the commands in question.

■ **Note**   Many users try to avoid running anything as root, if it is at all possible. Therefore, when adding timed tasks to your home, it is recommended you add them to the crontab for a special myhouse user and assign it only the specific rights it needs.

The crontab, as provided, is accurate to within one minute. If you're one of the very few people who need per-second accuracy, then there are two ways of doing it. Both involve triggering the event on the preceding minute and waiting for the required number of seconds. The first variation involves changing the crontab to read as follows:

```
00    7   *   *   1-5  sleep 30; /usr/local/minerva/etc/alarm 1
```

The second involves adding the same sleep instruction to the command that's run. This can be useful when controlling light switches in a humanistic way, as it is rare to take exactly 60 seconds to climb the stairs before turning the upstairs light on.

For randomized timing, you can sleep for a random amount of time (sleep `echo $((RANDOM%60))s`) before continuing with the command, as you saw in Chapter 1.

There will also be occasions when you want to ignore the cron jobs for a short while, such as disabling the alarm clock while we're on holiday. You can always comment out the lines in the crontab to do this or change the command from this:

```
/usr/local/minerva/etc/alarm 1
```

to the following:

```
[ -f ~/i_am_on_holiday ] || /usr/local/minerva/etc/alarm 1
```

The first expression checks for the existence of the given file and skips the alarm call if it exists. Because this can be any file, located anywhere, it doesn't need to belong to the crontab owner for it to affect the task. One possible scenario would be to use Bluetooth to watch for approaching mobile devices, creating a file in a specific directory for each user (and deleting it again, when they go out of range, that is, have left the house). Once everyone was home, a cron job set to check this directory every minute could send an e-mail reminding you to leave the computer and be sociable!

For more complex timing scenarios, you can use cron to periodically run a separate script, say every minute. If you return to the "next train" script from earlier, you could gain every last possible minute at home by retrieving the first suitable train from here:

```
NEXT_TRAIN=`whattrain.php 30 35 | head -n 1`
```

In this scenario, a suitable train is one that leaves in 30 to 35 minutes, which gives you time to get ready. If this command produces an output, then you can use the speech synthesizer to report it:

```
if [ `echo $NEXT_TRAIN | wc -l` -ne 0 ]; then
  say default $NEXT_TRAIN
fi
```

The same script could be used to automatically vary the wake-up time of your alarm clock!

In Chapter 7, you'll learn how Minerva supports even more complex actions by sending a status message to different places, according to whether you are at home, at work, or on the train.

Occasional Control with At

In addition to the periodic events, you will often want to invoke extra events, such as a reminder in ten minutes to check on the cooking. Again, Linux is prepared with the at command, such as the following:

```
echo "say default Check on dinner" | at now + 10 minutes
```

This syntax is necessary because, by default, at accepts the commands interactively from the command line (finishing with a Ctrl+D). Every at event goes into a queue, enabling complete recipes to be produced for multipart events.

Alas, this example works fine in its current scenario but has a fatal issue for tasks requiring finer granularity as the scheduler works only with whole minutes, meaning that a task for "now + 1 minute" actually means "at the start of the next minute," which might be only five seconds away! So, you need to employ the "sleeping seconds" trick:

```
echo "sleep `date +%S`; say default Check on dinner" | at now + 10 minutes
```

It is also possible to use at to trigger events at a specific time:

```
echo "say default Time for CSI" | at 21:00
```

This always takes place when that time is *next* reached, meaning that it could be on the following day.

Error Handling

In any development, reporting and handling the errors are the most time-consuming parts of the project. HA is, unfortunately, no different. You have some things in your favor, primarily that you're in control of the house and (most of) the other software running on the machine, so you can work out in advance if there are likely to be problems. But if you send a text message to your video, for example, you have no way of knowing whether the command worked or where in the chain it failed. There are three rules here:

- Always acknowledge commands and requests

- Always reply using the same medium

- Always log the replies into a local file and optionally send them by e-mail

The second one is probably the nonobvious one. If someone sends a command by SMS, then the reply should also go back to SMS, even if it's more costly. This is because the sender is using SMS for a reason—maybe they don't have access to e-mail or the web site has broken—so they'll only be reassured of its delivery by the same route. Certainly, it's acceptable for the message to ask that replies are sent elsewhere, but the default should take the same route.

This rule applies at every stage in the pipeline. So, in a chain of SMS to e-mail to IR, if the IR unit has a failure, then the script that invoked it (and is processing the e-mail) must pass that error back in an e-mail. At this point, the SMS to e-mail gateway picks up an e-mail–based error and passes it to the end user as an SMS.

An adaptation of the ideas in HTTP are useful here, where you adopt a three-part response to every request in the form of number, argument, description:

- The number is a numeric code describing the result of the operation. Use 200 for OK, perhaps, along with the various error codes for "device not found," "disk full," and so on. This means that on the lowest-bandwidth devices, you will get an error that is descriptive enough to start diagnostics.

- The argument covers the specific device or unit involved.

- The description contains a device-specific error, which should not repeat any information pertaining to the error number or the device name (as they're already present).

Because the size and format of the various error messages will be unknown to everyone in the chain, this layout ensures a unified view of the system and means that a custom formatting script is able to prepare the information for the target medium, maybe by including full descriptions of the numeric error code, or maybe it will crop the description text on SMS and tweet messages.

Conclusion

There are essentially two phases to data processing in a smart automated home. The first is the collection, usually by screen scraping, RSS feeds, or API access, to provide a copy of some remote data on your local machine. This can either occur when you request it, such as the case for train departure times, or when you download it ahead of time and cache it, as you saw with the weather forecasts and TV schedules. The second phase is the processing, where the data is converted into something more usable such as a short, spoken, weather report or a list of CD tracks that can be clicked to play that track. You learned about a wide variety of different data formats, including private calendars and public news feeds. All are available to the geek with a little time to spend. As I mentioned in the introduction to the chapter, content is king and is a great stepping stone to making it appear that your computer can think for itself and improve your living.

CHAPTER 7

■ ■ ■

Control Hubs: Bringing It All Together

Most people are interested in features and benefits, not the minutia of code. Unfortunately, the barrier to entry in home automation is quite high, as basic features require a lot of underlying work. The comparatively simple process of being able to e-mail your video at video@myhome.com requires preparing a DNS record, e-mail server, message parser, network functionality, and IR transmission. Now, however, you have these individual components and can look at combining them into processes and features and abstracting them so they can be upgraded or changed without breaking the home's functionality as it stands.

Integration of Technologies

As I've mentioned previously, your home technology is based around Node0—or, more specifically, a Linux machine or Raspberry Pi based in a central location that performs all the processing and thinking tasks. This is your single point of failure in several ways. Most obviously, it means you lack media control or playback when the machine is offline or broken. Being Linux, this is fortunately a rare occurrence. But it is the standard security model of Linux itself that makes it the most vulnerable. Ironic, huh?

Linux provides access to every file and device[1] through a three-stage set of permissions: user, group, and other. Additionally, each file can be designated ownership by one user and group. This is normally enough control for standard files and documents, but in HA you are controlling devices that are used by several different systems. Audio in /dev/dsp, for example, is used for MP3 playback, speech synthesis, and the soundtrack of a movie playing. It is easy to see from this how several programs and users should be allowed to use the audio device to report errors through speech but not be allowed to control the whole house audio system. Similarly, the use of the serial port to back up a mobile phone SIM over Bluetooth needs different permissions when the same port is used for reprogramming an Arduino or sending IR signals. Unfortunately, there is not a fine enough granularity of control because the only genuine protection is offered by the operating system. And because of that, you can only restrict access to the devices as a whole. You can't even limit access to software because you could simply write the MP3 playback script (or rebuild the package from source in a local directory) and run it as any user to avoid any restriction placed on the software. Again, you are limited to whatever access rights you place on the device file.

■ **Note** Some distributions, such as SELinux, provide explicit access rights for each program that allow this level of fine control. It is time-consuming to set up, however.

---

[1] Because every device is also a file.

Our solution, as it has been throughout the book, is to ignore the problem! There are two components to this. In the first instance, you simplify the situation by creating only a minimum of local users on the Linux box, preferably one, and add only the primary users to a group called homecontrol, for example. You can then apply permissions for this group to each of your devices. When you allow control to this device through a web or SMS interface then, naturally those daemons must also be added to the group so that they have access to the device.

■ **Note**   Remember that most daemons, like Apache, need to be restarted after any changes to group membership are applied.

The secondary part of the solution involves, as it always does, the knowledge that anyone in the house has both a level of physical access and a level of social coercion that prevents users from abusing the system as others might do.

Both of these, in the given scenario, are acceptable tradeoffs between security and ease of use. After all, most other family members are unlikely to be using the server directly and instead through an interface (such as a phone or the Web) where security can be applied.

The Teakettle: An Example

When discussing my home automation system to people, one topic that always comes up is that of my online electric teakettle. Its functionality includes the ability to initiate a boil from a web page or command line and have a fresh cup ready the second that I get home from work. From a hardware level, this requires nothing more than a basic pair of X10 modules—a CM11 from which the computer sends the message and an appliance module like the AM12 to control power to the teakettle—but the subtleties are in the software and attention to detail.

■ **Note**   In all cases, the teakettle must be always switched on and plugged into the AM12. Furthermore, there must always be water in the teakettle to stop it from boiling dry.

Making a cuppa from the Web is the same as triggering one from the command line or anywhere else. Namely, there is a basic trio of commands:

- "Switch on"
- "Wait"
- "Switch off"

Traditionally, you might implement a script for this like this:

```
heyu turn kettle on
sleep 215
heyu turn kettle off
```

And it works! This script can be triggered from anywhere, at any time, to provide the necessary function. Naturally, if it is executed directly from a script on a web page, the page will take 215 seconds to return and will usually have timed out, so it should be run in the background:

```
shell_exec("/usr/local/minerva/bin/kettle &");
```

The next subtlety comes from the configurability of the teakettle itself. Each has its own peculiarities with regard to boiling times, so you create a configuration file for your home indicating the X10 address of each teakettle and its respective boiling time.[2] This is then processed by the main `kettle` script. I use a configuration script like this:

```
#!/bin/bash
DEVICE=$1
CMD=$2

# DEVICE here refers to a particular kettle, for those that need
# to differentiate between one in the bedroom, and kitchen.

if [ "$CMD" == "time" ]; then
    # report the number of seconds the kettle takes to boil
    echo 215
fi

if [ "$CMD" == "device" ]; then
    # the x10 device
    echo e3
fi
```

This allows me to add other kettles as needs require, which makes the configuration script look like this:

```
DEVICE=$1
homedevice default on `kettle.conf $DEVICE device`
sleep `kettle.conf $DEVICE time`
homedevice default off `kettle.conf $DEVICE device`
```

Note the abstracted script `homedevice`, instead of heyu, which I'll discuss later.

There is then one detail to add—once the teakettle has switched itself off, you can use the speech synthesis module to announce the fact. You could alternatively issue a popup window on your terminal, like this:

```
kdialog --msgbox "The kettle has boiled!"
```

Providing a fresh boil when you return from work is a similar combination of simple scripts. In this case, you need to know the time the teakettle takes to boil (as shown earlier) and the travel time from work to home. You then perform a basic subtraction and issue a sleep before the `kettle` script is called. What calls the script is then a matter of taste (no pun intended). If you're used to working on the command line, then a simple script could initiate a sequence to awaken the teakettle, switch on lights, and so on.

Naturally, this same code could be run from a web page or triggered on receipt of an e-mail.

This works in the specific case where the journey duration is consistent, as it is for walkers, cyclists, and anyone *not* reliant on public transport or at the mercy of traffic.

More complex solutions are also possible by looking at the live train departure boards (as covered in Chapter 6), for example, and letting the computer work out which train you are most likely to have caught and check for its arrival time before beginning the boil. This is left as an exercise for you!

Naturally, if you have a fast-boiling teakettle, there might be enough time to trigger the script from a pressure mat sensor under the front door mat or when the Bluetooth dongle detects your phone coming *into* range for the first time that day. In that case, by the time you've approached the house, opened the door, and taken off your shoes and coat, the teakettle is ready.

---

[2] The boiling time of most kettles shortens when there is less water, so empirically test the boil time with a full teakettle.

Minerva

Minerva is a complete, easy-to-use home automation suite. Using Minerva you can make your home easier and cheaper to run and can make it more secure. With Minerva you can switch on your lights from anywhere using a mobile phone or PC, e-mail your video, check your security CCTV footage, control your central heating, and do much more. It is the epitome of the modular design goals outlined in the introduction, and it's an example of how you can bring all the technologies you've learned so far into a single unified whole.

Minerva runs on GNU/Linux (including the Raspberry Pi) but exists in its own mini-ecosystem, with its own list of users, set of scripts, and functionality. It relies on native command-line tools to perform its many tasks and can therefore be run from virtually any platform (smartphone, PDA, laptop, or remote PC) with identical functionality. It also relies on the security model outlined earlier, where only a few users have access to the machine directly, expecting them to go through alternate interfaces so that their user credentials can be controlled on a case-by-case basis.

There is a guide to the basic structure in Figure 7-1.

Minerva Basic Control Diagram

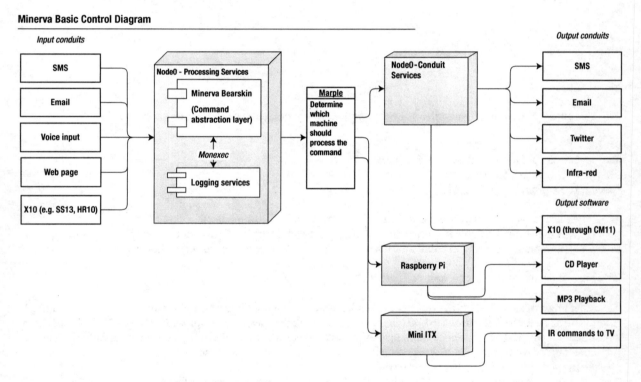

Figure 7-1. Minerva Block Diagram

Overview

The Minerva system isn't really a collection of software. It's more akin to a bundle of protocols, each giving a unified interface to other programs and scripts in the system. This allows each script to abstract the tools underneath it so that if, for example, heyu becomes unable to support the necessary features or needs to be replaced, then only the X10 control script needs to be replaced—and none of the code that uses it. Similarly, as it is possible to replace, or supplement, X10 with the other systems outlined in Chapter 1 there is a further layer of abstraction so that alternate methods can be used, should the need arise.

There are abstractions and interfaces for each part of the system. Minerva's visionary grand design is to provide a means whereby every piece of home technology can be interfaced together through a common technology. This architecture consists of three parts: input, process, and output. Each part is completely distinct, meaning you can control any of the house *processes* from any supported *input conduit* such as the web browser, remote control, or SMS text message.

Similarly, any reports or notifications can be sent to any of the available *output conduits*, which may (or may not) be the same as the input. One common example is to trigger a process (such as switching the teakettle on) using an IR input conduit but receive confirmation through the voice output conduit where the computer speaks to you.

From this you can see that the web page input conduit is built on top the existing command abstractions. Furthermore, the web page has its own abstractions (called Zinc) so that if you want to build a smaller slimmed-down web page (which doesn't have the dependencies on the WARP system), you can do so without replacing any of that code.

Like the best Linux software, Minerva adopts many open standards and has code released through the GPL, which provides a platform that can encompass every user and system without vendor lock-in. You can reach its home and download page from `http://www.MinervaHome.net`.

■ **Note** Most examples here use the variable `$MINBASE` that is set to the install directory of Minerva, which by default is `/usr/local/minerva`. It is omitted for the sake of brevity.

Underneath `$MINBASE` is a directory structure that is not unlike that used by most Linux Filesystem Hierarchy Standard–compliant distributions. It has the following:

> `bin`: The scripts that send and receive messages between conduits and the abstractions for the devices themselves.

> `conf`: Personal configuration data, such as external accounts and address book contacts. This has been separated from the traditional `etc` directory to allow sharing and updates to happen without accidentally exposing this private information.

> `etc`: Configuration data regarding the Minerva system itself, its users, settings, and its appliances, such as the teakettle boil time.

> `house`: Global configuration concerning devices for this and other machines in the house. It dictates which specific devices (such as `/dev/dsp` or `/dev/dvd`) should be used with each particular command. This is also used with Marple (covered later), which allows other devices in the house to be controlled from a single location.

> `media`: Any sound, image, or text file used by the base-level system, such as chimes to begin a vocal announcement or recorded speech used in an alarm clock. These are generally called by the sfx utility that translates the argument of ok, `error` or `end`, for example, into a corresponding wave file in the `minerva/media/wav` directory.

> `var`: All data generated by the user, as a consequence of using Minerva, is stored here. This includes the sampled messages generated by projects such as the Arduino dictation unit, presented in Chapter 2. For Linux compliance, it stores log information from the commands themselves in `/var/log/minerva` so that tools such as `logrotate` can be used normally.

Installing Minerva requires an invocation of the basic `install.sh` script. This copies the files to the appropriate directories, changes the file permissions, and generates the default users for the system. It is also capable of downloading the current day's weather reports and TV schedules. The script is fairly all-inclusive, so you can access the web-based applet for the CD player without explicitly granting read/write permissions to `/dev/dsp` to the web server. The downside of this permissive process is that potential vulnerabilities are opened up. Furthermore, anyone outside the U.K. area will need to rerun the update scripts describing their locale for Minerva to report accurate weather forecasts and TV schedules.

Linux Users Are Not HA Users

The desire of Minerva to have its own ecosystem, with distinct usernames and passwords, is not egomaniacal for the sake of it; it's merely a case of practicality because not everyone using the system will have (or should be able to get) a Linux-based account. After all, you eliminate Linux accounts for most users, as you want users to control the system through means that can be more easily authenticated on a fine-grained level. This gives you a multistage approach:

- Everyone living in the house or a family relative has a Minerva account. This gives you the option of allowing them to view family photos, see what you're listening to, and so on. It also means they can use your services to retrieve shows from the TV guide or view the weather report.

- Everyone living in the house will generally also have a web username, which should match their Minerva user, to provide them access to this input conduit. They will be a subset of total Minerva users. This allows them to control their music selection and review certain house stats. Each web user has controllable read and write authentication to the various facilities.

- Most people living in the house will have access to the other input conduits, such as SMS or e-mail.

- Few users, usually just one, will have a Linux account allowing them to directly control the filesystem and users. A guest account will usually exist to allow read-only access to the Samba file servers so that music can be played locally. Other users will be created for the purpose of e-mailing light switches, for example, but will be made inaccessible to other dwellers by setting the shell to /bin/false.

Therefore, you will introduce your own read-only hierarchy within the Minerva filesystem (all relative to $MINBASE) covering each user, the applications, and their appropriate rights. The passwords for each input conduit will not be included here because the files must be publicly readable for the various commands to work. Instead, you rely on the input conduit (such as the web browser) to store its own passwords and validate the user. After all, you're more likely to trust the experience of Apache in providing robust username security than yourself.

First you can add users to the system with a line such as this:

```
addminervauser steev "Steven Goodwin"
```

This will create a directory for them, beginning here:

```
$MINBASE/etc/users/steev
```

to hold all the user-specific settings and data, including the following:

- Full name

- Personal address book

- Default Minerva preferences (such as preferred style of synthetic voice)

- Access rights to various devices

- TV search terms

- External account references (such as links to their Google calendar)

Each application in the system has a specific code (homedevice, cdplayer, and so on) and an associated directory that holds files for determining the access rights such as r (for read-access) or rw (for read-write). I use r and rw as standard terms, even though their meaning isn't directly analogous because, in the case of the CD player, *read access* means "can you look at the current track playing," whereas *read-write* means "can change the current track." You have a simple command to query this status, which returns a true or false response by setting 1 or 0 as an exit code, retrievable with $? if the specified user can query the state of the CD player:

```
minuser auth steev cdplayer get r
```

The currently supported codes are as follows:

- `cdplayer`
- `Bluetooth`
- `system`
- `mixer`
- `mp3jukebox`
- `photos`
- `videostream`
- `vlc`
- `x10`
- `sms`

These can be added to as necessary, without configuration, as the lack of an access file is considered as "no access allowed."

The Minerva User

In the same way that Linux has an all-powered root user, so do you in the realm of Minerva. And that user is called, er, Minerva! Although it doesn't have the same level of OS control that root does, it does have the responsibility of dealing with any housewide (that is, user-agnostic) data collection and processing. This includes the nightly collection of weather reports and the searching of the TV guide, which are processed by the scripts inside its update directory.

The Public User

You also have a public user that is used for storing housewide information such as the family address book. Because you can't communicate with Minerva except through a conduit—and each conduit authenticates you as a user—this is used primarily to store default data.

Device Abstractions

In the code samples throughout this book I have used standard Linux tools such as heyu and cdcd. However, as I've outlined previously, these tools might (and probably will) be superseded by others in the future, and you don't want to be tasked with rewriting every script and program to fit. Therefore, you should pledge to use only abstractions for these commands.

Bearskin is a series of command wrappers that creates a common interface for controlling all the devices under Minerva's control. It also maintains the state of that device in those cases where the underlying software does not support it.

The format chosen is simply as follows:

```
bearskin_command <device> <command> [command arguments]
```

The concept of a *device* relates to the protocol in question and allows you to pass the command to an alternate machine for processing. This is useful in cases where the server cannot be physically located in the best position, which includes the example given in Chapter 4 where the Computer-to-X10 gateway (such as a CM11) is unable to communicate with the rest of the appliances because of other electrics suppressing the signal. It can also include cases where you want to play the music from a machine that isn't the local /dev/dsp device or to control the CD player in a different machine. It is part of *Marple*. Consequently, most commands begin with the following:

```
DEVICE=`$MINBIN/finddev x10 $*`
if [ $? == 0 ]; then
  echo $DEVICE
  exit 0;
fi
```

Under the hood, the finddev script looks through the $MINBASE/house/marple/x10/devlist file to discover how to address the X10 module on the current machine, that is, localhost. The devlist file might appear as follows, indicating that the module is attached to /dev/ttyS0:

```
localhost dev /dev/ttyS0 - -
```

You will see how this is able to communicate with other machines in the "Marple" section later in this chapter.

Additionally, all Bearskin commands support init as a command argument so that it can prepare temporary log files, adjust ownership permissions, and launch any daemons as necessary.

Typical Application Abstractions

The currently supported abstractions are held in $MINBASE/bin and include all the necessary functionality. I'll cover these briefly, pointing out the subtleties as necessary:

homedevice: This is a simple abstraction that invokes heyu (for X10 control) to switch lamps and appliances on and off and dim lights. Because the arguments are unified between all Bearskin commands, the invocation of this looks reversed to heyu, making a typical call of heyu turn bedroom_light on look like homedevice default on bedroom_light.

cdplayer: For those still in love with those shiny plastic discs, this controls the CD player (with cdcd) and retrieves its track listing using the cddb-tool package. Because the retrieval of this data can be quite slow, the track data is temporarily stored in /var/log/minerva so that it can be queried instantly with commands such as cdplayer default currentname.

mp3player: This is a general-purpose media player that also processes the ID3 tags inside the MP3 to report the current artist and album with mp3player default artist, for example. It uses /var/log/minerva to store this information, along with the current process ID, which allows you to move through the tracks with mp3player default next. It abstracts mplayer, while making use of mp3info to parse the ID3 tags.

wavplayer: This is a simpler, primarily synchronous, audio player used for general house alerts using play.

mixer: This adjusts the relative volumes of each channel in the audio mixer, the names of which have also been abstracted so that user-friendly words such as *master*, *cd*, and *recording* can be used. It allows you to set the volumes as either a relative or absolute value between 0 and 100 percent, even when the underlying mixer application doesn't. The current implementation uses aumix.

say: This is the most interesting abstraction, despite being the simplest, because this queries the default voice (stored as a name in $MINBASE/etc/defaults/festvox, if present) and invokes festival. When called on behalf of a specific user, it uses their customized voice settings. There is also a sayfile variant for longer phrases using Festival's more efficient --tss argument.

announce: This is an important extension because its context is different. Namely, it's used for announcements to the house that something (important) is happening. It wraps the call to say by playing a chime sound and lowers the volume of any music that might be playing, before making the announcement and returning the volume levels to normal. Because of the importance of such messages, the device should generally be different from that of mp3player to prevent audio device conflicts in some systems.[3] In the worst cases, this can require using a second sound card or making use of the sound card in an external machine that generally has no use for audio, such as a wall panel. The wavplayer is often configured to use this same device.

report: This produces preformatted information about train times, time, date, and calendar. It is a useful way of creating a homogeneous way of presenting this data, and eliminating injection attacks.

tweet: This is a way of publishing an announcement via microblogging site Twitter. This can be used by multiple users in the house, as it queries a set of stored credentials for each user in $MINBASE/etc/users/[username]/external/twitter.

irsend: This is a means to send predetermined infrared remote-control codes to the connected IR transmitter. It will then be picked up by any sensor in range. For this reason, most IR-enabled equipment is held in Node0 where a single transmitter can service them all. It takes two arguments, the name of the equipment and the message that needs to be sent, and retrieves the code from a file held in $MINBASE/etc/ir/[equipment]/codes/[command]. The format of the data in this file is governed by the name in $MINBASE/etc/ir/[equipment]/method.

The <device> in each case will generally be default to indicate the default output stream, which is the set of devices attached to the server machine, mentioned earlier.

■ **Note** Most Bearskin commands are controlled by killing and restarting the Linux process. This means that in many cases you cannot amend the mp3player process from a user who didn't initiate it. That is, if you began MP3 playback using the web interface, you can't stop the music using Cosmic or the command line, unless the governing user has the user privileges to do so.

Monexec

Monexec is a script that is called manually by the various Bearskin commands mentioned earlier to log each action. When the CD player is started, for example, the cdplayer script calls the following:

```
$MINBASE/bin/monexec cdplayer play
```

---

[3] Always determine whether your sound card (and its drivers) allow you to play audio from several applications at once.

That in turn invokes a script:

```
$MINBASE/conf/exec/cdplayer/play
```

This play script can then perform any imaginable task, such as tweeting the currently playing track or using another command (like say) to announce "Good night" when the bedroom light is turned out. It is for these reasons that a simple log file is not enough. Although, naturally, monexec can also log commands, too.

TODO: A Worked Example

To cement these ideas, you are going to be the brand new writer of a brand new module! It will be the TODO application and will be a fully worked example consisting of a Bearskin command, output conduit, messaging system, and web applet. The design is such that when someone performs the following:

```
todo add steev "Take out the rubbish"
```

the message will be added to the list of tasks in steev's area and will be available for review on a web page or at the command line, with this:

```
todo list steev
```

This output could even be piped through Festival as part of the alarm call in the morning!
So to begin, you need to create a file such as $MINBASE/bin/todo and process the basic arguments:

```
#!/bin/bash
MINBASE=/usr/local/minerva

CMD=$1; shift
USER=$1; shift
MSG=$*

TODOFILE=$MINBASE/etc/users/$USER/todolist

if [ "$CMD" == "add" ]; then
  date +"%Y-%m-%d $MSG" >> $TODOFILE
fi

if [ -f $TODOFILE ]; then
  if [ "$CMD" == "list" ]; then
    cat $TODOFILE
  elif [ "$CMD" == "clear" ]; then
    rm $TODOFILE
  fi
fi
```

You then need to ensure the script is executable with this and test it for a little while:

```
chmod ugo+x todo
```

(It's okay—I've done the testing step for you!)

That's your first step done; once you've understood conduits, you'll see how to add entries into your to-do list from elsewhere.

Conduits

All communication is two-way, so naturally there are both input and output message conduits. The concept of which part is input and which is output depends on the direction of communication, so you consider them from the point of view of the Linux server, meaning an output conduit is the one that sends messages *to* devices, primarily for reports and error messages, and an input conduit is one that the server receives from a human to tempt it into action.

The current version supports the following conduits, retrievable from the command `msgconduit list`:

- `echo` (output only)
- `email` (in/out)
- `ir` (output only)
- `log` (output only)
- `sms` (in/out)
- `twitter` (output only)
- `vox` (in/out)
- `weblog` (output only)
- `winalert` (output only)

Each conduit has a directory hierarchy afforded to it, existing underneath `$MINBASE/etc/msg`. Each is identical in structure and may contain none or more of the following directories:

addr: This contains two flat files formatted in the same way. The first is `alias`, which is a list of Minerva-oriented usernames and a conduit-specific address. This would be a mobile phone number in the case of the SMS conduit, for example. The second is `contacts`, which is a list of address for people you might want to contact but who are not Minerva users. This latter file is available only when sending messages to the output, thereby allowing you to send text messages to your friends but not permit them to query or change the state of your home appliances in any way.

auth: This is reserved for future expansion, although it's rarely used as most authentication is currently done through the `$MINBASE/etc/user/[username]` hierarchy.

cmd: This directory contains a list of command aliases used with input conduits. In this way you can send short messages to the conduit, such as "wakeup," which in turn runs a `cmd/wakeup` script, allowing it to perform several commands at once, without you having to explicitly specify them all. Additionally, the script could perform smart contextual operations, so commands such as `lightson` would determine your location and control the most applicable light. I'll cover location deduction later in this chapter.

xmit: This contains a file called `cmd` that is usually a symlink to an abstracted Bearksin command that processes the argument list whenever this conduit is used as an output.

I'll now cover the method by which each of these functions so you know how to add new ones in the future and utilize them to best effect.

Echo

Output only.

This is the simplest to understand because it merely reflects all the input parameters to the current console. It is used primarily for debugging the conduits and address book.

Email

Input/output.

Like most of the conduits that support input and output methods, the two are separated by a large expanse of code. For the input side of the conduit, procmail is triggered automatically from the mail server after parsing the incoming mail to determine whether it's originated from someone who is able to send messages. This is covered fully in Chapter 5.

The output conduit uses the standard mail program directly.

Infrared Remote Control

Output only.

This calls the irsend code to determine the device and protocol necessary.

Logging

Output only.

This writes all messages into /var/log/minerva/msglog and is also used primarily for debugging.

SMS

Input/output.

The output conduit works through mxsms, which is symlinked to one of three possible driver scripts, mxsms-gnokii, mxsms-intelli, or mxsms-txtlocal, depending on who is providing the current output service. If adopting the ideas of Chapter 5, you can make mxsms a script in its own right to consider the priority of the transmitting user and determine which service to use.

For input, you will have Apache triggering the code when a specific web page is downloaded from a remote SMS-PC gateway or from a custom script checking message through Gnokii (courtesy of crontab).

Twitter

Output only.

This uses the tweet command to update their Twitter status, thereby using the configuration information from the given user, with their credentials being stored in $MINBASE/etc/users/[user]/external/twitter.

The Voice Conduit

Input/output.

In its current state, all voice recognition input is taken from an HTTP request on a separate page that triggers the msgrcv script with the given command. The output conduit has a direct connection to the Festival speech synthesis suite, which has already been abstracted through Bearskin with say and announce. Vocal output is also a very good debugging conduit, since the output is immediately accessible.

Web Log

Output only.

This is the same as the standard logger but writes its output to a different file, `/var/log/minerva/weblog`.

Window Alert

Output only.

This displays the message on an X Window terminal using the basic `kdialog` program. The existing script exports the `DISPLAY` variable to display the box on the current system but could be set to any suitably configured installation of X Window on the network.

If you need this to support Windows users, then you must install some software (such as Apache) onto those machines to listen for an incoming message and then use it to trigger a small script once the appropriate message is received. The following code, called `message.js`, will use the Windows Scripting Host (WSH) to display a suitable box:

```
message = "";
for (i = 0; i < WScript.Arguments.length; i++) {
  message += WScript.Arguments.Item(i) + " ";
}
Wscript.Echo(message);
```

Note that the file extension is important, as this is used to determine the particular scripting engine.

Administering Conduits

The administration of conduits is simple, as the major work is handled by the commands themselves. The task of adding conduits to the system is processed by the `msgconduit` command. This command can either list the existing conduits, shown earlier, or add a new one, like so:

```
msgconduit create newconduitname
```

or add a new command into an existing conduit:

```
msgconduit add conduitname conduitcommand original command with arguments
```

■ **Note** There is also an `msginstall` command, which is executed automatically during the installation process. Its sole purpose is to create the existing conduits, listed earlier. You should never need to call this.

Messaging Conduits

Having now gotten some conduits to send and process messages, you need to abstract them one stage further so they can be controlled from a single script. This is because each conduit has a lot of common functionality, such as address book lookups, which can be unified into a single place. You therefore create two commands: `msgxmit`, which sends messages into the output conduits, and `msgrcv`, which is called by the various daemons when an input conduit receives a message.

Output Conduits: Transmission

These are based solely on the `msgxmit` script, which is a method by which messages are sent to one or more (comma-separated) users by one or more (also comma-separated) conduit protocols. This allows you to use this master script to separate the target addresses, as well as perform address book lookups, so that each conduit driver script needs to accept only a single destination address.

Like all commands, you need a standardized format. This one will be in the form of conduit, address, and message:

```
msgxmit sms myphonenumber "An SMS from the command line, but could be anywhere"
```

This avoids the complication of a subject line, priority levels, attachments, and embedded links. They could be added but would only make logical sense in specific transport conduits. Consequently, you do not try to process them (or remove them with preprocessing) and instead pass the message through directly to the appropriate driver script. The conduit may, at its discretion, elect to choose a subject line based on the message if it desires.

For example, the SMS transmission in the previous example would determine that the SMS conduit was to be used and call the specific driver function like this:

```
mxsms sms 012345678 "An SMS from the command line, but could be anywhere"
```

The naming convention follows that the transmission script is always called `mx`, followed by the conduit name. In some cases, two abstractions are involved. Speech output, for example, occurs with the vox conduit:

```
msgxmit vox default "I am talking to everyone in the house"
```

This trickles down into the `mxvox` script, which in turn will call `say` through:

```
mxvox vox default "I am talking to everyone in the house"
```

The conduit type is included as an argument at each stage as a sanity check and to allow one underlying command to be used by more than one conduit.

So that new conduits can be added without changing the `msgxmit` script, you create a directory structure that details each of them. For example, the folder will detail the SMS account credentials, address book aliases, and the all-important command that transmits the message as I covered earlier:

```
/usr/local/minerva/etc/msg/sms
```

So, given a conduit type (or comma-separated list of several conduits) in the argument $1 and a list of addresses similarly separated in $2, you can process them with the following:

```
SAVEIFS=$IFS
 IFS=","
 declare -a CONDUIT_ARRAY=($1)
 shift

 declare -a TO_ARRAY=($1)
 shift
IFS=$SAVEIFS

MSG=$*
```

and then enumerate each conduit with the following:

```
for CONDUIT in ${CONDUIT_ARRAY[@]}
do
  CMD=$MINBASE/etc/msg/$CONDUIT/xmit/cmd
  if [ -f $CMD ]; then
    # existing conduit - send the message to each user
  fi
done
```

Knowing the conduit, you can consult the conduit-specific address book in $MINBASE/etc/msg/[conduit_name] to replace the username with a number. You use a space-separated list as follows:

```
steev 012345678
teddy 012347890
```

As mentioned previously, this results in the SMS-specific script dealing only with the canonical form of phone number and limits the complexity in each of the protocol scripts. Obviously, if the address is already in its canonical form, then it won't appear on the left side of the list, and you can revert to the original input. When sending information, you also check a second list of addresses that consists of non-Minerva users and can be used to store your work numbers. This code appears thus as follows:

```
ADDRBOOK=$MINBASE/etc/msg/$CONDUIT/addr/alias
if [ -f $ADDRBOOK ]; then
  ALIAS=`grep -m 1 "^$TOADDR " $ADDRBOOK | sed "s/^[^ ]* //"`

  if [ "$ALIAS" != "" ]; then
    TOADDR=$ALIAS
  fi
fi
```

It is then a simple case of calling the driver script and optionally logging the message details to a file:

```
$CMD $CONDUIT $TOADDR $MSG
```

Input Conduits: Receiving Messages

This uses the same set of abstraction principles as transmission but in reverse. Minerva has a basic script, called msgrcv, which processes any commands found in the message, regardless of where the message originated. This script then checks to see whether the sender is allowed to issue that command and refuse it if not.

■ **Note** This process is the most obvious example of the insecurity present with the system, since any Linux user is able to call the script with valid parameters and bypass your security. Even if you made all the files read-only, it is no effort for someone to copy or retype these locally and execute the commands. This is yet another reason why Linux-oriented local users should be banned from the server.

There are various complications with receiving and processing messages, since every type of communication is different, both in how the text format is used and the way in which messages are picked up the system. In Chapter 5 you saw examples of how e-mail and SMS require significantly different code to process the incoming message.

My approach is to let the software that receives the communication in the very first instance (the web or e-mail server, for example) to authenticate the user. Most of these daemons will be running as a privileged user of some description and therefore less vulnerable to abuse. In addition to deducing the Minerva-oriented user account of the sender, the receiving code will also be in charge of stripping out all message information that is not pertinent (in the form of header, footers, signatures, and so on) before sending a much-reduced command to your msgrcv script. This pushes the workload to where it belongs and gives your script a unified appearance to all input conduits.

Taking the example of SMS, you already have a web page in place that is invoked whenever someone sends a message to your house. This page might process the input and call the receiver script using the following:

```
$command = "/usr/local/minerva/bin/msgrcv sms ";
$command.= $_POST['from'];
$command.= " ";
$command.= $_POST['text'];

system($command);
```

which evaluates down to a command such as the following:

```
msgrcv sms 012345678 bedroom on
```

The command code can then look up the phone number in $MINBASE/etc/msg/sms/addr/alias and deduce who is issuing the command and whether they're allowed to use it.

From here you can determine how to process the command and its arguments in a uniform way. However, allowing arbitrary access to the entire Linux command set is very dangerous, particularly given the privileges under which software such as the web server is run. As you've just seen, even the seemingly inconspicuous SMS control requires Apache and is therefore vulnerable. Therefore, each user has a list of applications it is allowed to use, as controlled with the minuser command.

Furthermore, you can kill two proverbial birds with one stone by preparing your own set of aliases. Some commands, like kettle, are short and simple and effective for SMS messages. Others such as the following are not:

```
homedevice default on bedroom_light
```

Consequently, you will create a directory /usr/local/minerva/etc/msg/sms/cmd that contains a number of command scripts with short names. bedroom, for example, would perform the full command given earlier. You could also create an aliased command called sleepover, which runs the following:

```
homedevice default off bedroom_light
homedevice default off studio_light
homedevice default off lounge_light
```

This would eliminate a lot of typing and limit the scope for command injection attacks. This also allows you to add new SMS-controllable commands without changing the SMS input handler code inside the web directory.

Notice that in this example and all others like it, you always pass the conduit type and address through to the underlying script as you did with msgxmit. You suffer no performance penalty for doing so, and it ensures that error reports are sent back to the correct user, using the same conduit.

One powerful example of this is with voice control. In Chapter 5 you used Apache to trigger individual scripts when a specific web page was accessed. With this input conduit abstraction, you can extend the scope of your voice input very simply. Like SMS, you create a simple web page that picks up each request and invokes `msgrcv`. You have created `voxcontrol.php` that reads as follows:

```php
<?php
$cmd = $HTTP_GET_VARS['cmd'];
$auth = $HTTP_GET_VARS['auth'];

if ($auth == "") {
  $auth = "public";
}
system("/usr/local/minerva/bin/msgrcv vox $auth $cmd &");
?>
```

This causes any existing command script called $cmd present in /usr/local/minerva/etc/msg/vox/cmd to be executed and includes typical commands to control the lights (`lightson`, `lightsoff`), audio mixer (`mute`, `quiet`, `next`), and status reports (such as `time` and `status`).

Also, you know that any text written to the output is returned by the same conduit. Because this uses the vox voice input conduit, the output will be via the voice output conduit (Festival through `say`). You can therefore persuade the computer to enact simplistic conversations by creating scripts such as `hello`:

```
# /usr/local/minerva/etc/msg/vox/cmd/hello
echo Hello
```

and `time`:

```
# /usr/local/minerva/etc/msg/vox/cmd/time
$MINBASE=/usr/local/minerva

$MINBASE/bin/hdate
$MINBASE/bin/htime
```

TODO: Building a Conduit

Although there are many necessary small files and directories in the creation of a conduit, the process has been made simpler by a short script that generates them all automatically, so you need only to call the following:

```
msgconduit create todo
```

You should see the extra directories created:

```
$MINBASE/etc/msg/todo/addr
$MINBASE/etc/msg/todo/auth
$MINBASE/etc/msg/todo/cmd
$MINBASE/etc/msg/todo/xmit
```

By default, the output command ($MINBASE/etc/msg/todo/xmit/cmd) is symlinked to $MINBASE/bin/mxtodo. This is currently empty, and there is no reason to bend the standard for the sake of it, so you can edit this file to create the code that will run whenever a message is sent into the TODO conduit. Because you have a Bearskin command that does all the processing, it's simply a matter of taking out the arguments and passing them into $MINBASE/bin/todo:

```bash
#!/bin/bash
$MINBASE=/usr/local/minerva

CONDUIT=$1; shift
USER=$1; shift
MSG=$*

$MINBASE/bin/todo add $USER $MSG
```

And, again, you need to ensure that this script can be executed:

```
chmod ugo+x /usr/local/minerva/bin/mxtodo
```

And that's it! It's ready for testing:

```
msgxmit todo steev "Write the web applet for TODO"
```

Message Relays

Minerva also includes a message-relay system to pass information between different conduits whenever a new message is received. This works in a similar way to monexec, except that rlyexec is always, and only, called from msgrcv. A typical invocation would be as follows:

```
rlyexec email steev command arguments
```

This would trigger each executable script in the $MINBASE/etc/users/steev/relay/email directory, giving ample opportunity for the command or message to be processed, which might include retransmission as an SMS, for example. Each script is executed alphabetically and stops on the first script who's exit code is nonzero. Consequently, you would adopt the convention by giving each script in the directory a sequential number, similar to how you ordered your virtual hosts in Chapter 5.

Time-Based Messaging

Some systems aim to be smart. It is, after all, the next stage of home automation. So, being able to target a message according to certain parameters, such as time, introduces a new level of convenience for the user.

Unfortunately, to be truly accurate, you would need to make every personal and work calendar you have accessible to the system. And then you would need to understand how to parse it. Neither one is a realistic goal for the short term. However, you can create an approximate description of your daily routine as it is, for most purposes, routine.

The Minerva Timing System (MTS) sits in a layer above the messaging conduits to determine which of the conduits should be used at any given hour of the day or night. So, the computer might want to issue the following warning, and be sure to send it in the manner where I'm likely to receive it soonest:

```
mtsxmit steev warn "Disc space is getting low on /dev/sdc1"
```

It does this with a two-stage process by first working out where I'm likely to be and then, knowing that, how I'd like to be contacted while I'm there.

The first part works through a series of personalized timetables, found in $MINBASE/etc/users/steev/mts, which describe where that user is likely to be at the times given for a particular type of message. That one-line design document has already created four sets of variables for us:

- The user

- The type of message or priority

- The day

- The time of day

By arranging them in order, you can probably guess the directory structure already, because each category sits in a directory beneath the other! The priority is one of mesg (for standard informational messages), warn (for warnings about the hardware or software of the house), and error (for severe problems, security issues, and possible intruders).

You will be pleased to know that the day can be determined with less than 365 separate files. In fact, you only need as many files as you have *types* of day. Most employees will have three: weekday, Saturday, and Sunday. Consequently, the configuration for the 240 working days of the year would be "get up, go to work, work, come home, sleep." This equates to a file called weekday that could appear like this:

```
! hourly
# 00 01 02 03 04 05 06 07 08 09 10 11 12 13 14 15 16 17 18 19 20 21 22 23
* -- -- -- -- -- -- -- hp tr wk wk wk wk wk wk wk wk wk tr hp hp hp hq
```

The format used by MTS is simple but very strict. The first line indicates the format of the file, in this case, an hour-by-hour report. The second is a comment, reminding us (me!) of the format, while the last line represents the data itself.

In addition to a file for every identical weekday, you can also create one for Saturday (called Sat) and Sunday (called Sun). Furthermore, if there's something specific on a particular date, you can override this by creating a file called Dec25, for example, that indicates you don't want to be disturbed at all! The MTS code will look for the most restrictive date first and work through to lower priorities finishing on the default. The order in full is as follows:

- Festival (Christmas, Eid, and so on)

- Specific dates (Jul30, Feb14)

- Days of the week (Mon, Tue, ...)

- Type of day (weekend or weekday)

- Default (called daily; this should always exist)

Each two-letter code corresponds exactly to one of the hours in the day and indicates where you are expected to be at that time. These codes are arbitrary to each user, so let's consider a fairly typical set, along with the potential protocols you'd use:

hp = Home, public. Use the speech synthesizer.

tr = Traveling. SMS only.

wk = Working. E-mail or work e-mail if it's important.

hq = Home, but be quiet about it! Use e-mail and SMS.

The location can be determined with the `mtspick` program, issued as follows, where a two-character code is returned:

```
mtspick steev error
```

You can then look up this value in a key to determine how (and to whom) the message should be sent. To allow multiple receivers and protocols, you create a script for each two-letter code that takes a username as input and outputs a conduit protocol and username. This also allows you to consider the importance of the message and vary the e-mail address, as I discussed earlier.

This is then combined with the original message and passed onto the `msgxmit` code that I've already covered.

We shall later cover a technology called mashmodes that allow you to change house-wide on a large grain basis. This allows the mts configuration file to change between working and holiday schedules, for example.

Other Uses for MTS

The `mtspick` part of the procedure accepts two parameters, a user and a priority. This is normally hidden from the user by `mtsxmit`. However, it can be reappropriated to create some additional home-spun functionality.

You could create a user called `mixer` and prepare a crontab so that the master volume of the house changes over time, automatically lowering over the last few hours of the night so you're naturally lulled to sleep. The same effect can be used to dim the bedroom lights gradually.

It can also be used to trigger preprepared e-mails asking whether you got into work okay and, if it receives no reply, issues an alert.

You can also create your own radio station by using the codes as program schedule slots. These can govern which particular MP3 folder is used to randomly select music for a given time of day or night. Some codes might initiate Festival into reading news items and reporting the weather.

Location-Based Messaging

Being able to deduce your location can have its uses too, as a way of directing output more accurately. As we've just seen, MTS can provide a very large part of that functionality. But there's always room for improvement.

We can enlist the support of hardware, such as PIRs, or doormat pressure sensors to get an approximate idea of which room you're in. If you use two pressure sensors on the stairs (one at the top and one at the bottom), then you could work out the direction of travel to enable the current audio loom, flooding your music to only where you'd hear it.

If you've adopted a voice recognition system and you're using a separate machine for each room, then you can create a simple voice command like here to inform the server of your location.

By using the Bluetooth monitor software, you can determine the strength of the signal that, with experimentation, you can sometimes use to deduce your position within the house. It works better when you have a large house and/or lots of obstructions in the signal, both of which create an obvious distinction between near and far.

For fine-grained location-based determination, an RFID tag can be used to give more accurate details, although you will need a fairly powerful tag for it to be detected naturally as you move around the house. One possible solution here is to mount them *in* the soles of shoes or slippers, for example, so they can be detected when you walk over the threshold of any particular room.

And, finally, the best method for determining the location is to employ your local knowledge of the problem. If the request came from a web page at 192.168.1.132, then you can determine its MAC address (from the DHCPD log) and therefore which machine it is and where it's located. Furthermore, if you always send personal e-mails from your laptop in the lounge, then build that information into the system so that any messages sent from that e-mail account controls the devices in the lounge. Sometimes you can look at the e-mail headers for the last "Received: from" line that appears to determine the IP address of the sender, but this is not foolproof.

Cosmic

Cosmic is an RF-to-PC gateway that uses Heyu to intercept the X10 signals that have been placed on the power line by an X10 RF transmitter (such as an HR10 or SS13E) and triggers an arbitrary piece of code. This could be to control the volume of the currently playing music, skip tracks, or start timers to aid with the cooking. This is probably the cheapest method of introducing stand-alone wireless control panels to your home.

There are two main issues with this approach. The first is that these devices have no feedback mechanism. Consequently, you will need to design your interface such that every button causes a noise, speech output, or visual cue upon each key press. It is your responsibility to ensure that the server processing these commands understands where the switch is located so that it can make these feedback noise cues in a location where they will be heard.

The second problem concerns X10. Because the controlling messages are X10 signals, they will also control any lights on the same addresses. Depending on the size of home, you may either have to split your X10 address into two or utilize two house codes. In the case of the former, you can split the addresses into two sets, with 1–8 to control the lights, teakettle, and standard appliances as normal, and with 9–16 working as the second set that is not found on any devices and used solely by Cosmic. There is a switch on most remotes to toggle between these particular address sets and so is no coincidence that they've been chosen here. Consequently, the button is reappropriated as a home control/Cosmic control task switcher.

Configuration

Assuming that you have eight available addresses, this gives you 16 workable buttons—on and off for each of the eight. In case these later change, you can alias them within the /etc/heyu/x10.conf file like this:

```
ALIAS cosmic1 E9
ALIAS cosmic2 E10
ALIAS cosmic3 E11
ALIAS cosmic4 E12
ALIAS cosmic5 E13
ALIAS cosmic6 E14
ALIAS cosmic7 E15
ALIAS cosmic8 E16
```

You can configure the heyu daemon, which is always watching the power line, to invoke specific commands whenever a message for these addresses appears. In its default configuration, Cosmic splits the commands into three groups:

- Media control

- State-based operations

- State control

The media control ones are global and functional all the time. This is because of their relative importance. They allow you to increase and decrease the volume, as well as mute/unmute the music, and they provide a way to pause all the currently playing media. They occupy the top four buttons (two rows) of a standard HR10. The commands they run all use the abstracted Bearskin commands and are added to x10.conf like this:

```
SCRIPT cosmic1 on  :: /usr/local/minerva/bin/mixer default dec master 10
SCRIPT cosmic1 off :: /usr/local/minerva/bin/mixer default inc master 10
SCRIPT cosmic2 on  :: /usr/local/minerva/bin/mixer default toggle
SCRIPT cosmic2 off :: /usr/local/minerva/bin/pmedia default
```

Remember that these commands will be executed by whichever user invoked heyu engine initially. They must therefore have appropriate access rights to the audio output and mixer devices for this to work.

■ **Note** You always affect the master volume, not the individual device volumes. This is so the relative volumes of the radio, CD, or MP3s aren't changed, and the only inaccuracy occurs at the top and bottom of a single range—that of the master volume.

The state-based controller is a little more involved. It consists of four predefined buttons to query and change the state and eight that are mode-specific. This is configured as follows:

```
SCRIPT cosmic7 on  :: /usr/local/minerva/bin/cosmic default modestatus
SCRIPT cosmic7 off :: /usr/local/minerva/bin/cosmic default nextmode
SCRIPT cosmic8 on  :: /usr/local/minerva/bin/vstatus
SCRIPT cosmic8 off :: /usr/local/minerva/bin/cosmic default clear
```

Notice that you cycle through the modes in only one direction because this sequence is easier to remember. Also, you have used what would have been a previous button to reset Cosmic to its initial state. The modestatus report reminds you where you are in the cycle, lest you forget, and there's a general-purpose status report to even up the rows.

This assignment is specific to devices laid out in two columns like the HR10, which have the on button on the left. This allows you to line up both status reports on the left side and separate the two sets of global buttons into media at the top and Cosmic state at the bottom. Notice that the software within Linux never changes, only the configuration.

To control the Cosmic system, you assign the remaining buttons to arbitrary c1, c2, and so on, commands.

```
SCRIPT cosmic3 on  :: /usr/local/minerva/bin/cosmic default c1
SCRIPT cosmic3 off :: /usr/local/minerva/bin/cosmic default c2
SCRIPT cosmic4 on  :: /usr/local/minerva/bin/cosmic default c3
SCRIPT cosmic4 off :: /usr/local/minerva/bin/cosmic default c4
SCRIPT cosmic5 on  :: /usr/local/minerva/bin/cosmic default c5
SCRIPT cosmic5 off :: /usr/local/minerva/bin/cosmic default c6
SCRIPT cosmic6 on  :: /usr/local/minerva/bin/cosmic default c7
SCRIPT cosmic6 off :: /usr/local/minerva/bin/cosmic default c8
```

As you can see, the cosmic script is technically stateless, so you must use the /var/log/minerva/cosmic directory to hold the current mode.

■ **Note** Because the heyu daemon needs to be restarted after any change to x10.conf, you can improve the maintenance aspect of this script by redirecting all Cosmic scripts to an indirect form, through the invocation of a script such as /usr/local/minerva/bin/cosmic default base1.

Creating Modes

You then have the fun (!?) part of designing the states and their interfaces. The Cosmic system places no limits on the number of modes possible or how the commands inside them must function. However, it is recommended that every button press result in some kind of feedback, either directly because something happened as a consequence of the command (such as a light turning on or some music playing) or indirectly with auditory feedback to indicate the command happened, although it was invisible to you.

Each mode exists in its own directory, numbered sequentially, from $MINBASE/etc/cosmic/0. This holds all the files necessary to control that mode. It includes the following files:

name: A text file with the mode name. This is read aloud when you cycle to the mode.

status: A script that writes the status report for this mode to STDOUT. In the case of a multimedia mode, it would be the currently playing song, for example. This is read out at the end of each mode status report. If no file exists, the mode name is simply reread.

c1, c2, c3, c4, c5, c6, c7, c8: These eight files are the scripts that are executed when any of the eight corresponding command buttons are pressed. By running scripts in this way, you can change the system without reprogramming the x10.conf file or restarting the heyu daemon.

All of the main work is done in those eight c1–c8 scripts. There are three sample subsystems in Minerva: media control for the CD player, a set of status reports, and a set of timers. This latter mode uses the wireless controller to begin timing a set period, such as five minutes. Once the time is up, the voice announces its completion, with several timers able to be run concurrently.

■ **Tip** The output from all c1–c8 scripts should be written to STDOUT. In this way, you can debug Cosmic configurations much more quickly (and easily) by changing the code in Cosmic to read REPORT=/bin/echo.

To Yaks

Although Cosmic has many benefits, it wasn't as expansive as some people wanted. So Yaks was born. As an acronym it stands for "Yet Another Kontrol System," and is a method for processing arbitrary messages (from X10 device) into Linux-bound commands. There are a series of scripts, held in /usr/local/minerva/etc/x10/scripts/ which are called when a button is pressed from a specified controller. Each controller lives in its own subdirectory, and each button has a subdirectory from that. So, for example, button 8 on the control panel for the shower unit would be in the directory,

/usr/local/minerva/etc/x10/scripts/Shower/8

bECAUSE the X10 addressing protocol isn't as user-friendly as this, you must also configure Yaks to map the X10 messages (such as D9) into their equivalents here. This information is stored in a code-based configuration script at /usr/local/minerva/etc/x10/controls which looks like this:

```
$c = $config->addController(new YaksController("Keyfob", "c", 1, 8));
$c = $config->addController(new YaksController("Shower", "d", 8, 8));
```

■ **Note** This configuration looks like code because it is! This file is loaded as part of the yaks program, which creates the $config object, and declares the YaksController class. Using code as data is a cheat, but allows for more flexibility in the configuration.

From this, you can see that the Keyfob occupies house code "C", and 8 unit ids of 1 through 8, while the shower is working on house code "D", with 8 units numbered 8 to 16. All that is then necessary is to ensure **every** house code and unit is set-up in /etc/x10.conf to trigger the yaks program.

```
SCRIPT b1 on :: /usr/local/minerva/bin/yaks control b1 on
SCRIPT b1 off :: /usr/local/minerva/bin/yaks control b1 off
# etc
```

Note If you use mashmodes to upload new `/etc/x10.conf` files to system, remember to include these lines in each configuration, or `cat` a template to each version before it is uploaded to the CM11.

Living Modes

The mode system in Mineva is called Mash, and is short for "Minerva Automated Smart Home" (no, really!) and is a way of placing the entire house into a particular state. Your house can only exist in one state at a time, and so each mode is mutually exclusive. Some examples of a mashmode are:

- Being on holiday

- Being at work

- Being at home, normal

- Being at home, working

- Being at home, while sick

Therefore, it is simple to issue the command:

```
mashmode set holiday
```

and, whether triggered by a script, text message, e-mail, MTS (time-based messaging) or web interface, can put your house into a state of readiness for your holiday. Think of it as an e-mail auto-responder for home automation. This might include:

- Changing the automatic lighting schedule

- Randomly playing music and TV channels during the hours of 18:00–23:00

- Send an SMS to your milkman to cancel the milk

- E-mail a holiday reminder to your family

Note Regardless of your security arrangements, there is no benefit in publicly announcing the fact that you're holiday. Although the reports of burglars monitoring twitter feeds to time their breakins are largely apocryphal (there are easier ways to determine if someone's home) there's no point being blase.

Setting up a mashmode is very simple as they consist of two directories containing scripts, one when the mode is begun, and another when another mode supplants it. Note that there is no differentiation if the holiday mode is replaced by "work" or "work from home". Begin by creating a new profile:

```
mashmode create holiday
```

which creates the directories mentioned earlier:

```
./etc/mode/holiday/onenter
./etc/mode/holiday/onexit
```

Each directory is processed in exactly the same way, so regardless of whether you are entering or leaving the mode, the files in the directory are scanned and:

- If an x10.sched file is present, it is uploaded as a new schedule to your x10 unit

- If a script named process is present, it runs the script with whatever arbitrary commands it contains

- If there is an xmit directory, it transmits a message to the designated parties

The third case is the interesting one. The file name indicates which conduit is used to send the message (email, sms, and so on), whereas the file contents indicate to whom it is sent, and the message.

```
$ cat etc/mode/holiday/onenter/xmit/sms
#mum,sis
#!/bin/bash
date +"We're off on holiday, beginning on the %dth %B"
```

As you can see, the first line is a comment that contains the comma-separated username(s) to whom the message is sent. The rest of the file is a script that determines the message to be sent.

For a reminder of which conduits are supported you can use:

```
msgconduit list
```

Routines

A routine is a sequence of timed events, beginning at a specific moment in time, and is no different from a traditional script. The example of a "wake-up" script that prepares your shower in the morning might be:

```
MINBIN=/usr/local/minerva/bin
sleep 0
$MINBIN/alarm 1
sleep 300
$MINBIN/homedevice default on bedroom
sleep 600
$MINBIN/homedevice default on shower
sleep 60
$MINBIN/homedevice default on shower_speaker
sleep 10
$MINBIN/report say shower calendar
sleep 1200
$MINBIN/say shower Hurry up
$MINBIN/homedevice default on shower_speaker
$MINBIN/homedevice default on shower
$MINBIN/homedevice default on bedroom
```

This is triggered, indirectly, by cron with several internal timings to cope with the walk between the bedroom and the shower. Instead of writing a direct crontab line such as:

```
10 7 * * 1-5 /usr/local/minerva/bin/routine start 1
```

it is instead better to write:

```
* * * * 1-7 /usr/local/minerva/bin/routine process
```

Because while a lot more processing takes place with it running every minute, it moves control from a (fixed) script in cron, to a more dynamic script in Minerva's configuration directory. This allows you to use variable times in your routine scripts, as these are not supported in cron. For example you could put lights on automatically at sunset, as determined by the utility script sunset.

Structurally, each directory describing the process of a routine includes three files:

```
$ ls /usr/local/minerva/conf/routine/1
name normal script
```

name is a single line text description, which is human-readable and rendered on `routine list`

normal is the normal time this event should be triggered, for example, 7:00

days lists on which days the even can run, for example, sat,sun. Consequently, you need to create two different routines to handle your weekend wake-up schedule, and your weekday one.

script is the executable to run at that time

There is also one optional file, override, which (if present) uses the time present within it on the following day—and only the following day. The time returns to "normal" for the day after. This is a simple way of introducing the concept of "I need to be up at 6:00 tomorrow, instead of 7:00, for the meeting", and eliminates a lot of temporary configuration changes.

By having the script and time separate from the cron also allows you to:

- Begin with a random sleep delay, to delay events by a few minutes, making the house feel more human.

- Look at your current location, with the time-based processor MTS, and disable/enable various events.

- Check the weather, and delay your alarm if it's raining and it knows you'll be taking the car, instead of walking.

- Check the weather, and wake you earlier if it's snowing, knowing you'll need more time to defrost the windows.

- Check the train times, and delay the alarm if it's late. Or automatically e-mail your boss if it's cancelled.

- Prevent the event (e.g., starting shower) from happening if it's detected you've already taken a shower.

The use cases may involve starting something sooner, or later, than normal. Because it's impossible to rewind time, the script should always be triggered on the earliest applicable time for the event, that is, the worse case scenario, and delay the event until the best case. This naturally solves the problem of "dual reality", where a 6 o'clock alarm might determine that it's acceptable to wake you at 7 . . . while the 7 o'clock alarm might decide that, due to a change in circumstances, it should rely on the 6 o'clock event to trigger.

Known exceptions to the rule (such as the early meeting example) are still best served with the override file.

As a very developer-centric implementation, this can be easily reprogrammed from the iOS remote application, or tied to the calendar.

And finally, I present a real-world example from my own shower routine! This routine is trigger by my "night time" event, and prepares the shower for me. In addition to basic lighting, it also reads me my schedule for the following day. The last point, amusingly, requires additional logic because, if I'm home after midnight, then the "following day" is actually the same day, and we need to amend the process accordingly:

```
# For early morning/late nights
if [ `date +"%H"` -le 4 ]; then
        REQUEST_DAY=today
        MESSAGE="Back late - I hope it was a good night. Let's talk about the morning"
else
        REQUEST_DAY=tomorrow
        MESSAGE="Let us talk about tomorrow"
fi

CONDUIT=vox
$MINBIN/report $CONDUIT shower echo $MESSAGE

# ... other messages here ...

$MINBIN/report $CONDUIT shower echo Let me look at the calendar
$MINBIN/report $CONDUIT shower calendar $REQUEST_DAY
$MINBIN/report $CONDUIT shower echo Checking house events
$MINBIN/report $CONDUIT shower lstatus $REQUEST_DAY
$MINBIN/report $CONDUIT shower weather $REQUEST_DAY
```

Minty

Minty serves two purposes. First, it is a timeout system in which devices will auto-turn off if they are not used within three minutes of their last usage. Second, it is a reference counting utility, to ensure the first component acts intelligently. Therefore, if two people switch the light on, then it switches off three minutes after the *last* person to switch it off. This is essential in an automated house as it's possible for one person to switch it on locally, another to do so remotely, and the computer to do it automatically . . . and for all three to expect the device to be on while they're interacting with it.

To facilitate this, each device has a Minty on event, and a corresponding off event, described in two scripts such as:

```
/usr/local/minerva/conf/minty/shower_speaker/on
/usr/local/minerva/conf/minty/shower_speaker/off
```

So, when the device is first required to switch on, the script minty start shower_speaker is called, and the time is noted. If this is the first time that the shower speaker is being turned on, then the script above is run. If not, its count is incremented. Once you've finished using the device, and turn it off (with the predictably named minty end shower_speaker) the count is decremented and, if the count reaches zero, the three-minute timeout begins.

Because the on script is only called on the first invocation, you can trigger the same event from lots of different places. So, for example, the shower speaker remains on if:

- you're playing music in the shower

- listening to the computer voice reading your calendar

- the shower light is on

Each of these event triggers make an identical to call to minty start shower_speaker so only after you have stopped listening to music in the shower, *and* you're having your schedule read to you, *and* you've switched the light off, does it get ready to switch it off.

Of course, if you return to the shower within three minutes and play more music, then the three-minute time out begins again.

The Universal Remote Control

This is an iOS app[4] that lets you control any part of your home automation setup, whether run by Minerva or not. It is able to do this because the remote sends only HTTP requests to a web server, and all configuration then happens on the server. This has parallels to the various bridge solutions for communications covered in Chapter 3. While introducing an extra link into the chain, it does mean that you only need to set up the end point for this server on the controlling client device, consisting of:

- URL (it defaults to the Minerva home page at www.minervahome.net)

- Port (usually 80)

- Script (urc/echo.php)

These are combined into the HTTP request:

```
GET http://www.minervahome.com:80/urc/echo.php?command=menu.1.region.6.index.23&code=nocode
```

The command argument details the specific button pressed, and will be in the format:

```
command=menu.[index].region.[icon_reference].index.[position_on_screen]
```

The code parameter is also configurable from the app, and sent as a passcode, to provide a basic level of security. Your server-side script may choose to process (or ignore) this parameter as it sees fit.

We shall now see how the index, icon_reference, and position_on_screen references are determined.

Configuration

Because we've already said that the app is configured by the server, it makes sense to feature such a configuration file.

```
<homeremote>
        <menu>
                <button text="TV"/>
                <button icon="20"/>
                <button icon="19"/>
                <button icon="35"/>
                <button icon="36"/>
                <button menu="1"/>

                <button icon="0" text="Film"/>
                <button icon="38"/>
                <button icon="37"/>
                <button icon="40"/>
                <button icon="39"/>
                <button menu="2"/>

... cut for brevity ...
        </menu>
</homeremote>
```

---

[4]http://itunes.apple.com/us/app/universal-remote-control/id538062489?ls=1&mt=8

The first GET request made by the app is for a file called "config.xml" in the root of the servers URL. The display is broken up into 6 x 6 areas (the index first referenced as the position on screen, in the command argument), reading left-to-right, then top-to-bottom, with each area being either a piece of text, a function button with an icon, or a link to another menu. In this case, our first menu (called zero) begins with a line of controls for the TV, which have various icon references, and is following by a link to menu 1 (i.e., the second). The icon for the menu is predetermined.

The available icons are:

0. Blank	11. Film	21. Right/next	31. Pause
1. Ellipsis—reserved for menu change	12. Photographs	22. Plus/more	32. Stop
	13. Mail	23. Minus/less	33. Volume lower
2. Power off	14. Weather	24. Cross/delete/remove	34. Mute
3. Power off	15. CD	25. Magnify/show/status/info	35. Volume higher
4. Book mark	16. Documents on a server (or cloud)	26. Grow	36. Rewind
5. Mixer levels		27. Battery or power	37. Previous
6. TV output	17. Friends	28. Chat messages or conversations	38. Next
7. Music	18. Up		39. Fast forward
8. Photographs	19. Down	29. Document	40. Favourites
9. House control	20. Left/previous	30. Play/start	41. Tags
10. News or information			

■ **Note** Because there is a lot of typing involved in the configuration file, sample ones can be downloaded at http://www.minervahome.net/homeremote.htm

---

Once a button is pressed, the full URL is called as mentioned previously. You can then split the command at the dots, and parse each according to the specifics of your app. An example processing script works like this:

```php
<?php

$cmd = $_GET['command'];
$code = $_GET['code'];

if ($code != "nocode") {
        echo "Invalid code";
        return;
}

preg_match('/menu\.(\d+)\.icon\.(\d+)\.index\.(\d+)/', $cmd, $match);

$menu = $match[1];
$icon = $match[2];
$index = $match[3];
```

```php
$minbin = "/usr/local/minerva/bin/";

$menuActions = array();

// Main menu screen
$menuActions[0] = array(
 10=>'media default next music 5',
 16=>'media default next music 5',
 19=>'mixer default toggle', 20=>'mixer default quiet', 21=>'mixer default loud',
 25=>'weatherstatus',26=>'ldbquery get lut stp',27=>'todo list steev',28=>'getcalendar steev 1',
 29=>'media default status',
 30=>'media default stop', 31=>'media default toggle', 32=>'manifest default next music',
 33=>'housenight', 34=>'homedevice default on bedroom',
);

// ... other menu actions here ...

$result = "Unknown command";
if (array_key_exists($menu, $menuActions)) {
        if (array_key_exists($index, $menuActions[$menu])) {
                $command = $menuActions[$menu][$index];
                $command = $minbin.$command;
                $command .= " >&1";

                $output = array();
                exec($command, $output);

                $result = join("\n", $output);
        }
}

print $result;
?>
```

Whatever is printed as a consequence of this script is passed back to the app, and displayed in the status window. The default echo.php script will simply repeat every argument passed in, back to the app. This is helpful to verify your assumptions about which menu, position on screen, and icon are being pressed. It is simply:

```php
<?php
print_r($_GET);
?>
```

and worth keeping around during the development your own scripts.

Web Applets

For most people, controlling the house through the web browser is the secondary goal (after voice recognition, that is!). As I mentioned in Chapter 5, this is the ubiquitous means of communication in the 20th and 21st centuries, so you are obliged to provide access to all the Bearskin commands through such an interface, hidden behind the security that SSL and usernames and passwords provide.

At the simplest level, you can build your own site to provide a list of links that execute the Bearskin commands on the server. But the web provides a richer canvas with which to work and can be used to present house-friendly features that the existing commands do not provide.

In addition to controlling your home from a desktop PC or laptop, you might want to consider the purchase of new machine(s) to be used as kiosks or house terminals. These can be in the form of a tablet PC, mobile phone, or a home-brew machine with a touchscreen monitor and miniature form-factor PCs (like the Raspberry Pi, covered in Chapter 8, or the Fit-PC2 and Mini-ITX machines from Chapter 4). This machine can be powercycled according to your waking hours and set up with a small and fast version of Linux, such as Webconverger mentioned in Chapter 3. Having one in the kitchen, for example, would allow you to read recipes from the Web, while the use of a touchscreen (as opposed to a keyboard and mouse) would make it easier to control when your hands were covered in dough.

There are a small number of subtle, but important, differences when designing an interface for a touchscreen. First, there is the absence of any hover control for when your pointer moves over (or into or out of) the button area. So, you should avoid using tool tips to present additional information or explain the button. Furthermore, the button areas themselves will generally need to be larger, with some conceptual space in between them. When controlling a pad with your finger, for example, you will generally only be accurate to within 20 pixels or so, so each button should probably be a minimum of 32 pixels in size. And, finally, the use of touchscreen usually implies a lack of a keyboard. When this is the case, your ability to type into text boxes is much reduced. There are several on-screen keyboards to solve this problem, but they need to be large enough, for the reasons given earlier, and have a mechanism to direct the input to more than one input control. It is also advisable to avoid screens that have to scroll in one or more direction—ideally, none at all.

Zinc: Between Web and Native

Before you get to the web pages themselves, there is one final layer to unwrap, Zinc. This is a small library of server-side code that abstracts various types of device and allows them to be controlled through WARP. This is also known in Minerva parlance as a *web gateway conduit*.

It consists of several very thin wrapper classes, which allow the PHP applet code to make system calls in a safe and structured way. For instance, if you were to use the mp3player script, the web page would not finish loading until the entire piece had been played. And if you start it in the background, then any output (such as errors) would appear in your web page at some arbitrary location. This layer protects against that. It also allows you to use alternate device names through the configuration files in zinc/conf/mp3player.conf, for example, which let you replace either the Bearskin commands or the web site without affecting the other. Without Zinc, the code necessary to correctly run mp3player from a web page would be as follows:

```
$cmd = MP3PlayerDevice::$binary." ".MP3PlayerDevice::$device;
$cmd.= " play $track";
$out = system("($cmd 2>&1 >/dev/null) >/dev/null 2>&1  &");
```

Of Web Pages and Applets

The web interface supplied with Minerva is based on WARP and as such allows you to have several applets appearing on a single web page. Figure 7-2 shows a typical screen.

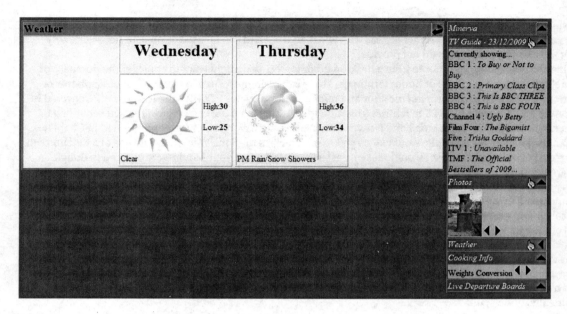

Figure 7-2. *Various Minerva applets all running on a single page*

Each applet is rendered as a small "panel" view (as shown by the cooking information) with the maximized applet (the weather) being shown in a full window. All of these applets are available from a single page, such as wnews.php, which consists of code like this:

```php
<?
require_once 'warp/warplib/appletmanager.inc';
require_once 'warp/applets/main/main.inc';
require_once 'warp/applets/weather/weather.inc';
require_once 'warp/applets/tvguide/tvguide.inc';
require_once 'warp/applets/photoframe/photoframe.inc';
require_once 'warp/applets/cookery/cookery.inc';
require_once 'warp/applets/ldb/ldb.inc';

include_once 'system/master_standard.conf';

$appman = new Warp_Applet_Manager();
$appman->init();

$appman->AddApplet(new Warp_Main_Applet());
$appman->AddApplet(new Warp_TVGuide_Applet());
$appman->AddApplet(new Warp_PhotoFrame_Applet());
$appman->AddApplet(new Warp_Weather_Applet());
$appman->AddApplet(new Warp_Cookery_Info_Applet("Cooking Info"));
$appman->AddApplet(new Warp_LiveDepartureBoards_Applet());

echo $appman->renderPage();
?>
```

You can build your own pages using any combination of applets that you desire. This flexibility allows you to ignore certain applets if they come from an IP address range outside the local network or even build a page specifically for the machine. For example, knowing that your DHCP server always provides your kitchen PC with an IP of 192.168.1.140, you can build a page that only includes a list of recipes and cooking information.

■ **Note**   If you access a web page through any form of proxy, including routers, you may not be able to get the correct address, because the server will only see the IP of the proxy unless the proxy is so configured with "X-Forwarded-For" header.

With version 3.0 of Minerva, this process was grown by means of a browser factory. If you have multiple kiosk-like devices at home, you can now write:

```
$appman = getBrowser()->createManager();
$appman->init();
```

This code creates an application manager specific to the client machine. The getBrowser method is held in system/browserlist.conf, to translate the client IP into a specific browser object that details its function and approxiamate size. This is a two-step process. The first maps the IP to a browser type (e.g., touchscreen, PC), like this:

```
$ipaddr = getIPAddress();

$style = $_GET['WRPOOOXO_style'];
$dostyle = array_key_exists('WRPOOOXO_dostyle', $_GET) ? $_GET['WRPOOOXO_dostyle'] : "";

switch($ipaddr) {
    case "192.168.1.132": // kitchen tablet PC (height accounts for border)
        $style = STYLE_TABLET_LARGE;
        break;

    case "192.168.1.131": // hall-mounted iPod Touch
        $style = STYLE_TABLET_SMALL;
        break;

    default:
        $browser = $_SERVER['HTTP_USER_AGENT'];
        if (strstr($browser, "iPhone")) {
            $style = STYLE_TABLET_SMALL;
        } else if (strstr($browser, "iPad")) {
            $style = STYLE_TABLET_LARGE;
        }
        break;

}
```

The second step uses the $style argument to construct the object, with sizes:

```
switch($style) {
  case STYLE_TABLET_LARGE:
    return new WebBrowser(new WAM_FactoryTouch($style), 1024, 740);

  case STYLE_TABLET_SMALL:
    return new WebBrowser(new WAM_FactoryTouch($style), 480, 320);

  case STYLE_FULL:
  default:
    return new WebBrowser(new WAM_Factory(STYLE_FULL));
}
```

In each case, the WAM_Factor* class indicates which applet manager to create is currently either Warp_Applet_Manager or Warp_Applet_ManagerTouch, the latter uses large clickable icons rather than small icon and text for its interface.

Instead of using a single page containg all the applets, you can produce several pages and use the main applet to switch between them. This is shown in its maximized view in Figure 7-3.

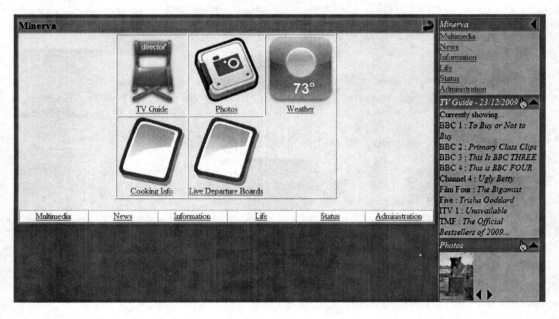

Figure 7-3. *The main applet*

The main applet has two functions. The first is to enumerate each applet added into the applet manager on that page, thus providing similar functionality to the minimized boxes on the right but with larger graphics (that is, better for touchscreen users). Its second is to provide a way of moving between separate pages. These are determined by the configuration file system/master_standard.conf, which looks like this:

```php
<?php
class MasterBar
{
    public static $automaticInclude = false;
    public static function getPages()
    {
        return array("Multimedia"=>"wmm.php", "News"=>"wfeeds.php",
            "Information"=>"wnews.php", "Life"=>"wlife.php",
            "Status"=>"wstatus.php", "Administration"=>"wsystem.php");
    }

    public static function generate(&$appman)
    {
        if (self::$automaticInclude) {
            return $appman->getMasterBar(getPages());
        } else {
            return "";
        }
    }
}
?>
```

The details of this should be obvious! Because you can now build your own custom pages using the existing applets, and adapt them according to the browser using the getBrowser method above. Now, let's look at what applets are available.

Existing Applets

The supplied applets are split into several broad categories—media, lifestyle, information, and administration. Most applets use the Bearskin abstractions since one of the many benefits of using a loosely coupled component-based development model is that many small tools can be combined into larger ones. These web applets are one such case. Each applet presented here relies on underlying code and data from simpler front ends. With this in mind, the configuration of each applet will be given in its entirety, from basic data to web-oriented page, so as to give an immediate understanding of the entire data flow, without scattering the information between its subcategories of Bearskin command, abstraction, configuration, and on.

Media

These applets allow you to control the playback of media in its various forms and include a CD player, a volume mixer, an MP3 jukebox, a VLC server and client, and a front end for displaying the TV guide.

The CD player is a very simple abstraction of the Bearskin cdplayer command that allows control of the disc, as shown in Figure 7-4, along with the album and track names present. The bridge between the PHP applet code and the Bearskin system command is handled by zinc/system/cdplayer.inc, with zinc/conf/cdplayer.conf being used to indicate the location of the executable and device to use.

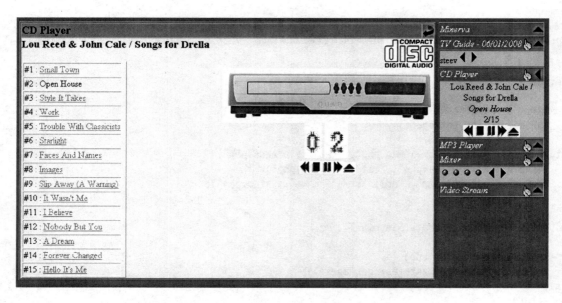

Figure 7-4. *The server's CD player being controlled through the web*

The audio mixer follows the same idea as the CD player and simply calls out to the underlying Bearskin command, although its settings and parameters are configured by `zinc/system/mixer.inc` and `zinc/conf/mixer.conf`, respectively.

There is an MP3 jukebox that allows you to explore the various directories under a given root, set at initialization with the following:

```
$appman->AddApplet(new Warp_MP3Play_Applet("MP3 Player", "media/mp3"));
```

If the folder name (second argument) begins with a /, then the path is absolute to the filesystem, whereas a relative path (as such shown here) means it's relative to the web server itself (but not relative to the Minerva directory). The MP3 jukebox can either play the music on the server itself or be streamed across the Internet to the browser. (Follow the hints in Chapter 5 regarding media access to prepare this.) The consideration of the root folder is important here if you want to support streaming, since it can work only if the music directory is accessible by the web server, that is, it is underneath the Apache root server directory, such as `/var/www/sites/homecontrol`. To this end, you may need to create a symlink to your music collection and enable `FollowSymLinks` in the configuration.

The TV guide uses the data downloaded every night by the Minerva user. It generates a large block of PHP code that stores program information for every show over the next three days inside `$MINBASE/etc/users/public/tvresults.inc`. This can be parsed out by the Bearskin commands such as `tvonnow default` and `tvreport default public` or processed by the applet directly.

In addition to the list of all programs held by the public user, the daily `crontab` is able to search user-specific criteria and generate a customized schedule. It does this with a search string provided as a comma-separated list of terms, on a single line, in a file such as `$MINBASE/etc/users/[username]/tvsearch/list`. The `tvsearch` directory also may optionally contain two extra files. One is called `e-mail` and is the e-mail address to which this list is also sent; the other is `sms`, which is the SMS phone number to which a shortened form is sent. If the file in question doesn't exist, then no message is sent.

Adding new TV channels requires the addition of disparate settings, since the TV configuration for the guide and control is unified into a single set of arrays held in $MINBASE/conf/tvconf.conf.

```bash
#!/bin/bash

tuner=( a1 a1 d1 d1 a1 d1 a1 a1 d1 )
channel=( 55 0 0 65 0 0 59 0 )
names=( BBC1 BBC2 BBC3 BBC4 "Channel 4" "Film Four" Five ITV TMF )
stations=( bbc1 bbc2 bbc3 bbc4 ch4 film_four five itv1 tmf )
```

As you can see, this holds the tuning information for the TV card (the channel number and whether it uses the analog or digital tuner[5]), along with the station ID and its full, printable name. The only restriction on the station ID is that it must match the one being used to retrieve the TV guide data. In this case, this is discernible from the list at http://bleb.org/services/tv/data/listings/0.

These data arrays are supplemented by the web-only data for the station icons, held in $MINBASE/media/images/tvguide. The filename stubs must match the IDs given earlier and end in .png to be correctly read by the applet. Furthermore, since these icons must be available to the web server, it is necessary to ensure a symlink exists from a web-friendly directory (such as warp/conf/tvguide/images) back to the original folder. By default, this is created by the Minerva installer, so you needn't worry.

The final media applets covered here support streaming video and come in a pair. The first is the VLC streaming applet that allows you to browse a series of predetermined folders (such as /net/media/videos) and select one for playback. This creates a media stream on the server and port specified in $MINBASE/conf/videostream.conf, which can then be read by a VLC client on any connected computer. The other half of the pair is a client applet that is able, by using a plug-in (available for Firefox when you install VLC), to stream the video clip into the browser window itself.

■ **Note** The streaming generally occurs over the local network only. To make it accessible from the outside, you need to open a port on your firewall or router to redirect traffic on the VLC port (8080, by default) to the given machine.

Lifestyle

These applets are generally for use in and around the house and include an X10 control panel for switching your appliances on and off in a visual manner, as shown in Figure 7-5.

---

[5] Analogue TV transmissions are all but extinct in the United Kingdom, and other countries, so this functionality will soon follow suit.

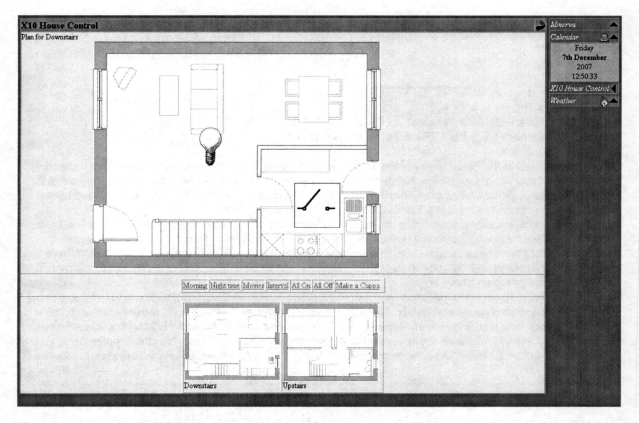

Figure 7-5. *Using the web to switch your lights on or make a cuppa*

This has a number of configuration files because of its complexity, which I will cover now. (All paths are relative to the Minerva's web home directory.)

> `warp/conf/x10/x10.conf`: This controls the mood or scenes bar that appears underneath the main X10 control map. This normally includes references like "all lights off" and "film mood." You need to program a list of scenes and the code that will be run when the corresponding scene is selected.

> `zinc/conf/x10floorplan.conf`: This contains a list of X10 devices in the house and their respective floor index, X, and Y positions on the floor plan maps. These names must match the devices in either Hu format (such as E3) or by alias names, as provided in the `heyu` configuration file (`/etc/heyu/x10.conf`). This file also contains the names for each floor in the house.

> `warp/applets/x10/img`: In addition to the standard X10 graphics for lightbulbs and appliance switches, this directory should also contain the floor plan maps, stored as `floor0.png`, `floor1.png`, and so on.

The calendar, shown in Figure 7-6, retrieves the Google Calendar information for both the public calendars and the current user. These are determined from the `ical` and `gcal` configuration files held in the user's Minerva directory, `$MINBASE/etc/users/[username]/external`. The `ical` file is parsed to look for today's events, while the `gcal` file is used to present links to external calendar files. The clock used is a piece of freeware Java, but you can easily change this to any design that takes your fancy.[6]

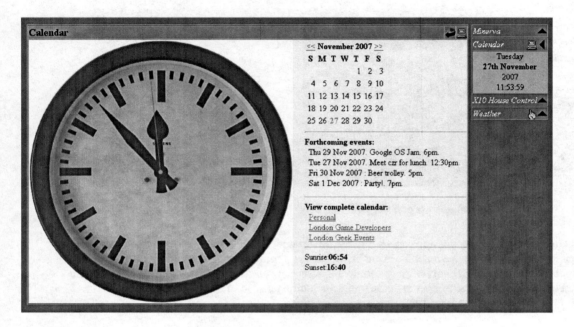

Figure 7-6. *A calendar that extracts personal data from a public site*

The applet for cookery information is very simple, because it is a basic lexicon of cooker terms and basic conversion units, each loaded from a separate file found in `warp/conf/cookery`. If you plan on building an applet that is based around static text files, then this is a good starting point.

The contacts applet provides full details of all your friends and relatives and is available on a per-user basis. Whenever a user is logged in, their contact information is read from the `$MINBASE/etc/users/[username]/contacts.xml` file, parsed, and presented in this applet. If they're not logged in, then you will get those belonging to the public user.

Finally, the photo frame applet is unique to the web conduit in Minerva. It reads a list of photographs from `warp/conf/photoframe/photoframe.conf` (the images themselves being held in a subdirectory called `photos`) and displays them one at a time, as shown in Figure 7-7.

---

[6] Such as `http://toki-woki.net/p/scroll-clock` or the HTML5 clock from
`http://sgxengine.com/examples/clockface/html5/default.htm`

Figure 7-7. *The photo frame can operate as a slide show on kiosk machines*

By clicking the main image, this app can work in the full browser window, making it suitable as an interactive photo frame for those times when a machine is not being used as a control panel. You can cycle through the images using hotspots on the left and right of the image, while the lower portion returns you to non-full-screen mode. The Internet has a lot of available images to fit the frame, including those for the culture vultures at http://www.most-famous-paintings.org.

Information

These applets provide information about the real world, which is also useful and valid when outside the house. There is potential overlap from these and your lifestyle, but it's a good enough distinction for now!

Moonbeam is an applet that relies on MySQL to store a list of bookmarks, each with multiple tags. It is similar to http://del.icio.us, except that all data is held on your own server. To prepare the database, you can run the build/applets/moonbeam/createdb.sql script using your existing root account:

```
$ mysql -u your_username -h your_machine_name -p < createdb.sql
```

Then enter your password to build an empty database. You can populate it with sample links by adding the same credentials to the config.php file in the same directory and running the following:

```
php init.php
```

You can then add this account information to the Moonbeam's web configuration at conf/moonbeam/config.php and use the applet as normal. If you want to create an alternate user to access the Moonbeam database (which is recommended), then log into MySQL and enter the following:

```
CREATE USER 'moonbeam'@'localhost' IDENTIFIED BY 'some_pass';
GRANT SELECT on moonbeam.* TO  'moonbeam'@'localhost';
```

And amend the web configuration, as shown earlier. The moonbeam user is consequently granted read-only permission to the database for security, while the real user (e.g. steev) is able to add, change, and remove bookmarks through the database as normal.

The weather applet simply reads the precached forecasts (made earlier in the day by the Minerva user's `crontab`) stored in `/var/log/minerva/cache/weather.txt` and `/var/log/minerva/cache/weather_info.txt` to look for matching strings that determine which icon will be drawn on the page.

There is also a currency calculator, based on the `http://xurrency.com` web service that you saw in Chapter 6. Its inclusion is primarily educational.

Another applet that merely wraps an existing Bearskin command consists of live departure boards. It calls `$MINBASE/bin/ldbquery` to determine the next trains from your predetermined stations. There is no configuration here, since the `ldbquery` script accepts arguments designated as the source and destination stations on your journey from hard-coded values in the applet.

And finally, the RSS news applet makes use of the `news-read` command to render the most recent news stories into your browser. Each news feed is governed by the unique pairing of a site ID and username, which presents a file stored in `$MINBASE/etc/users/public/news/slashdot`, for example, that holds the site name and URL for the RSS feed:

```
Slashdot
http://rss.slashdot.org/Slashdot/slashdot
```

This news is downloaded on demand, either explicitly with `news-get public slashdot` or implicitly when a story is read with `news-read slashdot public text 0 headline`. At this point, the RSS content is downloaded and stored in a local cache where the various elements can be read. The system is smart enough to not redownload content if it is fairly fresh and can render the output in text, HTML, or vocal-friendly text. The latter case removes any markup. The WARP applet displays the elements, headline, URL, and story, individually, using the `news-read` arguments shown earlier. The same approach can be used on the command line, allowing the alarm clock to include a line such as the following to give you the headlines in the morning:

```
$MINBASE/bin/say default (`news-read slashdot public vox 0 headline`)
```

Administration

These are all very simple applets to quickly review the status logs, processes, and server, without you having to log in through SSH. You will need to have authority to use these tools, so give yourself permission with the following:

```
minuser auth [myusername] system set rw
```

The typical applets available here report the following:

- Free disk space (the specific devices can be specified in `warp/conf/diskfree/diskfree.conf`)

- User agent of the browser (for debugging mainly)

- Samba status

- Processor top

- UPS status

- Various log files

- Bluetooth scanner results

Creating Your Own Applets

To fully appreciate the development methodology of applets, it's necessary to know a little about WARP. WARP is a system built on WebFace that abstracts the basic elements of web design to ensure that the control logic and presentation elements are strictly separated. This means that it's not possible to add a link in your page with the following:

```
<a href="process.php?bedroom_light=on">Switch Light On</a>
```

but instead you have to ask an applet manager to generate one for you:

```
$html = $appMan->getAppletLink($applet, "on", "bedroom_light", "Switch Light On");
```

You would then pick up the argument like this:

```
$prm = $appMan->queryParameter($applet, "bedroom_light");
```

This approach has several benefits. Naturally, it forces a separation between logic and display, which encourages more structured code, and it means you can place the applet onto any page you like, since the page itself isn't mentioned. But more important, it allows for an easy upgrade path. WARP is based on something akin to a RESTful approach. Because HTTP is a stateless protocol, there is no way of remembering the user action from one page to the next. Some web sites do this by using lots of different pages, where the page itself is an implicit reminder of the state. Some will create server-side objects that remember the state and last for as long as your browser is looking at the page or until an arbitrary timeout. WARP does this by recording the state as part of the URL. And with several applets appearing on each page, each applet must therefore have its own part of the URL indicating its own state. A typical URL might appear as follows:

```
http://my.minervahome.net/minerva/wmm.php?WRP001X1_user=0&WRP001X1_day=0&WRP002X3_dpage↵
=0&WRP002X3_fpage=0&WRP004X6_current=/&WRP004X6_dpage=0&WRP004X6_fpage=0&wintype↵
=main&content=WRP002X&max=WRP002X
```

If you dissect this carefully, you can see that each parameter fits the pattern of WRP, followed by a three-digit applet code, an X separator and parameter index number, an underscore, and then a name/value pair. There are also some parameters that describe WARP's internal state in the form of wintype, content, and max. Naturally, attempting to generate or parse this URL manually would be foolhardy!

The WARP Directories

There are three directories of note inside minerva/warp:

> applets: The code and assets for each of the applets, inside their own subdirectory

> conf: The configuration data for the earlier applets, inside an identically named subdirectory

> warplib: The base and operational classes for the applet and applet manager

The Components of WebFace

Each abstraction in WebFace covers one of the four areas in WARP code design. References to each can be retrieved from the applet manager with functions and functionality as follows:

getAuth(): Authorization. This module will let you know whether the user has logged in and been authenticated by the Apache server using the method getUser. Since the Apache user ID is administered manually to match the Minerva username, this can be used to present the TV guide and other user-specific data on a web page. This module also connects to the minuser code, through isUserValidFor, to provide fine-level control over the various applets. This makes it possible for many people to see the currently playing CD or MP3 track but for only a privileged few to change it (warp/warplib/appauth.inc).

getCtrl(): Control. Generates anchors for web links; I'll cover this in detail later in this chapter.

getView(): Viewport. This is used to combine multiple blocks of individual data into a single frame. The metaphor used here is *pane*, since they are combined to form windows. The default functionality allows you to combine these into horizontally or vertically, aligned windows of two, three, or four panes (webface/webview.inc).

getDbug(): Debug. This is a utility submodule that allows individual errors, warnings, and information lines to be logged. Once the HTML has been built, the complete list can be written out using dumpAll. This is done as output written to arbitrary parts of the web page can break the formatting badly and, in the case of cookies, prevent the page from loading altogether (webface/webdbug.inc).

The Basic Structure

Almost every applet begins the same way, with a directory inside warp/applets and a new applet class taken from the template as follows:

```php
<?php
require_once 'system/setup.conf';
require_once 'warp/warplib/applet.inc';

class Warp_TODO_Applet extends Warp_Applet
{
    function Warp_TODO_Applet($caption = "TODO List")
    {
        parent::__construct($caption);
    }

    function getID()
    {
        return "MY_APP_V1A";
    }

    function getDirectory()
    {
        return "todo";
    }
```

```php
    function init(&$appMan)
    {
        Warp_Applet::Init($appMan);
    }

    function renderPanel(&$appMan)
    {
        return "";
    }

    function renderWindow(&$appMan)
    {
        return "";
    }

    function renderInfo(&$app_man, $fast=false)
    {
        if ($fast) {
            return "-";
        }
        return "Instructions...";
    }
}
?>
```

You can easily see the blanks in which you fill the HTML code to form the panel, main window, and help screen. These are the easy bits. The interesting code is in `init` and the hitherto unseen `getRefreshParams` that control the parameters.

TODO: Controlling the Applet

With everything being controlled by parameters, you must take care to use them effectively. The best way to do this is to think of the GET request as featuring two sets of parameters. The first set reflects the refresh parameters and are those that you'd want to appear in the URL so that this state could be rebuilt at a later date. The second set is the command parameters, indicating how that state is to change when the page is reloaded.

In the TODO example, your applet should be able to list the to-do list for the current user or the public and optionally be able to sort it alphabetically.[7] This will ultimately provide you with five potential parameters:

- *Refresh state parameter*: Which user is visible?

- *Refresh state parameter*: Is the list sorted?

- *Command argument*: Switch to user X.

- *Command argument*: Sort list.

- *Command argument*: Unsort list (aka, show in order).

This demonstrates the next point—there is redundancy here. It is technically possible to combine the refresh state and command parameter in one, as they both control the same data. However, when you are building a web page, you need to know all the refresh state parameters so that the other links on the page have the correct values.

---

[7] To correctly delete an entry from the TODO list, you'd need to lock the file in case the file got corrupted when two people tried to delete at the same time. I have a truly marvelous solution to this, which this margin is too narrow to contain!

Unfortunately, that would require a lot of work to know which state parameter would be overridden later by the command parameters. You can simplify this by writing a refresh function that describes the current state and that every other applet will indirectly call when it requests a URL from the applet manager:

```
function getRefreshParams(&$appMan)
{
  return
    $appMan->getArgument($this, "user", $this->_viewuser)."&".
    $appMan->getArgument($this, "sort", $this->_sortlist));
}
```

You next add links that contain command parameters, which are similar to those you've seen already:

```
$html = "Show: ";
$html.= $appMan->getAppletLink($this, "dosort", "0", "Chronologically")." ";
$html.= $appMan->getAppletLink($this, "dosort", "1", "Alphabetically");

$html.= "   For: ";
$html.= $appMan->getAppletLink($this, "douser", $user, $user)." ";
$html.= $appMan->getAppletLink($this, "douser", "public", "Public");
```

These parameters, by convention, are prefixed with do, indicating that they should change the refresh state. That is, new state = old state + do changes. The applet manager generates a suitable link by gathering the refresh parameters from every applet present on the current page and appending these do links to the end.

When the page is loaded, a new state is built based on these parameters and done in two stages. The first is to retrieve the refresh arguments:

```
$this->_sortlist = $appMan->queryParameter($this, "sort", false);
$this->_viewuser = $appMan->queryParameter($this, "user", "public");
```

The second is to look for any do parameters to change this state:

```
$this->_sortlist = $appMan->queryParameter($this, "dosort", $this->_sortlist);
$this->_viewuser = $appMan->queryParameter($this, "douser", $this->_viewuser);
```

In both cases, you're using a default argument to queryParameter that covers the case when the applet is first used and no parameters at all are available and for when there are no command parameters.

You can then flex your creative muscles in displaying the output from the Bearskin command todo (remember writing that all those pages ago?!) and write the list into the HTML:

```
exec("/usr/local/minerva/bin/todo list ".$this->_viewuser, $todolist);

if ($this->_sortlist) {
  sort($todolist);
}

$html .= "<ul>";
foreach($todolist AS $item) {
  $html .= "<li>$item</li>";
}
$html .= "</ul>";
```

To add a layer of polish to these, you could move the exec call into Zinc, but that can be left for another day!

Global Configuration

There are a small number of configuration files used in the web portion of Minerva to cope with the different directories structures you might adopt, as detailed in Table 7-1.

Table 7-1. *Web Configuration Directories*

Include Filename	Function	Default Directory	Description
minerva.conf	getMinervaRoot	/usr/local/minerva	The base of the Minerva system itself.
system/setup.conf	getURLRoot	/minerva	The name used by Minerva web components. Can be changed for protection against bots that attempt to break any web pages held in a Minerva-named directory.
system/setup.conf	getPathRoot	/var/www/sites/homecontrol	The filesystem path of the web root. Used when you need to access files in the conventional manner.
system/utils.inc	getServerName		Varies. Use this, instead of IP dotted quad if virtual servers are used.
system/utils.inc	getServerPort		80.
system/utils.inc	getRemotePort		Varies by client.
system/utils.inc	getIPAddress		Determined by client. Might actually be IP of router.

Applet Configuration

There are two different types of directory you, as an applet writer, need to consider. The first are those that are used to serve web data to the client, such as images, configuration data, or supplementary files. There are several methods inside each applet class to retrieve this, each accepting a filename and returning its full path, such as getConfFileName (taken from the configuration directory), getAppletFileName (the applet code directory), and getImageURL (the images directory inside the applet folder).

The second type of directory is one that refers to a location in the filesystem and is referenced with getFilesystemPathStub and concatenated with the relative filename. In reality, any relative web path can be converted into a filesystem path by joining it with WarpSetup::getPathRoot, but these methods provide a clean way of writing code.

There is also an intriguing method called getRefreshTime, which causes the current web page (with all its applets) to automatically reload itself every *n* seconds. This allows the applet to more easily reflect changes to data without needing to implement specific push protocols. If more than one applet supports getRefreshTime, then the shortest time is used. This is provided as an alternative to the use of Ajax (as demonstrated in the Bluetooth, currency, and recipe applets) that asynchronously responds to requests from the main server. Remember that most browsers support only two concurrent Ajax requests, so their issue should be staggered with a timeout.

Utilities

Various utility methods are included as part of the applet manager, as well as the individual applet base class itself. Indeed, there are even full classes that can be derived from to create near-complete applets with very little work. Warp_Browser_Applet, as used by the MP3 player and video streamer, lets you traverse an entire directory structure without writing a single line of code; you only need to overload the renderFileLine and renderDirectoryLine methods to generate appropriate actionable links. Additionally, Warp_Static_Text_Applet can be used select and render one of many given HTML files, as demonstrated with the cooking applet.

Caching is one of many utilities provided by the appletUtils class, located in warp/warplib/appletutils.inc. Code like this will download the contents of $url to the local data file but only if the file doesn't exist or is older than 6,000 seconds:

```
$contents = appletUtils::getContents($url, "local_data_file", 6000);
```

The cache contents are stored in /var/log/minerva/cache.

Release

If you're developing an applet for yourself, then the job is now done! Otherwise, you should package it ready for others. The addminervaapplet script is used to install new applets into the correct locations. Because there can be several components to an applet (Bearskin, WARP, and Zinc), you should create directories for each so that it matches those used already. Here's an example of the FM radio applet:

```
fmradio/example.php
fmradio/Readme
fmradio/version
fmradio/fmradio/bearskin/fmradio
fmradio/fmradio/install/install.sh
fmradio/fmradio/warp/app/ [contents of applet directory go here]
fmradio/fmradio/zinc/conf/ [Zinc configuration here]
fmradio/fmradio/zinc/cmd
```

Manifest

The Manifest system is a method of presenting multiple elements in a sequential pattern in a way that can be interactively terminated, interrupted, or extended, with the commands stop, next, and more, respectively. This is better explained by working through the two supplied examples, News and Music, whose audio-based output is typical of the usage of Manifest.

The news manifest reads headlines from a given news feed one at a time. If the more command is given at any point during the headline, the full story is then read, before continuing with the next headline. (In the case of the music manifest, the more command is a null operation but could be used to speak the title and artist of the previous track.)

The manifests can be invoked with a simple command like the following:

```
manifest default start music 10
```

and, because the current manifest is known, can be controlled without naming it:

```
manifest default next
```

Note that the start command is synchronous and doesn't return until all the items have been played, which will be either when there is no news left or the maximum number of items have been read, in this case 10.

Every manifest has the same set of driver commands, based in a suitably named directory under `$MINBASE/etc/manifest`. These commands are held in files:

> `onstart`: This is an optional script that triggers an introduction to the manifest as a whole. This could be an initial "here is the news" kind of announcement. The first element of the manifest should *not* be played here, however.

> `onmore`: This is another optional script, covering the additional information to be played. The script should exit with an error code of 1 to terminate the playback.

> `onnext`: This is obligatory and called once at the start to initiate the first piece of information and repeated for each element in the manifest. Like `onmore`, it should return an exit code of 1 to prevent any future results.

> `onstop`: This is called, optionally, at the end of the sequence and usually initiates a chime or conferment that the manifest has completed. This happens regardless of whether it ended naturally or by forcible termination.

> `terminate`: This kills any process spawned from an `onnext` output. It is optional and needed only for those scripts that launch additional programs, such as the media player that must invoke `mp3player default stop`. If this doesn't exist, the process is killed using the standard Linux command.

■ **Note**   You can connect the music manifest to Cosmic in order to trigger a few random songs at bedtime or read the news in the morning. There are some fulsome examples of this in the earlier section on routines.

The news manifest is programmed, by default, to read the top headlines from the BBC news site, whereas the music one will randomly search a given directory and play music it finds there.

Naturally, after a while, the same songs will repeat (such is the nature of *pseudo*-randomness) that you'll be sick of hearing them. Therefore, it is a blessing that you can prevent the currently playing song from ever being heard again with:

```
manifest default block
```

or prevent any song from the current tracks' directory (which is useful when only one track exists within it) with:

```
manifest default blockdir
```

The details of what is blocked is held in a mirror of your media directory structure inside `/var/log/minerva/manifest/block`.

■ **Note**   If a file can be accessed by two different paths, the system only blocks files whose name matches exactly, and so you might need to reblock files that are symlinked from different locations.

You can review the list of blocked files at any time by either recursively listing the directory, or with the command:

```
manifest default blocklist
```

Marple

Marple stands for the Minerva Appliance Routing and ProtocoL Engine. This is a mechanism whereby you can control a device, such as a TV card, from a command on one machine while using the command and resources of another. This allows you to spread the hardware load between machines or to distribute commands to remote servers that service peripherals that are ineffective in other locations—X10 gateways, notably. The low cost of the Raspberry Pi now makes this a very real possibility.

You can use the same mechanism to invoke software-only devices, such as WiFi-enabled media players and speech synthesis units, allowing music to be streamed into locations where physical speaker cabling is not possible. The system is bidirectional, so you can also get a remote machine to send any commands it gets to the main server for processing.

Marple was introduced in version 2.2.0 of Minerva and is now supported by all the current Bearskin commands and used transparently to the user.

The Workings

There are two files necessary to enable Marple's full range of functionality, both are called `devlist` and exist for each of the Bearskin commands that have been enabled. They are formatted thusly:

```
localhost dev    /dev/dsp       -       -
default   dev    /dev/dsp       -       -
bedroom   soap   192.168.1.123  19781   localhost
```

The columns are as follows, in order:

The device name: This is always the first argument to any of the Bearskin commands, such as the bedroom in `cdplayer bedroom play 1`.

Protocol type: This currently may be `dev` or `soap`. If the protocol is `dev`, then the protocol device represents a Linux-style device on the local machine. If it's `soap`, then the device specifies the IP address of the machine to talk to.

Protocol device: This indicates which address is to be used for the device. It's usually a device or IP address (see the previous item).

Protocol parameter: This is used in conjuncture with the protocol device. This is mostly unused, but in the example earlier it represents the port number associated with the IP address.

The remote device name: When the command is being executed on the remote device, this name is used instead of the original one given. This parameter is unused for `dev` protocols.

Handling Protocols

When the user invokes the `cdplayer` command for example (from either the Web, command line, or Cosmic), the script will examine the local `devlist` file located at `$MINBASE/etc/devices/cdplayer/devlist` for a matching device name in the first column. If no matching device name can be found, it then reads the global `devlist` file (in the same format but located at `$MINBASE/house/marple/cdplayer/devlist`) and tries again. If a match still can't be found, then the original device name is used by `cdplayer` in the hope that it is application-specific and the `cdplayer` application can understand it.

Once a matching device name is found (regardless of which file contained it), the device is evaluated. In the case of `dev` protocols, the protocol parameter (such as `/dev/dsp`) is passed back to the application for immediate use.

All other protocols, such as soap, are handled by external commands located in $MINBASE/bin/xmit/ [protocol_name]/cmd. This combines the new protocol information (IP address and port) with all the parameters from the original command, with the remote device name (column 4) in place of the original one, and passes it to the appropriate cmd script. Here it is in geek parlance:

```
$MARPLEPROTOCOL/cmd ${DEVARRAY[2]} ${DEVARRAY[3]} $COMMAND ${DEVARRAY[4]} $ALLARGS
```

This command can then issue an appropriate network packet to the server listed. In the case of SOAP, a call is made to minerva/marple/cmd.php where the arguments are extracted, and a brand new Bearskin command is formulated like this:

```php
<?php

function getCommand($cmd, $args) {

    # in case someone tries exec'ing other programs, in different directories
    # we'll try and stop them.
    $cmd = str_replace("/", "", $cmd);
    $cmd = str_replace("..", "", $cmd);

    $minervaPath = "/usr/local/minerva";
    $fullCommand ="$minervaPath/bin/$cmd $args";

    return $fullCommand;
}

function marple($cmd, $args) {
    $fullCommand = getCommand($cmd, $args);
    $result = array();

    exec($fullCommand, $result);

    $rts = "";
    foreach ( $result as $v ) {
      $rts .= "$v\n";
    }
    return $rts;
}

$server = new SoapServer(null, array('uri' => "urn://www.minervahome.net/marple"));
$server->addFunction("marple");
$server->handle();
?>
```

Note that the only commands available are under the /usr/local/minerva hierarchy, with all instances of pruned out to stop malicious code from being run.

■ **Note**　If you add your own protocols but they're not addressed by an IP/port pair, then you can reappropriate the two columns to your desires, provided your $MARPLEPROTOCOL/cmd script can understand them.

Using the `cdplayer` example again, the remote machine processes a command that now looks like this, if it were to be processed locally:

```
cdplayer localhost play 1
```

Bearskin Compatibility

To make your own commands compatible with Marple, you need to begin your scripts with a few extra lines of code. Here's an example:

```
DEVICE=`$MINBIN/finddev mixer $*`
if [ $? == 0 ]; then
  echo $DEVICE
  exit 0;
fi
```

This rather strange-looking piece of code makes use of both the `finddev` output and its exit code. It returns a 0 in those cases where the device name was found but wasn't intended for this machine. In other words, it has dispatched a SOAP request or similar and 1 when a genuine device was found. The latter is more usual and ends up being `/dev/dsp` or similar. As far as the command scripts go, this is all that's necessary.

The extra work comes from creating a local `devlist`. But each is generally a carbon copy of the others. Namely, a file called `$MINBASE/etc/devices/new_app_name/devlist` should be created and appear like this, replacing `/dev/dvd` with a suitable device for your app:

```
localhost dev    /dev/dvd       -        -
default dev      /dev/dvd       -        -
```

Note that the local `devlist` file should always include a `default` and `localhost` reference. This ensures that every query can terminate and stops recursive loops from happening.

■ **Note** Some low-level software, such as the CD player program `cdcd`, requires `$HOME` to be set up before the program can be run. This requires the machine charged with processing SOAP requests to add this extra line of code and sometimes prepare a `.cdcdrc` file in the home directory of the `www-data` user.

Utility Scripts

A quick perusal of the `$MINBASE/bin` directory will reveal a number of commands that haven't yet been covered. These divide into status and user tools.

Status

These are the simplest to consider and are basic scripts that perform read-only tasks to report on the various elements of the system. Because of the architecture, this is usually nothing more complex than reading text files in the `/var/log/minerva` directory or querying the existing commands.

Every status command, except vstatus, issues its report to the standard output stream. In this way, it can be incorporated directly into a web page output or piped into announce:

netstatus: Calls the user tool $MINBASE/bin/ipcheck to determine whether the external network is available, in addition to your local web server. Because ipcheck is synchronous, this can take a short while to happen, particularly if there's no available Internet.

lstatus: Life status, reporting what should generally happen today. For example, "empty the bins tonight." This is a housewide message and so appears on everyone's status reports. It also accepts an (optional) argument to indicate a day of the week (0 meaning Sunday, 1 for Monday, and so on) or "tomorrow".

weatherstatus: A simple echo of the weather forecast that has been downloaded and processed previously with ~minerva/update/weather.

mstatus: Reports on the media currently playing, including both MP3 and CDs, detailing the artist and album when they're known.

status: All of the earlier reports are combined into one, along with the time and date, making it an informative alarm call.

tvonnow: Provides a list of the TV programs currently showing. The list is downloaded every night and stored locally, where this code rips out only those programs in the current time slot.

vstatus: A wrapper to status, presenting all the information in a spoken form with announce, meaning there's a single chime at the beginning and end of the whole phrase, and not one between each individual report.

Variable Constants

Although computers are very rigid devices, real life isn't. The mantra/cliché of 'the only constant thing is change' is true. So, as we saw when using the routine code to vary our alarm call, there are some tools which help with those things that always happen . . . but we just don't know when they happen.

easter: A short script that computes the date of Easter Sunday for the current year, in the form 31 March 2013. If Easter has passed (which can be determined by passing the single argument ispassed) you can determine the date for the subsequent year and call easter $((`date +%Y` + 1))

sunrise: The time of sunrise, at your current location, in the form 06:35. This is good for affecting the lights around the house, particularly if your work means you're getting up before sunrise, and want your lights to brighten naturally in the morning. You can specify your location with longitude and latitude coordinates in the file /usr/local/minerva/etc/location.inc.

sunset: The opposite of sunrise, obviously, with your current location specified in the same file.

User Tools

As I've mentioned several times, the differences between an automated house and a smart home are the subtleties and extras and make people go "Wow!" These tools generally fall into this category:

hdate: This reports the date in a natural, humanistic manner such as Tuesday the 15th of December 2009 instead of Tue Dec 15 10:40:03 GMT 2009. This not only makes it user-friendly but machine friendly, too, as the output can be sent to a speech processor where you'll get a better-sounding voice because it understands how to vocalize words and sentences better than the computerized form.

housenight: This is a simple shutdown script for putting the house to sleep. The default script says "Goodnight" and switches off a predetermined set of lights. You may want to extend this to send shutdown messages to secondary PCs (as shown in Chapter 4) or initiate overnight download scripts.

htime: This reports the time in a natural, humanistic manner in the same way that hdate does for the date.

vtime: This produces a vocal version of the time using piecemeal samples, as covered in Chapter 5.

ipcheck: This pings each web site listed in $MINBASE/etc/ipcheck.conf to determine whether the Internet, as a whole, is currently available.

pmedia: This is a utility script to pause any, and every, media device that is currently playing such as MP3 and CD. If the media is already paused, then it resumes it. This is a useful emergency cutoff command, especially when issued remotely through Cosmic, when you're trying to listen to what someone else in the house is saying.[8]

timedscale: This blocking script repeatedly calls a given command, scaling the input parameters over time. So, a call like timedscale 0 100 60 homedevice default dim e3 will vary the light output from 0 to 100 over the next 60 seconds by appending the scaled numbered to the end of the command. When the program does not take the value as its final parameter, you will need to create a small wrapper script to rearrange the arguments.

Topology Ideas

Every house is different. And for the most part, so are the network and wiring configurations necessary to run it. I will now present a couple of standard configurations as inspiration.

Networking

Figure 7-8 shows the simplest of networks. It uses an off-the-shelf router to hide your Node0 server and your other machines on a local address range (such as 192.168.1.x). The router is then configured to open specific ports, redirecting those requests to the main server or other machines on the network as appropriate. The additional machines can be laptops, media head units, or secondary administrative machines such as file servers.

---

[8] Having music available in every room increases the ambient noise, making it more difficult to hear others calling you, so some of these commands exist to solve the problems that we have created.

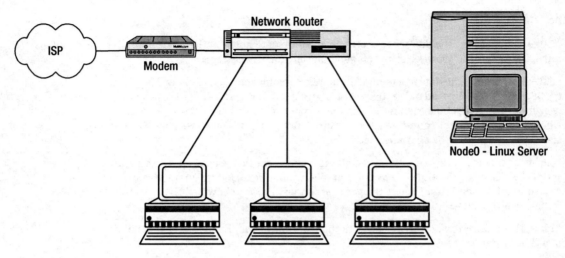

Figure 7-8. *A simple network configuration*

This allows you to reuse the router as a network switch and employ servers with only one network port, such as the majority of small low-power mini PCs on the market. If this configuration is too limiting, such as when you want to use Linux as the router itself, then you can adopt a configuration like the one shown in Figure 7-9. With this setup, you will need two network cards and a separate network switch.

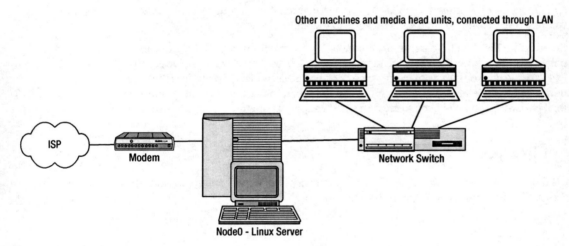

Figure 7-9. *Using a Linux server to separate the two network domains*

In either case, you use a remote server, such as a colocated server or a virtual machine located in a data center, to accept and process all traffic, thereby hiding the identity of your home machine.

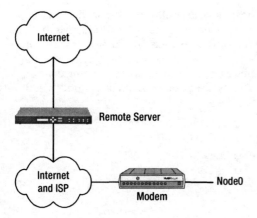

Figure 7-10. *Using an external server*

Wiring Looms

Whole-house audio and video with media accessible in every room can happen in one of two primary ways. The first is by using small PCs in each room, connected to the network to decode the audio locally. This is easier to upgrade and allows audio and video data to be streamed and controlled locally with very little effort. It is, however, expensive because of the hardware needed in each room. It is also inconvenient in those cases where you want to move between rooms while watching or listening since you have to manually restart it.[9]

The cheapest way of distributing AV data is by running cables to each room. This involves a combination of amplifiers and switchers, as shown in Figure 7-11.

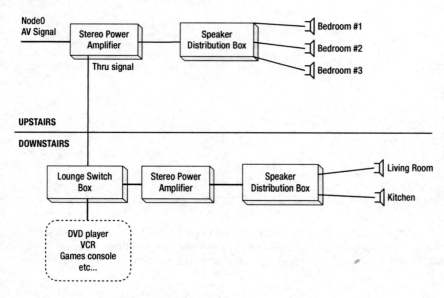

Figure 7-11. *A simple AV distribution network*

---

[9] The software to manage this is currently minimal to nonexistent.

In all cases, the generic term of *AV* is used to refer to audio and/or video data, according to your needs. You will notice that distribution among the rooms upstairs is easier, since the cables can be run up into the attic, across the attic space in any haphazard manner you please, and down into the other rooms. Here there is a single set of AV cables running down the downstairs, giving full control to the living room.

The primary limitation with this setup is the single AV channel coming from the Node0 server, meaning that any media not held on Node0 cannot be distributed or used elsewhere. The PVR, for example, can be controlled and viewed only in the living room. This is solved in Figure 7-12.

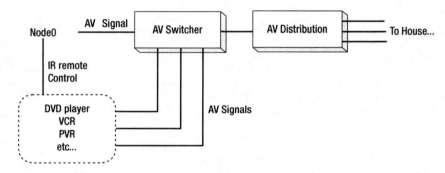

Figure 7-12. *Placing all the AV in Node0*

In this environment, all the AV equipment is placed physically within Node0, making for short cable runs and easy-to-install IR transmitters. And there is still only a single AV cable to lay into each room wanting media. This is both a benefit, because the installation is much cheaper, and a hindrance, because only the *same* media can be experienced in each room. This is solved with a matrix switcher, shown in Figure 7-13, which allows any input to be sent to any room.

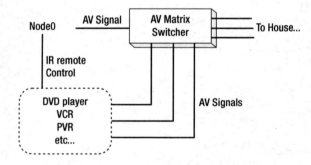

Figure 7-13. *The benefits of a matrix switcher*

Notice that in all cases, the placement of the particular amplifiers will be determined by the amps themselves. Some provide two power outputs, allowing all speakers to be passive (that is, unpowered), while others provide only a line-out level requiring an additional amplifier (and therefore power socket) for each room in which they're installed.

Conclusion

As you've seen with the example using the teakettle, there are comparatively few pieces of software needed to smartly automate a house. Once you can process incoming e-mails or text messages and issue an X10 command, then the task of "e-mailing your teakettle" becomes a simple matter of combining the two scripts in a trivial (almost banal!) fashion. The next level of interest is generated from the usability features and the specificity of function. Usability is something you can add only after living with the configuration for a while—having Festival use speech synthesis to say "the teakettle has boiled" is an easy technological change but is something so uniquely specific that only a geek living in the environment could actualize it with such effortless precision. Make the most of the opportunity.

CHAPTER 8

■ ■ ■

Raspberry Pi

The Raspberry Pi, shown in its full glory in Figure 8-1, is one of computing's modern marvels-a credit-card-sized single board computer, capable of running Linux, its applications, and capable of handling playback of HD video. Launched on Febuary 29, 2012, it has now been released in three different versions, with the current two versions being the Model A (256 Mbyte with USB) and the Model B (512 Mbyte, with 2 x USB and Ethernet). For the sake of an extra $10, there's no reason to not consider the Model B! Neither machine is sold with a power supply, case, keyboard, mouse, or anything necessary to make it work (which provides users with their first dose of education!), so it is as cheap as it could possibly be.

Figure 8-1. *The barebones Raspberry Pi, at 85.6 x 56.0 x 21.0mm*

The Raspberry Pi within HA

For many people, the Raspberry Pi is a small, cheap, Linux machine. But to think of it *only* in these terms is missing the point. When broadband was first introduced, people thought of it as "a fast dial-up service," with a nice benefit of being online all the time and nothing more. In reality, having a permanent connection changed the way everyone used the Internet. Having home servers, and consequently HA, was a viable possibility for the first time, allowing people to have a private data store and control system. In a similar fashion, having a computer this small isn't a question of having more space on your desk, it's a question of being able to automate devices that otherwise would become to cumbersome to use if there was a full-size machine connected to it. Similarly, having one this cheap means that you can experiment more and automate more (and more esoteric) devices.

Obvious Benefits

Despite my comments in the preceding paragraph, being small and cheap *does* have its benefits. The size allows us to connect it to other devices and in other places. Surprisingly, an Raspberry Pi can fit into a light switch! Because the plan for HA is to remove old manual technology, such as the light switch, this means that you can reuse the hole where the switch once was for a Raspberry Pi and some additional add-ons. This is especially true for peripherals such as webcams,[1] which are dumb pieces of technology that require complex software drivers to work. If you were so inclined, you could use SimpleCV add face recognition to the switch by your den, or study, and limit access in this way! Or, with the addition of a small screen, you could turn the switch into a conferencing or VOIP terminal.

▧ **Note**   For those with more money, replacing each wall switch with an iPod Touch or Android tablet can achieve the same effect!

It is also worth considering that the Raspberry Pi is easier and cheaper to hack than any existing gadget off the shelf. In the past, developers would spend months reversing engineering a $35 gadget just so they could add one feature or get it to run some version of Linux or BSD. Now, with the Raspberry Pi costing the same amount, there is little need to do this work because a Raspberry Pi can become that gadget through minimal hardware, and a prominence of software-software that is mostly already available and released under an open source license.

Towards Full Local Control

The cost of a Raspberry Pi means that it's no longer unreasonable to have one (or two) computers in every room in the house. What's more, because it is more powerful than an Arduino, it can be used as both a media streamer and a control system, particularly as it runs Linux, and therefore capable of using all the traditional Linux software for these tasks.

As already noted, the Raspberry Pi can fit inside a light switch so you can replace the "hard" switch, through which current flows to control the light, with a "soft" switch. In the HA context, this means that the switch doesn't (directly) control the current flow. Instead, the switch is connected to the Raspberry Pi, which in turn sends the open/close message to Node0. Node0 picks up this message, interprets it, and sends an appropriate control signal to the light. If the light is on X10, or a Hue bulb, then the commands we've already seen can control the light. However, you can also implement a similar system yourself by connecting the GPIO of the Raspberry Pi to a relay, which in turn controls the existing circuit with the light bulb. The circuit in Figure 8-2 is of use here, although more details of the Raspberry Pi GPIO interface will be discussed later.

---

[1]Although some web cameras (particularly HD ones) have been known to cause issues, since the Rapsberry Pi CPU isn't as capable of handling them as one might like!

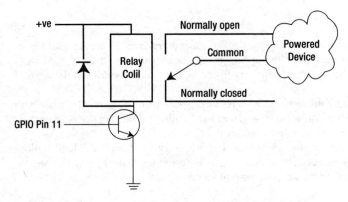

Figure 8-2. *A method to control a relay from a Raspberry Pi*

The low power demands of the Raspberry Pi make soft switches a very simple proposition, and so to preserve the low-energy footprint it is recommended to use individual LEDs for status lights, instead of a power-hungry (and expensive) display. It is then up to you whether you add a USB charging station to the switch . . . or a speaker . . .

The Joy Of Community

By saving lots of money on the cost of the boards, developers are able to instead spend time helping other developers. Aside from the Arduino, the Raspberry Pi probably has the largest community for any single piece of hardware currently on the market. In addition to the official boards (`http://www.raspberrypi.org/phpBB3/index.php`) there is also a (often more technical) forum at Element14 (`http://www.element14.com`), which is part of Farnell.

■ **Tip**   If you're looking for more detailed community support then avoid the official Raspberry Pi forum and use the ones on Element14-despite the arduous and unnecessary sign-up procedure! As the thread `http://www.element14.com/community/thread/19436` shows, people have been banned and threads removed from the official site when the conversation does not present the foundations ideals, which can hamper your efforts to find an answer to a question, or even provide prove that such questions exist.

Case design is another area where the Raspberry Pi community has come together to discuss ideas. This is particularly pertinent for those with older boards that lack screw holes. Cases have been made from LEGO, old Playstations, and paper. There have even been professional versions made from aluminum, and several kickstarter projects initiated to provide a case. Although there is currently no official case, the Pibow Color Case is picking up a lot of fans at the moment.

■ **Caution**   Not all prebuilt cases provide access to the GPIO pins, which are necessary for interfacing with homebrew periperals, so be aware.

The Drawbacks

Of course, if the Raspberry Pi were perfect we wouldn't need to invent any more computers. Ever. However, aside from its lack of power to do modern tasks (even speech synthesis is limited to a much simplified, and less aurally pleasing, algorithm), there are some issues that limit the places in which a Raspberry Pi can be used. Whether or not these are important issues will depend on your use case.

The first point to raise is that you cannot boot across the network with PXE or similar technologies. Therefore, you will always need an SD card or (less usually) a hard drive, connected. So, if you're planning on putting the Raspberry Pi in a confined space, bear in mind that the SD will stick out further than the case.

Another caution when physically mounting the device is that the power supply is connected via a USB lead, which adds another few millimeters to the total dimension, as does the composite cable, Ethernet plug, and so on. The more usual dimensions of a Raspberry Pi is actually 175.0 x 85.0 x 25.0mm, as seen in Figure 8-3.

Figure 8-3. *The effective size of a Raspberry Pi, without bending the cables excessively*

Also, talking of mounting, remember to buy version 2 boards because these are the first ones to have mounting holes so they can be fixed into cases and attached to arbitrary devices, using the two holes.[2] Previous revisions relied on being tightly wedged into a case, and laid horizontal, which limited their location.

As you might notice from looking at the board, there is no on/off switch. Given the amount of current it draws, this is probably unimportant for most people. Indeed, the hacks necessary to make an NSLU2 or Mini-ITX work around the issues of the power switch might mean this was a sensible choice. However, if you think you'll need such a button, you'll have to insert one into the USB cable, manually.

Another missing element is a real-time clock. Without one, you have to manually set the clock every time you plug it in. This means that log files and file stamps can get into a mess if you don't reprogram the time, or reprogram it incorrectly. Normally, the clock circuit would consist of a resonator or crystal and backup battery, to retain the time and date when the machine is switched off. However, this was considered too much extra circuitry and therefore omitted from the design. Therefore, any solution requiring knowledge of the time or date (which includes anything that might log data) will either need to synchronize the clock with a networked time server (NTP), keep it permanently remain on, or buy/build an external USB clock such as the one at http://ahsoftware.de/usb-rtc. For a software-based solution, you could write a short script that looked for the most recent date in the log files, and use that. The time would be wrong from a human's perspective but, with the date stamps being sequentially, the machine wouldn't cause problems.

---

[2]These were originally added by the factory at Sony to aid their production processes.

When considering the low-level hardware implications, be aware that the full documentation for the Broadcom BCM2835 chip (which does all the main work) is unavailable without an NDA. Most people will be happy using it at a higher level, even programming the GPIO, or working from the kernel source. But if you're hoping to be educated on the internal workings of a SoC, or wanting to investigate the drivers, then you're out of luck and should look to the fully open options out there.[3]

From an interfacing point of view, the lack of VGA port is the one with which most people will be concerned. Although the Raspberry Pi foundation considers VGA to be an antiquated technology, the reality is that there are many good value monitors available that don't support HDMI and so requiring you to buy a separate converter. This problem is expounded when looking for small monitors, as there are very few of the smaller incarnations of HDMI available and (as yet) no definitive compatibility list. (HDMI on Raspberry Pi seems to have a worse issue of compatibility than HDMI on desktop PCs.) Consequently, you may be forced into using the composite video to make use of a small display, at which point you're using an even older technology than VGA, and worse visual quality to boot. Other visual hook-ups include the Kindle (needs a jailbreak and a terminal emulator, as covered at http://www.ponnuki.net/2012/09/kindleberry-pi), iPad (just use a standard terminal emulator), or even an existing digital photo frame (http://www.cjb.im/2012/06/raspberry-pi-wireless-display-using.html).

■ **Caution**   If your HDMI device is not correctly detected you will need to edit the /boot/config.txt file to include parameters to explicitly define it. This appears as two lines, such as hdmi_group=1 and hdmi_drive=2 with the parameters indicating the type of HDMI (CEA or DMT) and the resolution. Both are described at http://www.raspberrypi.org/phpBB3/viewtopic.php?f=26&t=5851.

The biggest single problem with the Raspberry Pi appears to be the implementation of the USB stack, with issues in both hardware and software. Although the situation is improving, anything that needs USB to be of a "mission-critical" nature might need to be redesigned. This, unfortunately, includes Ethernet as that is provided through USB. (This is also why you can't have gigabit Ethernet on the Raspberry Pi–you're limited by the speed of the basic USB port.)

At the time of writing, the USB issues haven't been entirely solved, but the crux is thus. The hardware component inside the Broadcom chip, which handles the USB port, isn't particularly good and the driver (dwc_otg) that attempts to tame it has some issues whereby if a NAK packet is received, the processor gets interrupted. At this time (but only some of the time, it seems) the hardware portion of the USB stack resends an IN packet . . . that generates another NAK packet… that causes another interrupt on the processor. And so on. This very quickly leads to an interrupt cascade problem that can render the Raspberry Pi unusable for 20 seconds or so. For an interesting discussion on this topic, and why the Raspberry Pi has 8000 interrupts per second when idle, the thread is still open at http://www.raspberrypi.org/phpBB3/viewtopic.php?f=28&t=7866&start=111.

One fix to this problem is to disable the USB entirely:

```
echo 1 > /sys/devices/platform/bcm2708_usb/bussuspend
```

Naturally, this prevents the keyboard from working. And with Ethernet being controlled through USB also, this means that you can't remotely control it to make it communicate with the outside world. It is possible to connect a keyboard or similar device through the GPIO, but such circuitry is outside the scope for this book. There is also some online discussion on whether the Raspberry Pi (Model A) avoids this problem, or whether it hasn't been witnessed as often. A thread, more detailed than the official one, can be found at http://www.element14.com/community/thread/18568.

---

[3]A partial list of these alternatives can be found at http://www.bigboardlist.com.

Typical Projects

The Internet is awash with uses for the Raspberry Pi; so much so, that many might think that is it a solution looking for a problem! This is standard behavior. With any new technology, there is always a cry of "could I do X on the PI," where X equates to any task they wanted to do on another machine. We shall now consider some of these projects, and how they can be realized but, more importantly, cover many more that are *only* possible because the Raspberry Pi is cheaper enough, or small enough, to allow such ideas to come into fruition.

The Telephone

The widespread use of mobile phones and the Internet have changed many businesses. Some, like the postal service, continue to argue for an "e-mail tax" to supplement their dying business model. Others, like the telecoms, are looking for new ways to sell their existing sevices in a world where the Internet providers can undercut them in most areas. One obvious area is in voice over IP, where traditional telephone calls can be made for virtually nothing using the Internet, instead of land lines. Indeed, you can even use an "all you can use" data package to run Skype on a mobile phone and bypass the phone charges of your mobile provider!

For those interested in VOIP solutions, you can leverage the Raspberry Pi's small size by including it inside the drawer of the telephone table (for those that still have such things!). This can then be loaded with Asterisk, or other PBX software, to provide an internal phone system that may be as effective as another VOIP-based intercom systems. A Raspberry Pi placed in this location also provides a suitable excuse to use it as a charging and sync station for your mobile phone. As you return home, your phone can be placed in the Raspberry Pi-connected cradle, and the day's photographs can be copied (i.e., backed up) to your home network server automatically.

Child Minding

The Raspberry Pi's size also gives you the opportunity to mount one inside a teddy bear, to provide a comforting story telling device for the kids, while doubling up as a child safety monitor once they've gone to bed, by using a basic webcam and microphone combination. This can work both ways to include VOIP functionality, with all data streamed through Ethernet or a separate WiFi board. There is a Raspberry Pi–approved camera module in development, which should be ready by the time you read this.

Construction of such a model is simple. A "bedtime bear" is best, as they are largely devoid of stuffing, as the child is intended to place their nightclothes inside them. Instead of nightclothes, however, you can stuff the bear with a Raspberry Pi! This is one of those projects that is only possible because the Raspberry Pi is small enough. So much so, in fact, that you will need to add some stuffing back, as most bears are large enough to take a cased Raspberry Pi, a battery pack, and assorted peripherals!

As it is made of fabric, there is no easy way to screw a Raspberry Pi board into the bear, so sew a small pocket into the inside of the bear, and slot the Raspberry Pi (in either a case or an antistatic bag) into it and pierce holes for the cables to enter and leave the bag.

The UK TV children's series Teletubbies had teddy bears who had television displays in their stomachs. You could replicate this, too. Or include a pico projector to show the child cartoons on the ceiling of their room. Maybe a different cartoon depending on where the bear is sat in the room, as detected by either QR codes, or with RFID or NFC sensors.

ToyTalk (`http://www.toytalk.com`) have recently begun work on the modern day Teddy Ruxpin that can interact with your child through stories and songs so, along with Kinectimals, you should be able to find a slew of good ideas for your virtual child minder.

If your child is older, then maybe it'd be better to build such child minding facilities into an arcade games cabinet, rather than a teddy bear!

Photo Frames

The low cost of the Raspberry Pi has also meant that manufacturers of other home gadgets have had to up their game, and bring down prices. A good quality digital photo frame used to be very expensive. Now, with just a Raspberry Pi and a cheap display, you can better the best products on the market, providing a slideshow with images, videos, and sound clips.

From the software point of view, this couldn't be easier. You could even use a standard screen-saver, or the slideshow functionality of OpenElec or XBMC. If you're avoiding the web-based solution (and unless you want the additional cost of adding a wireless board, or running Ethernet cable, there's no reason to connect this to the network) there are a multitude of other solutions out there-eog (`https://help.gnome.org/users/eog/stable`), gthumb (`http://gthumb.sourceforge.net/home.html`), a kiosk system (`https://github.com/csldevices/sweb`) or fbi. The latter uses the frame buffer device, so you don't need a full desktop install, which can be helpful in reducing the boot time and footprint of your system.

By running the photo frame through software, instead of firmware, means that you can upgrade the system easier to incorporate the changes for daylight savings hours, show the weather, or render the days schedule periodically during the morning time, or to add alarms or messages sent from Node0 (as detailed in Chapter 7) to multiple photo frames in the house. You can also more easily adapt the images that are shown, maybe to introduce images of Christmas past in the month of December, or to add more of the family when you know they're coming to stay, and remove them shortly afterward!

Weather Stations

You could also consider building, or enhancing, a weather station. Most come in two varieties—the cheap versions that might report the temperature, wind speed, and chill factor, for example, but provide no means of exporting that data outside of the device. The expensive versions provide a wireless or USB component for data export. However, the difference in cost usually exceeds that of a Raspberry Pi, so it makes an interesting project to hack your own.

The specifics of each hack depend on the weather station itself. You can either trap the messages made by the device (`http://hackaday.com/2011/09/06/lacross-weather-station-wireless-data-acquisition`) and reverse engineer the protocol, or reappropriate the sensors and feed the results directly to the GPIO.

If you intend to study the protocol, buy a weather unit that has a separate outdoor sensor. In this way, the protocol will have a definite end point, which makes it easier to engineer. (None of the ones I've seen encrypt the weather data!)

The idea of buying a complete unit, only to cannibalize it for parts, might seem wasteful, but it is often cheaper to do this, than it is to buy the sensors alone! Plus it's usually easier to find product specifications for the sensors, than it is to find a description of the protocol. To this end, I would recommend looking for a project that's already happened in this space (such as the Hack-A-Day example) and buy an identical device.

One such is Pywws, by Jim Easterbook. This Python program reads information from a Maplin USB weather station and his project is documented `http://www.weather.dragontail.co.uk/index.php?page=station_setup`. From here, the data can be graphed, analysed, and presented on a web page. The interest factor is replaced by the utility function when you consider adapting your thermostat to reflect the temperature, especially when returning from holiday.

Raspberry Pi as a USB Host

Looking at USB devices that need powerful drivers to operate, you could turn an old printer into a modern networked printer with a Raspberry Pi by simply connecting one to the network and installing a CUPS server on it. This is a standard package and prepared thus:

```
sudo apt-get install cups
sudo usermod -a -G lpadmin <your_user_name>
```

The rest of the configuration can then happen through the web browser:

```
http://127.0.0.1:631
```

If you plan on using the Raspberry Pi as a headless printer server, then you must edit `/etc/cups/cupsd.conf` to listen for other machines:

```
Listen 192.168.0.100:631
```

And continue with an amendment to the /admin section to include the IP addresses of which machines can use the interface:

```
<Location /admin>
Order deny,allow
Encryption IfRequested
Satisfy All
AuthType Basic
AuthClass System
Deny All
Allow 127.0.0.1
Allow 192.168.0.100
</Location>
```

Continuing with the USB theme, the low cost provides the opportunity to treat it as a throwaway device, in much the same way as a USB memory stick is, already. However, since you also have a CPU on board, it is possible to carry an entirely secure device (a personal cloud, if you will) with you holding login credentials, and a data mirror for those times when you're without Internet access and/or you can't trust the local Internet café, as can happen when you're abroad and your smartphone is lacking battery or signal. This is the same method used for having a personal Bitcoin wallet discussed on several websites, including `https://coderwall.com/p/9i4g9a,` which uses the `http://electrum.org` client.

Or, for a more frivolous use, connect any of the USB novelty gadgets, such as warming slippers, Christmas lights, hamsters in wheels, miniature fans, missile firing units, or beverage chillers and include the Raspberry Pi as part of your toy room!

As A Device Host

In theory, all of the plug-in modules and utilities for desktop PCs are available for the Raspberry Pi. In practice, it can be rather pointless. For example, why would you want to run a high-powered desktop machine to switch your lights on and off, if the power it saves is dwarfed by the kilowatt hours consumed by the PC? A similar argument can be levelled at the devices which monitor power consumption around the house-by the time you've factoring in the PC, it's cheaper to just leave everything on!

Considering those two use cases, the Aeon Labs Z-Stick is a low-power USB dongle that has good compatibility across Linux, including the Raspberry Pi and OpenZWave (see Chapter 2.) The project outlined at `http://thomasloughlin.com/z-wave-controller-setup-on-my-raspberry-pi` allows you to control ZWave devices with a minimal power footprint. The writeup also exemplifies the idea that each Raspberry Pi should do only one job, by providing a single SD image that comprises of a full install of Linux and the necessary software.

For energy usage, the OWL system has received compliments of late, particularly as it is possible to connect its Owl Sensor Receiver to a Raspberry Pi and recover the data. The project detailed at http://www.raspberrypiusers.com/?p=7486 shows the simplicity involved, thanks in part to OWL multicasting its data to the network, allowing you to open a socket and retrieve data with the Pi's language of choice, Python, using code such as:

```
import socket
import struct

MULTICAST_ADDRESS='224.192.32.19'

s = socket.socket(socket.AF_INET, socket.SOCK_DGRAM, socket.IPPROTO_UDP)

s.setsockopt(socket.SOL_SOCKET, socket.SO_REUSEADDR,1)
s.bind(('', 22600))

mreq = struct.pack ('4sl', socket.inet_aton(MULTICAST_ADDRESS), socket.INADDR_ANY)

s.setsockopt (socket.IPPROTO_IP, socket.IP_ADD_MEMBERSHIP, mreq)

buffer = s.recv(800)
```

Proximity Sensing

For those wanting the Raspberry Pi to play a more serious role in a smart home, the BlueProximity project (http://blueproximity.sourceforge.net) provides a means to automatically lock, and unlock, an X Window session based on how close your Bluetooth-enabled phone is to the machine in question. Naturally, this doesn't need to be plugged into the machine you want to lock! You can place a Raspberry Pi, and its Bluetooth unit, in the doorway of the den, or by the front and back doors. The simplest way of sending messages between machines involves an HTTP GET request from one to the other, and a small script checking for the correct parameters (as they should include a password of sorts.)

This idea can be extended by using several proximity sensors placed around the house, to work out an individual's location. To facilitate this, work is underway on a version 2.0 of BlueProximity which will monitor the Bluetooth signal strength on several different machines, and use this to deduce your location.

This location information can be used to target feedback messages and alerts to your current location. So if, for example, the software has detected you're in the living room it can display the message on your TV screen. By being able to target specific devices in this way eliminates the need to send all the messages to your phone. Also, it allows to you use your phone as a remote control that can intelligently target whichever device is closest to your current location. As I say, this project is still in development, but has potential, and is an excellent example of a solution that would not otherwise be possible if the controlling PC was much larger, or more expensive, than the Raspberry Pi!

Coffee Machine

In the 1970s and 1980s, a teasmaid was the middle-class gadget du jour! At night you'd fill the machine with water and tea, or coffee, and set the alarm for the following morning. Then, acting like an alarm clock, it would automatically make your first cuppa in the morning. Through the X10 project we covered in Chapter 2, this is now again possible. But with the Raspberry Pi capable of greater control opportunities, its scope can be improved.

The benefit of a Raspberry Pi over X10 is that you can have a feedback loop from the teasmaid to a web page, and you can control more parameters of the device, since the modern espresso machine has a multitude of buttons for the different coffee types, it isn't enough to just switch on the power as it is for a teakettle. As an example of this, Shawn Wallace and Matt Richardson built a Raspberry Pi–controlled coffee machine, as covered at http://blog.makezine.com/2013/02/11/raspberry-pi-for-web-initiated-coffee.

For those wanting something stronger in the morning, `http://brewpi.com` discusses a Raspberry Pi–based solution for controlling the temperature of a home brewery!

Clock Radio

If tea (or an early morning beer!) is not to your taste, then the Raspberry Pi makes a very advanced clock radio. Such a project is a suitable starter into the world of self-penned home automation, as it needs very simple software, and can suffice with a very basic display.

Instead of using an actual radio, there's no reason why it can't stream music from your local media server, or read the news from the RSS feeds, or your schedule, or any of the other ideas presented in Chapter 7. As a bonus, and unlike most clock radios of their day, it can also adjust itself for daylight savings. It this happens, however, it should always issue feedback to say that it has changed the time, because (as we've learned) every action should have a feedback message, and we don't want to update the time twice.

Without Mains Power

Moving away from the benefits of small and cheap, one can utilize the Raspberry Pi's ability to be powered by battery to use it in locations that might be considered dangerous or illegal to have mains power.[4] For example, a shed, shower, kitchen, or garden, where the introduction of water or steam could have an adverse affect on mains powered devices.

This allows you to build your own garden robot to feed and water the plants at specific intervals and, without any additional effort, report the results back through a web page. The keyword here is "interval" because computers, even the Raspberry Pi, are high-power devices so permanently running it from batteries is going to ensure a short-lived robot. For example, the Adafruit power pack (`http://www.adafruit.com/products/962`) lasts around 5 hours, while a basic AA battery pack (`http://www.raspberrypi-spy.co.uk/2013/02/running-a-raspberry-pi-from-6-aa-batteries`) can last over 16 hours.

One of the biggest drains on battery power (other than a screen) is WiFi connectivity. Because you wouldn't want to forgo a power cable, only to find yourself tethered by a network cable, it's best to store all the data locally, and write an rsync script to offload the data periodically to another machine, such as a laptop.

Installation

The Raspberry Pi, as supplied, is capable of doing nothing. Indeed, the board as supplied needs both additional hardware and software before it comes as smart as a brick. Let us now look at those steps.

Software

As with a traditional Linux system, the first step is to choose a distribution. The Raspberry Pi occupies an interesting place here, since while some traditional distros (like Debian) have versions of their offerings available, many others have shied away. The community, at large, has adopted an interesting approach of treating distributions as if they were applications – if you want to use the Raspberry Pi as a media centre, then use a pre-installed media centre distro such as XBMC[5] or OpenElec.[6] If you want thin client, then use RPTC.[7] And so on.

---

[4]Many jurisdictions have a minimum distance for power sockets to taps, for example.
[5]`http://www.raspbmc.com`.
[6]`http://www.openelec.tv`.
[7]`http://rpitc.blogspot.se`.

The process for installation is the same, regardless of distribution. In this example we shall use the official, general purpose, distribution Raspbian that is based on Debian Wheezy. You must first download a pre-installed version in the form of an image for the SD card, from a web site, such as `http://www.raspbian.org/RaspbianImages`. This image must then be written to an SD card (of a size appropriate to the image, obviously, with 4GB being a good entry level) with the commands:

```
sudo dd bs=4M if=raspbian.img of=/dev/sdd
sudo sync
```

▓ **Warning**   Refering to the wrong device here can (and will!) wipe your hard drive or other SCSI-based device connected to your machine. Measure twice—cut once, as the makers say!

---

you can then unmount the SD (shown here on `/dev/sdd`) and insert it into your Raspberry Pi, and turn it on.

If this is your first foray into Linux, you will need either PiWriter[8] (Mac OS X) or ImageWriter[9] (for Microsoft Windows) to perform the equivalent dd step.

The current version of the Raspbian image does not have a root account, so you cannot log in directly. One of the benefits of this is to prevent you doing major damage on your first time logged in. However, the default user on many distros is "pi" (with its password of "raspberry") has sudo privileges that allow you run commands as root in order to carry out system administration tasks.

Hardware

With no on/off switch, you need only to plug in the SD card, and then the power lead, and you're away. All the standard disclaimers, about shutting down the before inserting or removing the SD card, still apply.

The Raspberry Pi power lead is a micro-USB plug that supplies 5v from either a host computer, or a mains adapter plug connected to the equivalent USB port on the board. As we've seen there are battery packs available, but these are not intended for long-term use.

Once the OS is installed, it's time to power down and begin physical installation. This is optional! The compact elegance of the Raspberry Pi design means that a lot of people (myself included) prefer to forgo a case, or maybe use a transparent case to keep out dust. Otherwise, you will need a version 2 board, two nuts, four bolts, and two spacers that are slightly longer than the height of the nuts and bolts. Double nuts are recommended so they can be used as "lock nuts" that prevents them from accidentally coming lose. Of course, for geek chic, you can never go wrong with a LEGO case, such as the one shown in Figure 8-4.

---

[8]`http://sourceforge.net/projects/piwriter`.
[9]`https://launchpad.net/win32-image-writer`.

Figure 8-4. *One of many LEGO cases, from LegoPunk.com/?q=node/210*

Interfacing With Hardware

When your Raspberry Pi arrives, it comes as a circuit board in a small static-free bag. This is a far cry from the big box and fancy packaging of a laptop, or desktop machine. It might be this that makes people more inclinded to connect wires directly to the board for the purpose of interfacing, in a way they're never likely to do with a desktop.

Given the previous mentioned problems with USB, and the fact that the USB sockets are slow and usually full of keyboards, mice, and hard drives, means that USB isn't the usual way of interfacing with a Raspberry Pi. That accolade is shared between the GPIO, I2C, SPI, and Arduino-related technology.

Hardware Caution

Debugging software, although painful and difficult, is comparatively easy when compared to debugging hardware. Especially, when you come from a software background. The debuggers available to hardware engineers (e.g., a voltmeter, and an ammeter) are positively antiquated when compared to even the most basic version of GDB. So, unless you're a rich kid with a good logic analyzer, you will have modify your development approach! Particularly as a hardware bug can destroy the circuit you're trying to build, and the computer connected to it. When this happens you might not even realize it, and waste time trying to fix a circuit that can never work.

It is for this reason that many interface boards exist, as they generally have protection buffers built-in so even if you put too much voltage on an input in, or try and drive the current the wrong way around the circuit, then you won't destroy your hardware. They can also help fix the voltage levels needed to run the various pieces of hardware. A lot of discrete socketed components use 5v, which is why the Arduino can work simply with them since it's is set to use 5v by default. However, with the Raspberry Pi running at 3.3v, you need adjust the voltage level when communicating with such chips. An interface board can help in this regard.

If your development approach could be described as cautious, then adopting I2C or SPI might be preferably to GPIO because they both need a chip to effectively handle the protocol-such as the MCP23017 or MCP3208, respectively. Not only do they allow many more channels than the GPIO, but they also provide a form of buffering to help protect the Raspberry Pi itself.

■ **Caution**   Linux is not a real-time operating system, as your software can't run exactly when it wants, or for as long as it wants, because there is always the opportunity for the OS to task switch to another process. Therefore, if your task requires precise timing of sensors or switches, then it is better to use an Arduino where you can guarantee control over every clock cycle and time your code accordingly.

With the GPIO

The GPIO (General Purpose Input/Output) is a set of 26 pins on the Raspberry Pi circuit board. These include 3.3v and 5v power rails, a clock, and several pins which can be controlled directly by the processor, and therefore by your software. These can communicate with external hardware. Like the Arduino, these pins can be reconfigured and our case they can function as an I²C interface, UART (Universal asynchronous receiver/transmitter), SPI (Serial Peripheral Interface Bus) and PWM (Pulse width modulation), as detailed in Figure 8-5. The biggest draw back is that it is more difficult to program this functionality with a Raspberry Pi, compared to an Arduino, because the Raspberry Pi is a multitasking operating system, and so the vagaries in timing can vary by very small amounts. Whether these microseconds are noticeable will depend on your application, however, it is very unlikely that anyone just starting out with the kit will experience problems for a while.

	Left bottom, pin 1	Left top, pin 2	
3.3v			5v
GPIO 0 (SDA)	I²C		5v
GPIO 1 (SCL)	I²C		Ground/0v
GPIO 4 (GPCLK0)		UART	GPIO 14 (TXD)
Ground/0v		UART	GPIO 15 (RXD)
GPIO 17			GPIO 18 (PCM_CLK)
GPIO 21 (PCM_DOUT)			Ground/0v
GPIO 22			GPIO 23
3.3v			GPIO 24
GPIO 10 (MOSI)	SPI		Ground/0v
GPIO 9 (MISO)	SPI		GPIO 25
GPIO 11 (SCLK)	SPI	SPI	GPIO 8 (CE0)
Ground/0v		SPI	GPIO 7 (CE1)

Figure 8-5. *The GPIO pins*

Both Raspberry Pi and Arduino have the same process of configuring pins for either input or output, and then writing high or low signals to them. So, after connecting an LED and resistor (in series) to physical pin 11 (and ground, on pin 1) you can control it using the command line:

```
gpio mode 0 out
gpio write 0 1
```

This gpio program is part of the WiringPi package, which can be found at https://projects.drogon.net/raspberry-pi/wiringpi. We use this package also to help solve the complication of understanding the differences in pin nomenclature. The WiringPi code allows us to refer to *wiring* pin 0 as the output of our system, which is mapped to the *physical* pin 11 because that's where *GPIO* pin 17 happens to live. (Now pause and reread that until you understand the difference between each type of pin, as it will save much pain later.) The odd numbering of the pins is just how this particular chip is configured. So if we were to port the code to an alternate processor, where GPIO-17 was on physical pin 9, we could keep our code exactly as it, and simply rebuild the circuit with our LED on the appropriate pin.

Of course, the name "Pi" references the original intention of being programmed primarily in Python. So, if that language takes your fancy, you would instead write:

```
import Raspberry Pi.GPIO as GPIO

GPIO.setmode(GPIO.BOARD)

GPIO.setup(11, GPIO.OUT)
GPIO.output(11, GPIO.HIGH)
```

As with the Arduino, and most micro controllers, the Raspberry Pi cannot provide enough current for an electric motor. (It is recommended that you draw no more than 50mA from any pin, and less than 150mA in total.) Therefore, you will need to employ a driving circuit with a relay that follows the same design as previously shown in Figure 8-2.

The code for input signals, such as from a switch, require the code changes you'd expect:

```
GPIO.setup(12, GPIO.IN)
inputValue = GPIO.input(12)
```

allowing you to build the same level of circuits as you might with an Arduino, but also allow you to hardness the power and connectivity of a full Linux machine.

■ **Tip** To learn more of this style of programming, along with some examples, head along to http://elinux.org/RPi_Low-level_peripherals.

Once a motor is connected to the Raspberry Pi you'll need an effective way of controlling it. Depending on the use, it will depend on the type of motor to buy, although a feedback loop that tells the machine how far the motor has moved is always recommended.

For cases in which a significant amount of motion is required, such as a curtain rail, then a stepper motor or a standard DC motor can be employed. In the former case, feedback is automatic because the motor is programmed to move in a specific number of discrete steps. For a DC motor, either limit switches or slotted disc counters can be used. If you notice the motors used in LEGO Mindstorms projects, you'll understand how to build this from more solid components. If your feedback is of a Boolean variety, that is, you only need to know if a limit has been reached, then a simple microswitch at the extent is all that's necessary.

Alternatively, for light applications such as robots, the best solution is to employ servos where the position of the motor can be controlled by the pulse width of the output signal. Accurate control of this pulse is vital, and while it might be difficult programming for the newbie, especially since there is only one PWM pin available, there is already a library to solve this problem by emulating PWM in software.

▨ **Note**   Servo motors that work through pulses may only be able to turn around a portion of their axis, maybe less than 270 degrees, and so can not be used in all applications.

ServoBlaster (`https://github.com/richardghirst/PiBits/tree/master/ServoBlaster`) is a library that is capable to driving up to eight servo motors through the GPIO port of the Raspberry Pi, meaning it requires no additional hardware. In its most basic form, it is nothing more than a user space daemon (which still needs to be run as root, given it needs access to the GPIO) that detaches from the shell when you first run it:

```
$ sudo ./servod
```

However, you can also use the kernel space implementation that works by creating a new device `/dev/servoblaster` that handles all the timing, and you just need to specify the pulse width. A 1.3ms pulse width, on motor 4, would be addressed:

```
$ echo "4=130" >/dev/servoblaster
```

A value of zero will turn it off. With 8 servos, each taking 2.5ms to be serviced the maximum latency-the time from issuing a command to seeing the effect-will be the cycle time, 8 * 2.5ms, or 20ms.

Given this cycle time, it is not possible to have a longer pulse than 2.5ms, or 12.5%. If you're working with LEDs, then longer pulses are necessary and made possible with a fork of the servoblaster code, called Pi-Blaster (`https://github.com/sarfata/pi-blaster`). Give it's obvious heritage, it is invoked in an identical manner, but using a fractional percentage for the pulse width, instead of an absolute time. A 12.5% pulse would therefore be:

```
echo "0=0.125" > /dev/pi-blaster
```

To expand the number of motor controllers, for building a robot perhaps, you will need to switch out your debugger for a soldering iron and install a physical add-on such as the Adafruit module from `http://adafruit.com/products/815` that provides up to 16 channels for servo motors.

For more advance analogue I/O you would do well to consider a more recent development-the Gertboard. Although it is a very expensive board, it does come with a wealth of interfacing options using the full scope of the GPIO. The SPI is pressed into service for both an A2D (MCP4002) and a D2A (MCP4802) converter, while the sole PWM pin is used as a motor controller (L6203, buffered to a mighty 48V/4A). The UART is configured to take with an Atmel AVR microcontroller,[10] and the remaining GPIO pins used for various buttons and LEDs for utility purposes. Being a predominantly analogue controller this is a better match for most projects because our (real) world is analogue, not digital!

▨ **Tip**   If you plan on including an Arduino in your Raspberry Pi setup at some point, then it's worth considering getting just the Gertboard and the chip, as this will probably work out cheaper than buying a separate/additional shield and Arduino board.

---

[10]A variety of chips can be used with the Gertboard (48A/PA, 88A/PA, 168A/PA, 328/P) but none are supplied with it.

Programming the Gertboard is much like the low-level Arduino code. That is, you are writing directly to the memory-mapped IO and therefore need the careful skill of an assembly programmer. This code might appear banal like this:

```
PWMCLK_DIV  = 0x5A000000 | (32<<12);
PWMCLK_CNTL = 0x5A000011;

PWM_CONTROL = 0;  // i.e. off
PWM0_RANGE = 0x400; // all values between 0 and 1023

PWM0_DATA = 0x100; // write output
```

This, seemingly natural code (albeit a little heavy on the magic numbers), is all that's necessary to set up the PWM. However, hiding behind these macros are pointer indirections such as:

```
#define PWM_CONTROL  *pwm
#define PWM_STATUS   *(pwm+1)
#define PWM0_RANGE   *(pwm+4)
#define PWM1_RANGE   *(pwm+8)
#define PWM0_DATA    *(pwm+5)
#define PWM1_DATA    *(pwm+9)
```

So all that's necessary is a missed warning about incorrect data types, and you'll be corrupting the subsequent register and be tracing nonexistent bugs for hours! More information on this board can be found on the Element14 site at http://www.element14.com/community/docs/DOC-51726?ICID=raspi-group.

Naturally, other interfacing boards are available, with Pi-Face from Manchester University, Pi Crust, and Quick2Wire. More are coming out each month, so a quick web search for "buffer boards" or "expansion boards" will let you know of the current state of the art.

With the Arduino

The simplest way to connect the Raspberry Pi to the outside world is through an Arduino, as we already have many years experience with the device. Furthermore, there are many useful shields already available. For most people, this is a waste of effort because the Arduino is capable of processing most input devices that we care about. However, it does provide a level of security knowing that if you make an error, it is the (cheaper) Arduino that will blow up, and not your beloved Raspberry Pi!

USB

Despite the issues mentioned previously about USB on the Raspberry Pi, this is the simplest and safest way to connect the two machines. You simply plug one into the other!

As far as software goes, the Arduino processes its input and writes data out using the traditional:

```
Serial.begin(9600);
pinMode(inputSwitchPin, INPUT);
pinState = digitalRead(inputSwitchPin);
Serial.println(pinState ? '1' : '0');
```

and there is a program on the Raspberry Pi reading this from the serial device. You'll need to set-up the device with:

```
char *szUSBDevice = "/dev/ttyUSB0";

FILE *fp = fopen(szUSBDevice, "r");
```

and then read data from the serial device in a tight loop, executing something not dissimilar to:

```
if (fread(&v, 1, 1, fp)) {
    if (v == '0') { }
    if (v == '1') { }
}
```

Naturally, this is very slow and has considerably latency between an event occurring, being discovered by the Arduino, and then transmitted and processed on the Raspberry Pi. To improve this, you need to look at using the I²C bus.

I²C

I²C is a two-wire interface called Inter-Integrated Circuit. It is a bus protocol, designed originally by Philips, to connect slow peripherals directly to a computer motherboard. By putting data directly onto the bus, latency between devices can be drastically reduced. Furthermore, you can connect up to 128 devices on an I²C bus which far exceeds the rather timid USB solution we covered earlier.

▓ **Caution**   When connecting devices directly onto the bus of another, you have no isolation or protection that other methods (such as USB) provide. It is therefore easier for one device to (physically) harm another, or allow through inaction harm to come to it. In the specific case of connecting Arduino and Raspberry Pi, remember that they work at 5v and 3.3v respectively, and need a level shifter to correctly harmonize the voltages.

The hardware component is as easy as it should be for a two wire protocol-you connect the SDA of the Raspberry Pi to the SDA of the Arduino, and the SCL of the Raspberry Pi to the SCL of the Arduino, and that's it. Granted, you need the level shifters that we used previously (and you might like to add some pull-up resistors for safety) but, otherwise, all that's necessary is as it appears in Figure 8-6.

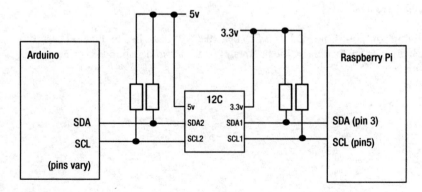

Figure 8-6. *Connecting an Raspberry Pi to an Arduino*

Build it, then power on and run the software on the Arduino, so that it is able to register itself on the I2C bus:

```
#include "Wire.h"

int i2cAddress = 0x03;

void setup() {
  Wire.begin(i2cAddress);
}
```

The rest of the software is as simple as the hardware! First check that the Arduino can be found on the bus. So, on the Raspberry Pi, simply run:

```
$ sudo modprobe i2c-dev
$ sudo i2cdetect -y 0
     0  1  2  3  4  5  6  7  8  9  a  b  c  d  e  f
00:          03 -- -- -- -- -- -- -- -- -- -- -- --
10: -- -- -- -- -- -- -- -- -- -- -- -- -- -- -- --
20: -- -- -- -- -- -- -- -- -- -- -- -- -- -- -- --
30: -- -- -- -- -- -- -- -- -- -- -- -- -- -- -- --
40: -- -- -- -- -- -- -- -- -- -- -- -- -- -- -- --
50: -- -- -- -- -- -- -- -- -- -- -- -- -- -- -- --
60: -- -- -- -- -- -- -- -- -- -- -- -- -- -- -- --
70: -- -- -- -- -- -- -- --
```

From this, you can see that your Arduino is successfully connected to the bus, and on address 03. If you don't see the Arduino, then it's likely you're using a revision two board, and therefore need to use bus 1, and not bus 0, so change the i2cdetect command above, and SMBus reference below.

Sending data from the Raspberry Pi uses the smbus library and code such as:

```
#! /usr/bin/python
import smbus
bus = smbus.SMBus(0)

address = 0x03
dataToSend = 42

bus.write_byte_data(address, 0xC9, dataToSend)
```

Notice that we send two bytes, even though only one is needed. This first byte (0xC9) is like a header that indicates the type of data we're sending. The Arduino can then watch for data on the I2C bus, at address 3, and respond accordingly. We therefore amend our program above to read:

```
#include "Wire.h"

int i2cAddress = 0x03;

void setup() {
  Wire.begin(i2cAddress);
  Wire.onReceive(receiveEvent);
}
```

```
void receiveEvent(int size) {
  if (size == 2) {
    int header = Wire.read();
    int dataRead = Wire.read();
    if (header == 0xC9) {
      // Do something
    }
  }
}
```

The equivalent, but more rare, code to send data from the Raspberry Pi back to the Arduino is left as an exercise for the reader!

With SPI

As a de facto standard, the Serial Peripheral Interface Bus is a method of communicating between a single master (the Raspberry Pi in our case), and an arbitrary number of slave peripherals. Although it is only possible to control, or query, one slave at a time, its high speed of operation along with full duplex operation makes this a useful approach for many microcontrollers and other such projects.

The hardware necessary involves just five pins of the Raspberry Pi's connector, SCLK (the clock), MOSI (master out), MISO (master in), and CE0/CE1 (both select which slave to use.) The MOSI/MISO pair provides the transmit/receive pairing for the full-duplex communication channel, while the SCLK is used to keep all the slaves in sync with the master. As a consequence of this, there is no need to run separate clocks on the slave machines, which makes it easier to find suitable oscillators and they don't need to be precise. This effort of simplifying the circuitry is also demonstrable by the fact that, unlike I²C, no pull-up or pull-down resistors are needed to you can simply connect the MOSI on the master to the MOSI on the slave (repeat for OISO and SCLK) and you're nearly ready!

The slave select indicates to which of the slave devices the master is talking. The Raspberry Pi hardware provides two of these, CE0 and CE1, which utilize /dev/spidev-0.0 and /dev/spidev-0.1. As a protocol however, SPI allows you to control as many slaves as you like. Therefore, it is possible (and indeed, suggested) that you use the other GPIO pins to select the necessary slave, using a low logic 0 to indicate the slave in question. Since you can't use the standard SPI library, you must manually handle the slave selection by writing to the GPIO as we saw earlier. Timing between the GPIO and SPI is a question of ordering it correctly-first take all the GPIO pins used in slave selection high to logic 1, wait, and then take the appropriate pin low.

■ **Tip** If you write your own slave select driver, then you should always begin by sending the selection pins high, and then low, since some slaves are only awoken by the falling edge.

The projects possible with SPI are much the same as if you were using GPIO or I²C. What you gain in the simplified electronics, you lose on the software, so you need to write your own error handling and hand-shaking code since there is no way of knowing if the slave received the messages sent to it, nor is there any error checking in the protocol itself. If your project is to be in an electrically noisy environment (maybe the utility room, with the powerful motors of a washing machine and tumbler dryer) then this is a valid concern, since SPI is more susceptible to noise. If you have no SPI slaves with which to experiment then you're probably wrong (!) because anything capable of communicating on four different pins can be pressed into service . . . the Arduino is a suitable candidate for this. A proof of concept can be found at http://hackaday.com/2013/01/06/hardware-spi-with-python-on-a-raspberry-pi.

From a programmatical point of view, the software is a simple to write as for any of the other protocols. In Python you can use the standard library and write:

```
import spi
spi.initialize()
spi.transfer((1,2,3))
```

Or, with C, there is a test program from the Linux kernel itself at http://git.kernel.org/cgit/linux/kernel/git/torvalds/linux.git/plain/Documentation/spi/spidev_test.c.

With Arduino Shields

Although it's true that the Arduino shields are a big selling point, it's not necessarily true to say that you must have an Arduino to use them. Cooking Hacks (http://www.cooking-hacks.com) have produced a connection bridge that sits atop of your Raspberry Pi and allows you to add Arduino shields to the Pi directly.

The bridge comes with the arduPi library that mimics the API of the Arduino; so all the traditional functions of digitalRead and readBytes are still available. You can therefore write standard Arduino code, provided that you add your own main function:

```
#include "arduPi.h"

// Insert your usual setup and loop methods here

int main (int argc, char *argv[]) {
    setup();
    while(1){
        loop();
    }
return (0);
}
```

The rest of the code can be copied directly from the original Arduino source, and then compiled and run in the normal way.

■ **Note** The arduPi library has been released under the GPL, and so is usable for other Linux machines, should you wish to emulate the Arduino, test your software in another environment, or even try and to connect the shields to a desktop machine!

The hardware component involves a little more work because the voltage level of the Raspberry Pi GPIO is 3.3v, whereas the original Arduino uses 5v throughout. Unfortunately, the bridge doesn't handle this hardware conversion as well as it does the software. Therefore, all 5v input signals need to be scaled down to 3.3v, which can be done with a 5K/10K potential divider circuit. Alternatively, look to the more recent versions of Arduino, and their clones, as many of the new ones can be switched between 5v and 3.3v that eradicates this problem.

Similarly, the 3.3v digital output will need to be upgraded, perhaps with a transistor switching circuit as we saw in Figure 2-5. For those with more exotic components, you can build a level shifter with two 2N7000 MOSFETs and a circuit not dissimilar to http://www.hobbytronics.co.uk/mosfet-voltage-level-converter, or buy a prebuild level converter such as http://www.skpang.co.uk/catalog/logic-level-converter-p-511.html.

The big question, however, revolves around whether it is worth it. Currently, it costs €40 for the bridge, which is around the same price as the Arduino Due, and twice the price of an Uno. So, although it is an interesting idea, this device is only worth using if the cost (in time) of connecting an Arduino directly through I²C exceeds €20.

However, in those cases in which there is a good Arduino shield available for use, and there is nothing similar to the Raspberry Pi, then this shield can easily justify the cost. (Provided, of course, that you couldn't alleviate the need of a Raspberry Pi by processing the data on an Arduino, and transmitting the data to a suitable machine for display.)

Software Options

Being a Linux machine in its own right means you are able to run any of the traditional open source software on the Raspberry Pi. The official Raspbian distribution is recommended for this because they have compiled most of the Debian packages to be suitable for the Raspberry Pi's ARM chip. Software that is not *open* source, or has been distributed in binary form, will need a Raspberry Pi–specific version, as you'd expect for any non-Intel architecture.

If you find you need to compile your own packages from source, then you may need to amend the make file to ensure it uses hard floats:

```
CFLAGS="-O2 -pipe -mcpu=arm1176jzf-s -mfpu=vfp -mfloat-abi=hard"
```

The "hard float" options ensure that all floating-point operations are done in hardware, on the CPU, and not emulated in software. The reason for this is that software emulation is at least 10 times slower than the hardware-based solution.

■ **Tip** If you have an old install of the Foundation's Raspberry Pi Linux distribution (based on Squeeze), it is likely to have been compiled with the soft float version, making your hard float compilation incompatible. Although it is possible to recompile the libraries to use hard floats, and regain some speed, it is easier to simply download a new image and reinstall. These newer images are called Raspbian and all use armhf. Also, the memory controller on the Model B changed (when they doubled the RAM), so you will need a new install image in this case also.

Even without building (or rebuilding) your own packages, there is a lot of standard software already available. You can therefore turn your Raspberry Pi into a print server, BitTorrent client (such as with Seed Field), NAS server, and so on, without any effort whatsoever. Note that, whereas its small size would suggest a nice compact file server, the interrupt cascade problems on the USB could mean issues if you intend to use it for media streaming as opposed to data backup. Also note that the Raspberry Pi is sometimes temperamental with USB hubs. (The newer drivers are better, but the issues still exist.) Therefore, it is recommended to fit a single drive to the system, which is as large as you can currently afford. It might not be able to do software-based RAID, but because it's a predominantly read-only device (as you have original media files on DVD, or there's a backup), it's not necessary.

As you know, the Pi in Raspberry Pi stems from Python, the scripting language intended to be the de factor standard for the machine. However, with the inclusion of a full development tool chain, most other languages are available for use. If you're writing small programs (of, say, fewer than 10,000 lines), then you can happily build out your Raspberry Pi software on the device itself. For larger projects, it's usually better to build (and test) on a full-size Linux box, and then cross-compile it for the Raspberry Pi.

Cross-compilation is the process of building an executable for one machine, using the compiler on another—more specifically, building for one architecture, using the architecture of another. For example, this could be compiling for the ARM processor while on an Intel machine. This means that you can use the improved processing power of a desktop machine to quickly compile for the smaller, less able, machine.

In order to cross-compile software, you will need a suitable toolchain that comprises of the compiler, libraries, headers, and other assorted tools for the language in question. Determining *what* compiler, libraries, headers, and other assorted tools you need can be a tiresome activity, but-in true open source fashion-other developers have already done the heavy lifting. The team at `http://crosstool-ng.org` has provided a toolchain for a number of systems and languages, including our Raspberry Pi. The installation process is straightforward but not overly quick. However, when building large software, the time taken to install a cross environment will be recouped with your first large compile. Full instructions for the installation process can be found at `http://www.kitware.com/blog/home/post/426`.

Conclusion

The Raspberry Pi is a capable machine, able to support many maker-oriented projects in the home automation arena. Its moniker as a small, cheap, Linux machine isn't necessarily accurate as it lacks many of the components that one takes for granted in a PC, such as a real-time clock, VGA output, or a solid USB stack, and building around these limitations can cost money. However, the provision of an easy-to-program GPIO port makes this into a superpowered Arduino that is capable of running several services at once, which means that it can be easily expanded with new features and update much more easily than other, similar, devices. Being so young in its development cycle, and such a charming device, has ensured that a number of specific modules are already available for its expansion that will hopefully ensure a long shelf life and a lot of new projects.

Index

CPSIA information can be obtained at www.ICGtesting.com
Printed in the USA
LVOW09s0947021213

363439LV00012BA/68/P

9 781430 258872